A

· · ·

BOOK

The Philip E. Lilienthal imprint
honors special books
in commemoration of a man whose work
at the University of California Press
from 1954 to 1979
was marked by dedication to young authors
and to high standards in the field of Asian Studies.
Friends, family, authors, and foundations have together
endowed the Lilienthal Fund, which enables the Press
to publish under this imprint selected books
in a way that reflects the taste and judgment
of a great and beloved editor.

The publisher gratefully acknowledges the generous contribution to this book provided by the Philip E. Lilienthal Asian Studies Endowment Fund of the University of California Press Foundation, which is supported by a major gift from Sally Lilienthal.

Vicarious Language

ASIA: LOCAL STUDIES / GLOBAL THEMES

Jeffrey N. Wasserstrom, Kären Wigen, and Hue-Tam Ho Tai, Editors

1. *Bicycle Citizens: The Political World of the Japanese Housewife,* by Robin M. LeBlanc
2. *The Nanjing Massacre in History and Historiography,* edited by Joshua A. Fogel
3. *The Country of Memory: Remaking the Past in Late Socialist Vietnam,* by Hue-Tam Ho Tai
4. *Chinese Femininities / Chinese Masculinities: A Reader,* edited by Susan Brownell and Jeffrey N. Wasserstrom
5. *Chinese Visions of Family and State, 1915–1953,* by Susan L. Glosser
6. *An Artistic Exile: A Life of Feng Zikai (1898–1975),* by Geremie R. Barmé
7. *Mapping Early Modern Japan: Space, Place, and Culture in the Tokugawa Period, 1603–1868,* by Marcia Yonemoto
8. *Republican Beijing: The City and Its Histories,* by Madeleine Yue Dong
9. *Hygienic Modernity: Meanings of Health and Disease in Treaty-Port China,* by Ruth Rogaski
10. *Marrow of the Nation: A History of Sport and Physical Culture in Republican China,* by Andrew D. Morris
11. *Vicarious Language: Gender and Linguistic Modernity in Japan,* by Miyako Inoue
12. *Japan in Print: Information and Nation in the Early Modern Period,* by Mary Elizabeth Berry
13. *Millennial Monsters: Japanese Toys and the Global Imagination,* by Anne Allison

Vicarious Language

Gender and Linguistic Modernity in Japan

Miyako Inoue

UNIVERSITY OF CALIFORNIA PRESS
Berkeley / Los Angeles / London

University of California Press, one of the most distinguished university presses in the United States, enriches lives around the world by advancing scholarship in the humanities, social sciences, and natural sciences. Its activities are supported by the UC Press Foundation and by philanthropic contributions from individuals and institutions. For more information, visit www.ucpress.edu.

Chapter 1 was previously published as "The Listening Subject of Japanese Modernity and His Auditory Double: Citing, Sighting, and Siting the Modern Japanese Woman," *Cultural Anthropology* 18 (3): 156–93, and is © 2003 by the American Anthropological Association. Chapter 2 was previously published as "Gender, Language, and Modernity: Toward an Effective History of Japanese Women's Language," *American Ethnologist* 29 (2): 392–422, and is © 2002 by the American Anthropological Association.

University of California Press
Berkeley and Los Angeles, California

University of California Press, Ltd.
London, England

© 2006 by The Regents of the University of California

Library of Congress Cataloging-in-Publication Data

Inoue, Miyako, date.
   Vicarious language : gender and linguistic modernity in Japan / Miyako Inoue.
      p.   cm.—(Asia-Local studies/global themes ; 11)
   Includes bibliographical references and index.
   ISBN 0-520-24584-9 (cloth : alk. paper)—ISBN 0-520-24585-7 (pbk. : alk. paper)
   1. Women—Japan—Language.   2. Japanese language—Sex differences.   I. Title.   II. Series.
PL698.W65I56   2006
306.44'082'0952—dc22   2005010545

Manufactured in the United States of America

14 13 12 11 10 09 08 07 06 05
10 9 8 7 6 5 4 3 2 1

Printed on Ecobook 50 containing a minimum 50% post-consumer waste, processed chlorine free. The balance contains virgin pulp, including 25% Forest Stewardship Council Certified for no old growth tree cutting, processed either TCF or ECF. The sheet is acid-free and meets the minimum requirements of ANSI/NISO Z39.48-1992 (R 1997) (Permanence of Paper).∞

This book is dedicated to

Kuniharu Inoue

Kazumi Inoue

This is my *shinshoarikomachi!*

Contents

List of Illustrations and Tables — *xi*

Acknowledgments — *xv*

Note on Japanese Names and
the Romanization of Japanese Language — *xix*

Introduction: Women's Language
and Capitalist Modernity in Japan — *1*

PART ONE: LANGUAGE, GENDER, AND NATIONAL
MODERNITY: THE GENEALOGY OF JAPANESE WOMEN'S
LANGUAGE, 1880S–1930S

1. An Echo of National Modernity:
Overhearing "Schoolgirl Speech" — *37*

2. Linguistic Modernity and the Emergence
of Women's Language — *75*

3. From Schoolgirl Speech to Women's Language:
Consuming Indexicality in Women's Magazines, 1890–1930 — *108*

PART TWO: THE NATION'S TEMPORALITY
AND THE DEATH OF WOMEN'S LANGUAGE

4. Capitalist Modernity, the Responsibilized Speaking Body,
and the Public Mourning of the Death of Women's Language — *163*

PART THREE: RE-CITING WOMEN'S LANGUAGE
IN LATE MODERN JAPAN

Introduction — *207*

5. "Just Stay in the Middle": The Story of a Woman Manager — *217*

6. Defamiliarizing Japanese Women's Language:
   Strategies and Tactics of Female Office Workers — *252*

   Afterword: This Vicarious "Japanese Women's Language" — *278*

   Bibliography — *283*

   Index — *309*

Illustrations and Tables

Figures

1. List of schoolgirls' "vulgar" speech forms cited by Ozaki Koyo — 59
2. Comparison of final particles attached to the auxiliary verb *da* in *Ukiyoburo* and *Sanshiro* — 94
3. Comparison of utterance-endings in *Ukiyoburo* and *Sanshiro* — 96
4. NHK "Women and Language" survey of Japanese women (1986) — 186
5. Selected NHK survey responses, by age, marriage status, and education (1986) — 187
6. NHK "Linguistic Awareness" survey (1989) — 190
7. The passage from the section titled "Gender Difference in Language Use" in "Deferential Expressions in Modern [Japanese] Society" — 199

Plates

1. "Bijutsuka to Reijō"(Artist and his daughter). *Fujin sekai*, 1930. © Jitsugyo no Nihan Sha, Ltd. — 132
2. "Modāngāru no shitai sono roku" (The pose of a modern girl, act 6). *Fujin sekai*, 1930. © Jitsugyo no Nihan Sha, Ltd. — 134

3. Untitled image of a moga. *Fujin sekai*, 1931. © Jitsugyo no Nihan Sha, Ltd. — *135*
4. Advertisement by Sekiguchi Yōhinten (Sekiguchi Costume Store). *Fujin sekai*, 1911. © Jitsugyo no Nihan Sha, Ltd. — *137*
5. Advertisement for Bigan Taoru (Beautiful Face Towel). *Fujin sekai*, 1909. © Jitsugyo no Nihan Sha, Ltd. — *138*
6. Advertisement for Puresuto Araiko (Presto Washing Powder). *Jogaku sekai*, 1907. © Hakubunkan Shinsha Publishers, Ltd. — *139*
7. Advertisement for Pāru Nerikōyu (Pearl Paste Perfumed Hair Oil). *Jogaku sekai*, 1912. © Hakubunkan Shinsha Publishers, Ltd. — *141*
8. Advertisement with geisha for Rēto Nyūhaku Keshōsui (Lait Milk Lotion). *Jogaku sekai*, 1909. © Hakubunkan Shinsha Publishers, Ltd. — *143*
9. Advertisement with schoolgirl for Rēto Nyūhaku Keshōsui. *Fujin sekai*, 1909. © Jitsugyo no Nihan Sha, Ltd. — *144*
10. Advertisement for Bikutoria Gekkeitai (Victoria Menstrual Garment). *Fujin sekai*, 1925. © Jitsugyo no Nihan Sha, Ltd. — *146*
11. Advertisement for Misono Mizuoshiroi (Misono Liquid White Powder). *Fujin sekai*, 1929. © Jitsugyo no Nihan Sha, Ltd. — *148*
12. Facing pages in *Fujin sekai*, 1915: Advertisement for travel cosmetics cases and photographs from the Patriotic Women's Association. © Jitsugyo no Nihan Sha, Ltd. — *152–53*
13. The cover page of "The Collection of Women's Model Language Use," supplement to *Fujin kurabu*, August 1932. © Kodansha — *156*
14. Kimiko and Kikue chatting in the garden, in "The Collection of Women's Model Language Use," supplement to *Fujin kurabu*, August 1932. © Kodansha — *158*

Chart

1. The location of Yoshida-san's Facility Management Office within the Personnel and General Affairs Unit — *221*

Examples

1. An exchange between Yoshida-san and a male vendor — 234
2. An exchange between Yoshida-san and Sasaki-san, a younger male worker — 236
3. An exchange between Yoshida-san and Kimura-san, another woman manager — 242
4. An exchange between Tanabe-san and Ikegami-san, interrupted by a customer's phone call — 256
5. An exchange between Sugimoto-san and Fujiwara-san — 263
6. Examples of Sawada-san's use of *kashira* — 268

Tables

1. Demography and rank system at MJL — 210
2. Job allocation for newly graduating MJL recruits, 1993 — 211

Acknowledgments

I learned the craft of scholarship from my doctoral dissertation advisor at Washington University, John Bowen. I also am in enormous intellectual debt to Michael Silverstein, whose work has been my inspiration since graduate school. On the day when I first read one of his articles, I knew I wanted to become a linguistic anthropologist. My interest in linguistic anthropology was definitively shaped by taking Steven Caton's linguistic anthropology classes at Washington University, and Joel Robbins taught me how to read books seriously, as a scholar. With much admiration, my deep thanks go to Sakai Naoki and Miriam Silverberg, whose work gave me many productive but sleepless nights of exhilaration and inspiration, and helped me to see the power of creative, critical, and sustained analysis that challenges existing conceptual boundaries.

I extend special thanks to Penny Eckert and Aminata Saho, who generously indulged me for many hours as I tried to figure out what I really wanted to say in this book. Kitamori Eri and Kawamura Kunimitsu gave me both moral support and intellectual guidance for my research. Ann Anagnost, Tim Choy, Claire Fox, Joan Fujimura, Takashi Fujitani, Sue Gal, Liz Hengeveld, Ide Risako, Celia Lowe, Matsuki Keiko, Carol Maxwell, Sally McConnell-Ginet, Bonnie McElhinny, Okamoto Shigeko, Beth Povinelli, Mary Pratt, Satsuka Shiho, Bambi Schieffelin, Janet Smith, Tamanoi Mariko, Anna Tsing, Pat Wetzel, Sunaoshi Yukako, and Kit Woolard have read and commented on various versions of the chapters of in this book. I thank them for their passion for scholarship and their remarkably creative intellectual imaginations, which made their comments and suggestions all the more useful. I am also indebted to Mary

Bucholtz, who in different professional capacities read many versions of the manuscript and tirelessly helped me to clarify points and to make the text more intelligible.

I thank my colleagues in the Department of Cultural and Social Anthropology at Stanford University for providing me with a truly exciting intellectual environment as well as warm support. Other Stanford colleagues, Yoshiko Matsumoto, Ray McDermott, John Rickford, Lucia Sa, and Karen Wigen, offered me encouragement. I am indebted to Stanford University for generous funding through a Center for East Asian Studies Faculty Grant, a grant from the Center for East Asian Studies, a Vice Provost for Undergraduate Education Faculty Grant for Undergraduate Research, an Alden H. and Winfred Brown Faculty Research Fellowship, a grant from the Iris F. Litt, M.D., Fund of the Institute for Research on Women and Gender, a Hewlett Faculty Grant, a grant from the Institute for International Studies, and a grant from the Office of Technology and Licensing Research Incentive Fund. I also gratefully acknowledge staff members at Tenri University Central Library and the Waseda University Central Library, who made available to me their collection of early-twentieth-century Japanese women's magazines.

I also want to thank Reed Malcolm at the University of California Press for keeping faith in my project, and my copy editor, Ellen F. Smith, whose informed and intelligent editing helped to make my prose more readable. I am deeply indebted to Yoshitomo Nara, who generously allowed me to reproduce his painting *The Girl with the Knife in Her Hand* on this book's cover.

During my research in Japan, Prof. Ide Sachiko and her graduate students at Japan Women's University, Prof. Kawasaki Akiko of Rikkyo University, and Kawahashi Noriko provided me with a stimulating intellectual network. The late Prof. Matsumoto Mikio, my undergraduate advisor, initially introduced me to the managers at the company I call MJL in this book. Without his help, my book would not exist.

I am truly indebted to the people at MJL, including the CEO, who generously endorsed my research. I have no adequate words to convey how much I owe the people I describe in my book and how much I enjoyed working with them. Hirata Kazuko and Suzuki Masayuki not only put up with my clumsiness as a clerical worker, but also took me under their wings and gently guided me through the everyday world of life in a corporation. I learned more from them than I could ever have imagined. I also thank Hagiwara Junji, my *sararīman* friend, for sharing with me his experience of working in a large corporation, as well as uncountable clippings from his own research.

I thank Dora Cañas and Rachel Brown for the priceless gift of peace and order. Tom, Chibby, and Noah Shintaro helped keep my sanity. And thank you, Kei-chan, Miyuki-san, Takkun, Nao-chan, Mana-chan, Hiroyuki, Yuki-san, Ryo-chan, and Obaa-chan, for putting up with my wild dream of writing a book. This book is dedicated to my parents, the hardest working people I have ever known, who will never know how much they have given me.

Note on Japanese Names and the Romanization of Japanese Language

In this book, Japanese proper names are denoted with the family ("last") name preceding the given ("first") name. The modified Hepburn system (Hebon-shiki) is used to romanize the Japanese language. Accordingly, long vowels are marked with macrons (ā, ē, ī, ō, ū), with the exception of the transcription and quotation of actual speech, in which the lengthening of vowels is marked with additional vowels (e.g., "aa" instead of "ā").

INTRODUCTION

Women's Language and Capitalist Modernity in Japan

> *There's a sign on the wall but she wants to be sure*
> *'Cause you know sometimes words have two meanings.*
> Jimmy Page and Robert Plant, "Stairway to Heaven"

"Japanese women's language" (*onna kotoba* or *joseigo*) is a socially powerful truth.[1] By this, I do not mean that the phrase refers to the empirical speech patterns of women but that Japanese women's language is an obligatory cultural category and an unavoidable part of practical social knowledge—for both women and men, urban and rural—in contemporary Japan. By using the phrase *women's language*, I refer to a space of discourse—understood as a complex ensemble of practices, institutions, representations, and power—in which the Japanese woman is objectified, evaluated, studied, staged, and normalized through her imputed language use and is thus rendered a knowable and unified subject both to herself and to others. Doxic statements, such as "Women and men speak differently," "Women speak more politely than men," or "Women are not capable of speaking logically," are commonly heard in daily conversation. Scholars, too, have perennially produced a highly reflexive and abstract—and therefore privileged—knowledge of how women speak differently

---

1. The indigenous terms are *onna kotoba* (*onna* = women, *kotoba* = speech/language) or *joseigo* (*josei* = women, *go* = language). Although neither of the Japanese phrases includes a term specifically referring to "Japan" or "Japanese," I affix the term *Japanese* in my English translation because of its specific connection with the development of the Japanese nation-state since the late nineteenth century.

I

from men. Using both empirical and anecdotal evidence, they have systematically located male-female differentiation at all levels of language—phonology, semantics, morphology, syntax, speech acts, and discourse (in the technical linguistic sense), as well as extralinguistic features, such as pitch, and have accounted for how female-specific values, attributes, and social roles are registered in speech forms and in the management of conversation.[2] Particularly notable are certain parts of speech, such as pronouns and final particles, that are said to function as mutually exclusive gender markers indexing femininity and masculinity. Women's language is thus understood as a set of linguistic forms and functions of language exclusively or statistically used by women and very often associated with certain feminine demeanors, roles, and attributes, such as being soft-spoken, polite, hesitant, empathetic, gentle, and nonassertive. In addition, women's language is often represented as having a higher pitch.

Women's language also is a national issue, a self-conscious parameter of civil order and social change. Nationwide opinion polls are regularly conducted on whether women's language is becoming "corrupted" and, if so, how. Public sentiments regarding the perceived disappearance of women's language are thereby crystallized and circulated in the form of numbers and statistics.[3] This linguistic consciousness of how women speak is closely connected with notions of culture and tradition in the assumption that women's language is uniquely Japanese, with unbroken historical roots in an archetypical, imaginary Japanese past, and inescapably linked to an equally traditional and archetypical imaginary Japanese womanhood. Kindaichi Kyosuke, one of the founders of modern Japanese linguistics, noted in his discussion of women's language: "Japanese womanhood is now being recognized as beautiful and excellent beyond comparison with the other womanhoods of the world. Likewise, Japanese women's language is so fine that it seems to me that it is, along with Japanese womanhood, unique in the world" (1942:293). Kikuzawa Sueo, one of the first modern linguists to bring attention to women's language, observed: "Women's speech is characterized by elegance, that is, gentleness and beauty. Moreover, such characteristics correspond with our unique national language" (1929:75).

2. See Ide 1982 and Shibamoto 1985 for classic sociolinguistic studies of Japanese women's language.

3. NHK (Japan Broadcasting Corporation) and the Agency for Cultural Affairs (Bunkachō) in the Ministry of Education, Culture, Sports, Science, and Technology, for example, regularly conduct surveys on language awareness, including items regarding women's language.

Women's language is thus viewed as an emblem of nation and tradition—as against the West and even modernity itself—whose most authentic form has been feared to be lost.[4] As Mashimo Saburo, another scholar of Japanese women's language, puts it, "We cannot hope for contemporary Japanese women to be as witty and tactful as were those in the past, but, at least, I would like them to have a sincere and humble attitude and to preserve the cultural heritage passed down from the ancestors without destroying it" (1969:81). Such an image of the loss of women's language is widely shared by the public. Talk of women's language implicates the perceived continuing contradiction between Japanese tradition and modernity.

Japanese women's language also is a transnational social fact. An article appeared in 1995 in the *New York Times* titled "Japan's Feminine Falsetto Falls Right out of Favor." The subtitle reads: "Traditionally, women have spoken in a falsetto pitch, but now they're beginning to find their own deeper sounds." In this article, Japanese women's voices are described as being "as sweet as syrup, and as high as a dog whistle. Any higher, and it would shatter the crystal on the seventh floor," and "they are not speaking, but squeaking" (Kristof 1995:A1). The article compares the pitch of Japanese women's voices and that of American women's voices and reports that Japanese women's voices have significantly dropped these days because of the change in women's status in Japan. Japanese women's speech—as if merely one other disassembled and fetishized part of a woman's body—now draws intensive international attention as indexical of how far Japan has progressed or caught up with America in terms of "equality" and "modernity."

But here is a little public secret: the very simple, yet obstinately disregarded, fact is that most women in Japan do not have access to—did not systematically learn and cannot skillfully produce—the speech forms identified as women's language in their habitual speech repertoire; particularly people in the cultural, class, and regional peripheries would tell us that statements such as "men and women speak differently" do not apply to *their* everyday linguistic experience. Why, then, does it *make sense* to talk about how men and women speak differently? Why is women's language use a national obsession? What kind of social, historical, and political conditions are necessary to make possible the normalization of

---

4. See Ivy's (1995) important analysis of the reflexive projection of an unsullied Japanese essence into the past, in which "longing" for something brings it into cultural existence even if it did not actually exist. Likewise, any statement about perceived "corruption" functions to affirm the ontology of the essence by logically implying that there was once a pure women's language.

a stubborn self-referential and self-contained discourse about language, culture, and gender? Why are people so compelled to engage with the assiduous production and reproduction of the sociolinguistic knowledge of women's language? Why are the densely heterogeneous linguistic practices of people in Japan so radically reduced to one single binary, that is, gender—male and female—and to a single set of speech forms?

This book is about this vicarious language that universally represents and speaks for the voice of Japanese women that is not theirs. The almost theological avowal of gender difference in language use, reified in the cultural category of "women's language," derives not from women's characteristically—much less, universally—speaking it, but from its culturally reflexive role in scaffolding the foundational narrative of modern Japan as a nation-state—with universal tropes of progress, modernity, tradition, the middle class, and homogeneity. The book thus begins with the observation that "Japanese women's language" is not simply a set of speech forms and functions that operate in the interpersonal micro-context as a gender marker. Rather, the cultural tenacity and condition of the possibility of women's language are intimately bound up with the emergent social formations of modernity, capitalism, and nationalism, which Japan has experienced since the late nineteenth century. Drawing both on historical research and on ethnographic fieldwork in a Tokyo corporate office to study the everyday linguistic experience of white-collar female office workers, and challenging the ontological underpinnings of the cultural category of women's language on historical, ethnographic, and linguistic grounds, this book seeks to unravel the hard-tied knot of gender, language, and political economy in modern Japan and to understand how it is lived by contemporary historical actors.

In this book, I seek to understand the historical and structural linkages among Japan's experience of modernity and modernization, gender, and language use. "Japanese women's language" emerges in the contingent mediation of these three mutually constituting domains of social form in a particular geopolitical location at a particular historical juncture. Modernity entails a particular temporal experience whose terms are set by those of the global circuit of capitalist accumulation, expansion, and abstraction of social relations. But it is definitively a *cultural* experience in the sense that such a global economic and political process, accompanied by technological development and concomitant nation-formation, constitutes the cultural condition of who we are, or, simply put, modern subjectivity. Under cultural idioms centering on "progress," "Westernization," and "newness," modernity shapes human lives by temporalizing them, while concealing the increasing spatial unevenness and contradictions among them in their concrete social conditions.

Accordingly, the cultural form of Japanese modernity and modern subjectivity is not to be conflated with those of the West. Japan's experience of modernity is one of many modernities that simultaneously coexist. As Harootunian puts it, "co-eval modernity . . . calls attention to the experience of sharing the same temporality, that whatever and however a society develops, it is simply taking place at the same time as other modernities. But the experience also, and necessarily, marks a difference. What co-eval suggests is contemporaneity yet the possibility of difference" (2000b:xvi–xvii).[5] Harootunian gives us the framework for making sense of the modernity of Japanese women's language and the auditory and gendered nature of Japanese modernity. Women's language is perhaps "unique" to Japan, but it is not a vestige from the premodern past, ready for the dustbin as Japan catches up with the West. It is fully modern, but an example of modern difference as made visible by Harootunian's model. This allows us to avoid cultural essentialism—the proposal that things that are not obviously modern or Western are rooted in Japan's cultural or historical deep structure—but still allows us to attend to intensely local matters such as speaking and hearing. Such local matters are real and historical as well as critically connected with broader economic and political processes, and demand not only linguistic but also social and cultural analysis.

The notion of co-eval modernity allows us to understand the cultural category of women's language not as unintended surplus but as what modernity structurally produces at a particular historical and geopolitical juncture. Women's language is one of the key differentiations—if not *the* key differentiation—that marks the specificity of Japan's modernity on the global stage. It inaugurates a distinctively gendered modernity within the nation and a different modality of being connected with the national and the global. The discourse of women's language is a complex regime that governs social awareness and reflection about not only gender and speech but also about "Japaneseness." It is a historical product of modernizing forces in the state, the family, and the market that mobilized the "I" in women's language to interpellate the female population into the citizen, the subject of capitalist reproduction (the wife and the mother), the subject of consumption, and the imperial subject. But at the same time, the construction of women's language centrally partakes of the structural

---

5. See also Fabian 1983 for the similar conceptualization of the co-evalness in his discussions on the relationship between anthropologists and "natives."

and temporal condition of Japan's modernity. Gender is foregrounded by the nation-state, negotiating its cultural or spatial terms in which the temporality of modernity is experienced. This takes the form of binaries such as West and East, tradition and modernity, center and periphery, and culture and economy, and gets transposed onto the ontological binary of male and female.

But we also need to recognize a co-eval modernity *within* Japan. The speech forms characteristically identified as "women's language" are not characteristic of the speech of many millions of Japanese women—particularly in the regional peripheries, among metropolitan working-class women, and in other socially or culturally "marginal" populations. This fact of linguistic heterogeneity, when recognized in Japan, is conceptualized in precisely the way that Harootunian meant to critique: it is understood as "lag," " nonstandard," or some other concept that denies its co-evalness. In other words, it is understood as an indicator of the incompletion of Japan's modern, national integration. This book will focus squarely on the political process of dislocating heterogeneity to gain an understanding of how the standard became the standard.

The Epistemology of the Abject

Growing up in a regional area in Japan, where no one speaks women's language, I never experienced as a child a face-to-face context of talking with or hearing someone who used the speech forms identified as women's language. Women's language was, for me, language not to speak but only to hear on television. The only exception I can remember was when my friends and I were playing house with Licca-chan (Rika-chan), an extremely popular must-have girl doll, the Japanese equivalent of Barbie. She had among her accessories everything we did not have, including a Western-style house without a *tatami* floor, a sofa, a piano, stylish clothes, a sports car, and a good-looking boyfriend, Wataru-Kun. We ventriloquized her and let our Licca-chan "speak like women on TV," or what we understood as "women's language," characterized by certain utterance-ending forms such as *dawa, noyo, nano, kashira*, and so on, with exaggerated rising intonation in what we thought of as "standard" Japanese accents.[6] Our Licca-chan did not speak her (our) local dialect.

6. Contemporary Japanese language scholars commonly classify speech forms such as *dawa, noyo, nano,* and *kashira* as *"shūjoshi,"* which is normally translated into English as

I vicariously experienced women's language through the media. When I was a child, I encountered women's language as foremost the language of *whiteness*. On Sunday evenings at 9:00 P.M., my father's favorite TV program, *Sunday Western Movie Theater* (Nichiyō Yōga Gekijō), aired. It would show mostly American movies dubbed with Japanese voices. I was not allowed to watch because of my bedtime (and also because of the claimed unsuitability of the content for a child). But since I slept in the room adjacent to the TV room, partitioned by a sliding rice-paper door, I used to listen to the "voices" of foreign actresses as dubbed over in Japanese. I heard white women "speaking" (Japanese) "women's language," perfectly. With my ears keenly attuned in my futon, I imagined what these white actresses looked like from their "Japanese" voices and impeccable women's language.

Women's language was also the language of commerce in selling products. I always associated it with the speech style of TV advertisement. From

---

"sentence-final particles," or "final particles." Together with other grammatical units such as verbs, auxiliary verbs, adjectives, and copulas, a final particle comprises a compound predicate, or a sentence-ending form. There are, however, at least two problems with using the grammatical term "final particle" to refer to elements of women's language as understood by native speakers. First, what is conventionally classified as a final particle itself can be broken down further into smaller units, depending on which system of grammatical categorization one uses. For example, *teyo* is classified as a final particle, but can also be classified as a compound form made up of *-te* (a conjunctive or gerund inflectional ending of a verb, or a suffix attached to an adverbial inflectional ending of a verb) and *yo* (a final particle), depending on which linguistic analysis one is using. Or *dawa*, which is commonly classified as a final particle, is actually a compound of the auxiliary verb *da* and a final particle *wa*. Second, some of the speech forms identified as women's language do not necessarily belong to the class of final particles, and yet they are treated like final particles by native speakers. For example, *chatta*, which, as will be seen in chapter 2, some Meiji intellectuals identified as part of schoolgirl speech, is not a final particle, but is a contracted form of the verb *te-shimatta* (have done). The point is that grammatical categories used by scholars do not necessarily correspond with units and categories used and understood by nonlinguists to talk about salient linguistic features of women's language, and nonspecialist speakers do not use the term *shūjoshi* in conversation about Japanese. As will be seen later in this chapter and other chapters, nonspecialist native speakers simply gloss the relevant women's language forms as *gobi* or *kotobajiri*, which literally mean "the end or the tail of words or utterances." A technical linguistic distinction between a final particle and a verb inflection is not meaningful to native speakers. Since one of the key goals of this book is to examine how historical actors themselves reflexively represent language and language use, I will rely on the categories *gobi* or *kotobajiri*, with their English translation as "utterance-ending." Because Japanese is a S-O-V (subject-object-verb) language with its word order positioning the predicate at the end of the sentence, "utterance-ending" refers to a predicate part, including a verb (inflection), an auxiliary verb, a final particle, or a combination of those. I will use the term *utterance-ending* in places where it is important to reflect categories and units that are *pragmatically or culturally meaningful* to historical actors. In places where grammatical specificity is relevant to the discussion or analysis, I will rely on linguistic terms such as final particle and auxiliary verb.

soaps and rice vinegar to vacuum cleaners and rice cookers, TV women addressed the viewer in women's language, individuating a viewer as "you" and hailing her as a consumer. Women's language worked like an arrow pointing to all the commodities, particularly "female" commodities, which promised to make one modern and middle class.

It was also the language of Tokyo. The place associated with women who speak women's language is Tokyo, an unmarked place, in the world of television, where everybody is middle class, every man wears a tie and commutes on trains and subways, and every woman wears a frilled apron or high heels. For me, women's language was the language spoken on the other side of the TV screen. The original speakers of women's language for me were cartoon characters, stuffed animals, Midori-sensei (Teacher Midori) on *Romper Room,* the Onēsan (Big Sister) on *Okāsan to Issho* (Together with Mother), women in cooking shows, actresses in dramas, and popular singers. I heard the most authentic women's language from such inauthentic—electronically mediated—bodies, not the bodies of real people in face-to-face interaction with me.

It was on my first visit to my uncle's house in Yokohama (within the greater Tokyo metropolitan area) that I heard for the first time what I thought was women's language spoken by the organic human body. Upon arriving at Tokyo Station, I heard people speaking like those on TV: men sounded like TV announcers, and women sounded like those on TV commercials and in dramas. I felt the vertigo of being thrown suddenly into a television set. Watching TV at my uncle's house was most surreal; the language I heard around me and on the TV screen was, for the first time, identical! My cousins were speaking like kids on my favorite kids' drama, my uncle like a TV announcer, and my aunt just like Elizabeth Taylor! Or, at least, that is how I remembered it.

"Women's language" excessively signified for me things more than, or even other than, femaleness. It figured an excess of meaning that the gender binary fails to contain, such as commodity consumption, whiteness, nonhuman (female) automatons and creatures, the middle class, Tokyo, the modern, and the media. The temporal order that underwrote my encounter with women's language also inverted the naturalized history of women's language, which presupposes its natural spontaneous evolution out of the inherent traits of the Japanese femaleness of real Japanese women. My first encounter with women's language was a series of disembodied and synthetic copies and imitations, and only ex post facto did I discover—to my pleasant surprise—the living organic bodies that used women's language. For me it was the "copies" that were the original.

I tell my story not because my experience is terribly special, but precisely because it is not at all uncommon, particularly for those in regional areas and in the working class, for whom women's language is language not to produce but only to consume, and not so much to hear as to *overhear*. It is inherently disembodied and vicarious as a tele-aural phenomenon, in which the copy precedes the original. Furthermore, women's language for these subjects is not reducible to gender difference, because their sense of women's language rests also on those differences that are not contained within the gender binary—an unproductive or "inessential" extra of meaning with no sign value that contributes to the binary system of gender. But this seemingly "inauthentic," or "secondary," experience of women's language is necessary for the very identity of women's language. In other words, such experience, seemingly external to the identity of women's language, in fact essentially constitutes it, and such elements that cannot be contained within the gender binary are excluded and are presented as external to its identity. For women's language to assert its pure identity, that is, normalized "gender" identity, other elements—class, history, and politics—need to be rendered invisible.

It is "the supplement" (Derrida 1976:144–45), an inessential surplus, which is added to that which is already complete and, at the same time, supplants the absence in what claims to be complete. In this contradictory move, the supplement is posited as exterior and extra to the identity and yet is necessary for the identity to be full and complete. The fact that the identity needs the supplement means that it is deficient and can be complete only with the presence of the supplement. It follows that the supplement is inside the identity that excludes it. "It adds only to replace. It intervenes or insinuates itself *in-the-place-of*" (145; italics in original). The supplement's absent presence then endlessly defers and thus wrenches the stability and fruition of the identity.

Consider Saussure's (1959) structuralist account of the system of language. For the word *cat* to mean what it does, it must be differentiated from, for example, *cut*. There is no inherent meaning attached to the word *cat*. It is only its distinctive features in relation to other elements in a system that makes *cat* mean something distinct from *cut*. Without this system of differences, *cat* makes no sense. But when we hear or see the word *cat*, we think we know what it means without hearing or seeing the other paradigmatic elements of the system without which *cat* has no meaning. Derrida extends this analysis to the supplement. *Cut* is an apparently insignificant addition and exterior to *cat*, which appears to present itself self-sufficiently. Yet *cat* always requires the "absent presence" of *cut* (and other elements). In other words, from the original moment, *cat* cannot present itself without *cut*. It is *originally* incomplete and deficient, and *cut* is not actually exterior to *cat*, but interior to it. The logic of the supplement thus exposes the internal contradiction of the seemingly stable essence. An apparently inessential surplus is necessary to that which seems already complete and, at the same time, supplants the absence in what claims to be complete.[7]

It is this logic of supplementarity immanent in the experiences of women's language from the cultural and economic peripheries that I would like to make operative in this book as the ground of knowledge to retell the story and history of Japanese women's language. What can we learn about women's language when we see it from the position of the supplement, the place where the temporal relationship between the origin and the copy is inverted? This is the epistemology of those for whom neither "speaking women's language" nor "not speaking women's language" is a viable or meaningful choice and for whom there is no organic origin of women's language. Occupying the place of the supplement, their experiences of women's language are designated as secondary and derivative (failed) representations of the original and the ideal of women's language. By virtue of being the supplement, however, they lay bare traces of difference prior to being recalled and suppressed by the gender binary. By "taking the place of" the gender binary as the ontology of women's language, the supplement exposes what the discourse of women's language fails to contain and thus threatens the claimed temporal and spatial origin of women's language and undermines its stable and direct identification with the equally essentialized notion of "Japanese culture."

Derrida's concept of supplement is reworked by Butler as the notion of the "abject" (1990:133–34, 1993a:3, 1993b). Abjects are those "who are neither named nor prohibited within the economy of the law" (1993b:312), whose domain is produced to define the domain of the subject. The abject is neither the sovereign subject nor the object because it is what was

---

7. Derrida's full comment thus notes, "The supplement supplements. It adds only to replace. It intervenes or insinuates itself *in-the-place-of*; if it fills, it is as if one fills a void. If it represents and makes an image, it is by the anterior default of a presence. Compensatory [*suppléant*] and vicarious, the supplement is an adjunct, a subaltern instance which *takes-(the)-place [tient-lieu]*. As substitute, it is not simply added to the positivity of a presence, it produces no relief, its place is assigned in the structure by the mark of emptiness. Somewhere, something can be filled up *of itself*, can accomplish itself, only by allowing itself to be filled through sign and proxy. The sign is always the supplement of the thing itself" (1976:145).

originally and inherently part of the subject but was abjected and posited as exterior in order for the subject to be the subject. Here Butler examines the construction of "normative" sexuality and the way in which homosexuality is systematically abjected as secondary and derivative in order for heterosexuality to be normalized. Heterosexuality as the origin, the natural, and the normal is established by its claim of temporal anteriority to homosexuality; homosexuality is a time-lagged, failed copy of the original. What Butler (1993a:3) shows us is the extent to which the normative subject can constitute itself only "through the force of exclusion and abjection" of homosexuality. Thus homosexuality cannot be posterior to heterosexuality. If the heterosexual can emerge only after the homosexual is abjected from it, then there is no heterosexuality prior to homosexuality, nor can the heterosexual be more normative than the homosexual.

The domain of those for whom neither "speaking women's language" nor "not speaking women's language" makes sense, and for whom the copy is the original, is that of the abject and its enabling ground to invert the temporal order and thus to "expose the fundamental dependency of 'the origin' on that which it claims to produce as its secondary effect" (Butler 1993b:314). My strategy thus is not so much subversion as inversion. Rather than turning the abject into an ethnographic subject as positive knowledge, say, "the language used by working-class women," and thus positing those women as external to the identity of women's language, I would like to invoke the very category of women's language and to look at moments of its own epistemic failure from within, by foregrounding the absent presence of the abject and the present absence of its subject, origin, and identity within the discourse of women's language.[8] The ethnographic focus of this book is the urban middle-class white-collar women working at the heart of the cultural and economic center in downtown Tokyo, who are, in many ways, in closest proximity to women's lan-

---

8. While I am not examining the actual speech of the marginalized here, my aim is emphatically not to discount historical or ethnographic accounts of the underrepresented. But my project has more to do with the specific problematics of the representation of Japanese women. Given the persistent tendency for "Japanese women" to be exoticized, eroticized, and objectified, turning them into the positivity of scholarly knowledge needs much more care and caution than has been shown. Whether as heroines bravely resisting the system of oppression and dominance or as victims who fail to pursue their own gendered interests, constructing "Japanese women" as the self-consolidating other, we should be reminded, creates a seductive space where we are tempted to insert our own fantasy, redemption, and frustration. In thinking about the question of how to represent the abject, particularly in the form of an ethnography in the context of modern Japan, I am indebted to the works of Ivy (1995) and Yoneyama (1999).

guage in terms of both habitus and acquired linguistic capital and discipline. And it is among these women and their linguistic practices that I will seek traces of what the subject of women's language attempts to abject, the "real" of which returns, if momentarily, to haunt that subject.

This is, of course, neither to exclude nor to dismiss those who "speak" women's language, who have long been considered the most legitimate subjects of sociolinguistic studies of women's language. On the contrary, the epistemology of the abject compels us simply to convert normative subjects into denaturalized, denormalized, provincialized "marked" subjects. Instead of taking it for granted that a certain speech style of a particular segment of the population is empirically in close proximity to the style identified as "women's language," we need to ask what kind of social, economic, and historical conditions make it possible for some segment of the population to cite the law of women's language so faithfully and successfully to the extent that they can identify themselves, or that they can be identified by others, as the "original" speakers of women's language and thus claim its ownership as habitus.

The *politics* of women's language, in other words, is not only about its power to name as deviant those who might consciously resist or to exclude those who do not take sufficient steps to discipline themselves to its regime. Nor is it only about the power of the discourse of women's language to designate the positions from which "resistance" to it is thinkable or possible. Nor is the politics of women's language only about its linkage with sexism and patriarchy as a key site and means of their perpetual reproduction and their violent recasting of politics as aesthetics. All of these forms of power are important, surely. But this book will argue that we must include in our vision of the politics of women's language its status as a materialization of the logical contradictions of Japan's industrial modernity. This politics dissimulates the ever growing hierarchy and inequality *among women* and recalls differences and surplus that those who would belong to the domain of the abject—dialect speakers, the working class, or the non-Japanese—produce vis-à-vis women's language to the "nationalized" gender binary.

What is abjected in the production of the subject of women's language approximates what is abjected in the production of Japan as a modern capitalist nation-state. In other words, what defines the boundary between the subject and the abject in the cultural category of women's language and guarantees its stability has to do with the multiple forces constituting the social formation of Japan as a modern capitalist nation-state. The order of gender in the realm of "speaking" is in an interdependent relationship with other systems of order that undergird a complex of culture, economy, and politics, identified as "Japan" and "the Japanese." I will thus seek to highlight how both language and gender centrally matter to political economy and cultural identity.

What Is Women's Language?

Gender is a system of ideological representation, allocating meanings and positions to concrete individuals and rendering them gendered subjects as men and women. Thus, it is also a social relation marked by practices of power and inequality with concrete material consequences. Language (use) is necessarily a social relation involving both a semiotic system and social action, through which images, ideas, identities, and meanings of gender are constituted, and individual speakers are thus engendered in the very process of everyday linguistic activities. Gender is both made by language and productive of language. In Japanese, the representation of female gender-in-language is a culturally salient category, whose various forms of reflexive, practical knowledge and practice are often referred to as "women's language." This body of knowledge/practice is a cultural conception of the relation of gender to, and its representation in, the realm of language use. Women's language is a set of linguistic beliefs about forms and functions of language used by and associated with (Japanese) women. To put it differently, it is a culturally salient category and knowledge about "how women speak," how they "usually speak" or "should speak." The production of such knowledge takes a wide range of forms, including commentaries and statements such as "Women speak more politely than men" or "less logically," or "to say the same thing as men, women use such-and-such a final particle."

Women's language is an established subject of scholarly inquiry with its own system of historical classification and periodization, and this scholarship is not autonomous from, but an integral part of, the culturally salient practice of representing gender in language. Sociolingusitic studies have systematically located gender difference in all the linguistic levels of Japanese — phonology, morphology, syntax, speech acts, discourse, and beyond — in both the Japanese of the present and that of the past.[9] They have found,

---

9. Unless otherwise specified, I will use the Western categories of *sociolinguistics* or *sociolinguists* to cover all the scholars and scholarly works involved with the study of Japanese women's language, including both *kokugogaku* (national language studies) and *shakaigengogaku* (sociolinguistics).

for example, formal features of women's language, which include a specific set of vocabulary, first-person pronouns (*atashi, atakushi*), final particles (*wa, dawa, no, noyo*), and a so-called beautification prefix, *o-*. These are all said to be "exclusive" features of women's language and to be used exclusively by women, whose pragmatic effects are tautologically explained as sounding "soft," "nonassertive," "gentle," and so on.[10] While such pragmatic effects are not necessarily locatable in discrete forms such as pronouns and final particles, scholars have also located them at the level of speech acts. For example, the social act of "being polite" can be linguistically realized, and researchers examine how men and women differently execute speech acts that create the effect of politeness. What is at work here is a relative—as opposed to mutually exclusive—system of gender difference, which is beyond the linguistically conscious grasp and rationalization of laypeople, ascertainable only by using empirical and quantitative methods. Notably, such studies have been conducted generally among the middle-class female population of standard Japanese speakers who live in Tokyo and its greater metropolitan environs.

In this study, I pursue a different direction and seek to understand women's language as a *network of cultural practices of objectifying femaleness/femininity and mapping a reified gender binary onto the sounds, figures, manners, and organizations of talk*. Through this network of practices, women are objectified, subjected, and abjected through their imputed language use. Scholarship on women's language is clearly part of this network. The diverse modes of this discourse emerge through the everyday social practices of commenting on, interpreting, evaluating, criticizing, classifying, abstracting, and studying how women speak in various sites of social life, in the present and the past. And we must add to this list the reflexive and self-conscious monitoring, evaluation, and interpretation of one's own use of (or failure at) "women's language." The relevant discursive activities encompass not only everyday commentaries by ordinary people, but also the institutional production of authorized knowledge of women's language in academia, the public sphere, mass culture, the

---

10. It is impossible to draw a complete list of what formally constitutes "women's language" because the pragmatic effects of language use are inevitably contingent upon the context. This is not to mention—and this is the point of this book—that people in different social locations have different ideas about what constitutes women's language. For some people, for example, a final particle *no* sounds "feminine," whereas for others it sounds neutral, since they claim that they hear men use it on regular basis. Any list is thus vulnerable to contestation. See Okamoto 1995 and Shibamoto 1985 for the best attempt to provide a general view of the linguistic features associated with women's language.

government, Japanese pedagogy, and formal education. And it is my contention that these pervasive and quite day-to-day and mundane cultural practices of engendering speech and languaging gender specific to modern Japanese society not only occasion the production and reproduction of gender as an ideology and a category, but also operate as the entailed condition of *other, broader regimes of power* at specific historical junctures. The discursive construct of women's language *necessarily* implies *Japan* and its historical and cultural modes of address—nation, class, race, modernity, and tradition—in particular historical moments. To speak of "women's language" is *necessarily* to speak of Japan as a unique cultural thing-in-the-world.

If we recognize women's language not as mere gender difference in language, but as a mode of the broader social formation and of the constitution of the subject, historically and politically bound up with other domains of cultural practice, then we need to recognize the productivity of discourse, which Foucault defined as "practices that systematically form the objects of which they speak" (1972:49).[11] Inseparably linked up with the exercise of social power, the discourse of Japanese women's language produces the very condition that makes it possible for people to talk about "women's language" by assigning it particular modalities of existence. It is a truth-producing practice by which the subject (of women's language) is brought into being by delimiting the zone of the normative, the possible, and the intelligible at the cost of the simultaneous constitution of the abject, the unthinkable, and the unnamable. The discovery—or "birth"—of women's language as a scholarly object and the impassioned pursuit of identifying its linguistic features and workings can be understood as *a function of the discourse*. The goal of this study is therefore neither to identify gender difference in language use empirically or otherwise nor to engage in empirical discussions about the language-gender relationship (for example, whether women's language use has been changing or whether there is actually gender difference in language use). Instead of asking whether or not linguistic characterization of women's language use is empirically valid, I ask how such empirical questions are possible and thinkable to begin with, what kind of "truth" of women's language they produce, and how social power is

---

11. As it is sometimes misconstrued, "discourse analysis" means neither linguistic analysis nor text analysis. Furthermore, in Foucault's sense of discourse, it is a matter neither of representation nor of meaning. Discourse delimits the possibilities within which the subject comes into being and provides the very condition under which a certain mode of being—and not others—is possible. For his painstaking account of discourse, see Foucault 1977a.

exercised through the articulation of such discursive practices with those in other discourses.

Whether we examine a scholarly thesis or everyday conversation, what is important in this book is not so much the content or meaning of what is said about women's language, but the sheer fact that it is said, or can be said in certain contexts by certain agents, and the fact that what is said is intelligibly repeatable in other domains of the society. Discourse is an ensemble of "what is said" or "statements" that belong to a single discursive formation. Foucault explains what "statements" are in the following way:

> We must grasp the statement in the exact specificity of its occurrence; determine its conditions of existence, fix at least its limits, establish its correlations with other statements that may be connected with it, and show what other forms of statement it excludes. We don't seek below what is manifest the half silent murmur of another discourse; we must show why it could not be other than it was, in what respect it is exclusive of any other, how it assumes, in the midst of others and in relation to them, a place that no other could occupy. The question proper to such an analysis might be formulated in this way: what is this specific existence that emerges from what is said and nowhere else? (1972:28)

The critical task of this book is to describe the conditions and the principles within which statements about women's language are generated, dispersed, and repeated. I will explore these processes in concrete cases, both historically and ethnographically. I ask where, how, and by whom a particular statement is made, under what conditions the statement is possible and makes sense, and what other kinds of statements are excluded or rendered unthinkable in the process of some statements becoming possible. The object of my analysis is thus the mode of existence of statements about how women (should) speak and the dispersion and material effect of such statements (see Young 2001:399, 401–2). From the academy to everyday conversation, why do we have such passion and determination to talk about gender difference in language? What makes possible such an impassioned will to truth and knowledge of women's language? What are the incitements to speech such that we never stop talking about women's language?

The will to "know" and to talk about what women's language is or how women speak (or should speak) is never an "innocent" desire flowing out of "pure" intellectual curiosity. The rendering of women's language into a knowable and intelligible object is precisely the operation of discursive power, for the constitution of any subject, be it "woman," "women's language," or "Japan," is, as we saw above, secured through a process of exclusion and abjection. Foucault's discourse analysis, which should not be mistaken for a mere textual discourse analysis, thus postulates, and pays careful attention to, the exteriority of discourse. He thus urges us to ask "why it could not be other than it was, in what respect it is exclusive of any other, how it assumes, in the midst of others and in relation to them, a space that no other could occupy." If "women's language" means something, its identity does not come from a stable text or referent, accessible to us by hermeneutic interpretation or empirical observation, but from the boundary-making of the discourse itself that divides what is women's language from what it is not. By presupposing other possibilities of existence, discourse analysis thus enables us to ask what is excluded and abjected, what is dissimulated, and who is silenced at the cost of the plentitude of the identity that the discourse produces. And it is this theoretical supposition of the space of the "could have been otherwise" that is precisely the architecture for the epistemology of the abject. Speaking from there might be a lost possibility, but looking at the idea of women's language from this space nonetheless provides us with a moment of critique.

Women's Language as Linguistic Ideology

Women's language is a specific kind of discourse, that is, a discourse about speech or language use, or reflexive meta-level statements about language use. Linguistic ideology, as such discourse is termed, has been a central conceptual tenet in contemporary linguistic anthropology, and is broadly defined as "sets of beliefs about language articulated by users as a rationalization or justification of perceived language structure and use" (Silverstein 1979:193).[12] The concept of linguistic ideology concerns how the

---

12. See also Joseph and Taylor 1990; Kroskrity 2000; Rumsey 1990; and Schieffelin et al. 1998 for other definitions of *linguistic ideology* or *language ideology*. Note that the term *ideology* here does not necessarily refer to a Marxist notion of ideology. The relatively recent conceptualization of reflexive activities of language and language use as metapragmatics is indeed groundbreaking, given the fact that speakers' reflexive accounts of how they (or others) speak have often been dismissed as "anecdotal" and empirically unreliable linguistic data "contaminated" by the speaker's consciousness, whereas the accounts of linguists are treated as "theory." Concepts such as linguistic ideology and metapragmatics thus allow us not only to integrate reflexive linguistic activities into social and cultural analysis, but also radically to dismantle the hierarchy among divergent metapragmatic activities, some of which are treated as "theory" and others as mere "murmuring."

structure of language, the use of language, and beliefs about language—both its structure and its use—are necessarily interconnected and dialectically constitutive of each other. Rather than treating the linguistic and the social as isomorphic and assuming the former simply reflects the latter, the concept of linguistic ideology focuses attention on the mutual mediation between the linguistic and the social as *historical* entities, which develop and shift in the material world.

Linguistic ideology consists of "metapragmatic" statements, which encompass a wide range of reflexive social practices of language use, including representing, evaluating, reporting, quoting, citing, classifying, scripting; reifying in the form of dictionaries, etiquette books, scholarly theories of language use, and everyday commentaries about how people speak.[13] Voloshinov calls such metapragmatic statements "reported speech," which he defines as "speech within speech, utterance within utterance, and at the same time also speech about speech, utterance about utterance" (1973:115). It is a way to take others' voices into one's utterance, and, by doing so, to construct and, potentially, to transform them. Reported speech thus entails social issues of authenticity, authority, responsibility, evidentiality, and various performative effects such as parody.[14]

Some metapragmatic activities can take place temporally and spatially apart from linguistic activities in the form of reflection and retrospection, and others are what we can call "metapragmatic activities-in-talk." These work as evaluative acts that are incorporated into concurrent linguistic acts and display how they are to be interpreted.[15] In other words, metalinguistic activity and linguistic activity work like a double signal within the same utterance or statement. Imagine, for example, a comedian impersonating a powerful politician. The manner of impersonation conveys and displays not only what and how the politician would speak (linguistic activity), but also how the comedian reflexively evaluates—making fun of, for example—the politician's manner of speaking and by extension his character and policies (metalinguistic activity).

---

13. See Lucy 1993; Silverstein 1993; Silverstein and Urban (1996). Note that in this book I will use the terms *metalinguistic* and *metapragmatic* interchangeably, since discourse about any level of language, from structure to use, is ultimately about *using* language. See Lucy (1993:17) for further discussion on this point.

14. Some of the classic works on reported speech are included as essays in the following edited volumes: Hill and Irvine 1993; Lucy 1993; Silverstein and Urban 1996.

15. Lucy (1993:17) calls this type of implicit metapragmatics "metapragmatic functioning." See also Silverstein 1993 for further theoretical explications of the difference between metapragmatics and metapragmatic functioning.

To examine the discursive formation of women's language, I will look at a wide range of activities of reported speech and metapragmatic statements in various historical and social locations, including male intellectuals' social commentaries on the linguistic and moral corruption of schoolgirls in the late nineteenth century (chapter 1), novel writers' scripting of dialogues in the late nineteenth century to early twentieth century (chapter 2), new prose genres and commodity advertisements using women's language in women's magazines in the early twentieth century (chapter 3), public opinion surveys on women's language in the late twentieth century (chapter 4), and women in the late twentieth century working at a white-collar corporate office who narrate their language use and perform "women's language" (chapters 5 and 6). These historical instances of metapragmatic activities iterate a set of ontological statements about women's language and thus performatively materialize and avow its historical and contemporary existence. One set of statements concerns its temporal origin, positing that there was once a pure "women's language" in the past, which was supposedly spoken by most, if not all, Japanese women—or at least by more women than do now. At both the beginning and end of the twentieth century, the supposition of the ancient existence of an unsullied women's language took the form of deploring women's contemporaneous linguistic (and moral) corruption. In the early twentieth century, this corruption was attributed to rapid Westernization, and at the end of the century, blame was laid on the rapid economic and social changes that increased women's presence outside of the domestic sphere, as both workers and consumers. Talking about women's language makes sense in such a way that the absence of, or the perceived disappearance of, women's language all the more attests to its ancient existence: women's language, which once existed in pure form, is now lost as a *consequence* of women becoming morally and linguistically corrupted in the present.

Another set of statements, which is subsumed under the first set, has to do with the spatial origin of women's language, positing that women's language, and therefore gender difference in speech, as a culturally unique category *exists* because there are or have been actual living women who speak it. In other words, it identifies a particular segment of the female population—urban middle-class female speakers of standard Japanese—as the direct heirs of the authentic women's language. Metapragmatic activities in various sites thus construct and retroactively discover an authentic and original speaking body as the *cause* and *initiator* of the cultural category of women's language, as opposed to it being a mere ideal or ideology. The spatial origin narrative is conjoined with a temporal narrative to secure the ontology of women's language, claiming that the difficulty of finding authentic women's language speakers in the present results from, again, women's linguistic corruption. As I will discuss extensively in later chapters, both the temporal and the spatial orders produced by the discourse of women's language allegorize Japan as the modern nation-state and link up with similar sets of bifurcations, such as modernity and tradition, economy and culture, the West and Japan, and Tokyo and the "regions."

From Speech to Speech about Speech

Taking the linguistic forms of citing, reporting, and quoting, metapragmatics encompasses practices of representing what is said (or imagined to be said), whether in statement, text, discourse, or sign. These practices' crucial capacity is to transport spatially and temporally what is said from one context to another as a carrier in an endless loop of contextualization, decontextualization, and recontextualization.[16] Derrida (1977) recognizes such a capacity of the sign to break with the context and to function in another context as a general condition of any utterance, not just of reported speech. He calls this universal capacity of the sign "iterability," the ability of a sign to be repeated in difference, in unforeseen contexts. Relatedly, he writes of "citationality," the ability of an utterance to be extracted from one context and contextualized in another.[17] It follows that speaking and speaking about speaking share the same quality, as far as the necessary condition of the sign is concerned. In other words, the existence of any utterance—even though it has no formal trace of being reported or cited—is possible *only as the effect of reporting and citing*, because to be a sign it must be dissociable from the original context and

---

16. See also Bauman and Briggs 1990; Briggs and Bauman 1992; and Hanks 1989 for programmatic essays on the concept of contextualization, decontextualization, and recontextualization.

17. We can see Derrida's (1977) most engaged and elaborate discussion of his conceptualization of iterability and citationality in his critical dialogue with Austin's speech act theory. In addition to plays on stage and fiction, Austin (1962) excluded the act of quoting and reporting from the scope of his speech act theory, saying that it is parasitic and nonserious. It is "parasitic" in the sense that it does not and cannot accommodate the speaker's intention or the presence of his/her being. Derrida's reading of Austin's speech act theory is to point out that those excluded as parasites nonetheless share the same quality—in fact, the essential quality of being a sign—of being iterable and mobile from one context to another. The act of citing and reporting, in this sense, is a viable and necessary linguistic means to materialize such iterability of the sign.

must be citable and repeatable in contexts different from its original. Any utterance thus can be understood as having quotation marks around it, visibly or invisibly. Some are cited with formally visible quoting devices, and others come with invisible quotation marks, as if they were uttered for the first time.

Identifying iterability and citationality as universal qualities of the sign means two things. First, it recognizes that the *absence* of the original speaker's intention is the precondition of the sign. The "origin" is irrelevant to defining the effect and meaning of the sign, since what makes something a sign lies in its historical accumulation of repetition. It is impossible for us to locate the first-time sign and its original speaker. Second, by virtue of the contingency of the location and manner in which the sign will be repeated in the next context, it is vulnerable to unpredictable futures. Thus, the sign's iterability and citationality structurally entail its failure, and that is where and when the possibility of resignification lies and where and when we can locate the moment of agency and resistance (Butler 1993a, 1993b, 1997).

A shift in focus from speaking to speaking about speaking and to metapragmatics as a citational practice, and from women's language as an observable or ideal category of speech to a form of discourse, is fundamental to the epistemology of the abject, which I have laid out above. This shift is necessary to develop a framework that will allow us to imagine space for the abject and the linguistic practices that belong to that space, which are customarily considered frivolous, parasitic, and illegitimate. We need a framework that takes the *vicarious experience of women's language*—experienced citationally, derivatively—as seriously and legitimately as we do the actual women speaking women's language. We need to treat this vicarious experience itself as a scholarly object and as a proper basis of and for theory. We need a framework that can theorize my estranged childhood rendition of "women's language" through Licca-chan's inorganic body, experiencing the copy as the original utterance of women's language.

Speaking "women's language" can be then understood as repeatedly citing in repetition its norms, its (constructed) historicity. What are the discursive "regulatory ideals" at work here? (See Butler 1993a:1.) Recognizing linguistic practice as repetitive acts of citing and quoting is to wrench speech from the speaking subject as its origin and to break the imputed *causal* relationship between the speaking subject and speech. This move radically divests "speaking" of its epistemological privilege as the exclusive object of study and as the singular means by which identities—subjects—are constructed. The productionist ideology—"I speak; therefore, I construct my identity"—logically identifies the middle-class urban standard-Japanese-speaking female population as the subject of women's language, and materializes the idea of "Japanese women speaking women's language"—which is in fact an effect of the discourse of women's language—into tangible, real speaking bodies as the origin, cause, and initiator. The majority of women in Japan are thus relegated to the domain of the abject, as secondary or "failed" copies. Furthermore, the productionist ideology reduces women's language exclusively to "gender" as a depoliticized, abstract, and culturally naturalized expression of femaleness, and prevents us from understanding how the construction of women's language involves multiple systems of difference, such as class, region, and even race.

The productionist ideology subscribes to the fundamental assumption inherent in the discourse of women's language that the speaking subject precedes speech, or that the "I" in the discourse of women's language is caused by the speaker's subject-ness. As Butler persuasively argues, this is a function of *metalepsis*, the inversion of cause and effect, by which "the subject who 'cites' the performative is temporarily produced as the belated and fictive origin of the performative itself" (1997:49–50).[18] *It is the discourse that makes the person who invokes it look like its agent.* The discourse thus dissimulates its agency as that of the subject, who cites its norms and historicity. Metaleptic substitution of the discourse for the subject is ideologically complicit with the functionalist narrative of women's language, the proposition that it exists because women of multiple generations voluntarily spoke it as the expression of their female identity.

In describing discourse, Foucault (1972:25) tells us to keep in suspense any self-evident grouping of statements that accords itself unity and continuity and to disturb the "tranquility with which it is accepted." The horizon of the discursive field must be sought beyond immediate unity and continuity. Foucault thus notes, "Once these immediate forms of continuity are suspended, an entire field is set free. A vast field, but one that can be defined nonetheless: this field is made up of the totality of all effective statements (whether spoken or written), in their dispersion as events and in the occurrence that is proper to them" (26–27). To describe the discursive field therefore necessarily questions the limits and distinctions imposed by a deceptively unified theme such as "Japanese women speaking women's language." Instead, discourse analysis enables us to envision other modes of experience and existence of women's language such as

---

18. For a brief definition of *metalepsis*, see also Spivak (1990:122).

reading, seeing, listening, consuming, writing, stage-performing, quantifying, and surveying, and to imagine all these for people in the zone of the abject, and thus agents other than "speakers."

To recognize multiple modalities of citational practices that constitute the discursive field of women's language is also to go beyond the limits imposed by the production of knowledge on women's language; not only by experts, but by ordinary people; not only in the process of production and reception of speech, but also in retrospection when one does not engage in any actual linguistic activity; not only about language or language use, but also about identities, values, and life opportunities, which are indexed by such citational practices. Discourse analysis thus breaks down disciplinary and analytical boundaries and distinctions such as folk belief vs. scholarly work, the standard vs. dialects, the linguistic vs. the social, the spoken vs. the written, speech vs. speech about speech, and the ideological vs. the real, and reveals the contradiction in those binaries. Surpassing boundaries and binaries allows what is dismissed as "folk," "nonstandard," or "anecdotal" to enter into the scene of "theory" and to help us to see how imposed boundaries and binaries serve to normalize the idea of women's language, indeed to conjure it into existence.

Finally, delinking speech from the speaking body also shifts the terms in which we return to familiar concepts such as agency and resistance. How can we imagine forms of resistance and locations of agency, especially for those in the domain of the abject, which derive not from the act of speaking *against* women's language but from speaking *within* women's language? If it is true, as I argue, that people are not so much the origin of language as the *invokers* of language—and here we recognize language's accumulated historicity and effects—we can envision multiple ways, sites, and manners of citing by multiple parties, including those for whom women's language is a resource neither for maintaining social hierarchy nor for resistance. Citation produces copies in difference. As Derrida (1977) says of signature, it must be identical from one instance to another, but each instance is also different. Butler (1997:10–11) sees this in the performativity of the speaking body. Precisely because the body which cites and speaks exists in an ongoing historical world, the inevitable contingency of here and now means that each act, however much disciplined, "says more, or says differently, than it means to say" (11). It is precisely in such repetition in difference, in the unforeseen context, that we can look for the dislocation of the regime of power and, perhaps, the articulation of what we could call "agency." But these acts are not necessarily calculated, strategized, or organized with clear oppositional consciousness. Viewed from the epistemological ground of the abject, in particular, they are often unintended and incalculable, and their effects ambiguous. What will be foregrounded in this book are such enigmatic traces of doers and their deeds that are irreducible either to submission or to resistance, either to structure or to agency.

Butler's discussion of performative contingency as an occasion for the sign's own failure, and therefore as an occasion for the future possibility of resignification, means that we must pay attention to the *temporality* of performativity, which is potentially autonomous by virtue of the sign's ability to break with prior contexts. Butler thus notes, "Understanding performativity as a renewable action without clear origin or end suggests that speech is finally constrained neither by its specific speaker nor its originating context. Not only defined by social context, such speech is also marked by its capacity to break with context. Thus, performativity has its own social temporality in which it remains enabled precisely by the contexts from which it breaks" (1997:4). It is this social temporality of performativity that we must seek in everyday metapragmatic activities. As I mentioned earlier, women's language is a gendered terrain in which the temporality of national modernity is encoded and reproduced. It intimates what Bhabha (1990a:297) calls "nationalist pedagogy," the cumulative sense of time passing from a mythical origin to the present, in which citizens are embedded in—the objects of—a master historical narrative of the nation. At the same time people are the subjects of the nation's narrative by "performing" it in the everyday contingency of social life, which inevitably creates multiple and heterogeneous temporalities. As Bhabha argues, it is this split between the "pedagogical" or the homogeneous and linear narrative of the nation, not unlike the "empty, homogenous time" of Benedict Anderson's (1983) "imagined community," and the recursive enunciation of the "performative," that creates a liminal space for potential disruption of the nation's master narrative.

The Outline of the Book

This book examines two pivotal historical moments in the emergence of "Japanese women's language." One is at the end of the nineteenth century and the beginning of the twentieth, the threshold of Japan's modernity and modernization, when "women's language" came into existence as a discourse through multiple modernizing agents citing and constructing the knowledge of how modern Japanese women (should) speak. The other moment is the early 1990s, at the height of Japan's late capitalist economic boom, which resulted in shifting gender relations and changing struggles over gender. At both historical junctures, "women's language" (re)surfaced as in danger of "loss" as a result of significant shifts in the social formation. The emergence of women's language was simultaneously the mourning of its loss.

PART I: LANGUAGE, GENDER, AND NATIONAL MODERNITY: THE GENEALOGY OF JAPANESE WOMEN'S LANGUAGE, 1880S–1930S

The goal of part 1 is twofold. First, I will historicize the idea of women's language in the context of Japan's modernization. Against the pervasive ontological statement that women's language has ancient roots and represents the essence of a uniquely Japanese tradition, I will show the extent to which the core linguistic features associated with women's language emerged only in the late nineteenth century. Furthermore, originally called "schoolgirl speech," the group of speech forms associated with "women's language" today was far from being considered "feminine" or "elegant," and was, in fact, considered vulgar and low class. Educators and intellectuals were scandalized by such speech. Drawing on Foucault's method of genealogy, I will present a critical history of Japanese women's language and demonstrate its fundamental discontinuity and contingency in the face of the linear historical narrative that claims its premodern origin as part of a distinct and continuous national culture and tradition. Second, I will trace the historical process by which what was once considered "vulgar speech" came to be re-resignified as the ideal "women's language," and show how the emerging capitalist mode of consumption—and its hailing of women into gendered consumer subjects—enabled such resignification.

Chapter 1 considers the historical moment in the late nineteenth century when male intellectuals heard the voice of schoolgirls on the street and cited their speech as "strange" and "vulgar." The term "schoolgirl" referred to girls and young women from elite families who attended women's secondary schools, modern institutions that were part of the early Meiji modernization project inspired by Western Enlightenment and liberal thought. This speech came to be scornfully glossed as *"teyo-dawa* speech" *(teyo-dawa kotoba)* or "schoolgirl speech" *(jogakusei kotoba)*. Ironically enough, many of the actual speech forms identified as "schoolgirl speech" are associated today with "women's language." In this chapter, I will describe how the practices of male intellectuals citing schoolgirl speech actually gave birth to "schoolgirl speech." I will underscore the "derisive" origin—as vulgar and low class—of women's language, which has been erased from the nation's public memory and will analyze the semiotic process by which the "vulgar" speech of schoolgirls came to be reified, and, in turn, schoolgirls as a sign of the Japanese modern came to be a culturally meaningful category through their acoustic presence.

At the same time, this chapter highlights the historically situated listening practice on the part of male intellectuals who overheard the voice of schoolgirls, and traces how this listening practice that produced the auditory appearance of schoolgirls, in turn, constituted the male intellectual as a particular historical subject who "heard" in schoolgirl speech the echo of his own voice, the voice of ambivalence toward his experience of Japan's modernity. The genealogy of women's language shows its birth—as derisive and frivolous as it was—as an aural specter of Japan's modernity and modernization, an annoying iteration of the male voice. This ghostly female voice needed to be abjected, so as to constitute Japan's male modernity. Schoolgirl speech came to be the positivity of a discourse, not simply so much because schoolgirls were engaged in such a way of speaking as because it embodied a surplus of Japan's modernization and modernity that had to be excluded.

Chapter 2 examines the relationship between the language modernization movement, called *gembun'itchi,* and the emergence of "women's language" at the turn from the nineteenth to the twentieth century, when state formation, capitalist accumulation, industrialization, and radical class reconfiguration were taking off. This chapter considers another "derisive" origin of "women's language" in the context of modernizing Japan, specifically in the realm of various events of linguistic modernization, including language standardization and print capitalism. While the language modernization movement aimed to create a standard colloquial Japanese that would serve the purposes of the state administration, the education system, the military, and nationalism, for writers in particular, who were also part of this movement, the aim was to create a new modern Japanese language by which they could represent modern subjectivity. My focus in this chapter is on a group of writers who envisioned modern Japanese literature and its possibility of representing the modern Japanese subject. I will examine how they cited the imaginary modern Japanese woman's voice in the form of dialogues in the modern novel.

Taking a cue from the Western realist novel, Japanese writers sought a language that would allow them to represent reality as faithfully as possible. One of the critical aspects of this modern language is its subordinated linguistic space in the form of dialogue and reported speech. This is a formal space where the object-world is to be represented as literally as possible and is neatly kept apart from the narrating self. The novel thus formally created a hierarchical relationship in which the narrated is always already objectified by the male gaze of the narrating subject or of the modern Japanese citizen. It was in this linguistic space, a quoted space, objectified by the imbricated gaze of the male, the national, and the modern, that "schoolgirl speech," once considered vulgar and low class, was quoted and represented as "the voice" of an increasingly differentiated modern Japanese woman. I will argue that the idea of "women's language," commonly understood to derive from ancient Japanese tradition and culture, is in fact a modern invention, a "hazardous effect" of multiple forces bent on modernization.

Chapter 3 focuses on commercially successful magazines for young women, launched and circulated between the 1890s and the 1930s. These magazines were one of the key sites where young women encountered and experienced "women's language" and where its indexical meaning dramatically shifted. Not only were these magazines one of the first readily available consumer goods for young women, they were also one of the first media of consumer goods in general by virtue of their print advertisements. Such magazines, with their unique format, effectively socialized middle-class literate readers to be desiring gendered bourgeois-citizen-consumers, as readers engaged in the indexical labor of connecting particular speech forms identified as schoolgirl speech to images, ideas, and things in the magazines.

I examine diverse citational practices within these magazines, by which "schoolgirl speech" was transformed from the quoted to the quoting voice, and came to be resignified as "feminine speech style," genuine and universal "women's language," the index of the ideal, urban, middle-class woman. Particularly notable are new textual genres in which schoolgirl speech came to be the quoting voice, in which, instead of being quoted and represented, the "I" of schoolgirl speech talks and represents herself as metalanguage. In these new genres, this self-representing "I" of schoolgirl speech was variously mobilized as the voice of the bourgeois subject to be incited to disclose her inner truth, to assert her consumer-individual taste, style, and choice, to talk about romantic love, to embrace same-sex friendship, and to avow her commitment to the family and the nation. In the women's magazines, schoolgirl speech thus emerged as a linguistic technology to construct and to display the subject position of the modern Japanese woman as a consumer, citizen, wife and daughter, imperial subject, and (petit) bourgeois.

Particularly notable is the way in which commodity advertisements in the magazines used schoolgirl speech as a quoting voice. There, schoolgirl speech was shaped in, through, and as commodity experience, and served as the index of the commodity, inciting the reader's desire and interpellating her into a consumer-subject. In this new context with a new citational practice, "schoolgirl speech" lost its marked reference and become a generic "women's language." Furthermore, consumption successfully mediated politics, specifically the state gender ideology of "good wife and wise mother" *(ryōsai kenbo)*, by translating it into class aspiration and bourgeois sociality through desire for commodity goods. Here, the resignification of schoolgirl speech as women's language had much to do with its semiotic role in mediating consumption and politics in the magazines.

Schoolgirl speech is always represented as in *the present tense.* It is the language of "here and now," by which the reader shares the same time and space with the speaker in the magazine. Unlike the voice of gembun'itchi, or modern standard Japanese, whose transcendental and universal body speaks from nowhere, schoolgirl speech puts forward the materiality and physicality of the speaker, her particularized body and voice, here and now. Commodity advertisements, in particular, made good use of this spatial and temporal immediacy that characterized schoolgirl speech.

Consumer culture caused amnesia, erasing the frivolous origin of women's language and reducing all the original historical and social particularities to the singular binary of gender. It then sublimed women's language to the level of the aesthetic by inaugurating a new "origin" of women's language that firmly established its indexical linkage with "the urban middle-class Japanese woman" as was repeatedly visualized, idealized, desired, and consumed in the women's magazines. This new origin, which modern Japanese society wants to memorialize, dissimulates the inequality and hierarchy among women—one of the inevitable contradictions inherent in capitalist modernity—as the aesthetics of gender difference. The transformation from schoolgirl speech to women's language thus attests to one form of the aestheticization of gender politics in capitalist modernity and inaugurates its new role as a language of interpellation to hail women into the modern subject position demanded by patriarchy, capitalism, nationalism, and imperialism.

PART 2: THE NATION'S TEMPORALITY AND THE DEATH OF WOMEN'S LANGUAGE

While part 1 focuses on the emergent period of Japan's modern nation-state formation, industrial capitalism and Fordism, and the attendant construction of the modern gendered subject, parts 2 and 3 will take the reader to the late 1980s and the early 1990s. As noted, the discursive formation of women's language, examined in part 1, resulted in a new "origin" that made women's language into a sublimed and aestheticized object and endowed it with a naturalized history—and the effects of that history. Citing women's language is thus citing such history and its effects, which constitute the subject of the modern Japanese woman. Parts 2 and 3 will examine how the regime of women's language as such is re-cited in the political-economic context of late-twentieth-century Japan.

A century after the initial emergence of women's language, there was a resurgence of metapragmatic activities in the public sphere about women's language in the form of commentaries, lectures, debates, academic articles, "self-help" strategies, and even products. The period of the late 1980s to the early 1990s was marked by the "bubble" economy and unprecedented affluence for some segments of the society, which resulted in a massive (re)entry of women into an expanding labor market and a substantial surge in their purchasing power as consumers. Gender relations and the gendered division of labor were perceived to be radically shifting. The Equal Employment Opportunity Law (EEOL), which was implemented in 1986, anticipated a coming age of "gender equality" in all realms of the society (while it had literally no authority legally to penalize employers for gender discrimination in hiring or promotion). At the same time, women were celebrated as "flexible" workers and avid consumers. The EEOL was co-opted both by key buyers in the labor market and by the patriarchical system in such a way that women were encouraged to enter the labor market only as *contingent* workers, so that they would not compromise their domestic role as housekeeper and reproducer, compete with male "heads of household" on the job, or require employers to provide a full benefit package. The content of "gender equality" was thus (strategically) shunted into the realm of consumption and disposable labor.

With the perceived increase in the visibility and presence of women in the public sphere as workers and consumers, the larger social and political-economic transformations of late Japanese capitalism were translated into an anxiety over the anticipated collapse of traditional gender roles and relations. It was in the political-economic regime of flexible capital accumulation (see Harvey 1989) at home that a surge of commentaries on women's linguistic corruption and the death of women's language saturated the mass media. Women's language was thus ontologized by the collective mourning of its loss, its degeneration following on "women's moral corruption" in the context of Japan's unprecedented economic growth (with all the creative destruction necessarily entailed). Chapter 4 will focus on this public mourning of the death of "women's language" as a historically specific modality of the discourse of women's language. "Women's language," in other words, is not a monolithic structure, but is inflected by distinct kinds of gender relations (and gender struggles) in different historical periods. In this sense discourse has the qualities of a "strategy," but without a determinant strategist. I will describe metapragmatic activities of women's language as "mourning rituals" in various sites where knowledge of women's linguistic corruption was created and authorized, including through public opinion surveys, in readers' columns (letters to the editor) in newspapers, in the academy, and in self-help books.

The discourse of women's linguistic corruption is unambiguously predicated upon the temporality of Japan's national modernity, a historically specific, complex impulse that aspires to be modern *and* "Japanese," in which the assertion of the nation's progress is translated into women's moral and linguistic "regression." The "gender crisis" in the 1990s is a symptom of the nation's larger recurrent memory crisis, in which an acute sense of the unmooring of Japanese tradition from modernity in general gets converted into collective mourning of the perceived loss of pure "women's language." In other words, the narrative resolution of the nation's memory crisis was sought through debating about and disciplining women's bodily act of speaking. Public opinion polls and letters to the editor in the newspaper featured debates about the "problem" of women's language and collectively expressed anxiety over rapid social change through the discourse of women's linguistic corruption. At the same time, such anxiety was highly capitalized upon by the publishing industry. Bookstores' shelves were filled with self-help books for women with advice on how to speak "effectively feminine speech" for purposes of career, relationships, and marriage. Thus the discourse of women's language rendered itself into a significant discursive terrain on which the nation-people came to be reflexive about its past and future on one hand and, on the other, into a set of commodified bodily techniques of governmentality for women to become modern subjects.

The death of women's language is paradoxically the rebirth of women's language in that the perception of its disappearance necessitates the premise of its unquestioned pure origin. For it to disappear or die, it is necessary to presume that it existed intact sometime in the increasingly remote past; only if there was once a pure women's language can it be said that "it" has disappeared. Or, to be more precise, women's language was born when it died. The public mourning is then inescapably an act of invoking the timeless essence of women's language. Citing women's language, in a literal sense, is an act of evoking and conjuring it from the other world. What was buried by the death of women's language was, then, the heterogeneous voices and speech, and the temporalities, of the majority of living people, along with their intelligibility and legitimacy. A linear and singular life cycle of Japanese women's language, in its birth, life, and death, temporalized by Japan's national modernity, abjects all those speaking bodies that fail to cite the law of women's language as secondary, deviant, nonstandard, rough, vulgar, not middle class, and "not womanly."

PART 3: RE-CITING WOMEN'S LANGUAGE IN LATE MODERN JAPAN

Part 3 takes the reader to a Tokyo white-collar corporate office in the late twentieth century, where I conducted ethnographic research on language use in the workplace. I introduce a range of female office employees with whom I worked at what I call May Japan Limited (MJL), a pharmaceutical company. My primary interest in the ethnography is these women's metapragmatic narratives about their own language use and the various linguistic enactments of these narratives. Here, I will ask how the historicity and norms of women's language are cited, and possibly displaced, by these real, historical actors whose bodies produce, in their act of speaking in the real world of contingency, an *excess,* something more than is supposed to be signified within the terms of the discourse of women's language. In accord with Bhabha's (1990a) theoretical formulation, which I discussed above, these women's metapragmatic narratives show us the diverse ways in which historical actors historicize and particularize the idea of women's language by performing it in their concrete everyday lives. Such intensely local and personal enunciations are performative in that they produce differences that the national and public discourse of "women's language" fails to assimilate and contain and highlight moments when things that are abjected from the discourse come back to haunt and displace, even if only momentarily, the certitude of the discourse.

Chapter 5 provides an ethnographic description of a woman manager at MJL whom I call Yoshida Kiwako, and details her metapragmatic accounts of language use, work, and her identity as a woman manager. Yoshida-san was promoted to a managerial position at MJL at a time when many large corporations created new positions to which they promoted a handful of women as managers; their main job was to give talks about gender equity in the workplace. Many of these women had been working at the companies for years, in low-level jobs that may have involved some minor supervisory responsibilities. The real significance of the EEOL, in terms of my ethnographic informants, is that it made these women visible within the company, and gave the company an incentive to redefine what they did as "management." The popular media trafficked in representations of "women managers," both in the form of fiction such as *manga* (comics) and TV drama and in the form of nonfiction reportage, interviews, statistics, and documentaries. As one of the very few women in a managerial position at MJL, Yoshida-san was put in a situation where she constantly self-monitored her language as a conscious, self-knowing, and skilled actor, and developed her own theory of how to (how she should) speak as a manager. Through examining her metapragmatic narratives and linguistic enactments, this chapter shows the everyday texture of how an actual actor lives the discourse of women's language as a manager. Yoshida-san's narrative about language use intricately meshes with her life history as it is shaped by the macro-structural factors of company organization and variable life chances associated with class, regional, and gender positioning in an evolving Japanese economy marked inevitably by uneven development.

Yoshida-san's highly localized linguistic practices and the cultural and social rationalizations that she provides along with them show that she "speaks" from within the regime of women's language in the sense that she does not necessarily violate its norms. Yet this new social context opened up for her by emerging political-economic conditions in Japan and the attendant changes in gender relations—which epitomized the figure of a woman assuming a managerial role in a white-collar organization—intensifies the contingency and complexity of the ways in which women's language as a discourse is cited in unforeseen contexts. It simultaneously reproduces and renews the idea of women's language, but—and this is critical—it still defies any search for a positive trace of the sovereign subject. While she is the "author" in her narratives, the citational acts that her body performs in the ongoing and unstable context exceed Yoshida-san's authorship. And this "more"-than-she-says does not necessarily reproduce the discourse of women's language so much as insert the possibility of its displacement. This is not a matter of an intentional resistance or a strategy of resistance with a resisting strategist, but a matter of new statements entering into new discursive relations with other new statements on moving discursive ground. I seek to understand how Yoshida-san is constituted as the woman manager that she has learned to be through her metapragmatic narratives, and how, as an effect, that process complicates the ideological working of women's language.

Chapter 6 introduces a diverse group of other women workers at MJL and their citational practices of "women's language." This chapter shows how women's language gets radically displaced when it is performed by actual women to mark and invoke various cultural boundaries and social differentiations, such as class and regional background at a particular historical juncture, and how those moments reveal mutually contradicting multiple temporalities of the experience of women's language. I describe several ethnographic moments when women diversely perform "women's language" to mark it as their radical alterity—the admitted (and celebrated) difference from the imputed subject of women's language. The effect of such metapragmatic engagements is to *defamiliarize* "women's language," to make something familiar and universal look strange and peculiar. Such moments of estrangement also insist that women's language "means" something other than what it is said to mean. These are precisely the moments when what is abjected comes to the surface, if only momentarily. Through both their linguistic and their metalinguistic performances in everyday workplace contexts, these women's metapragmatic citations are "performative" (in Bhabha's sense [1990a:297]); their contingent, diverse, and repetitious enunciations of the sign intervene in the pedagogical narrative of the nation by "introduc[ing] a temporality of the 'in-between' through the 'gap' or 'emptiness' of the signifier that punctuates linguistic difference" (299). The differences these women mark through citing the discourse of "women's language" cannot be assimilated into the other that the discourse designates and thereby contains, and thus lays bare the incompleteness of the identity of women's language and undermines its fundamental assumption of the spatial and temporal homogeneity of both the nation and its women.

PART ONE

Language, Gender, and National Modernity

The Genealogy of Japanese Women's Language, 1880s–1930s

CHAPTER 1

An Echo of National Modernity
Overhearing "Schoolgirl Speech"

From approximately 1887 through World War I, a surge of commentaries were written and circulated in the Japanese print media about the "strange" and "unpleasant" *(mimizawarina)* sounds issuing from the mouths of schoolgirls. Male intellectuals of various affiliations located the source of their dismay in utterance-endings such as *teyo, noyo,* and *dawa,* which schoolgirls used. They called such speech forms "schoolgirl speech" *(jogakusei kotoba)*. It was jarring to their ears; it sounded vulgar and low class; its prosodic features were described as "fast," "contracting," and "bouncing with a rising intonation"; and it was condemned as "sugary and shallow." Using the newly available modern textual space of "reported speech" (Voloshinov 1973), male intellectuals cited what they scornfully referred to as "teyo-dawa speech" *(teyo-dawa kotoba)* in an effort to convince parents and educators to discourage it as a corrupt form of speaking.[1] The irony here is that many of the speech forms then identified as schoolgirl speech are today associated with "women's language," or the "feminine" speech style, indexing the figure of the generic urban middle-class woman. The contemporary discourse of Japanese women's language erases this historical emergence from social memory to construct women's language as an essential and timeless part of culture and tradition. Public opinion, responding to a perceived social change toward gender equity, recurrently deplores what once again is described as linguistic corruption and the cultural loss of an authentic women's language.

1. Throughout the book, I will use "teyo-dawa speech" and "schoolgirl speech" interchangeably.

As a demographic category, the term *schoolgirl* referred to girls and young women of the elite classes who attended the women's secondary schools that had been instituted as part of the early Meiji modernization project inspired by Western liberal Enlightenment thought.[2] By the late nineteenth century, women's secondary education had been incorporated into the state's mandatory education system, and schoolgirls became the immediate and direct target of the state's constitution of the (gendered) national subject as they were educated into "good wives and wise mothers" for modernizing Japan and, thereby, transformed into "modern Japanese women." Although they constituted less than 0.09 percent of the female school-age population in the middle Meiji, schoolgirls and their (apparently cacophonous) voices were incessantly *cited*, just as their (apparently ubiquitous) presence was continuously *sighted*, as an ambivalent icon of modernizing Japan.[3]

What is significant is that male intellectuals were not simply distracted by schoolgirl speech but that they positioned themselves in the act of overhearing. Consider the scene of a modern Japanese male intellectual flâneur walking on the increasingly urban streets of Tokyo, pausing to eavesdrop on the conversation of schoolgirls. What possesses him as an urban ethnographer-observer to stop and listen to their unspeakably "strange" voice, which he identifies, not as inarticulate noise, undifferentiated from other elements of the sonic landscape of the modernizing city, but as a speech form that signifies in the order of social things? What were the historical conditions of possibility that predisposed intellectuals to hear this schoolgirl voice as "language"? Although hearing someone's voice on the street might seem natural and obvious, perception (whether auditory or visual) is never a natural or unmediated phenomenon but is always already a social practice. The practice of hearing and seeing and the subject positions of listener and observer are as socially constructed and historically emergent as are other corporeal sites and practices of subject formation, such as the body, sex and gender, and race and nationality. A particular

---

2. I want to emphasize that it is a *demographic* category, as opposed to a cultural or social category, for as this chapter shows, it was precisely the incessant citational practices that transformed a merely demographic category into a culturally meaningful one in its discursive connections with other culturally meaningful ideas, sites, and practices.

3. In 1890, there were thirty-one secondary schools (both public and private) for girls, with 3,120 enrolled students, constituting 0.09 percent of the female school-age population. In 1900, a year after the inauguration of the Directive on Girls' High Schools, there were fifty-two girls' secondary schools, with 11,984 enrolled students, or 0.38 percent of the female school-age population (percentages calculated from Monbushō [Ministry of Education] 1964:595, 607).

mode of hearing and seeing is, then, an effect of a regime of social power, occurring at a particular historical conjuncture, that enables, regulates, and proliferates sensory as well as other domains of experience. The moment of hearing schoolgirl speech not as noise but as a signifier—as *meaning* something to the hearer—is a critical sociohistorical horizon in Japanese modernity.

These auditory practices are embedded in a "language ideology," or a linguistic regime of the social, that underlies and produces social knowledge of the "structure" of language, retroactively regiments it, and delimits certain (pragmatic) effects of its use (Silverstein 1979).[4] This metapragmatic awareness, which is, in this case, the recognition of certain linear sequences of sounds as segmentable and as socially meaningful, is historically specific and contingent on a determinate language ideology that it, in turn, informs. Language ideology sets the boundary for what counts as language and what does not, and the terms, techniques, and modalities of hearing and citing.

This chapter thus concerns the liminal or interstitial space where noise and language are neither naturally pregiven nor phenomenologically immanent. It explores the conditions of possibility for the schoolgirl to be heard and cited and thus to be acoustically recognized as a cultural being by Meiji intellectuals as listening subjects. I argue that the modern Japanese woman came into being as a culturally meaningful category in and through her imputed acoustic presence. Citational practices amounted ultimately to consolidating the metapragmatic category of schoolgirl speech and thereby belong to a discursive space where male intellectuals produced and contained the knowledge of the schoolgirl and her "voice" in a way that "she," as an acoustic substance, became knowable only as an (assimilated) other. Undoing and denaturalizing this liminal space will render visible (and audible) the discursive and ideological work in the auditory construction of her as the other of the modern Japanese (male) subject.

This chapter therefore links the auditory emergence of the schoolgirl with various social forces and projects of Japanese modernity around the beginning of the twentieth century. These include a cluster of language-modernization movements *(gembun'itchi)*, the state's containment of "Japanese" womanhood, and the consolidation of a new temporality that underwrote the very concept of modernity itself—a sense of drastic social and cultural change, displacement, and progress, as well as a perceived

---

4. See Rumsey 1990; Silverstein 1979; Woolard 1998; and Woolard and Schieffelin 1994 for programmatic statements on the concept of language ideology.

temporal "lag" in comparison to the West. The chapter then examines metapragmatic commentaries by intellectuals on schoolgirl speech published and circulated in the print media at the turn of the century and shows the semiotic process by which they converted schoolgirl speech from mere sound or noise into a sign, constructing the schoolgirl as the other by containing her voice metapragmatically.

However, the citational practices that produced schoolgirl speech as an index of vulgarity and commonness also, in turn, constituted the male intellectual as a particular historical subject. This chapter therefore examines the formation of a listening subject beyond the level of the merely pragmatic (the sociolinguistic value of schoolgirl speech) to ask how the speech of schoolgirls became "the object voice" (Dolar 1996), a psychic object, through which the male intellectual was constituted as a listening subject uniquely situated in the context of late-nineteenth- and early-twentieth-century modernizing Japan. Despite the apparent stability of male subjectivity and its power to effect the auditory containment of the schoolgirl, male intellectuals were in turn interpellated by what schoolgirl speech psychically presented to them.[5] I argue that schoolgirl speech was "unpleasant to the ears" because it exposed the shakiness of Japan's modernity and the extent to which the Japanese (male) modern self as the subject of Japan's modernity was (and is) inherently fractured with

---

5. The phrase "male intellectuals" is not to be taken as a demographic category but as a subject position in Japan's modernity, into which both actual male intellectuals and others were interpellated. The observing male intellectual became an obligatory role for anyone who would represent modern Japan; therefore the metapragmatic commentaries printed and circulated at the turn of the century were authored predominantly by male authors who had access to the print media. More importantly, they were in the closest proximity to the structural position of the Japanese modern subject, allocated by the discourse of modernity. My point is that male intellectuals as historical actors and those interpellated into this subject position are not automatically to be considered identical. Furthermore, the biographical or demographic sense of gender and gender as a structural position are not necessarily the same. It is the process by which real historical actors came to be the modern subject through their auditory experience of hearing schoolgirl voices that is the subject of this chapter. In fact, as shown below, a handful of elite nationalist female intellectuals and educators, including Shimoda Utako and Tanahashi Junko, had authority and access to the print media because of their complicit linkages with the state authorities. They equally condemned "schoolgirl speech" and advocated the reform of its linguistic corruption. The social power that operates in the citational and auditory construction of self and other is, therefore, far more complex than simply male versus female or the powerful versus the powerless. Schoolgirls came to be subjected to the social power of listening and citing, but their voice, in turn, threatened those who listened and cited because it reminded them of their unattainable plentitude—the condition of modern subjecthood, which was always "partial" and "not quite" (Bhabha 1994). I will expand on this point later in this chapter.

internal contradiction and ambivalence. In the broader sense of Freud's term, schoolgirl speech was "uncanny" because it revealed "something which ought to have remained hidden but has come to light" (1990:364).

Through the examination of the auditory construction of the modern Japanese woman, this chapter engages the enterprise of comparative modernities by showing the primacy of sound as a locus of the experience and knowledge production of the modern. To develop my argument, I rely on Harootunian's (2000a, 2000b) eloquent assertion that we need to pay attention to "cultural forms" of modernity, which are spatially inflected experiences of, and historical consciousness of, the modern. The cultural specificity of forms and practices of modernity and modernization tends to be obscured by the homogeneous temporal progress often presupposed by various grand theories of modernization. The connection between vision and modernity has been explored in work influenced by Benjamin (1968) that points to the productivity, autonomy, and historicity of vision (Crary 1990; see also Fujitani 1996). Auditory experience (i.e., sound, the act of listening and relaying into the system of indexicality) has, however, been given relatively sparse attention in terms not only of its historical connection to modernity but also of its spatial or cultural connection to modernity. This chapter aims to complicate the hegemony of *vision* as well as the centrality of the Western sensory experience of the modern. The schoolgirl's voice was heard in Japan as an echo of an "other" modernity, or what Harootunian (2000a:62) calls "peripheral modernity," coming from the margin, and was thus heard as threatening to Japan's (male) modernity.

Jogakusei (Schoolgirls): Neither Producers nor Reproducers

The schoolgirl constituted an unprecedented category of Japanese women. Although the majority of young women were producers (workers) who eventually married to become reproducers (wives and mothers), schoolgirls occupied a newly defined interstitial space for the duration of their schooling, being neither producers nor reproducers.[6] However, outside

---

6. As I have detailed above, the term *schoolgirls* referred to girls and young women who attended women's secondary schools (which were considered "higher" education for women) after finishing compulsory primary education—and this at a time when the majority of young women, because of family and economic realities, barely finished primary

the direct control of their fathers and families, schoolgirls were nonetheless subjected to the modernizing projects of the state, the market, and civil society by their interpellation within the (ideal) gendered subject position designated by Japan's industrial capitalism as an urban, middle-class consumer-housewife.

The idea of "educating women" was nothing new.[7] What was new in the Meiji period was that women's education came to be a target of the newly centralized state and thus a project that was both *national* and *modern*. To put it differently, educating women came be to equated with "nationalizing" women (Ueno 1998). In the 1870s and early 1880s, a series of Western books on democratic rights and the Enlightenment by authors such as Herbert Spencer, John Stuart Mill, Jean-Jacques Rousseau, and Alexis de Tocqueville were translated and introduced to Japanese intellectuals. This body of Western liberal political philosophy not only became the philosophical foundation for "the People's Rights Movement" (*jiyūminkenundō*) but also informed progressive intellectuals on the modern (and Western) ideal of womanhood and "sex equity."[8] Such texts were the foundation for advocating women's status as citizens of the modern nation-state and, therefore, the importance of educating them. Nonetheless, the idea of citizenship under Japan's enlightenment project was essentially and inescapably gendered. For women, citizenship was ultimately to be achieved through motherhood. As Koyama (1991) and other historians have pointed out, the emphasis on motherhood was relatively absent in pre-Meiji primers. Motherhood became a discursive apparatus that defined the modern discipline of citizenship for women. The worth of women would be to raise the imperial and national subjects of the next generation, who would contribute to building modern Japan. The Education Order of 1872 stipulated mandatory primary education for both

---

education. Schoolgirls were the daughters of the elite: landowners, wealthy farmers, government officials, capitalists, salaried workers, professors, career military officers, and other white-collar professions. For example, a survey on fathers' occupations that was conducted in one of the women's schools in Tokyo in 1901 shows the results: government officials, 60; merchants, 39; bank employees, 19; landowners, 16; medical doctors, 13; schoolteachers, 11; industrialists, 10; professionals, 6; others, 14; no occupation, 61 (Fukei no shokugyō chōsa 1901).

7. Confucian readings on women's virtues had served as primers for the daughters of samurai and wealthy merchants since the early Edo period (1603–1867). By the mid-Edo period, a large number of more accessible texts, called *ōraimono*, were widely circulated for private literacy education among commoners.

8. Notable in this regard was the appearance of a Japanese translation of John Stuart Mill's 1869 work *The Subjection of Women* (see Fukama 1878).

genders (with school curricula, of course, being far from gender neutral) and supported the first normal school to train women as teachers, founded in 1874.[9]

Beyond the fact that schoolgirls were the daughters of the elite, who had access to the kind of education envisioned by the agents of modernization (including state officials, intellectuals, and Christian missionaries), their cultural significance lay in their intrinsic *modern publicness*. From the beginning, schoolgirls were public beings, objects of visual consumption who were subject to the distanced and objective male-national gaze. They were to be sighted in public space, particularly in *modern* space, as iconic figures essential to the new urban landscape, including parks, department stores, museums, zoos, train stations, and downtown streets. Whatever the social realities and actual experiences of the young women identifying themselves as jogakusei might have been, they were mediated beings, represented in various modern representational genres both visually and textually. They were, for example, aesthetic objects of "modern Japanese painting" *(nihonga)* (Inoue 1996), postcards, and photographs, as well as characters in novels and as images in print advertising.[10] Jogakusei in this sense were both the first subject and first object of the modern Japanese woman whose experiential realities were interchangeable with a "reality" that was accessible in mediated, imagined, and consumable forms. It was the *copies* of the schoolgirl that became "the original" in the process of citational accumulation, and these copies became complexly inscribed on the bodies of living young women.[11]

Debord calls such a mode of representation "spectacle," a commodified form of display and sight under capitalist circulation and exchange.[12] Stripped of the historical and material trace of having been manufactured, spectacle is sheer surface and appearance that conceal the exploitation, struggle, and antagonism that capitalist social relations inevitably entail. Analogous to what Marx said of wage workers and the commodities they produce, spectacle constitutes "a social relation among people, mediated by images" (1977: para. 4), where the relationship be-

---

9. Before 1874, however, several private women's schools had already been founded by Christian missionaries.

10. Sato Rika Sakuma (1995) describes how a geisha was dressed as a schoolgirl and posed for a photograph.

11. Baudrillard (1988) calls these phenomena—copies without originals—simulacra.

12. Debord declares: "In societies where modern conditions of production prevail, all of life presents itself as an immense accumulation of spectacles. Everything that was directly lived has moved away into a representation" (1977: para. 1).

tween the original and its image is inverted.[13] The schoolgirl was, in Marx's sense, fetishized.[14]

Because of her spectacular publicness, possessing neither history nor material social relations, the schoolgirl worked as an empty signifier masking the social and historical condition that made her cultural existence possible. The schoolgirl functioned as a sign to the extent that she represented something *other than herself*. As Cowie observes, "The form of the sign—in linguistic terms the signifier—may empirically be woman, but the signified (i.e., the meaning) is not woman" (1978:60). Furthermore, the schoolgirl is a sign of menace and transgression needing to be tamed because her publicness potentially blurs the boundary that distinguishes "modern women" from prostitutes or women in the pleasure quarters, another category of "public" (and "working") women.[15] Policing women's sexuality is all about policing class and other social boundaries. As the feminist art historian Griselda Pollock notes, "Woman as a sign signifies social order; if the sign is misused it can threaten disorder. The category woman is of profound importance to the order of a society" (1988:32). Modern social order in crisis is the male subject in crisis. In the context of the development of modern cities in eighteenth- and nineteenth-century Europe, male anxiety was projected onto transgressive female figures such as prostitutes, kleptomaniacs, and women who were seen as hysterical or mad.

It is not mere coincidence, therefore, that essays and commentaries on schoolgirl speech started to appear in the print media in the mid- to late 1880s, precisely when the political climate took a reactionary turn against what was perceived to be a too rapid Westernization and modernization. By the middle of the Meiji period, the major institutional infrastructure

---

13. Debord thus states: "One cannot abstractly contrast the spectacle to actual social activity: such a division is itself divided. The spectacle that inverts the real is in fact produced. Lived reality is materially invaded by the contemplation of the spectacle while simultaneously absorbing the spectacular order, giving it positive cohesiveness. Objective reality is present on both sides. Every notion fixed this way has no other basis than its passage into the opposite: reality rises up within the spectacle, and the spectacle is real" (1977: para. 8).

14. Feminist psychoanalytic film theory also takes notice of the cinematic representation of women in terms of spectacle and visual consumption. Classic works on gender in terms of seeing and being seen are de Lauretis 1984; Doane 1992; and Mulvey 1989.

15. See Walkowitz 1992 for a study of the narratives of sexual danger in late-Victorian London. Walkowitz examines how the class boundary was maintained through the policing of female sexuality and how feminists challenged and transcended it. Wilson 1991 also discusses the complexity and ambiguity of women's experience in the city. Positioned as a menace to the male social order, women experienced the city as a place of danger and, at the same time, a place for pleasure and liberation.

for the centralized government had come to include the Meiji Constitution (promulgated in 1889), the opening of the national legislature (the Diet) in 1890, and other nationalizing channels that facilitated communication between the center and the regional peripheries. But these changes characterized as Westernization did not go unchallenged, and reaction in some quarters, combined with the rise of nationalism associated with the Sino-Japanese War (1894–95), occasioned an increasingly nativist political impulse advocating a "return" to "Japanese tradition," including the emperor and Confucianism. This reactionary movement was reflected in the Imperial Rescript on Education in 1890 that emphasized the Confucian moral virtue of loyal subjects as the foundation of the national polity *(kokutai)*. The Imperial Rescript was memorized and recited in schools. In this political climate, the supposedly Western liberal ideal of women's education met with severe criticism that resulted in the decline of the missionary-run women's schools, the elimination of English and Chinese classics as a subject in many women's schools, and a proposal to abolish women's education entirely. Schoolgirl speech emerged as a "problem" precisely at the time when state officials and intellectuals attempted to reinvent "modern" Japan as autonomous from, uncontaminated by, and mutually exclusive with the West.

A turn-of-the-century trade dispute illustrates how social crisis was displaced by and projected onto a gendered moral crisis. The Ansei Commercial Treaties of 1858, which permitted commercial transactions by "non-Japanese" only within specific jurisdictions, were ratified in 1894 and began to be enforced in 1899. These agreements allowed for free commercial activity, including capital investment, by non-Japanese. Not surprisingly, public commentaries articulated fears about what would happen as a result of these treaties. Referring to the post-1899 situation as *naichi zakkyo* (*naichi* meaning "domestic," or, in this case, Japan, and *zakkyo* meaning "living together"), the public debate anticipated a "culture war," an attack by Western civilization on Japanese indigenous culture: Japan would be put in moral and cultural chaos through open and direct competition with "foreigners" (i.e., Westerners) in all areas of society, from commerce to morality. More precisely, however, the concern was that Japan would be held up to Western standards of modernity and would be found wanting. Would Japanese civilization and moral standards be strong enough to withstand Western influence and judgment on an everyday basis? This question focused attention on the need for the improvement of women's education. As Katayama (1984:91–94) and Fukaya (1981:160–62) rightly point out, it was the increasingly heated debate over *naichi zakkyo* that triggered the state's interest in establishing regulations on women's higher education. The purity and stability of national (and racial) identity was thus both marked and measured by the disciplining of women's sexuality and morality.[16]

The Directive on Girls' High Schools (Kotōjogakkōrei) was issued in 1899 and signaled the state's official incorporation of the principle of "good wife and wise mother" into its policy for women's education. The phrase "good wife and wise mother" presents the proposition that women should contribute to the nation-state as (gendered) citizens by helping their fathers and husbands at home and by raising children to be loyal subjects of the emperor. Although it undeniably invoked Confucian ideals of women's virtue, the idea of achieving citizenship through being a homemaker and mother—by providing a direct linkage between the state and the family—is complicit with, and necessary to, the modern industrial capitalist state and its gendered arrangements for production and reproduction. The figure of the good wife and wise mother was meant to consolidate a new class of bourgeois (and petit bourgeois) families.[17]

Under the 1899 directive, women's secondary education was incorporated into the state-regulated public education system. The law stipulated that at least one public women's high school be established in each prefecture. Under the new regulations, the school curriculum added a new emphasis on scientific and efficient home management, including hygiene, saving, and household accounting, in addition to a range of gender-specific skills and bodies of knowledge that constituted a new middle-class female sociality and forms of social distinction, including sewing, cooking, flower arrangement, and so on. At the same time, a series of everyday school routines, including the recitation of the Imperial Rescript on Education, was meant to ensure loyalty to the emperor.

As a result, although there were 37 women's secondary schools (out of which only 9 were public) in 1899, by 1915 the number had risen to 143, with 20,117 students, constituting 5 percent of the total female population (*Kōtō jogakkō kenkyūkai* 1994:25–26). Even more importantly, the

---

16. For an instructive comparative case, see Stoler 1991.

17. For example, in 1899, Minister of Education Kabayama made a speech addressed to women's school principals: "A wholesome middle-class society cannot be developed only by men. They can advance the welfare of the society only after working together with wise mothers and good wives to support the family. In order to become a wise mother and good wife, it is necessary to acquire academic knowledge and skills essential to the life of the middle class as well as cultivating a graceful and refined disposition and a gentle and virtuous nature" (*Kyōiku jiron* 1899:22–23).

new regulations dovetailed with the economic transformation after the Sino-Japanese War. Between the Russo-Japanese War (1904–5) and World War I, the boom accelerated industrialization and urbanization and ultimately precipitated the full-fledged formation of a new middle class in urban areas. Surplus laborers in the rural areas flowed into the growing cities, including Tokyo, as job-seeking wage workers. At the same time, a new managerial-professional class began to appear. These functionaries and their families particularly embodied the social relations of the new middle class, characterized by the nuclear family, the spatial separation of work and home, and the gendered division of labor between production and reproduction. Women's education had to respond to an increasing demand for educated wives and mothers for the new middle class of salaried workers.[18]

Linguistic Modernity and the Auditory Construction of the Other

The acoustic presence of the schoolgirl was represented by how she ended her utterances. Meiji intellectuals focused on the utterance-endings, such as *teyo, dawa, koto-yo, wa, chatta,* and *noyo*.[19] Such forms are glossed as *gobi* or *kotobajiri* (utterance-ending), a "pragmatically salient" unit, which is, unlike other structural parts of language, formally segmentable and extractable from the rest of the utterance.[20] Pragmatic effect is thus formally locatable in the segmented form, which makes speakers more aware of linguistic forms and functions. Such a conscious knowledge in turn allows the speaker reflexively to *use* this knowledge by objectifying and describing the given speech form and generating narratives about it (professional scholarly linguistic theory—an institutionalized narrative of language—is, of course, not an exception because it is not autonomous from its social formation).

---

18. It should be noted, however, that this history did not go unchallenged, and by the early 1900s, socialists and feminists (Seitō, or "Blue Stockings") had voiced strong criticism of the "good wife and wise mother" policy because of its failure to achieve genuine gender equity (see Sievers 1983).

19. Although contemporary linguists and sociolinguists have identified linguistic properties of women's language in other parts of Japanese language as well (Ide 1982; Shibamoto 1985), the Meiji intellectuals located teyo-dawa speech almost exclusively in utterance-ending.

20. For the concept of pragmatic salience, see, for example, Errington 1988; Silverstein 1981. See also Lucy's (1993) introductory chapter to *Reflexive Language* for a comprehensive discussion of the nature of linguistic reflexivity.

Although pragmatic salience accounts for a structural ground for focusing attention on utterance-ending forms, the key question is how this structural factor articulated with a particular historical moment. The motivation to act on this structural possibility is found in the historical processes of Japan's modernity and modernization, in which the consolidation of women as a category of alterity was a necessary condition for the modern Japanese subject. The metapragmatic construction of women's language underwrites a specific way in which alterity comes into the auditory realm, where the boundary between language and nonlanguage is contingent on a semiotic order that is functional for social formations in general and to the historical specificities of Japanese modernity in particular.

De Certeau's (1984, 1988) sustained discussion of colonial historiographies in the New World is helpful here, for it exemplifies a semiotic strategy for the containment of alterity that parallels the issue of Japanese women's language. He argues that imperial "writing" in the context of the New World was interchangeable with colonizing power. Writing entails a scriptural operation that collects and classifies information on exteriority or alterity and transforms it in a way that conforms to the systems of domination that writing caters to, including, as de Certeau asserts, science, the modern city, industry, and, more generally, modern political-economic institutions. Writing is, thus, "capitalist and conquering" (1984:135).

Essential to the working of a scriptural economy is the immutable separation that materializes in the text between its exteriority or alterity and its textual identity, whereby "writing" separates yet contains and thus conquers the other, whether this is a racial minority, "primitives," women, children, or the working class. This sense of writing approximates Anderson's (1983) discussion of the role of a vernacular "print language" in the rise of nationalism and the modern nation-state. Through the mediation of its semiotic structure, which may take concrete form through modern representational genres such as the novel and the newspaper, the individual comes to learn a sense of belonging to the nation-state. Thus, the import of print language lies not so much in its symbolic dimension (symbolizing, for example, the unity of a community) nor in its iconic dimension (where a unified form of language rationalizes a unified community), but in its *indexical* dimension—its mobility and mediality, its traffic in "shifters."[21] Print language works as an archetype of tele-tech-

---

21. See Irvine and Gal (2000:37–38) for a further discussion of how iconicity operates as a semiotic process. On "shifters," see Jakobson 1971; Silverstein 1976. "Shifters" are linguistic signs whose reference "shifts" according to the context. A good example would be pro-

nology, which spatially and temporally displaces, transports, and circulates events and ideas in an expanding and socially colonizing market of print capitalism.[22] It is an institutionalized process of dislocating and relocating the text, or of entextualization, decontextualization, and recontextualization.[23] In this process, novels and newspapers exemplify a specific mode of narrative that structurally positions the narrator, as the agent of tele-technology, as a rational and objective observer and spokesperson describing what is narrated. This subject position, as Lee (1997) so eloquently argues, forges a specifically modern subjectivity inhabited by the citizen of the imagined national community that necessarily has its outside or others, even when these are internal. The construction of modern subjectivity is constituted in relation to an alterity—the other is not an accidental by-product but is a necessary condition for the modern self.

Narrative structure, as in the novel, for example, makes it possible formally to distinguish self from other by the use of framing devices such as quotation and "reported speech"—the only way by which the other can "speak" in the text.[24] The notion of civil society as anonymous and blind to difference is made possible by masking the utter exclusion of those who are other to the bourgeois male. Likewise, modern textual space is seemingly "civil" by allowing a formally delimited space where the other is permitted to speak (as "different but equal"). This textual practice parallels the fetishism of capitalism. Just as labor and social relations are reified in capitalist society, the voice of alterity represented in print language is also stripped of its history and material agency and put on public display, incessantly dislocated, circulated, and subjected to the consuming gaze.

When alterity "speaks" in reported speech, it is no longer the speaker

---

nouns. For example, "I" is grammatically referential, and at the same time, its indexical meaning constantly shifts every time someone says "I." Shifters thus marks the sign's mobility.

22. It also circulates as a paratext attached to commodities in the form of transaction documents and advertisements (Irvine 1989).

23. See Bauman and Briggs 1990; Briggs and Bauman 1992; Duranti and Goodwin 1992; Hanks 1989; Hill and Irvine 1993; and Silverstein and Urban 1996 for the theoretical expositions of entextualization, decontextualization, and recontextualization.

24. On "reported speech," see Bakhtin 1981; Voloshinov 1973. Voloshinov defines reported speech as "speech within speech, utterance within utterance and at the same time also speech about speech, utterance about utterance" (115). De Certeau observes the parallel relationship between self and other on the one hand and the "scriptural" (writing) and oral on the other: "The oral is that which does not contribute to progress; reciprocally, the 'scriptual' is that which separates itself from the magical world of voices and tradition. A frontier (and a front) of Western culture is established by that separation" (1984:134).

who is speaking. As de Certeau (1986:53) reminds us, the logic of a scriptural economy is one of "displacements and distortions" (cf. Bakhtin 1981).[25] What makes reported speech sound as if the other were truly speaking is the institutionalization of the historical relationship between quoting and quoted. To put it differently, it is this "metaleptic split" (Sakai 1996:196–202) that allows reported speech to pass for "speech," a vocal event that actually took place in the past. Reported speech creates an "author function" (Foucault 1977b), an illusion of a real person speaking by assigning the grammatical subject ("I") to the (constructed and objectified) subjectivity of the person quoted. Reported speech, when made possible and appropriated by projects of modernity, is a powerful linguistic apparatus to conquer alterity and thus to consolidate the modern self.

Japan had its emergent moment of linguistic modernity at the turn of the century through a cluster of language modernization movements called *gembun'itchi*. These language reforms introduced those textual strategies and formal apparatuses described above, including the form of reported speech formally separating self and other and the development of language as a tele-technology to cite, dislocate, and relocate the ephemeral voice of the other. Various agents of modernization sought to create a modern standard Japanese language for their own ends, to rationalize it as a medium for government, education, law, commerce, print capitalism, and the military, as well as to make it a unifying medium for the spiritual bond of the nation. For the literary community, which eventually led the gembun'itchi movement, a new language and a new literary genre (i.e., narrative prose) were necessary to represent a (new) modern Japanese subjectivity. *Gembun'itchi* means "unifying speech and writing." Emulating the European realist novels, gembun'itchi writers sought to create a new mode of language by experimenting with colloquially based writing styles. This resulted in a new conception of language that gave primacy to "speech" as the epistemological basis of language for its immediacy and presentness and its presumed unmediated access to "truth" and "reality" through which the inner self of the modern subject

---

25. Bakhtin (1981) envisioned a polyvocalic utopian speech community through reported speech, the success of which relies entirely on the author's ethical commitment to representing the voices of the other. De Certeau's discussion of citation in historiography and Bakhtin's of dialogism in literary works present a striking similarity in that both recognize the discursive construction of social relations; and yet they equally present a striking difference in terms of the social relations between the citing and the cited. This contrast would certainly entertain an important question of whether to be cited or quoted always marks subjection to social power, which is, however, beyond the scope of this chapter.

(and the modern world he lived in) could be transparently and faithfully represented. The crux of this new language ideology lies, however, in its trick of *indexical inversion:* it actively constructs the very reality that it claims to be representing. Directly reporting the speech of the other became a textual device made possible by the realist imperative of verisimilitude, and the voice of the narrator became, in turn, an authoritative presence that, through "giving voice," silently reports, dislocates, and, thereby, constitutes it as other.[26]

Recognizing quotation as a textual strategy of containment and as the only means by which alterity—otherwise suppressed and excluded—can return to the text, de Certeau further argues that the intratextual hierarchy between the quoting and the quoted has to do with the way the latter is reduced to mere phonic matter—voice, scream, cry, grunt, or noise—that is not capable of signifying by itself. This sense of sound is precisely what Saussure's (1959) concept of "sound" (phoneme) precludes. The phoneme is part of a system of language. Therefore it is essentially *negative* in the sense that only the difference between one sound and another makes meaning. Phonic matter, as a material substance, is an extension or marker of the physical proximity of the body.[27] Whereas *his* language (modern/standard/written Japanese) is bound by neither space nor time, *her* language (speech) "never leaves the place of its production. In other words, *the signifier cannot be detached from the individual or collective body.* It cannot be exported. Here speech is the body which signifies" (de Certeau 1988:216, emphasis in original; see also Adorno 1990).

Referring to Jean de Léry's sixteenth-century ethnographic writing on the Tupinamba, an Amazonian native people, de Certeau describes how Léry's ear (in addition to, but independent of his eye, which discovered them as exotic and spectacular) heard their speech as "poetic" sound. De Certeau thus notes: "The suppression of the native's effective uncanniness corresponds to the replacement of his exterior reality by a voice. This is a familiar displacement. The other returns in the form of 'noises and howls,' or 'softer and more gracious sounds.' These ghostly voices are blended into the spectacle to which the scriptural operation has reduced the Tupi" (1988:231). Reduced to pure sonorous properties with no signifying ability, alterity is then represented by writing for "ex-

---

26. See Karatani 1993 for further discussion of the role of the gembun'itchi movement in the construction of the modern Japanese subject. On the relationship between gembun'itchi and schoolgirl speech, see chapter 2.

27. The functionality of this sense of sound is also similar to Jakobson's (1981) "poetic" function.

actly what is heard but not understood, hence ravished from the body of productive work: speech without writing, the song of pure enunciation, *the act of speaking without knowing*—a pleasure in saying or in hearing" (227; emphasis added). Alterity thus speaks but does so without knowing what she is saying. She cannot signify by herself and therefore possesses neither objective knowledge nor truth, a position that de Certeau refers to as "fable": "To define the position of the other (primitive, religious, mad, childlike, or popular) as fable is not merely to identify it with 'what speaks' *(fari)*, but with a speech that 'does not know' what it says" (1984:160).

The kernel working at the core of linguistic modernity reduces alterity to an ephemeral acoustics with neither mobility nor signifying power and thereby translates it into a "message." This sense-making process is governed only by the one who does the citing. De Certeau concludes: "We have thus a first image of the voice simultaneously 'cited' (as before a court of law) and 'altered'—a lost voice, erased even within the object itself (the fable) whose scriptural construction it makes possible" (1984:161). To cite is, thus, to alter.

Such an intratextual hierarchy inherent in linguistic modernity is sustained by layers of dichotomies that effectively isolate alterity: writing and orality, past and present, truth and fable, citing and the cited, the subject and object of writing.[28] And these binaries are projected on the historical and social construction of gender, class, and race.[29] For example, we can think of the history of how hysteria became gendered as a female abnormality and treated in "appropriately" gendered ways. A woman's "hysterical" verbal language is dismissed as split and incoherent and is considered to bear no signifying faculty. The (male) analyst then "listens" to her bodily symptoms, and these can make sense only

---

28. The other is always past because in order to be cited, a speech event has to take place prior to the act of citing.

29. Derrida (1976) makes an extensive argument on the way in which the hierarchical distinction between writing and speech serves as the epistemological foundation of the Western metaphysical tradition. Derrida refers, for example, to Lévi-Strauss's ethnography of the Nambikwara. It shares the same hierarchical structure of writing and speech, where the ethnographer owns writing and the natives are illiterate with no writing technology. The Western metaphysics of phonocentrism informs Lévi-Strauss's association of writing with civilization and violence, and speech with a primitive and uncontaminated pure mode of being that was not violent. Derrida shows us how Lévi-Strauss's critique of civilization falls precisely into the trap of the ethnocentrism he attacks by according the Nambikwara only the narrow sense of "writing," whereas Derrida proposes writing as all kinds of traces, recording, and markings.

through the analyst's diagnostic exegesis built upon the language of modernity.

Warner's study of the cultural meaning of printing in the construction of the public sphere in eighteenth-century America similarly illustrates the reduction of the other to sonorous properties. He draws on the Maryland physician Alexander Hamilton's visit to New York City in the early 1740s, where he was amused to hear and record the encounter between his black slave, Dromo, and a Dutch-speaking black woman. He examines how Hamilton recorded the "fragmented" and "incomplete" speech (dialects) of the two women by quoting/citing them in his coherent narrative. The racial other of the elite white male was dissolved into "phonemic particularity"—illiterate, frivolous, and dialectal (1990:13–14). The key point is that this auditory construction of the racial other was the critical condition of cultural and political linkage between "printed-ness" and whiteness. The only way for the racial other to enter into the circulation of written discourse and therefore into the (white male bourgeois) public sphere was to be cited and quoted by a subject interpellated as both white and male.

As in de Certeau's "fable" and Warner's "phonemic particularity," alterity, once cited, is deprived of its semiotic capacity to provide itself with *metalanguage* (an authoritative representation of what the cited voice means). The epistemic violence of linguistic modernity lies, therefore, not so much in its erasure of what the other is saying but in the exclusion of what that other is saying about what he or she said.

The metapragmatic containment of the schoolgirl embodies a similar process. Key to this in the historical specifics of modernizing Japan is its linkage with the structural specificity of utterance-endings. As explained above, the schoolgirl's voice was represented typically not through what she said but how she said it. And this pragmatic effect was located and identified in her utterance-ending forms. Of particular importance are utterance-ending forms that contemporary linguists refer to as "final particles." They are *nonreferential* in that they do not contribute to the semantic meaning of the utterance.[30] Regardless of which final particle is attached to the end of the utterance, *dawa* or *noyo*, the propositional value of the utterance is not affected.

In addition to their being propositionally insignificant, it is important to note that final particles are syntactically positioned at the end of ut-

---

30. For the theoretical clarification of the difference between the referential and the nonreferential, see Silverstein 1976.

terances and phrases and are attached mainly to verbs and auxiliary verbs to constitute utterance-endings, but also to nouns and adjectives. Because of their given syntactic position and nonreferential nature, final particles are inherently unstable in terms of grammaticality: distinguishing between what counts as a final particle and what does not, or whose final particle counts as such and whose does not (in terms of the binary between the standard and the regional dialects), is a political task, handled in this case by authorities such as the National Language Research Institute (Kokuritsu Kokugo Kenkyūsho). Final particles literally hang on the edge of an utterance, on the borderline between language and noise. Some endings are classified as language and others as cries, screams, voiced breath, other vocal registers, or, at best, "dialects." They do not mark meaning so much as the sheer materiality of the speaker's voice, and they belong more to her body than to her language (or mind).[31]

The focus of citation on the nonreferential part of schoolgirl utterance is, therefore, neither a mere historical accident nor a linguistic-structural inevitability. Reducing the cultural significance of her speech to its nonreferential aspect denies and represses her *referential* voice, her will to mean and signify something in a rational manner. This is precisely a way of turning her speech into a "fable"—she is speaking, but she does not know what she is saying. In fact, this referential void became a caricature of schoolgirl speech (as "nonsense"). One of the most frequently cited phrases attributed to schoolgirl speech is "Yoku-(t)*teyo,* shiranai-*wa*," meaning "It is okay, I don't care (or I don't know)," or something that is equivalent to the presumably vacuous utterance "whatever" in Valley Girl speech in America. As a speech act, the reporting of schoolgirl speech produces the pragmatic effect of irrationality, incoherence, and garrulousness that contributes all the more to the imposed indexical meanings of *teyo* and *dawa*. Alterity is, thus, tamed and contained not by being silenced but on the contrary by being allowed to be loquacious.

This reduction to mere sound is also an effect of the particular mode of listening on the part of male intellectuals. Unlike the normative communication model (common in many cases of alterity construction), there was no sense of direct exchange between the listener and the schoolgirl. As with Warner's Alexander Hamilton, male intellectuals overheard and cited speech that was not addressed to them. The anonymous and detached objectivity of the male intellectual's ear thus follows his likewise anonymous and objective gaze, as demanded by his subjective positioning in

---

31. Barthes calls it "the grain of the voice" (1977).

modern (Japanese) language. Baron Ishiguro embodies this position of both seeing and hearing in a passage dating from 1911:

> In the old days, one used to be able to identify whether [a woman] is an artisan, the wife of a low-ranking samurai, or the wife of a lord, just by looking at the footwear left at the front door. But nowadays, the situation is such that even by clothing, much less footwear, one cannot easily tell what status her husband holds. Today, when you listen through the *fusuma* [paper sliding door] to a female guest talking in the living room, things are completely different from the old days. When you think that she is a teacher of either *samisen* [a three-stringed Japanese banjo] or dance, it surprisingly turns out that she is a wife of status. Or when you think that she is a dancing girl or an apprentice, she turns out to be a schoolgirl wearing a purple *hakama* [a long pleated skirt worn over a kimono]. This is because order in language has been disappearing. (1911:829)

Here is a communicative event without communication. The object of the gaze is similar to the prisoner in Jeremy Bentham's panopticon: "He is seen, but he does not see; he is the object of information, never a subject in communication" (Foucault 1979:200). Baron Ishiguro hears the woman without seeing her or verbally interacting with her. She registers in his text as an acoustic presence alone. This disembodied voice, which Chion (1994:128–31, 1999) would call *acousmêtre* (sound without an indication of its source), invites the listener to search for its owner and therefore begs for metapragmatic narratives about the identity of the speaker.

How, then, does a nonreferential form acquire "meaning"? There is no semantic origin from which certain analogical or etymological inference is possible. Speech that is overheard may not reveal how the pragmatic meaning of utterance-ending forms emerges intersubjectively in an exchange between two speakers. My point is that the foundational (first) order of indexicality was to be discursively created by metapragmatic citation. The nonreferential part of speech is context bound, and meaning cannot be understood without knowledge of the place and time, the sociological biographies of the participants, and other contextual information regarding where the utterance was made. To cite or to quote is to remove the utterance from its original context and to deprive it of any indexical grounding. To cite speech, then, is inevitably to (re)create—and alter—the context in which the utterance makes sense indexically. In addition, treating speech more as inarticulate sound than as signs, by focusing more on the materiality and physicality of the voice than on the symbolic, renders it particularly susceptible to metapragmatic framings. Reduced to utterance-endings and to sound and noise as opposed to the signification of meaning, schoolgirl speech makes sense only by the authority narrating and textualizing it. Just as the psychiatrist "listens" to the hysteric's body language, male intellectuals heard the bodily "female" symptoms that in themselves lacked any signification. Metapragmatic commentaries that framed and reported schoolgirl speech were, then, acts of manufacturing context—producing the social and cultural knowledge that gave indexical meaning to the given speech form, including a history (etymology and origin) of the form, a sociological and psychological profile of the speaker, and its pragmatic effects. As footprints index the presence of the person who left them or as smoke indicates the presence of a chimney nearby, there is always a sense of a time lag. Metapragmatic commentaries, which retroactively manufacture the context or what the given speech form indexes, simulate this temporal effect and normalize the indexical relationship, as if the manufactured context had actually preceded the given speech form. They inevitably point to the (imagined) truth.

The Semiotics of "Unpleasant to the Ear"

Below, I analyze the metapragmatic commentaries on schoolgirl speech in the light of the semiotic strategies of containment by which it was regimented and converted from sound to sign (that is, as signifying vulgarity and commonness). My point here is not simply to catalogue how schoolgirl speech was cited and attributed with pragmatic meanings but to examine the logic of semiotic mediation and rationalization that underlies the metapragmatic narratives of the schoolgirl as the other of modern Japanese subjecthood.

In the imputed world of the linguistic, the nonreferential signifies as an index by pointing to some contextual feature of speech: demographic, cultural, social, psychological, cognitive, and so on. For example, the use of *teyo* sounds vulgar because it is used by prostitutes. Or *teyo* is vulgar because it is not "grammatical" (and nongrammatical use of language is commonly heard among the "lower classes"). Thus the form, which does not generate a meaning by itself, needs to be latched onto an existing indexical relationship ("prostitutes are vulgar"), a metonymical or metaphorical extension in which *teyo* points toward a particular association. An "order" of indexicality is manufactured by connecting *teyo* to a semiotic chain of associations that links it to vulgarity, the "lower classes," the figure of the prostitute, and back again; and it is this indexical order that enables speech forms to function indexically. A particular social, cultural, and psychological domain (class, gender, region, affect, stance, and so on) becomes in this way a coded way to signify another domain. Thus, metapragmatic framing and citing craft a foundational narrative that rationalizes and naturalizes a causal and self-enclosed circuit of meanings to the extent that the given speech form—such as *teyo*—is fetishized as if there were some essential quality of vulgarity intrinsic to it.[32]

This is a critical part of the process by which speech reduced to inarticulate sound or noise is (re)organized and socialized into an indexical sign. For the Meiji intellectuals to analyze (i.e., to indexicalize) the schoolgirls' speech was a "strategy of containment" (Jameson 1981:10): the schoolgirl is turned from an unbridled, unknown other, exterior to the discourse of modernity, into a knowable and familiar other by structuring her (voice) into the *margin* of the economy of difference so that her identity makes sense (to the male intellectual) only as systematic difference from the center.[33]

ORIGIN NARRATIVES OF VULGARITY

One of the earliest commentaries on schoolgirl speech appeared in 1888 in a women's magazine, *Kijo no tomo* (The lady's friend). This short essay, titled "Vogue Speech," was by Ozaki Koyo, one of the best-known Meiji writers. In it he notes: "I do not remember exactly when, but for the last eight or nine years, girls in a primary school have been using strange language in their conversation among themselves." He then lists several examples of what he refers to as the "strange" speech of schoolgirls (see figure 1). Ozaki continues:

> In the last five or six years even those girls in the girls' high school have acquired such speech, and it has even reached the society of noblewomen. . . .
> The strange speech that schoolgirls use today was formerly used by the daughters of the low-class samurai [*gokenin*] in the Aoyama area before the

---

32. Irvine and Gal (2000) account for such a fetishization process in terms of "iconization." For the concept of indexing, see Silverstein 1976; Ochs 1992.

33. This is where the dialectics of language structure, language use, and language ideology (Silverstein 1979) come into play. Metapragmatic comments rationalize and organize the indexical relationship between the social identity of the schoolgirl and her alleged linguistic behavior. To explain language use necessitates the commentator's metalinguistic knowledge (or knowledge of linguistic structure). Once it is naturalized, it forms a metapragmatic category of schoolgirl speech, which in turn informs linguistic structure and, possibly, language use.

Meiji Restoration.... Thoughtful ladies must not let a beautiful jewel become damaged or a polished mirror become clouded by using such language. (1994:4–5)

Ozaki's comments on schoolgirl speech echo those by numerous other educators and intellectuals in pointing out its "dubious" origins and vulgar sounds, deploring its spread among middle-class and even upper-class women, and urging educators and parents to discourage it because *how* one speaks is *who* one is (and vice versa).

Other commentators, like Ozaki, identify specific locations, including "the seedy section of Ushigome" (Reijōsaikun no kotoba 1896:148) or "low-class" neighborhoods in the city of Tokyo. Origin narratives by the male elite commonly point to the "pleasure quarters" in the city of Tokyo and geisha of various sorts, including apprentices and prostitutes, as the origin of teyo-dawa speech. Teyo-dawa speech was thus identified as a form of private speech that spread (as a form of contamination) to the more presentable and bourgeois segments of the society. Takeuchi Kyuichi (1857–1916), a famous sculptor, observed:

> As to the question of how such private speech used in the geisha house came to permeate the upper-class family and became the common speech of respectable mothers and daughters: there are a number of former geisha among the wives of now powerful people who became influential as meritorious retainers at the time of the Meiji Restoration. Many other women with whom such women (former geisha wives) interact and closely socialize also have the same previous occupational [geisha] background.... They use such speech as *ii(n)-dayo* ["It is okay"] or *yoku-(t)teyo* ["That's fine"], even to their children. Then, those children acquire such speech and start using it outside their home. That's how speech such as *atai* ["I"] and *yoku-(t)teyo* ["That's fine"] became common usage today. I think this observation would probably not prove wrong. In support of my theory, it was around the time when the offspring of "the ex-geisha-now-upper-class wives" started going to school that such speech became prevalent. (1907:24–25)

Baron Ishiguro (1911:29) makes a similar point about geisha married to men of status in the time of social upheaval during the Meiji Restoration, when it was not considered shameful to have a geisha as a wife. This was how, he explains, the vulgar speech of the "seedy" section of town spread among upper-class women. In addition, he claims that women from the countryside contributed to the spread of teyo-dawa speech by misconstruing it as the noble language of the upper class and emulating it. Other commentators suggest that the 1899 Directive on Girls' High

FIGURE 1. List of schoolgirls' "vulgar" speech forms cited by Ozaki Koyo (1889); the parts of the utterances that Ozaki identified as "strange" are shown in boldface.

ume	wa	mada	sa-ka-naku **(t)te-yo**
plum trees	*COP*	*yet*	*bloom-not-PRES-**teyo***
"Plum trees do not yet bloom."			

ara	mō		sa-(k)i-ta-**noyo**
oh dear	*already*		*bloom-PAST-**noyo***
"Oh dear, they did already bloom."			

ara	mō		sa-(k)i-**teyo**[1]
oh dear	*already*		*bloom-PAST-**teyo***
"Oh dear, they did already bloom."			

sakura no hana	wa	mada	sa-ka-nai-n(o)-**dawa**
cherry blossoms	*COP*	*yet*	*bloom-not-PRES-**dawa***
"Cherry blossoms are not going to bloom yet."			

NOTE: Transcription conventions from Shibatani 1990 for Japanese glosses:
    PRES   present tense
    PAST   past tense
    COP   copula

[1] As I will discuss later, *teyo* is attached to a *renyō* form. The *renyō* form can be ambiguous in terms of tense because it does not contain grammatical information on tense. In other words, one cannot tell by the verb-phrase itself about its tense. I have translated this example as a past tense because of the adverbial *mō*, meaning "already."

Schools opened the door for the daughters of "the lower class"—meaning wealthy merchants and regional landowners—to make inroads into girls' high schools and to influence the daughters of the middle and upper classes.[34]

Whether it was the daughters of low-class samurai or the geisha, these origin narratives are symptomatic of a sense of moral panic over social unrest and the collapse of the traditional social order. The commentators felt—or (perhaps more appropriately) "heard" through their auditory senses—social change coming, not from the top, but from the bottom of the society (class, gender, and regional peripheries). Their familiar social order of class, gender, and the associated spatial boundaries such as those between private and public was collapsing around them. In the male intellectuals' metapragmatic narratives, this moral unease focused on the figure of the woman from the lower-class, seedy section of town who mar-

---

34. As in Europe at the dawn of capitalism, the bourgeoisie, along with peasants and proletarians, were considered low class by the Japanese hereditary elite.

ried to gain upper-class status, her speech spreading among upper-class ladies as a source of contamination. To begin with, it was outrageous for them to "hear" women in public space at all. This does not mean that there were no women allowed in public prior to Meiji. On the contrary, one can imagine the abundant presence of women—"working" women on the street, in the market, and other public "work" places. It was the particular kind of women who were supposed to be confined at home whose voices a keen observer could now hear in public places. A distinction among women formerly functioned as the sign that separated the private and the public—upper-class women and public commercial women were never supposed to share the same space. So not only were the private and public spheres collapsing into one another with modernization but the traditional social hierarchy itself was coming apart. The violation of the normative spatial boundary between private and public also mixed the social rules of the informal and the formal. As another anonymous author explains, using the analogy of bodily posture, "the speech in vogue among schoolgirls is one that comes out of their mouths while lying down [relaxed] and not while sitting upright [formal]" (Gengo no daraku 1906:1–2).

THE ICONIZATION OF VULGARITY:
THE IMAGINARY TRACE OF LINGUISTIC ERASURE

Although the vulgarity of teyo-dawa speech was rationalized through its *indexical* (metonymic) relations with the geisha, vulgarity was also claimed for schoolgirl speech through its lack of honorifics.[35] This "lack" or "absence" was attributed to "sloppiness," "laziness," or "impudence," signifying to male elites the schoolgirls' moral corruption and degeneration. For example, in an essay titled "The Corruption of Language" (Gengo no daraku 1906:1–2), the author deplored the use of "sō-*desu*" (it is so) as omitting an honorific form. *Desu* is a "polite" utterance-ending form that appeared during the gembun'itchi movement as one of the standard speech/writing forms. The author claimed that schoolgirls should say "sō-de-*gozai-masu*," a form of honorific that encodes proper deference by a woman. This and other similar commentaries attempted to invoke the

---

35. Honorifics are linguistic forms that encode deference to the interlocutor, particularly in a context where there is an asymmetrical social relationship between the speaker and the listener in terms of gender, status, or otherwise. Highly aestheticized and ritualized, the use of honorifics also indexes the speaker's refinement and good upbringing. It is in this sense that women in the elite families were expected to master the use of honorifics.

imaginary trace of the schoolgirl lazily skipping honorific forms and to recognize a simple *desu* as a failure (intentional or otherwise) to use the deferential form.

Another anonymous author writes in 1892: "Recently, a kind of language use is in vogue among schoolgirls. There are countless examples, such as *nasutte* [did? or have done?], which should be *nasari-mashita-ka*; or *i-(t)teyo* [I have gone], which should be *yuki-mashita-yo*" (Kotobazukai 1892:74). *Nasu-(t)te* is an adverbial inflectional form of the verb *nasa-ru*, the polite form of the verb *suru* ("do") with *te*, a conjunctive suffix.[36] An interrogative utterance that ends with *te*, which is necessarily conjugated with an adverbial inflectional form, is another linguistic property that the Meiji intellectuals identified as teyo-dawa speech.[37] The commentary above rationalized the linguistic corruption of schoolgirls by identifying the expression *nasu-(t)te* as a *failed* form of the polite form *nasari-mashita* in that it lacks the polite auxiliary verb *mashita* (*masu* [polite auxiliary verb] + *ta* [past tense]). In other words, the author sees the imaginary trace of the schoolgirls' "lazy" act of skipping honorific forms. One author claims that this kind of omission is caused by their speaking too fast. Note that the verb *nasaru* itself already encodes a higher degree of deference than the verb *suru*. The same logic works in the latter example, *i-(t)teyo*. This lack of honorifics is associated with not only rudeness but, in this case, the fact that this linguistic form is considered the *contracted* form of *yuki-mashita-yo*, which by an iconic analogy bespeaks indolence and laziness.[38] In other words, linguistic corruption is rationalized not only by its pragmatic effect of "rudeness" but, more importantly in this case, by its grammatical iconicity of "contraction."

The "laziness" of the schoolgirl is also "evidenced" by phonological contraction. For example, an article on schoolgirl speech (Jogakusei kotoba

---

36. Japanese verbs have several inflectional forms. The number and the classification of inflectional categories depend on a particular grammatical theory. The inflected form ending with *te* is variously called a gerund (e.g., Martin 1975), *te*-form, a gerundive (Kuno 1973), or a suspended form (Sakuma 1936). For this study, I use Hasegawa's (1996) grammatical explication of *te* as a connective suffix and will treat the inflected form with *te* as an "adverbial inflected form + *te* [connective suffix]." For the details of different inflectional categories, see Shibatani 1990.

37. In a regular sentence, this *te* is compounded with a final particle *yo* and becomes *teyo*.

38. Another example brought up in various commentaries is *so-desu* as opposed to *so-degozai-masu*. Omission of honorifics was the major target of the nationalist female educators who followed on the heels of male intellectuals who commented on schoolgirl speech. Shimoda Utako, for example, frequently contributed critical and programmatic essays on schoolgirl speech to young women's magazines.

1905) published in *Yomiuri Shimbun*, a popular newspaper, listed the utterance-ending *chatta*. Tanahashi explains that such a contraction (from *te-shimatta*) is caused by speaking too fast. She thus notes: "Speech with a rising intonation, or speaking with the ending contracted like bouncing, gives people an unpleasant impression. Speech would sound more feminine and refined if one spoke gently with the ending slightly falling" (1911:54).

Syntactic ambiguity is also mobilized as evidence of the schoolgirl's linguistic corruption. The utterance-ending form *teyo* is particularly susceptible to this semiotic rationalization. As I mentioned above, *te* (as in *teyo*) functions something like a connective suffix attached to the adverbial inflected form, connecting the verb (or adjective) to which *te* is attached to another (auxiliary) verb or linking multiple phrases and clauses, among which *te* establishes a temporal as well as other types of relations.[39] For example, *tabe* (to eat)-*te*, *neru* (to sleep) would be "to eat *and* sleep." When the predicate ends with a *te*, as in *teyo*, the sentential level of meaning gets suspended and made incomplete. In fact, the adverbial inflected form is sometimes called "suspended form" (Sakuma 1936). It is as though one ended a sentence with "and." Furthermore, the verb with *te* attached to it does not encode tense or mood. Without subsequent tense-marking devices such as auxiliary verbs, adverbs, or phrases, tense is unknown. Such structural ambiguity was rationalized by the modernizers as the linguistic alterity of the schoolgirl.

In his essay "The Reform of Teyo-Dawa Speech," Yanagihara Yoshimitsu observed:

> The recent speech of Tokyo has spread from the pleasure quarters to the upper class and has become habitual. For example, as with *iyada-wa*, *ikenai-wa*, or *nani-nani-shi-teyo*, etc., girls heavily abuse *wa*, *teyo*, and so on.[40] What is even more outrageous is that they use *nasu(t)te* when they mean to say *nasaru-ka* [Are you going to do such-and-such?], and thus they shamelessly mistake the past tense for the future tense (and this is called "low-class language"). (1908:14)

Yanagihara claimed that girls incorrectly used *nasutte*. He asserts that *nasutte* is the past tense, whereas the schoolgirls, he claims, use it for the future tense, for example, "Are you going to do such-and-such?" His rationalization derives from morpho-syntactic ambiguity in that *nasutte* could be either the past or the future tense and furthermore, from the fact that

---

39. Hasegawa (1996) emphasizes the extent to which *te* is not simply a syntactic device but functions as a semantic filter through which a certain cognitive normalcy is established.
40. In the original text, the utterance-ending forms are highlighted by a round mark.

both the past-tense-marking auxiliary verb *ta* and connective suffix *te* take the same adverbial inflectional form. Whereas Yanagihara heard *nasutte* as the past tense, it could also well be the future tense. As much as the schoolgirls' use of *nasutte* is considered "ungrammatical" by male authorities such as Yanagihara, his commentary in turn exhibits, to use Silverstein's (1981) term, his own "limits of awareness" of linguistic structure.

WOMEN READING, SPEAKING, AND LEARNING

Along with the lack of honorifics, phonological contraction, and "strange" utterance-endings such as *teyo* and *dawa,* the elite commentators also deplored the schoolgirls' presumed use of Chinese words *(kango)* and English words as "unpleasant to the ear" *(kikigurushii)*. Both kango and English were the distinctive province of the educated male elite, who were disturbed by hearing "the male language"—their "own" language—spoken by a *female* voice. The schoolgirls' mimicry of this language (kango and *keigo*), in what Bhabha calls "the uncanny fluency of another's language" (1990a:291), produced the effect of "sounds familiar but totally strange" to the ear of the male intellectual. Just as teyo-dawa speech was not so much about what the schoolgirls said but about how they said it, the schoolgirls' use of kango and English was understood not in terms of content but in terms of "the sound of it," as unmediated language, something that begs for metapragmatic commentary yet at the same time exceeds metapragmatic containment.

What made this speech particularly "unpleasant" was its transgression of the speech-gender nexus. Kango, words of Chinese origin, had been traditionally used for specialized texts in commerce, law, and administration and thus had been exclusively associated with the (elite) male writing style. The women of this class were expected to use *wabun,* or traditional Japanese writing, limited to writing letters, diaries, and epistles. With the establishment of women's secondary schools, women for the first time had legitimate access to kango as part of their school curriculum. But commentators urged schoolgirls to use expressions of Japanese origin (as opposed to Chinese); Japanese expressions were considered to be naturally feminine because, the commentators would explain tautologically, they sound more elegant and soft.[41] In a way similar to Chinese-

---

41. See Yoda 2000 for a compelling discussion of the historical and political process in which the division of labor in the mode of writing—native script versus kango—came to be gendered in the modern study of premodern Japanese literature.

origin words, English words were claimed as male in a gendered monopoly of access to, and assimilation and mimicry of, Western modernity and modernization. However, many of the first private girls' schools were founded by Christian missionaries, and English was part of the curriculum to enlighten and to civilize Japanese women. Schoolgirls' use of English words was cited (and often caricatured) as the epiphany of *haikara* (high-collar) or the modern.

The experience of hearing "his" language spoken by schoolgirls was doubly uncanny: he had to hear written language—kango and English—in oral speech and he had to hear it in a female voice. Using kango in conversation was reflexively stereotyped as the speech style of male high school and university students and was referred to as *shosei kotoba* (male student's speech). "Esoteric" and "bookish," kango-mixed language was used to talk about politics, economics, and world affairs. Many commentators were scandalized by the fact that the schoolgirls spoke shosei kotoba, mimicking masculine speech mannerisms. In fact, this male-student-like speech was cited in one of the earliest instances of reported schoolgirl speech, which appeared in 1885 in a short biography in *Jogaku zasshi*, a women's magazine. By 1887, however, as Honda (1990:113–18) notes, the same author had started using teyo-dawa speech to represent the dialogue of schoolgirls.

Let us listen to the scandalized commentators: Ogino Hajime observed: "Nothing is so unpleasant to hear and unsightly to see as women using kango" (1896:4). An anonymous writer to a women's magazine commented: "It is extremely unpleasant to the ear to hear women use kango. It sounds manlike. It sounds impertinent. When you see them talking in so-called Western language and walking at a late hour of the night, it looks as though high-spirited young men *[sōshi]* were dressed in women's clothes" (Onna tachi no kotoba bumi kotoba 1892:66–67).[42] Ogino later noted: "Whereas she should say 'Makoto ni kawaisō desu' [It really is pitiful], she says 'Jitsuni renbin desu' [It really is pitiful]. It goes without saying which is more gentle and modest for women's language use" (1896:4–5). Though they say exactly the same thing, kango words (*jitsuni* [really], *renbin* [pitiful]) are used in the latter sentence. What was even more disturbing was the woman's use of both kango and teyo-dawa speech all *in one breath*. An anonymous author deplored the fact that he occasionally heard ladies of the middle class and above mixing

---

42. In the early Meiji period, *sōshi* referred specifically to the advocates of the Popular Rights Movement.

(*chanpon*) the vulgarity and crudeness of teyo-dawa speech with the esoteric words of kango (Reijōsaikun no kotoba 1896:148).

The schoolgirls' use of vulgar speech such as *teyo* and *dawa* as well as the masculine language of kango was also attributed to their access to novels and newspapers. Those two semiotic genres are precisely what Anderson (1983:25) designates as "the technical means" to imagine the nation. Condemning schoolgirls' consumption of novels and newspapers as moral corruption is a testimonial to the fact that this particular mode of imagining the national community was an exclusionary practice and considered an illegitimate venue for women to imagine themselves as national citizens.

Ogino (1896:4) claimed that schoolgirls learned kango from reading newspapers and novels; others claimed that was where they learned teyo-dawa speech. What they mainly referred to as the novel, however, was the domestic novel, in which the main character was often a young woman. The writer Uchida Roan (1984:179) scornfully called it "the *yoku-(t)teyo* novel" because of the perceived excessive use of the teyo-dawa speech in dialogues. In an essay titled "The Schoolgirl's Language" (Jogakusei no gengo 1905:197), the author maintained that the schoolgirl learned and spoke vulgar speech as a result of reading such fiction. The author of the essay titled "The Corruption of Language" argued that the schoolgirl spoke the vulgar speech because she had been "carried away by the pen of the novel writer" (Gengo no daraku 1906:2). It should be noted that the domestic novel had not initially been "gendered," and that readers were both men and women. As Iida (1998) points out, however, as the novel form gained the status of the textual genre of modernity, it underwent a process of becoming "masculine." The domestic novel was carved out as a subgenre of the novel. It was severed from the mainstream novel, feminized as "sentimental," and thus excluded from the public sphere—that is, from the realm of serious fiction.[43]

Social crisis is indexical crisis. As much as metapragmatic comments allow one to imagine the expansive figure of the schoolgirl learning, reading, and speaking (out!), what also emerges is the figure of the male intellectual deeply disturbed by the familiar social, cultural, class, and gender boundaries becoming blurred, transgressed, and nullified. The kind of indexical order male intellectuals knew seemed no longer to work. They "heard" the loss of the primordial social order of the pre–Meiji Restoration and the anticipated chaos and crisis of social change. This change may well have been

---

43. See Huyssen 1986 for a discussion of the process in which "mass culture" increasingly became associated with women and became the other of male modernism.

heard as an "other" modernity, one that was led not by him, but by *her*, and one that would not come from the top (from the elite ex-samurai or the aristocrat) but from the bottom and from the periphery, or from the lower class, the seedy sections, the rural regions, and, most uncannily, women.

The signifying chain of teyo-dawa speech does not close at "the schoolgirl" and her alleged linguistic corruption as the final signified: it ultimately points to and signifies the figure of the elite male and his experience of the perceived drastic social change understood as modernity or modernization at the turn of the century. What ideologically motivated a set of speech forms, attitudes, and behavior to constitute the discrete metapragmatic category of teyo-dawa speech (and to signify the schoolgirl) was not so much that actual schoolgirls spoke that way as that a collective sense of disquietude was experienced by the male elite at the turn of the century over the perceived collapse of the familiar social and moral order and the particular temporality modernity names as "progress." Teyo-dawa speech came to reference not so much her but *his* experience of Japanese modernity. In the face of *his* perceived social crisis, woman turns into a sign—signifying anything but herself. Ultimately and paradoxically, teyo-dawa speech points its arrow back to the male intellectual himself.

The Return of Voice and the Construction of the Listening Subject

In a way, the scene of male intellectuals drawn to the schoolgirl's voice rehearses Althusser's (1971:174) image of a man hailed by a police officer and thereby interpellated as an acting subject in the ideological regime the officer embodies. To stop and follow orders is to reproduce the authority of the state. The male intellectuals were hailed by the schoolgirl's voice. As much as the schoolgirl came into being as a speaking subject through the ear of the male intellectual, the male listener was simultaneously constructed as the (listening) subject through his experience of hearing her voice. But what exactly was it in her voice that performed an act of hailing, given the fact that she never directly addressed him and he simply overheard her? What exactly did he hear in the schoolgirl's voice? Here we need to look at her voice as a *psychic object,* the quality of which exceeds indexicalization.[44] Just as de Certeau's Jean de Léry was "ravished"

---

44. Although beyond the scope of this chapter, a theoretical reconciliation between psychoanalysis and the metapragmatic understanding of language and identity has been given

by the Tupis' orality, whose voice "speaks" in his ethnography without his knowledge and beyond his historiographic metalanguage, however much male intellectuals attempted indexically to contain her voice as vulgar and low class, this "unpleasantness to the ear" could never be fully contained in the system of language. There is always a residue or excess that is irreducible to language and meaning, inconvertible into the signified, and not necessarily linguistically present and presentable. Žižek observes: "Voice is that which, in the signifier, resists meaning, it stands for the opaque inertia that cannot be recuperated by meaning" (1996:103). This "fantastic ghost," to use de Certeau's (1988:250) words, returns and haunts the male intellectual and potentially disrupts the plentitude of his identity as the embodiment of "Japan" *and* "the modern," exposing the extent to which its subjectness is inherently fractured and unstable.

The schoolgirl's voice is "unpleasant to the ears" because it disrupts the symbolic alignment between modernity and masculinity, for she is "female" *and* "modern."[45] "Female-and-yet-modern," as an index of inauthenticity and illegitimacy, is, however, precisely the expression that characterizes Japan's (male) modernity in its relation to Western modernity: the former is (dis)located as spatially peripheral to, and temporally lagging behind, the West with its originality, authenticity, and centrality infinitely absent and unattainable. As with many instances in the historical formation of the relationship between the First World and non-Western and (post)colonial places, this decentering is projected onto gen-

---

relatively little attention. For a cogent and provocative discussion of this issue, see Povinelli 1999, 2001.

45. The representation as "masculine" of those schoolgirls committed to education and politics interestingly paralleled the representation as "feminine," by its political opponents, of the Meiji oligarchy's promoting of Westernization. In other words, within the domestic power struggle, the antigovernment nativists used the same anomalous symbolic alignment of "female *and* modern" to criticize the oligarchs. The feminization of men and the masculinization of women thus emerged as mirror images, equally mediated through the notions of Westernization (and modernization), and equally morally suspect positions in late-nineteenth-century Japan. Furthermore, they are also equally alleged to entail (failed) acts of mimicry. Just as schoolgirls were condemned for mimicking men's speech as in their alleged use of kango and English words, so, as Karlin (2002) shows us, "Westernized" political leaders were ridiculed and caricatured by their opponents as, for example, "monkeys." As in the Japanese phrase *saru mane* (monkey's mimicking), the (male) Japanese mimicry of the West is likened to monkeys' mimicking humans, which is said to be "fake" and "superficial." What is remarkable is that this "not-quite-the-same" mimicry by men is taken as a sign of feminization. For provocative discussions on the degeneration of gender—the feminization of men and the masculinization of women—and its relationship to the shifting representation of Japan as a nation-state, see Robertson 1998a, 1999.

der relations both symbolically and materially. The figure of the schoolgirl embodying and performing a modernity from the periphery of the gender hierarchy in Japan thus repeats the figure of the Japanese male intellectual embodying and performing a modernity from the periphery of the national/racial hierarchy in the global context of geopolitics.

The schoolgirl's voice works as an "acoustic mirror" (Silverman 1988) or "auditory double" through which the male intellectual heard *his own* voice. As a psychic object, this voice becomes what Lacanian psychoanalysis refers to as *objet petit a*. The *objet petit a* is something that was part of the subject in the imaginary stage that is lost when it enters the symbolic (language). Lacan defines *objet petit a* as "something from which the subject, in order to constitute itself, has separated itself off as organ. This serves as a symbol of lack. . . . It must, therefore, be an object that is, firstly, separable and, secondly, that has some relation to the lack" (1977:103). It was part of the subject, in psychoanalytic terms, but was separated from the subject as a *thing* as he/she entered the symbolic. This "little otherness" includes feces, mother's breasts, and, among other things, the voice, or "the object voice" (Dolar 1996), particularly the mother's voice, with which the subject had unity as an infant.[46] In order for the subject to attain (imaginary) plentitude in the symbolic stage, the *objet petit a* (the lack) needs to be disavowed.[47] An encounter with the *objet petit a* in the symbolic stage therefore puts the subject into a crisis because he sees or hears himself as a thing, or sees or hears his uncanny double, and he is reminded of his incompleteness. In order to cope with it, the subject deploys a mechanism of "projection" (Silverman 1988:85), in this case, onto the female subject. In analyzing the male psychic response to the female voice in classic Hollywood cinema in these terms, Silverman argues that "the male subject later hears the maternal voice through himself—that it comes to resonate for him with all that he transcends through language" (1988:81). Cinema as a patriarchal apparatus thus works in such a way that "his integrity is established through the projection onto woman of the lack he cannot tolerate in himself. The male subject 'proves' his symbolic potency through the repeated demonstration of the female subject's symbolic impotence" (1988:24). Žižek also explains how *objet petit a* as the double is

---

46. This is because for the infant, the mother's voice is the first listening experience. It is also the mother's speech from which the infant first learns language, and through her verbal instruction, the infant recognizes himself and distinguishes himself from the other.

47. Whereas Derrida (1976) shows us how the voice grounds the full presence of the subject here and now, Lacanian voice is that which undermines it. As Dolar formulates it, it is *"the voice against the voice"* (1996:27; emphasis in original).

inevitably externalized because of the extent to which it is so similar but so strange: "This is why the image of a double so easily turns into its opposite, so that, instead of experiencing the radical otherness of his similar, the subject recognizes himself in the image of radical otherness" (2000:126). In the case of the Meiji male intellectual, such a psychic level of displacement of the internal other *(objet petit a)* into the external other (woman) took the form of converting the female voice into the sign through metapragmatic citational practice.

The schoolgirl's voice is "unpleasant to the ear" precisely because it is a (distorted) double of his voice, an object that returned from the prelinguistic stage (the real), when it was constitutive of the harmonious unity of the subject. Encountering his (auditory) double, or the little otherness in him, is a horrifying reminder that the subject is inherently split and insufficient and that the wholeness of the subject—in this particular case, Japan's male modern subject—is an impossible ideal. This is why the male intellectual had to convert the schoolgirl's voice into a sign metapragmatically in a way that made her the knowable other. It was an act of displacing (and projecting) the otherness that resides in him into the otherness of another subject (woman). I want to suggest here that it was himself, the displaced voice of himself, that the male intellectual heard when he heard the schoolgirl speaking. Her uncanny voice, heard partly as that of the other and partly as his own, exposes irresolvable ambivalence within the discourse of Japan's (male) modernity. The schoolgirl's voice *is* the male intellectual's voice, or at least, the distorted double of his voice.[48]

By the end of World War I, the commentaries on schoolgirl speech as linguistic corruption had quickly dwindled. This corresponded not only with the increased enrollment of girls' high schools but also with the rapid development of mass culture, the industrial capitalist regime of family and gender relations as well as of class structure, and, notably, an increasing confidence in Japan's male modernity in the form of adventurous colonial expansion in China and Korea. Various agents of consumer culture started "speaking" teyo-dawa speech to address young women as consumers. Advertisements in magazines for young women for cosmetics and hygiene products let the photo or illustration of a young woman—imaginable as a schoolgirl, a daughter of an aristocrat, or a young middle-class housewife—"speak" teyo-dawa speech (in the form of direct reported

---

48. Dolar notes: "Masculine and feminine positions are then two ways of tackling the same impossibility; they arise from the same predicament as two internally linked versions of the same voice, which retains an ineradicable ambiguity" (1996:28).

speech) to describe and point to a product. Teyo-dawa speech in advertisements thus came to signify the desired object on display in the magazines and at the same time, the desired subject who had access both to such an object and to the language (teyo-dawa speech) to describe it. More notably, however, real historical actors themselves started to claim teyo-dawa speech as their own. Readers' correspondence columns in some commercially savvy young women's magazines printed readers' letters peppered excessively with teyo-dawa speech. It came to be a key membership marker for the virtual community the magazines created.

By the 1930s, speech forms such as *teyo* and *dawa* had appeared in the model dialogues of urban middle-class and upper-middle-class women and had been resignified as a genuinely "feminine language," the language of the genuine Japanese woman. It is indeed remarkable that contemporary discourses on women's linguistic corruption recurred at a time of perceived social crisis and that the public deplored the loss of the language once condemned as vulgar and low class, a "genuinely feminine" language that it never was.

This chapter has traced the way in which Japanese male intellectuals around the beginning of the twentieth century, the critical moment in the takeoff of Japan's industrial capitalism and its attendant social and cultural formation, heard and cited the schoolgirl's voice, and in doing so gave rise to the new metapragmatic category of "schoolgirl speech," as well as "the schoolgirl" herself as a new social category. This was, in fact, the epistemic birth of "the modern Japanese woman." Japanese women's language at its emergence was occasioned by a never-ending process of citations, circulations, and dispersions of fragments of female voices in the newly formed publicity of print media. Essential to this process was the development of the tele-technology of the modern standard Japanese language in its ability to cite, dislocate, and relocate the ephemeral voice of the other.

Rather than assuming that the Meiji male intellectuals' reported speech of the schoolgirl was a more or less "accurate" reflection of how she actually spoke, I have examined her reported speech as a product of the modern observer's social practice of listening and citing, the specific mode of which is informed by the broader political-economic and historical context of modernizing Japan at the turn of the century. I have examined how the male elite crafted narratives of the indexical order of linguistic corruption of schoolgirl speech and how this metapragmatic practice was a form of strategic containment to domesticate competing forms of Japanese modernity and modernization, one of which the schoolgirl embodied and materialized. At the same time, however, as much as the schoolgirl's voice was objectified by the male intellectual, the excess of her voice, so "unpleasant to the ear," returns, reminding him that "the little other" that he projected onto the schoolgirl's voice indeed resided in himself as the eternally split subject of Japan's modernity.

Very often the experience of "modernity," particularly in non-Western locations, is understood simply as an event at the periphery of an "original" Western modernity—as diffusion globally from "the center." This chapter both questions the social reality of the Eurocentric assumption of global modernity and examines the effects of that assumption in a non-European context (see also Harootunian 2000; Pratt 2002; Rofel 1999). That modernities on the "periphery" have their own dynamics, contradictions, and syntheses can be apparent on two counts. First, although "vision" is the predominant trope and sensory channel by which modernity has been talked about and studied (see, e.g., Jay 1988 or Levin 1993), "listening" has been central here. Modernity (perhaps everywhere) is "heard" as well as "seen." Second, through the ear of the male intellectual we "hear" *another* modernity—the one experienced by young women—and this suggests the need to recognize different and separate experiences of modernity, competing modernities that are gendered and classed.

This chapter also argues the need to recast the notion of "the speaking self" (and its accompanying ideas, such as agency and resistance) within a framework of language and political economy. At stake here is a particular notion of the speaking subject—be it an individual or a group of individuals—as autonomous and self-consolidating. What is essentially a methodological-individualist take (assuming the autonomy and sovereignty of subjects) sometimes fails to deliver on what it purports to accomplish. In linguistic analysis, it often takes the form of conflating the grammatical subject ("I") with the initiator of enunciation as "subject-as-agent" or "speaker-as-agent." In this understanding of "I speak, therefore I am," the speaker's voice guarantees her full presence "here and now," and the equation of the act of speaking with the expression of human agency is fundamental to a particular mode of linguistic constructionism to which we are tempted to subscribe on political and other grounds. We are keen to recover and restore the subaltern voice deeply buried in historical documents. In the case of the schoolgirl, we might be tempted to depict her as the subject-as-agent who actively crafts and asserts identity, heroically defying the patriarchal discourse with a clear oppositional consciousness and to claim that *she* constructs her identity through her practice using her sovereign body from which her voice emerges.[49] But such an approach proves to be ineffective when we look at the subject formation of those who, in the real world, cannot speak for themselves and cannot do so for at least three reasons.

First, I have illustrated how the male elite heard the schoolgirls by eavesdropping. Such an "illicit" and solipsistic mode of communication (which would also include today's more technologically advanced and more explicitly power-laden acts of looking and listening, such as surveillance and wiretapping) complicates our familiar notion of communication, in which the speaking subjects of communication are mutually regarded and engaged and in which "understanding" is assumed to be a collaborative achievement (or failure) in *inter*subjective dialogue.[50] How can we conceptualize subject formation in such a form of social relations of communication? How can we study "linguistic voyeurism," where one is heard but one does not hear (or for that matter, *speak* in her own voice)?

This process is a good illustration of Foucault's "discursive power," in which the seemingly "objective" acts of "seeing" and "hearing" are in fact constitutive of—rather than neutrally receptive of—knowledge. "Madness," for example, as Foucault explains, "no longer exists except as *seen*. . . . The science of mental disease, as it would develop in the asylum, would always be only of the order of observation and classification. *It would not be a dialogue*" (1965:250, emphasis added).[51] The same point can be made regarding the act of listening on the part of the Meiji intellectual—the emergence of "the schoolgirl" without any involvement of her intention or even verbal exchange with him.

Second, I have argued that teyo-dawa speech as heard and cited has no sovereign origin or authentic identity. It emerged in the incessant citations, mediations, and disseminations of fragments of voices heard and reified as such by those who had access to the public sphere of the print

---

49. See Ahearn's (2001) deftly written review essay on the issue of language and agency, where she rightly cautions against conflating the notion of agency with free will or resistance.

50. "Lurking" in Listservs in computer-mediated communication would be another contemporary example. Even the more critical model of communication, which recognizes the power relation inherent in any form of communication, relies on the assumption that communication is interactive and intersubjective, and the linguistic reproduction of domination and inequality is explained as an emergent effect of the ongoing *inter*action in mutual regard among the participants.

51. As Žižek points out, the Lacanian notion of the (split) subject complicates the sociolinguistic sense of intersubjectivity because the primordial interlocutor (another subject) is the *objet petit a,* "that which prevents him from fully realizing himself" (2000:138–39).

media. And it was the circuit of citation and reported speech itself that performatively constructed the identity of the schoolgirl as the "original body" to which teyo-dawa speech belonged. Such a mode of existence of language defies our familiar sociolinguistic concentric model where the original speech emitted from its original speaking body diffused, through face-to-face communication, from the center to the periphery, like a wave or an epidemic disease on the basis of some sociopsychological determination. Even when historical actors themselves claimed or embodied teyo-dawa speech—as it was reified and cited—as their own (such as in the readers' correspondence column), it was performatively accomplished as an effect by the regulated appropriation of that which was foreign to them.

Third, if there is any possibility of agency on the part of schoolgirls as historical actors in the auditory emergence of schoolgirl speech, it was the moment when their voices arrested the Meiji intellectuals and destabilized, at the psychic level, the certitude of the latter's modern Japanese subjectivity by working as an acoustic mirror. Such a tacit yet tenuous psychic mode of agency and of the political resists the liberal notion of the (speaking) subject (Bhabha 1994:85–92, 102–22) and is critical for our understanding of linguistic subject formation. The figure of the lucid subject who is autonomous and self-consolidating, who masters language, speaks for herself/himself, founds knowledge, and constructs (and even "shifts" and "negotiates") his or her identities is problematic, especially when it comes to the subject formation of those who have historically been disenfranchised as the other, such as women. As Spivak (1988) argues, we cannot assume that "the other" can constitute herself and speak for herself in the same way as those at the center of the global political economy can. Similarly, invoking teyo-dawa speech as women's authentic and original voice and as the locus of their untainted agency and pure consciousness fails to account for the role of broader discourses rooted in social formations in facilitating both the possibilities and limits of modes of agency, resistance, and subjectivity. In the case of schoolgirls, their voices were heard only by being represented and cited by those with access to the tele-technology of writing and print media, and what drew them to schoolgirls' voices had to do with a significant political and economic transformation that Japan was experiencing as modernity and modernization. Teyo-dawa speech was not so much the sovereign voice of schoolgirls as it was the echo of the voice that the Meiji intellectuals had jettisoned in order to attain their plentitude as modern subjects. My analysis of the textual space of reported speech, made possible by a particular phase of Japan's political-economic development, renders visible the semiotic mechanism by which the schoolgirl—the ambivalent icon of Japan's modernity—was ventriloquized and ascribed voice, as if she were speaking for herself independently of the reporting voice. This is, of course, neither to argue that schoolgirls had no agency nor to abandon the notion of agency as a theoretical category. It is simply to suggest that understanding our political possibilities of linguistic practice necessitates going beyond observable and tape-recordable "realities."

CHAPTER 2

Linguistic Modernity and the Emergence of Women's Language

How and why did some speech forms and functions come to be identified as women's language? How and why have these speech forms and functions become promoted from unselfconscious sound to a universalized, national symbol that is both a socioculturally and a linguistically discrete index? Most importantly, how did such an indexical practice—a linkage of speech with social structure and cultural meaning—come to be possible to begin with? Scholars of the National Language Studies (Kokugogaku) often date the origin of women's language as early as the fourth century, and they commonly construct a seamless narrative of Japanese women's language passed down to the present.[1] Evidence of women's language is traced in premodern literary works and in records of terminology used by sequestered groups of feudal women such as court ladies, Buddhist nuns, and women in the pleasure quarters (geisha and prostitutes).[2]

This primordialist discourse, however, does not provide an adequate historical linguistic account of the development of contemporary women's language or of a continuous descent from ancient origins. Rather, it merely assumes an essence of Japanese women's language that originated at some ancient time and teleologically descended without interruption or trans-

1. National Language Studies (Kokugogaku) refers to a domestic scholarly circle for the study of Japanese language. It is aligned institutionally and conceptually with the government's national language policies.

2. See, for example, Horii 1993; Mashimo 1969; and Shiraki 1970. See also Ide 1994 and Ide and Terada 1998 for a concise introduction to the study of women's language in National Language Studies.

formation down to the present. The isolated and discontinuous examples are meant to illustrate the continuous essence assumed to lie behind them. For present purposes, I make the point that because it denies historical contingency and ignores emergent phenomena, this discourse paradoxically erases the material traces of women's diverse linguistic experience and affirms the transcendental national narrative of culture and tradition. It hides *histories* by articulating (teleological) *History*.

This teleological History often is insinuated into the way we conceptualize semiotic processes. Ochs's concept of indexing, for example, accounts for how final particles in Japanese—a set of utterance-ending forms—came to mark the gender of the speaker. Her model postulates a two-tier semiotic process, *direct* indexing and *indirect* indexing. Accordingly, certain contextual dimensions of speech, namely, affective and epistemological dispositions (or stances) of participants "are directly indexed in all languages, are central dimensions of all communicative events, and are central constituents of other dimensions of communicative events" (1990:296). Other contextual dimensions, however, such as the social identities of participants and the social relationships among participants, are less likely to be directly indexed. Rather, they are marked indirectly through the mediation of the direct indexing of affective and epistemological dispositions (or stances). In this two-tier semiotic process, Ochs observes "certain social meanings are more central than others. These meanings, however, help to constitute other domains of social reality. That is, a domain such as stance helps to constitute the image of gender" (1992:343). In the case of Japanese language, the final particle is an affective and evidential marker with which speakers signal their social attitudes or stances toward the statements that they make. Certain final particles index assertiveness and intensity, while others index uncertainty and hesitancy. Ochs observes that because of the culturally preferred symbolic association between gender and affect in Japan—women are associated with softness and men with assertiveness—use of those particles *indirectly* indexes the speaker's gender. For example, use of the particle *wa*, which directly indexes the affective disposition of softness, in turn, indirectly indexes the female identity of the speaker. Ochs thus explains, "Because of the strong conventional and constitutive relations between affect and gender, the direct indexing of affect evokes gender identities or gender voices of participants as well" (1990:295).

This widespread theoretical account of indexical processes entails what one could usefully call a "history effect." The account creates a simulated temporal order in which a direct index (affect) is assumed to have temporally preceded an indirect one (gender). The particle *wa* is recognized as the marker of female gender, and the tacit assumption is that this indexical linkage followed naturally from concrete speech situations in which women socialized themselves to speak softly by complying with the cultural expectation of female behavior. Over time, the account assumes, *wa* came to index softness, through women's long-standing cumulative and collective use of it—a mechanical, indeed, evolutionary, process of repetition out of individual choice, convention, or social conditioning. But this is a history with neither a beginning nor an ending. Barthes would call it a "myth" that "deprives the object of which it speaks of all History. In it history evaporates. It is a kind of ideal servant: it prepares all things, brings them, lays them out, the master arrives, it silently disappears: all that is left for one to do is to enjoy this beautiful object without wondering where it comes from" (1982:141).

This seemingly stable indexical order of affect and gender on the one hand, and of gender and speech forms, on the other hand, did not exist until the late nineteenth century. Prior to that time, the particle *wa*, for example, could be associated neither with softness nor femininity. Quite the contrary, educators and intellectuals considered it a vulgar speech form. The lesson to be drawn from this history is that the symbolic connection between softness and femininity, assumed today to be a natural outcome of repetitive practice, emerged at a specific point—a historical threshold in the recent past. Bringing this historical threshold into focus requires a critical method that allows theoretical appreciation of discontinuity in history, a goal Foucault (1977a:153–55) calls "effective history," the method of which is genealogy. This would permit location, not of the origin of a transhistorical essence, but of the *emergence* of a complex ensemble. To subscribe to the concept of emergence is to presuppose neither teleological continuity nor recalcitrant relativism; it requires seeking the history of the present not in the ideal but in the material and embodied context that entails multiple social forces in conjunction—in this case, Japan's unprecedented capitalist takeoff.

In this chapter, I examine the genealogy of Japanese women's language by locating the critical moment of its arising at the threshold of Japan's modernity during the late nineteenth and early twentieth centuries, when state formation, nationalism, capitalist accumulation, industrialization, radical class reconfiguration, colonialism, and foreign military adventurism were in full efflorescence. It was in this context that both language and women came to be problematized as national issues, and thus became political and cultural targets of state authorities and of intellectuals and entrepreneurs representing the progressive classes. I show how particular speech forms were carved out, selected, and (re)constructed as Japanese women's language and how that process was critically linked to a network of diverse institutional and individual practices of modernization, and the particular form Japanese women's language took in its complex mimicry of, and resistance to, the West.

The significance of this history lies not so much in the emergence of specific speech forms associated with women's language as in the conditions of modernization and modernity that, to begin with, made possible and thinkable the practice of the indexical signaling of "women" as a nationally regimented category. In other words, in this case, history involved the opening of a new cultural space where women became objectified through their language use, and thus their language use became the productive site of knowledge of Japanese women, a knowledge that was overdetermined by the production of knowledge of nation, race, and class. Using Hanks's (1996:278) insightful terminology, I take as my subject the historical construction of a "metalinguistic gaze" over women.

In order to focus on the emergence of women's language, I concentrate on the linguistic modernization movements variously pursued for different goals by government agencies, the literary community, the print media, and linguists and educators from the late nineteenth century to the early twentieth century. These independent initiatives eventually converged, and at the forefront was a literary movement called *gembun'itchi* (lit., speech and writing unification), which involved creating a colloquial written Japanese language and developing modern narrative prose (the novel form or *shōsetsu*). The novel is a distinctively modern institution, shaping and shaped by the advent of industrial capitalism, the rise of the middle class, and the development of mass print capitalism (Anderson 1983; Lukács 1971; Watt 1957). Most importantly, however, the critical linkage between the novel and modernity lies in the latter's epistemological commitment to realism and referentiality, or a modernist certitude that language is a transparent medium that can faithfully and truthfully represent reality. Followers of the gembun'itchi movement thus engendered a new "language ideology" (Schieffelin et al. 1998; Silverstein 1979; Woolard and Schieffelin 1994) regarding what language is and how language works. In this chapter, I argue that such a newly developed linguistic consciousness was both the instrument and the critical location of the birth of Japanese women's language at a time when the subject of "modern Japanese women" was emerging in the discourses of the state, civil society, and the market.

Nationalizing Women, Modernizing Women

In 1868, Japanese political and administrative power became centralized in the claimed sovereignty of the Emperor Meiji. Although the fiction was of a restoration of power to the emperor after the hiatus of the Tokugawa Shogunate, in fact the Meiji Restoration founded a spatially continuous national sovereignty unprecedented in Japanese history. The Japanese nation was an emergent social formation. In the years following the Restoration, a centralized state would replace the feudal Tokugawa government that had been composed of relatively autonomous regional spheres (headed by samurai-vassals), and industrial capitalism would replace the tributary mode of the Tokugawa period.

The late Meiji period, the two decades from 1888 to 1910, was critical for Japan's modern nation-state formation. This period saw the development of heavy and textile industries, mass communication and transportation systems, a legal apparatus organized through the promulgation of the Meiji Constitution and Civil Code, representative democracy established with the opening of the Diet (legislature), and the creation of a direct administrative channel between local and central government. The development of print capitalism (in the form of mass-circulation newspapers and magazines) and the instituting of compulsory education further created a sense of the population as not only an administrative and political body, but a nation-state where people came to identify themselves as Japanese and to imagine Japan as more than an arbitrary unit. Individuals also came to be directly—but unevenly—connected to the state through education, censuses, taxation, and new (liberal-democratic) legal rights. At the same time, citizens were differentially positioned, in terms of class, power, and culture, in the newly emerging mosaic of a capitalist society. Modern power, as Foucault suggests, is both totalizing and individuating (1982:208–26). These channels of power converged in the reorganization of the person as a modern (and imperial) subject in the late Meiji period. It was in this context of modern social power in the form of capitalist development and state centralization that "women" as a social category became radically renewed, and "modern Japanese women" emerged as an articulable social category burdened with new cultural meanings pertinent to its relationship with the nation-state.

Of particular importance to such a new configuration of gender in the late Meiji period were the political, economic, and cultural ramifications of Japan's first—and victorious—modern, industrialized wars, with China in 1894–95 and Russia in 1904–5. These both fostered and drew on nationalistic sentiments, which complicated the trajectory of the Meiji enlightenment project. As noted in chapter 1, those wars occasioned a shift in political climate toward a more reactionary position, skeptical of rapid Westernization, and people sought a "return" to Japanese tradition, including imperial absolutism and Confucianism. At the same time, economic developments fueled by the wars and facilitated by the opening of new overseas markets resulted in massive urban migration and increased labor struggle (Garon 1987). It was to address both the ideological demand for Japanese modernization and the practical demand for social control that the state returned to the (supposedly unique) Japanese principles of Confucianism, the emperor system, and an agrarian utopian ideology (Gluck 1985). The trajectory of Japan's modernization process thus entailed a complexly bifurcated construction of the traditional (or cultural) and the modern. This contradictory conjuncture, inherent in but not unique to Japan's experience of modernity, was the overdetermined context in which women increasingly became targeted as a national and social issue and were thereby rendered visible and articulable. As Ueno declares, women are "the very work the modern-civil-nation-state created" (1998:95).[3]

One concrete terrain on which "women" became consolidated as a social category in conjunction with the historical and cultural complexity of Japan's modernity was women's public education. As mentioned previously, in 1899 women's secondary education was incorporated for the first time within the state-regulated public education system, and the government actively launched a project to nationalize women and shape their roles vis-à-vis the state. Central to this endeavor was the idea of "a good wife and wise mother" *(ryōsai kenbo)*. The project advocated the traditional virtues and values of ideal womanhood, such as obedience to father, husband, and, later, eldest male child. Far from primordial, this ideology derived from the Confucianism espoused by the ex-samurai class and from the imported Western cult of domesticity. Eclectic yet decisively Japanese modern, the teaching of "good wife and wise mother" prepared women to take on a critical gendered role in an anticipated modern capitalist society, which in-

---

3. Ueno also observes the fundamental contradiction of women participating in the nation-state: *the nation-state entails gender*. Making women into the "subject of the nation-state embodies the irrationality the modern nation-state imposed on women. Total mobilization exposed such irrationality in an ultimately grotesque manner, and that, in turn, proved that women's liberation is impossible within the framework of the modern nation-state. And this shows women the reason why we need to go beyond 'the nation-state'" (1998:95).

cluded an emphasis on motherhood, rational and scientific house management (including hygiene and efficient home economy), and saving.[4]

Women, here as elsewhere, came to embody the shifting boundary between tradition and modernity, and the woman's body (and sexuality) became a concrete site where this irrevocable binary was negotiated and policed (Chatterjee 1990; Mani 1987; Stoler 1991). "Women's language" was one powerful effect of cultural work in the realms of politics, the market, civil society, and personal life—cultural work through which people sought to give the nascent signifier, the modern Japanese woman, her voice.

"Write as You Speak": Gembun'itchi and the Discursive Space of the Nation-State

The Meiji elite considered it critical to modernize language—which they recognized as an instrument for building a nation-state—for importing and simulating Western science and technology and achieving national integration. What I am dealing with here under the name of *language* is neither a system nor an object. Language here can best be understood as an assemblage of various statements, practices, and activities to produce knowledge about what counts as language and what does not. In discussing language modernization, therefore, I do not mean that some kind of structured object, premodern language, underwent a structural or systematic transformation into modern language. Here, I follow Sakai's approach: "I look for various differentiations and oppositions and their interactions, which, when put together, circumscribe an area in human activities called language" (1992:8).

In this section, I trace the historical process and various practices of language modernization in the late nineteenth and early twentieth centuries that resulted in a linguistic consciousness intimately connected with

---

4. See Koyama's (1991, 1999) discussion on the historical transformation of the idea of "a good wife and wise mother," particularly in its linkage with modernity and modernization. Koyama (1991) shows, for example, that the emphasis on motherhood is relatively absent in premodern primers. Taking a similarly critical standpoint, Muta (1996) compellingly argues that the notion of the family *(ie)* and women's roles in it became qualitatively discontinuous from analogous notions in premodern Japan. Both authors represent the increasing body of recent critical history that challenges the idea that institutions such as family and gender continuously and linearly evolve. See Nolte and Hastings 1991 on the importance of saving as part of women's domestic duties. See Smith and Wiswell 1982 for a rich ethnographic account of the ways in which women in isolated villages became nationalized in the mid-1930s.

the exercise of modern forms of power. The emergence of the metapragmatic category of women's language is predicated on such a modern linguistic consciousness, both as a technique with which new knowledge about (modern Japanese) women was produced and as an epistemological ground on which such new knowledge was made intelligible.

Language was one of the first symbolic terrains on which Japan was directly brought into concrete and invidious (self-critical) comparison with the (undifferentiated) West. Through translation as a sustained political institution, whose condition of equivalence was already set by the terms of the Western languages, any linguistic discrepancy between Japanese and Western languages—for example, the absence of a third-person pronoun in Japanese—was perceived by Japanese intellectuals as a lack, defect, or form of backwardness in their language. The call for language reform came from diverse elite communities intent on forging new modern institutions, such as education, academia, government service, the print media, and the literary community.[5] These communities commonly identified as problems the divergence between the written and the spoken, as well as the diversity across Japan—in a word, disorder—in writing and speech. At the time, there were divergent writing systems and literary styles, monopolized by diverse elite blocs. Spoken Japanese was characterized by a great diversity of mutually unintelligible dialects. All of this, from the reformers' points of view, was a barrier to national integration. In instrumentalist terms, education, communication, national culture building, and the spiritual bond of the nation would be hindered by these gaps.[6] A new metalinguistic vocabulary—well anticipated by capitalist logic—came to frame the public debate on language reform: modern Japa-

---

5. Although the members of each community or agency envisioned a language reform specific to their own immediate goals and interests, by as early as the 1870s some public space had been made available by newspapers and magazines such as *Meiroku zasshi* to debate language modernization as a universal national issue of the Japanese enlightenment—to which intellectuals were drawn from various constituencies.

6. For the purposes of this chapter, it is important to recognize in terms beyond those of the reformers precisely what reform did and did not do. To begin with, it did not eliminate the separation between the spoken and the written, a separation that continues to exist today. Furthermore, diversity between speech communities continues to exist in modern Japan. What has changed is not the existence of diversity but rather the emergence of an identifiable norm instituted through the complex actions of the state apparatus and the mass market—a norm that may serve (ideologically) to make the (real) gaps seem to disappear or at least become muted, go unheard, or be dismissed as (nonstandard) dialect in the popular, official, and scholarly representations of speech. The language reform under the state-building process needs to be critically examined in terms outside the instrumentalist framework of the reformers, terms that seek the genealogy of the modern subject in the project

nese language should be simple, accessible, and efficient.[7] Language reform was meant to eliminate the perceived gaps and to create a standard language, which would help the press gain a wider readership, the literary community pursue aesthetic production, and the government disseminate formal education, standardize the military, and execute successful colonial education in Japan's new and anticipated overseas acquisitions.

Gembun'itchi was the major language modernization movement and was initiated originally by the literary community.[8] It developed out of the concern of progressive Meiji writers with the lack of a literary style adequate for modern narrative prose as found in the Western realist novel they saw as a model. They developed the new colloquial written Japanese called *gembun'itchi-tai* (gembun'itchi style). It is not a coincidence that practitioners of gembun'itchi took the lead in language modernization. The novel—with its distinct origin in late-eighteenth-century and early-nineteenth-century Europe—was a technology that was as constitutive of the modern nation-state as were legislatures, laws, citizenship, policed borders, and standing armies. Its generic framing demands truth-telling about the realities of ordinary people and their daily lives. Thus, writers of novels attempted to put on public exhibition the Japanese citizenry—composed of individual, ordinary people. This realist metanarrative condition was inseparably mediated by, and inescapably linked with, forces emerging with capitalism in Europe, which involved the rise of a middle class, the articulation of possessive individualism, the precipitation of nationalism, and the birth of print capitalism. Through a culturally contingent reworking of the Western realist novel, the Meiji progressive writers encountered a new idea of language that enabled, and was enabled by, such elements of Western modernity.

---

of modernization, a point increasingly recognized by recent literary critics (Fujii 1993; Karatani 1993; Komori 2000).

7. Proposals for language reform included the simplification of lexicons, the abolition of Chinese characters (made by Maejima Hisoka [1835–1919], the first postmaster general, who wrote a petition to the shogun for dispensing with Chinese characters), and the exclusive use of the *hiragana* phonetic script system (as opposed to the mixed use of multiple systems). Mori Arinori (1847–89), the first minister of education, also proposed the use of English instead of Japanese and the use of the Roman alphabet instead of Japanese script systems. He wrote to William D. Whitney, a linguist at Yale University, characterizing the Japanese sociolinguistic situation as "chaotic" and asking for his opinion about the possibility of replacing Japanese with English.

8. See Twine 1991 for the general history of the gembun'itchi movement, which includes the comprehensive introduction to the massive philological work on gembun'itchi done single-handedly by Yamamoto Masahide (1965, 1971a, 1978, 1979, 1981).

In 1885, the writer and critic Tsubouchi Shoyo (1859–1935) wrote what is often considered the first book of modern Japanese literary criticism, *Shōsetsu Shinzui* (The essence of the novel; 1886). In it, he called for a radical reform of the prevailing literary form. The subjects of traditional Japanese narrative prose were mythic figures and heroes and their dramatic adventures. This literature was directed to a readership largely of women and children. Inspired by eighteenth-century British novels (such as those by Fielding and Defoe), Tsubouchi saw traditional Japanese prose as frivolous and superficial and advocated a form of serious aesthetic fiction that could be for male adults. For Tsubouchi, *shōsetsu* was just such an aesthetic form. Writers of novels depicted an unprecedented Japanese subject—*modern* individuals and their quotidian but complex and deep human experiences and emotions. For Tsubouchi and other early Meiji writers, the urgent task was to create a literary style that was truthful and faithful to reality. Their approach was to "write as you speak" *(hanasu yōni kaku):* "to write a passage as if it were actually spoken, even if the words that are used are somewhat obsolete, or even if the syntactic structure of the passage entails some difficulties and complexities" (Sakakura 1964:25–26). Tsubouchi and other writers turned to colloquial-based genres. Of particular significance here were orally transmitted written texts such as *rakugo* (storytelling performance)—some of which had only recently been committed to writing as a result of the introduction of stenography from the United States in 1872—and *gesaku* (popular literature from the Edo period).[9] Following Tsubouchi's advice, Futabatei Shimei (1864–1909) drew on Encho's rakugo as a model and wrote what is often considered the first Japanese modern novel, *Ukigumo* (Drifting clouds; published serially 1886–89).

The central problem was how to create a new colloquial style without the vulgarity and frivolity traditionally associated with non-elite forms of literature (Japan had its own forms of emerging bourgeois civility and distinction), while at the same time retaining "the spirit of vernacularism" (Futabatei 1906:12) that made the novel form modern and, I might add, directly useful in producing a *national* imaginary. "Write as you speak" was thus the formal strategy used to bring into writing the immediacy and the presentness of spoken sound. For the first time, it allowed writers to identify the voice of the narrator ("I") with themselves—

---

9. The significance of stenography is that it made available for the first time transcriptions of spoken language (Miller 1984). Massive records of oral proceedings in the Diet as well as storytelling performance were transcribed and published.

as if they were talking directly to the reader. "Write as you speak" signals a remarkable reconfiguration of writing as a signification system. For speech communities like Japan, where a hieroglyphic script system was the basis of written language, sound was not necessarily privileged as the carrier of truth. The idea that written language can and should faithfully represent and reconstruct the sounds of spoken language signaled a profound epistemological break in the discourse on language toward phonocentrism.[10] Speech became privileged as the repository of truth and reality, and speech and writing became hierarchically linked, with the latter being reduced to a mere supplement to—and derivative of—speech.

In their efforts to create a new colloquial style, practitioners of gembun'itchi faced the stylistic question of how to entextualize linguistic excess, the sheer physicality and materiality of the human voice.[11] In an actual face-to-face interaction, people not only exchange the semantic or referential meaning of what they utter, but, at the same time, they communicate pragmatic meaning by how they speak, with respect to elements of the immediate context of the interaction, including the social setting of the interaction and the social attributes of the participants (such as their gender, social rank and roles, age, and so on). The gembun'itchi writers sought to deal with this linguistic excess in the text by devising utterance-ending forms. For the writers, utterance-ending forms were the pragmatically salient sites where such linguistic excess could be encoded because, as I have described before, utterance-endings function indexically to mark an author's social and psychological position vis-à-vis the characters in the text and the readers in the context. In other words, utterance-ending forms are regimented into an indexical order of "different ways of saying the same thing" (Silverstein 1996:280). Depending on the utterance-ending form one chooses, different pragmatic effects, with the same referential value, are produced regarding how the narra-

---

10. Here is Derrida on phonocentrism: "When I speak, I am conscious of being present for what I think, but also of keeping as close as possible to my thought a signifying substance, a sound carried by my breath. . . . I hear this as soon as I emit it. It seems to depend only on my pure and free spontaneity, requiring the use of no instrument, no accessory, no force taken from the world. This signifying substance, this sound, seems to unite with my thought . . . so that the sound seems to erase itself, become transparent . . . allowing the concept to present itself as what it is, referring to nothing other than its presence" (1982:22). See also Ivy 1995:77 for an important discussion of the relationship between gembun'itchi and phonocentrism.
11. See Bauman and Briggs 1990; Briggs and Bauman 1992; Hanks 1989; and Silverstein and Urban 1996 for further theoretical discussions of the concept of entextualization.

tor (speaker) narrates (talks) to the reader (listener) about the characters and events.

The writers experimented with various utterance-endings. For example, utterance-endings such as *gozaru*, *gozarimasu*, and *gozaimasu* were understood as honorifics and conveyed the speaker's (the narrator's) deference to the interlocutor (the reader).[12] Likewise, *desu* and *de-arimasu* were perceived to be "polite" utterance-endings.[13] *Da* and *de-aru*, on the other hand, were construed as "plain style," which indexes the absence of (or potentially the willful disregard for) the reader.[14] Use of the honorific and polite forms presupposes the immediate presence of the reader, creating an illusion that the author-narrator and the reader-listener are shar-

---

12. Philological studies show that this group of verbs originated in the Chinese characters *go* + *za*. Later *aru* (to be or to exist) was added to it, making *gozaru*. This group of verbs is considered to have been used by the samurai class as *oyashiki kotoba* (lingua franca among the samurai elite) in the Tokugawa period. *Gozarimasu* and *gozaimasu* also are considered to have been used as polite forms by subordinates in interclass address (Twine 1991:71). In the early phase of the language reform movement, because of its origin in the elite class, *gozaru* was viewed as a strong candidate for standard utterance-endings and was extensively used, particularly in translation from Dutch and English to Japanese and in school readers in the 1880s (Yamamoto 1971a:522–35).

13. Neither *desu* nor *arimasu*, however, derive from the speech of the elite class in the Tokugawa period. Various works in National Language Studies show that both *desu* and *de-arimasu* were reconstructed to become the speech forms of women in the pleasure quarters, such as geisha, waitresses in teahouses, hairdressers, and courtesans in the Tokugawa period of popular literature (Twine 1991:71). *Kōgohō bekki* (Supplement to the grammar of colloquial Japanese; Otsuki 1917), the supplement to the first state-authorized grammar, *Kōgohō* (Kokugo Chōsa Iinkai 1916), explains the origin of *de-arimasu* as a false invention by samurai from provincial areas. It maintains that on first arriving in the city of Tokyo and hearing women in the pleasure quarters use it, samurai misrecognized *de-arimasu* as standard, and that is how it spread. Although today one hears *de-arimasu* only in political speech in the Diet or in election campaigns, *desu* is one of the most standard forms of utterance-endings in both written and spoken Japanese.

14. Yamamoto (1971a:451–68) maintains that *da* and *de-aru* derived not from the speech of the samurai elite, but from the script of orally conveyed Buddhist lectures around the fifteenth century. As in the case of *de-gozaru*, *de-aru* also was actively employed in translating the English *to be* and the Dutch *zijn* into Japanese in the mid–nineteenth century (see also Twine 1991:72). While *da* and its polite form, *desu*, are often categorized as "copulas" because they function like the English copula *to be*, they are also traditionally classified as auxiliary verbs in various traditional models of Japanese grammar. Treating them as copulas would be effective for certain linguistic analysis, particularly that of a comparative nature. Although their grammatical identity—copular or auxiliary verb—makes no substantial difference for my analysis, in this book I will refer to *da* and *desu* as auxiliary verbs (together with *masu*, another polite auxiliary verb), both to make grammatical explanations simpler and, more importantly, to emphasize that while functioning just like other auxiliary verbs, they construct an utterance-ending by inflecting and accompanying final particles and other elements and thus encode social information, including gender. See Maynard 1999 for one of the recent discussions on the limits of the identification of *da* with copula.

ing time and space. The plain style does not presuppose the presence of the reader, and therefore it can sound (read as) impersonal, distant, or potentially impolite.[15]

During the time between the Sino-Japanese War and the Russo-Japanese War, the literary gembun'itchi movement was appropriated by the state's nationalist effort to create a national language *(kokugo)*—and more precisely, a standard national language. For state intellectuals in the early Meiji, gembun'itchi was not a primary concern in language reform.[16] They were concerned mainly with writing or script reforms, for example, whether or not Chinese characters should be used—for modernization meant Westernization and a break with China. When the idea of a national language was introduced, however, the terms of the debate on national language policy shifted from questions of writing to speech matters. One of the central figures in this effort was Ueda Kazutoshi (1867–1937), a linguist trained in Germany and France who taught at Tokyo Imperial University and later became head of the Special Education Bureau of the Ministry of Education. In his multiple capacities as an academic, a government official, and an educator, Ueda managed to integrate the various local language reform movements (including the literary gembun'itchi movement) into a unified mission promising to achieve a national language suitable for a modern nation-state. In 1894, the year the Sino-Japanese War broke out, Ueda delivered a lecture titled "National Language and the Nation State" (Kokugo to kokka to) in which he introduced the concept of "national language" and emphasized its importance for uniting the populace, arguing that "the Japanese language is the spiritual blood *[seishinteki ketsueki]* of the Japanese people" (1968:110). The following year, Ueda (1895) called for the creation of a *hyōjungo*—his translation of the English phrase *standard language* and the German *Gemeinsprache*. What Ueda brought home from

---

15. For example, Futabatei wrote *The Drifting Cloud* using *da*, a plain utterance-ending form, for the narrative voice. He later recollected how he came to choose that form for the narrator's voice: "[The problem was] whether I should opt for *watashi-ga . . . de-gozaimasu-*style [honorific utterance-ending], or *ore-wa-iya-da-*style [plain utterance-ending]. Tsubouchi-sensei believes that it is better without honorifics. I do not say that I did not have any dissatisfaction with it, but . . . anyway I tried it without honorifics. This is how I started off my own practice of gembun'itchi" (1906:11). He further notes that he originally intended to adopt *desu-*style (a polite utterance-ending) and ultimately changed into *da-*style (a plain utterance-ending). Yamada Bimyo (1868–1910), another gembun'itchi writer, used *desu*, a polite utterance-ending form. Unlike Futabatei, Yamada tried *da-*style first but later switched to *desu-*style because the former sounded "rude" (Yamamoto 1965:552).

16. I use the term *state intellectuals,* in contrast with Gramsci's (1971) *organic intellectuals,* to refer to credentialed writers, educators, academics, and others whose roles and functions cut across state and nonstate boundaries, but whose intellectual work served and reflected state and modernizing interests.

Europe was a new way of producing knowledge of language. Having studied at the University of Leipzig, where he was exposed to the Neogrammarians' linguistic theory, Ueda focused on speech—as opposed to written language—in imagining a national language.[17] He also was aware that new (scientific) production of knowledge about language needed a new set of institutional apparatuses, including professional associations (of linguistics), scientific survey methods, and codification, as in the form of dictionaries and grammars.

The following ten years saw various institutional developments that applied the principles of the gembun'itchi movement to the government's language reform project. In 1898, Ueda organized the Linguistic Society (Gengo Gakkai), and in 1899 the government established the National Language Inquiry Board (Kokugo Chōsakai), by which, for the first time, language became officially an articulable national issue in which the state should intervene. In 1900, members of the Imperial Society for Education (Teikoku Kyōiku Kai), the government-sponsored assembly for educators, formed a branch organization called Gembun'itchi Club (Gembun'itchi-kai) to promote the extended use of the gembun'itchi style beyond literary practice. The members were drawn from a wide range of intellectual communities, including linguists, educators, journalists, editors and publishers, and writers—many of whom also were actively involved with the Linguistic Society. The Gembun'itchi Club represented and lobbied for the increasingly prevailing nationalist view that the achievement of linguistic unity and linguistic purification was a prerequisite for the advancement of the country as a modern state in parity with Western nations. A series of lobbying activities in 1902 by Gembun'itchi Club members resulted in the establishment of the National Language Research Council (Kokugo Chōsa Iinkai), headed by Ueda under the control of the Ministry of Education. In the same year the council members assigned themselves the following tasks regarding language reform:

1. On the assumption that a phonogrammatic system would be adopted as the official script system, an investigation was to be made into the relative merits of *kana* [the Japanese alphabet] and *rōmaji* [the Western alphabet].

2. On the assumption that gembun'itchi-tai [the colloquial style] would be adopted as the official writing style, an investigation was to be made into the ways in which gembun'itchi could be put into more general and extended use.

17. For the details of Ueda's linguistic theory, see I 1996.

3. The phonetic system of the national language [kokugo] would be examined.
4. A survey of the dialects would be conducted, and one would be selected to serve as "standard Japanese" [hyōjungo]. (Kokugo Chōsa Iinkai 1949:59; see also Kato H. 1902:124)

The decisions that were made on the adoption of colloquial Japanese had immediate effects on the policies of formal education. In 1900, the Ministry of Education issued "Rules for the Enforcement of Elementary School Regulations" (Shōgakkōrei shikō kisoku) in which colloquial Japanese was recognized as part of formal language education. In the following years, the colloquial style was officially recognized as standard in government-designated textbooks.[18] The ascendance of the gembun'itchi style into the national language (kokugo) was completed with its codification as the state-authorized grammar of colloquial Japanese. In 1916, based on a series of surveys with a view toward the creation of standard Japanese, *Kōgohō* (The grammar of spoken language)—the first state-authorized grammar book—was compiled and published by the National Language Research Council. The gembun'itchi movement reached its maturity during the first decade of the twentieth century when more than 90 percent of major literary works were written in the colloquial style (Miyajima 1988; Yamamoto 1965:51). Around the same time, the print media also began adopting the colloquial style.

The gembun'itchi movement itself underwent significant transformation as it became mobilized as a technology of the modern nation-state. Against the original advocacy of a "spirit of vernacularism," by the 1910s plain utterance-ending forms such as the auxiliary verb *da* had won out as the established literary style. Polite and honorific utterance-ending forms, which formally indexed context-bound relationships between the author and the reader and the author and the characters, eventually lost their status in serious literary style.[19] Concurrent with the predominance of the plain

---

18. Between 1903 and 1904, the first series of government-designated textbooks, *Jinjō shōgaku tokuhon* (Elementary primers; Monbushō 1904), were published, and *Jinjō shōgakkō tokuhon hensan shuisho* (The guiding principle for reading books in elementary school [an instruction guide for the primers]) stated that the colloquial style should be extensively used and that students should be informed of the standard of Japanese language (Yoshida and Inokuchi 1972:477).

19. The rise of the naturalist school and the Shaseibun (sketches in prose) school during the first two decades of the twentieth century in a way marked the culmination of gembun'itchi as a literary movement. Both schools shared the centrality of realist writing, the goal of which was to capture *aru ga mama* (reality just as it is) or to depict the nature and

style, the first-person narrative was superseded by that of the third person.[20] In the third person, the narrator's presence vanishes from the narrated event and the text ceases to acknowledge the context. Instead, standing outside the narrated event and commanding a God's-eye view, the third-person narrator rationally, objectively, and truthfully represents the scene (again, the linguistic version of Bentham's panopticon; Foucault 1979:195–228). Practitioners of "write as you speak" faced a contradictory task: creating the speechlike effect of immediacy, transparency, and physicality obtained with the plain style while retaining the pragmatic meaning (evacuated by the plain style) that would have given the speech realist context, polysemy, and indeterminacy. For this new narrative style, context and audience were no longer time-space bound but became the abstracted and imagined "Japan" and "the Japanese." Thus the linguistic technology of gembun'itchi semiotically helped to make an imagined community not only possible but also epistemically necessary, even if it did not really exist. The speaking subject of the gembun'itchi style literally necessitates and embodies the modern Japanese citizen and makes him imaginable.

I say "him" because this narrator, this citizen, was presumed to be (the middle-class) male, and he alone had full and legitimate access to the newly emerging liberal-democratic public sphere (Calhoun 1992; Fraser 1990; Habermas 1989; Warner 1990).[21] In fact, state language policy designated the speech of "educated Tokyo middle-class males" as the basis of standard language (Okano 1902).[22] The phrase "educated Tokyo middle-class males" alluded to the newly emerging petite bourgeoisie of salaried workers in Yamanote, the plateau section of the City of Tokyo. This class fraction was solidified during the process of rapid urbanization, the de-

---

quality of the ordinariness of objects and people's lives using simplicity and objectivity, which necessitated a subdued colloquial style.

20. Noguchi Takehiko (1994) argues that the third-person pronoun (or the grammatical concept of it) had been absent in traditional Japanese literary genres up until the gembun'itchi movement.

21. This, of course, is the gender of the genre and not that of the author insofar as the modern Japanese people interpellate their subjects as male. As noted in chapter 1, Warner's studies of the development of the public sphere in eighteenth-century America present a similar situation in which writing was integrated into a mode of being as male, bourgeois, and white. Exclusion of women is not simply a matter of access but of cognitive split; as Warner notes, "Women could only write with a certain cognitive dissonance" (1990:15).

22. The speech of the educated Tokyo middle class officially was designated as standard during the early twentieth century. *Jinjō shōgakkō dokuhon hensan shuisho* (The guiding principle for reading books in elementary school), issued by the government in 1904, states that "words that were adopted in the reading books were derived mainly from those used in

velopment of mass culture, and modern education. It included government officials, military officers, and other intellectual and white-collar workers. It was, however, neither an established community nor a sociolinguistically homogeneous group. Rather, these people were newcomers who had migrated from various regional domains and were the cultural and linguistic other for the natives of the City of Tokyo, who had a speech dialect rooted in the premodern City of Edo.[23]

Although philologists often point out that the speech of the Tokyo middle class in the late Meiji period was considered to be the direct descendant of *oyashiki kotoba,* a kind of lingua franca used among the samurai from outlying regions in late Edo (e.g., see Hida 1988:34), such a continuous descent is hardly clear given the linguistic elements authorized as standard. What was represented as the speech of the educated Tokyo middle class and the basis of standard language—including the modern colloquial utterance-endings—was pieced together from a variety of sources and is not reducible to the speech of any tangible individual speaker. But this heterogeneous origin of standard Japanese and the cultural and linguistic tension and disjuncture between the natives of the City of Tokyo and modernist newcomers from outlying regions were forgotten in the origin myth of standard Japanese language (Isoda 1979).[24] "The speech of the educated Tokyo middle class" served as an empty metapragmatic category in which disembodied and dislocated voices were integrated and assimilated into the voice of the modern subject, governed by state-mediated linguistic rules and principles. The origin myth served to naturalize the standard as an authentic voice by drawing on the authority of a hegemonic—if fractionated—social class. In other words, it was only after the speech of the educated Tokyo middle class was imagined that the social category of the educated Tokyo middle class developed. And such a semiotic inversion was instrumental in enforcing dialect reform at home and colonial education abroad.

In short, the gembun'itchi style has come to narrate the nation (Bhabha 1990b; Lynch and Warner 1996). Developed during the gembun'itchi movement, this narrating voice introduced a new linguistic consciousness: language is a transparent medium, purely and exclusively referen-

---

Tokyo middle-class society [*chūryū shakai*]" (Yoshida and Inokuchi 1972:477). The use of this speech as standard became a linguistic fact with the publication of *Kōgohō* (The grammar of colloquial language; Kokugo Chōsa Iinkai 1916), the first state-authorized grammar.

23. For example, in 1911, 45 percent of the City of Tokyo population had been born elsewhere (Tokyo Tōkei Kyōkai 1912).

24. On the transition from Edo to Tokyo, see Keen 1984; H. D. Smith 1986.

tial in its function, according to which nothing comes between language and the world; that is, there is an exclusive and context-free, one-to-one correspondence between sound and word, word and meaning, and language and the world. Language reflects what is already out there—always one step behind the world, docilely ratifying and confirming it. Such a realist conception of language is inherently ideological because it effaces the semiotic work of language in actively mediating and producing what is seemingly merely given, reversing the order of things as if the world existed as it is without the mediation of language. Linked up with the regime of modern power, language serves to turn things, categories, events, and ideas into faits accomplis.

In more concrete terms, the new narrating voice functioned at the metalinguistic level to signal that whatever it narrates, reports, describes, represents, and states is true, real, serious, and credible, and that it speaks not from a particular individual's point of view, but from the point of view of the modern rational and national (male) citizen—an omniscient point of view that purports not to be a point of view at all. This metalinguistic function was facilitated by formal (and diacritic) devices that separate the narrating voice and the narrated—whether it be people, events, or things (Komori 1988). Translating and appropriating the Western realist novel required gembun'itchi writers to develop subordinated linguistic space in the form of dialogue and reported speech. This is a formal space where *alterity* is constructed, highlighted, and neatly kept apart from the self. The novel thus formally created a hierarchical relationship in which the narrated is always already objectified by, represented through, and subjected to the male gaze of the narrating subject or of the modern Japanese citizen. And it is precisely this metalinguistic effect that various Japanese institutions and projects intent on their own modernization ultimately adopted from the literary gembun'itchi movement. Whether in school textbooks, newspapers, magazines, fiction, scholarly essays, public speeches, legal statements, military orders, advertisements, or colonial education, the new narrating voice not only provided semantico-referential information but also functioned simultaneously as "performative" (Lee 1997; Silverstein 1979) to authenticate and factualize that which is enunciated.[25] It is in this linguistic space, a "quoted" space, objectified, reified, and re-presented by the imbricated gaze of the

---

25. See Lee 1997 for an insightful discussion of the metalinguistic construction of publicity, as well as the semiotic explication of Habermas's and Anderson's notions of community (the public sphere and imagined community, respectively).

male, the national, and the modern, that women's language was pieced together from heterogeneous origins.

Quoting Women's Language: Producing the Modern Japanese Woman

Dialogues and reported speech became the new linguistic space where the maximum degree of verisimilitude was logically implied. And it was in this space that people "heard" modern Japanese women "speak" for the first time. The women's voice was, as mentioned above, centered on the use of final particles (or particular utterance-ending forms). Figure 2 compares the use of final particles attached to the auxiliary verb *da* in the popular fiction *Ukiyoburo* (The bathhouse of the floating world), written in 1813 by Shikitei Sanba (1952), and in the prose narrative titled *Sanshiro*, written in 1909 by Natsume Soseki (1985).

Shikitei Sanba was one of the traditional popular fiction *(gesaku)* writers of the late Edo period before the Meiji Restoration. *Ukiyoburo* is about people coming to a bathhouse and their frivolous interactions with each other. It consists of dialogues in which the characters tease, argue, compliment, gossip about, and comment on each other. The characters in *Ukiyoburo* are diverse in terms of age, gender, social class, region, and occupation, according to which Sanba carefully differentiates and characterizes individual speech styles. What is glaringly absent in figure 2 is anything that looks remotely like what contemporary women's language is believed to be.

Natsume Soseki was one of the best-known Meiji writers, and *Sanshiro* was published at the culmination of the literary gembun'itchi movement. By then, whether Soseki intended to or not, he and other early-twentieth-century Japanese writers had inescapably become deeply involved with narrating the nation and its modern subject. *Sanshiro* depicts the lives of young male and female intellectuals in Tokyo—new types of characters that did not exist prior to the Meiji. Soseki was also one of the first modern writers to depict the modern urban space and the accompanying new types of linguistic sociality by constructing dialogues that could take place in contexts such as a train, where anonymous modern Japanese citizens engage in conversations (Hirata 1998:137). The significance of *Sanshiro* is that the voices assigned to these young intellectuals contain both male-exclusive and female-exclusive final particles, identical to those of contemporary Japanese.

FIGURE 2. Comparison of final particles attached to the auxiliary verb form *da* in the works of fiction *Ukiyoburo* and *Sanshiro*.

Ukiyoburo (1813)		Sanshiro (1909)	
da-naa	M		
da-te	M		
da-te-na	M		
da-te-ne	M		
da-wa-i	M		
da-wa-su	M		
da-yoo	M		
da-ze-e	M		
da-e	F		
da-ne-nee	F		
da-no-ya	F		
da-yo-nee	F		
da-yo-noo	F		
da-mono-o	B		
da-na	B	da-na	M
da-ne	B	da-ne	M
da-nee	B		
da-no	B		
da-noo	B		
da-su	B		
da-wa	B	da-wa	F
da-wa-e	B		
da-wa-na	B		
da-wa-sa	B		
da-yo	B	da-yo	M
da-ze	B	da-ze	M
da-zo	B	da-zo	M
		da	M
		da-koto	F

NOTE: The data are drawn from Komatsu 1988. The reader should note, however, that I have rearranged Komatsu's data to draw my own conclusions and that I am using his data for purposes other than those he intended.

M: used by male characters only; F: used by female characters only; B: used by both male and female characters.

Note first, as figure 2 shows, that the gender-neutral final particles in *Ukiyoburo* have become gendered into either male-exclusive or female-exclusive final particles in *Sanshiro*. Second, the final particles in *Ukiyoburo* are idiosyncratic rather than gendered: there is a plurality of individual voices in terms of final particles. Sanba's commitment to the faithful reconstruction of people's voices in his stories is not regulated by the national discourse of language. He simply represents the unmediated physicality of people's speech as would a tape recorder (see Kamei 1993). In *Sanshiro*, on the other hand, final particles have become systematized and standardized so that they index gender in the modern nation. By this time male and female Japanese subjects are imaginable—indeed, inescapable—components within the nation, and the modern Japanese novel significantly flattens out the individual "grain of the voice" (Barthes 1977) so that one Japanese woman is interchangeable with another.

Figure 3 compares another set of utterance-ending forms in *Ukiyoburo* and *Sanshiro*, consisting of a final particle or a final particle attached to the auxiliary verb *da*. The right-hand column lists the male-exclusive and female-exclusive final particles appearing in *Sanshiro*, and the middle column is drawn from *Ukiyoburo*. The final particles marked with asterisks in the left-hand column are identified today as quintessentially female exclusive. Although the final particle *wa* appeared in *Ukiyoburo*, the other female exclusive final particles of contemporary Japanese women's language—*na-no, no-ne*, nominal plus *ne, wa-ne*, and *wa-yo*—did not appear at all in pre-Meiji work. The next two asterisked final particles, *da-wa* and *no-yo*, are particularly salient feminine final particles in the present but are not assigned to the female characters in the elite (samurai) class. *Da-wa* and *no-yo* were in fact considered to be vulgar and low class well into the late twentieth century, as we have seen in chapter 1, and educators and others strongly advised parents and teachers not to let their daughters use them. This is hardly a seamless history of a traditional Japanese woman's voice.

My point is not that *Sanshiro* represented women's language as it had come to be spoken by 1909.[26] The modern narrating voice may metalinguistically tell readers that what is being reported is merely that which is

---

26. It was socially possible for the author and the reader at that time to imagine that women spoke, ordinarily spoke, or should have spoken in a particular gendered way. My point about the emergence of women's language is similar to Foucault's point about the emergence of disciplinary power—that it could be socially imagined: "The [actual] automatic functioning of power, mechanical operation, is absolutely not the thesis of *Discipline and Punish*. Rather it is the idea, in the eighteenth century, that such a form of power is possible and desirable" (1980:20).

FIGURE 3. Comparison of utterance-endings in *Ukiyoburo* and *Sanshiro*.

	Ukiyoburo (1813)	*Sanshiro* (1909)
da-koto	B	F
no	B	F
NOM + yo	B	F
*wa	B	F
da(AUX)	B	M
da-ne	B	M
da-yo	B	M
na	B	M
sa	B	M
zo	B	M
*na-no	no example	F
*no-ne	no example	F
*NOM + nee	no example	F
*wa-ne	no example	F
*wa-yo	no example	F
*da-wa	B[1]	F
*no-yo	B[1]	F
da-na	B[1]	M
da-ze	B[1]	M
da-zo	B[1]	M
ze	B[1]	M
zee	B[1]	M
NOM + ne	B[2]	F
ya	B[3]	M

NOTE: The data are drawn from Komatsu 1988. The reader should note, however, that I have rearranged Komatsu's data to draw my own conclusions and that I am using his data for purposes other than those he intended.

AUX: auxiliary verb; NOM: nominal; M: used by male characters only; F: used by female characters only; B: used by both male and female characters.

*Utterance-endings exclusively identified today as "women's language."
[1] Not used by samurai-class females.
[2] Only a few examples of nominal + *ne* seen.
[3] Examples are many and diverse, regardless of gender, age, or status.

actually spoken in the real world, but they should not be deceived by this metalinguistic whispering. Reported speech (Bakhtin 1981; Voloshinov 1973) entails the authorial (and social) act of (re)creating and evaluating the women's voice within a socially produced—and self-reproducing— knowledge of how women speak. As Voloshinov (1973:82) argues, reported speech "is a social phenomenon"—a historical product welling up from a complex social field in ideological and political flux.[27]

The degree to which the speech of female characters in the modern novel was not, in fact, naturalistically represented during the early stage of the gembun'itchi movement is evidenced by the recollections of the Meiji writers themselves. For example, the writer Sato Haruo notes: "In those days, regarding women's speech in daily conversation such as *teyo* and *dawa,* a certain writer's invention came into general use (though I do not remember who he was)" (1998:173). Tsubouchi Shoyo also recalled the difficulties of writing the speech of female characters: "In those days, the language used by women in the middle class and above was filled with so many honorifics that one could not possibly manage to use it for translation" (1930:7). Many gembun'itchi writers developed their modern narrative prose by using *translated* Japanese—Japanese that had been translated (and thus filtered) from Western languages. Futabatei, for example, wrote *Ukigumo,* his first novel, while translating Turgenev's *A Sportsman's Notebook* into Japanese. Tsubouchi also translated into Japanese a large body of Shakespeare's work. The irony is that early gembun'itchi writers such as Futabatei and Tsubouchi needed the authentic speech voice of modern Japanese women in order to represent the (translated) voice of Western white women.

To solve their problem with women's reported speech, these writers turned to the speech of schoolgirls *(jogakusei)* that they overheard on the street. Tsubouchi exclaimed: "There were unimaginable obstacles and difficulties [during the early years of gembun'itchi] that today's writers who have been used to hearing *jogakusei-kotoba* [the speech of schoolgirls] since the end of Meiji could not have even imagined of. Oh, how blessed contemporary writers are!" (1930:7). As discussed in chapter 1, jogakusei represented a new social category of female. As the cultural construct of jogakusei became increasingly recognized, objectified, and imagined as a metonymy of Japan's modernization, their speech became the object of social imaginaries. In other words, the question of how schoolgirls speak no longer belonged to an innocent empirical curiosity, but to the discur-

27. See also Hill and Irvine 1993; Lucy 1993; Philips 1986; and Tannen 1989.

sive formation of Japan's modernity whose regularity allowed such a question to make sense. Schoolgirls were reported to use a set of distinctive final particles, including *teyo, dawa,* and *noyo,* many of which are the essential linguistic features identified today as women's language.[28]

According to Ishikawa (1972), the final particle *teyo* first appeared in a novel in 1888 (used by a young girl speaking to a man and to her friend), *noyo* in 1885 (used by a young girl speaking to a man), and *dawa* in 1886 (used by a young girl speaking to her maid and in her monologue). Such final particles were thus initially restricted to the speech of young women or schoolgirl characters. Later, however, they came to be used in a wider variety of dialogues, for example, those between wife and husband or between daughter and father (Ishikawa 1972). In early-twentieth-century writing, these particles were resignified and elevated to women's language, through the process of writers actively indexicalizing the speech of female characters as generic and universal yet increasingly feminized. The elevation of schoolgirls' speech to the generic women's language, the voice of the modern gendered subject, was thus far from a natural history. As we have seen, this speech was originally considered vulgar and low class by intellectuals and educators. For example, the writer Ozaki Koyo (1994:4–5) warned in 1888 that a certain speech style with "strange" *(iyōnaru)* utterance-endings, such as *teyo, noyo,* and *dawa,* now occurred among elementary schoolgirls between close friends and seemed to be spreading among high-school girls and even adult women. He insisted that sensible ladies would never use these utterance-endings because the endings were originally part of the vulgar speech used by daughters of low-rank samurai families. Intellectuals and educators also developed this origin narrative by locating the original speakers of these utterance-ending forms in pleasure quarters and teahouses. They claimed that the speech was adopted by daughters from the low-rank samurai families and later by the middle class and elites.

Indexicalization involved not only the active linking of signs to referents, but, more importantly, the active construction of the referents themselves. In other words, the speech of schoolgirls—as always already a constructed voice—could not be (re)signified as women's language unless the discursive and disciplinary space of "the modern Japanese woman"

28. As was argued in chapter 1, one should not assume that real schoolgirls spoke the way they were cited and reported to speak by the writers. The moment the schoolgirls' voices were cited (and therefore dislocated), the voices not only changed in Butler's (1990) and Derrida's (1982) senses of iterability, but also took on their own lives. In this sense, the copy becomes the original, apart from the living bodies of the schoolgirls.

existed. This critical move took place in the discursive space where the state's intended surveillance of women, print capitalism's interest in women as a market, and women themselves as new consumers intersected at a particular conjunction in Japanese history. This discursive space was also largely without a "head." Although it could be argued that the state "had power" because of its power to censor, this discursive space of the modern Japanese woman was, as Foucault said of disciplinary power, a "multiple, automatic and anonymous power" that functioned from "top to bottom, but also to a certain extent from bottom to top and laterally" (1979:176). In fact, it is the very lack of a clear actor "in control" within this field of discursive-space production that helps to erase the extent to which the Japanese woman was not found by language, but socially produced by it.

This process is most visible in the production and consumption of *kateishōsetsu* (the domestic novel). The domestic novel was originally serialized in newspapers as a technique to expand readership and to create a mass market for both newspapers and their advertisers (Ragsdale 1998). The intended readership included a growing body of wage workers and women.[29] Female characters in the domestic novel were women of the (imagined) new middle and upper classes emerging from capitalist modernization. Schoolgirls frequently were featured as protagonists, and what were to become female final particles were extensively employed in their dialogues (Morino 1991:247–48). Placed outside the novel considered as a serious art form, the claimed value of the domestic novel was its explicit sentimentalism and didacticism restoring wholesome taste and morality to the novelistic genre. The goal of the domestic novel is best explained by Kikuchi Yuho, one of the most successful male domestic novel writers:

> I wanted to write a story which would be a little more secular than the regular novel, not pretentious, but sophisticated, with good taste. I wanted to write it in such a way that it could be read in the family circle, that anyone could understand it, and that no one would blush. I intended to write a novel which would contribute to the joy of home and help to develop good taste. (1971:89)

29. Iida (1998) argues that the kateishōsetsu as a literary genre was originally viewed as nongendered. It simply referred to novels with wholesome taste and morality that could be read at home. With the assumption, however, that those who read and ought to read wholesome novels at home were women, the kateishōsetsu quickly came to be associated with the women's genre. More importantly, it was the perceived fundamental incompatibility between art and morality that eventually dislodged the domestic novel from mainstream Japanese literary history, so that it came to be feminized as popular literature. See Huyssen 1986 for a discussion of the ways in which femaleness came to be associated with popular culture against the rise of (male) modernism.

Kikuchi further emphasized that a good female character in his novel represented the ideal Japanese woman (90).

Contradictorily enough, however, the domestic novel covers a wide variety of seductive plots involving, for example, extramarital and premarital affairs, elopement, suicide, murder, lust for money and power, deception and betrayal, and so on. This paradox has been often pointed out and discussed by Japanese literary critics. For example, Shindo (2000:118) argues that the actual domestic novel, which was increasingly diverging from what it claimed to be, simply exposes the fundamental contradiction that the family as a modern institution was experiencing in the real world in the early twentieth century. But this paradox was what guaranteed the domestic novel would, while serving as didactic material, also sell successfully as a commodity. It framed stories as didactic, according to which readers were expected to learn moral lessons, albeit from juicy stories about immoral behavior and desires.

As the literary critic Komori Yoichi (1992) rightly argues, the domestic novel was clearly in a position to advance the nationalizing interests of the state apparatus by narrativizing and aestheticizing the state's ideal of modern Japanese women's role of "good wife and wise mother." The domestic novel was addressed precisely to women who were educated to aspire to fill that role. The novel's various themes developed around conjugal love, family happiness, women's self-sacrifice, virtue, and dedication to husband and children. *Family* no longer meant the traditional *ie* system but *hōmu* and *katei*, or the urban bourgeois nuclear family, and *love* alluded to the Western liberal notion of romantic love. The plots of the domestic novel involved events and relationships strictly confined to domestic space, and thus inscribed the capitalist gendered division of labor through the details of imagined new middle- and upper-class sociality, dispositions, sensibility, and material goods. In a nutshell, the domestic novel textually displayed the bourgeois gender ideology, in which class and gender differentiation are channeled and normalized through the politics of sentiment. By the early twentieth century, final particles such as *teyo, dawa, noyo,* and others, which were once viewed as vulgar, had thus come to be increasingly attributed to new middle-class and upper-class women in the novels. In combination with elaborate honorifics, these final particles were thus instituted as the voice of those who were depicted as *haikara* (lit., "high-collar," meaning modern, Western, and stylish).[30]

30. For the historical background on the emergence of the term *haikara*, see Karlin 2002.

This resignification process was linked to the specific ways in which the gembun'itchi style in popular novels was consumed. Unlike the elite literary circle—for whom gembun'itchi meant a serious aesthetic pursuit of Japanese modern subjectivity—in popular culture the gembun'itchi style, precisely because of the premise that the narrative faithfully recorded the real speech (lives) of real people, took on a more explicit commodity value as a device to stage the modern spectacle of the realist representation of reality. For example, the following advertisement for Kosugi Tengai's *Makazekoikaze* (Magic wind, love wind; 1951), one of the best-selling domestic novels published in 1903, appeared in a women's magazine in 1904:

> *Magic Wind, Love Wind* [henceforth, MW] is a realist novel, a romance novel, and an unheard-of masterpiece in the literary world. MW is a sketch of the world of the schoolgirls, and a lifelike description of the Meiji period. The writing of MW is excellent word for word, and is a model of the gembun'itchi style. The dialogues in MW are *the phonograph of the new, modern language,* and it is a reference book for those who pay attention to language. MW is infinitely poetical and allegorical of profound ideals, and is extremely suitable for family reading. (*Makazekoikaze* 1904:3; emphasis added)

Note the analogy made between the phonograph and dialogue. Just as the phonograph provided a spectacular reality of sound and a new mode of perceptual experience, the dialogue in the gembun'itchi novel was also showcased and advertised as a spectacle—the experience of a dislocated and yet realistic reality. The realistic representation of life was thus commodified and accrued market value. Readers enjoyed the pleasures of textual voyeurism and consuming the (realistic) image of women of the new urban middle and upper classes, ideas such as "romantic love," and (Western) commodity goods, such as bicycles, English dictionaries, violins, and cosmetics, which the female characters consumed in their imagined lives. The image, however, was interchangeable with the real for many readers, particularly those in the rural peripheries, who "knew" the urban modern elite women only in their (altered) *copies* through representations in novels. Like all commodity forms removed from the concrete situations of determinate social relations, "the modern Japanese woman" was susceptible as an evacuated signifier to any meaning ascribed to it in indexical practice. It is in this reifying, and therefore emptying, process that teyo-dawa speech became fundamentally reindexicalized. This indexical process was in no way developmental or natural.

The fact that the novels were consumed and not simply imposed as an elite or state-articulated project is critical because of the normalizing power of consumption. This consumption was central in dissemination. It was not long before the female final particles were not just reproduced in novels but also circulated in some of the commercially successful girls' and young women's magazines in the form of letters from real Japanese women.[31] The Directive on Girls' High Schools issued in 1899, by which girls' higher education officially came to be incorporated into the state education policy, stipulated the mandatory establishment of a girls' high school in each prefecture. As enrollment burgeoned, girls' magazines targeted the growing number of schoolgirls. These magazines embodied a gender-specific public sphere; they constituted a virtual speech community where virtual friends communicated with each other through letter writing. Using female final particles, they wrote to friends as if they were speaking to each other. Thus, they practiced their own version of "write as you speak."[32] "Women's language" was no longer merely a "quoted" voice—a process in which the active voice lies with "him" who "quotes"—but a "quoting" voice as young women claimed their new modern Japanese identity and constructed their virtual-speech community. Letters came from areas all over Japan (and even from its overseas colonies) where actual dialectal differences might have fatally fractured any sense of common (gendered) Japanese modernity. But in this unified virtual speech community, women spoke the speech style of modern Japanese women. Thus, they claimed—and were allowed to perform—the subjectivity of "modern Japanese women." In the emerging young women's (counter)public sphere, made possible by print capitalism (and thus disciplined by both the market and the state), young women staked claims to a new identity for women.[33]

Various surveys on reading and readership (Nagamine 1997) indicate that by the 1920s, these girls' and young women's magazines had expanded their readership to include factory girls (Tsurumi 1990) and young women

---

31. One of the first magazines to print letters of this sort was *Jogaku sekai* (Women's learning world) in 1909 (Kawamura 1993).

32. See Kawamura 1993 and Honda 1990 for more detailed sociolinguistic analyses of the letters and the letters column.

33. Hansen (1993) recognizes "counterpublic spheres" (composed of marginalized citizens excluded by the mainstream bourgeois male public sphere from participation) in places such as movie theaters, where disenfranchised citizens such as women had access as citizens-as-consumers. The readers' letters also included metacommunicative comments and discussions on how to maintain their virtual community by, for example, not including plagiarized poetry or letters from men or boys (Sato R. S. 1996). These metacommunicative comments created a sense—a well-calculated effect sought by the producers of the magazines—that the community was autonomous and self-governed by the girls.

in peasant families (R. J. Smith 1983; Smith and Wiswell 1982; Tamanoi 1998). These women were not, in fact, speakers of the *haikara* speech style. In 1902 the National Language Research Council administered the first nationwide dialect survey (Kokugo Chōsa Iinkai 1986). The council wanted to know how speech forms were used differently according to gender and position in the local social-class hierarchy. The assumption made by the elite members of the council was that there would be as sharp a social difference, including that of gender, in speech in outlying regions as there was in the City of Tokyo. It was their understanding that men and women spoke differently in terms of honorifics usage in the (ex-)samurai class. Such sociolinguistic differentiation was hardly reported by survey takers in outlying areas, however. Obviously disappointed, the council planned a second survey, and its instructions specifically directed the survey takers to pay attention to sociolinguistic differentiations including gender (Kokugo Chōsa Iinkai 1908:5; the results of the second survey were never published as an official document). By this, I do not mean to suggest that there were no gender differences in speech in local communities or to say that there was no way of indexing women in the peripheries. On the contrary, one could imagine the existence of sociolinguistic differences that were locally meaningful. My point is that, in the socioeconomic, cultural, and linguistic peripheries, there was no universal discursive space where gender was talked about, explained, understood, and articulated through its relationship with language. To put it differently, the gendered regimentation of the linguistic, and the linguistic regimentation of gender in turn-of-the-century Japan (which was metapragmatically glossed as "women's language"), made sense and became articulable only in the formation of the discourse of modernity and modernization.

The critical point is that the only place that people in Japan's periphery heard or perhaps spoke women's language in the late Meiji period was in print media—serialized novels and letters in girls' and young women's magazines. In other words (as I have noted before), the copy was "the original" for them. And the way that they experienced women's language was by consuming it as a metonymy of the modern, the urban, the national—everything that they were not. It was through the consumption of women's language that people in Japan's periphery were enabled to participate in the imagined national (speech) community. The dissemination of women's language, for these women, had little to do with gender and everything to do with class and region, as these elements became punctuated within the nationalist and capitalist project.

This act of consumption also facilitated internalization of the emerging gendered disciplines. Reading newspapers and magazines and writing letters to the editor necessarily involved imbibing a capitalist temporality bifurcated into leisure and labor. Women as efficient homemakers and reproducers learned that reading was leisure (something consumed, not produced), and they learned when to read and how to find time to read. This new economy of time often was exhibited in the readers' letters in the magazines. Many women wrote about taking care of housework efficiently, so they would have time to read magazines. Letters to the editor functioned as an "exhibitionary complex" (Bennett 1994) that helped produce a self-conscious national culture, much as museums and department store showcases also have functioned.

Consumption is critical here in another way. Speech forms referred to as "Japanese women's language" and those used in the letters simultaneously came to index gendered commodities in print advertisements for perfumes, ointments, menstrual garments, skin whitening creams, and other similar items. Also indexed were photographs of the young daughters of aristocrats and illustrations of beautiful, modern—somehow Western-looking, but also Japanese—young women. In other words, making the (gendered) Japanese nation also involved making the Japanese consumer (Silverberg 1991a). What is remarkable here anthropologically is the extent to which the constitution of the metapragmatic category of "women's language" is linked up not only with gender and nation-making but with consumption and market-making.

Toward an Effective History of Language, Gender, and Modernity

In this chapter, I have sought to account for the genealogy of Japanese women's language and to examine the historical process by which the practice of representing gender meanings through speech was brought into being in the early twentieth century in Japan. I also have argued that the social genesis of the metapragmatic category of women's language is not so much a natural or evolutionary outcome of indexing gender by women repeatedly and spontaneously using certain speech forms as it is a hazardous effect of modernity in which, far from being relics from feudal Japan, both gender and language became problematized as targets of national and capitalist interest and social reform. Both gender and language were significantly reconfigured as various domains of the society responded to the project of modernity and as its attendant social formations—

capitalism, nationalism, and colonialism—profoundly transformed the contours of all social relations. Historical beginnings are "derisive and ironic" (Foucault 1977a:143). Precisely the same new modern conception of language that enabled and was enabled by the development of rational bureaucracy, the universal education system, nationalism, the military, the print media, colonial education, science and technology, and modern mimetic apparatuses (such as stenography, photography, and the phonograph) made possible the emergence of women's language—one critical sign of Japanese culture and tradition. The representational technique of "write as you speak," which was instrumental in creating the speech forms of women's language, was made necessary by nothing less than Japan's engagement with the Western realist novel.

The emergence of women's language was and has been intensely modern and national. Indexing gender in early-twentieth-century Japan involved imagining the voice of (the yet to be imagined) modern Japanese woman. It was in the "vulgar" speech of schoolgirls that the Meiji writers discovered the linguistic forms to represent the voice of modern women. This type of speech became elevated to the rank of "Japanese women's language" only after it was displaced, grafted, quoted, recycled, and circulated in the network of newly available representational genres and media. In this sense, there is no original or authentic speaking body that uttered women's language. It is *no one's language;* indeed, it is disembodied language. It emerges from a series of entextualization processes (Bauman and Briggs 1990) in which the empty signifier of "the modern Japanese woman" became (imaginatively) fleshed out and given her voice. The rise of women's language is, thus, inescapably connected with the development of consumer culture. In short, the majority of women experienced women's language not so much as its producers but as its (gendered) consumers.[34] They "heard" modern women speaking in novels, magazines, letters from readers, and recipes for exotic Western dishes; and they "saw" modern women on magazine cover pictures and in advertisements for cosmetics and perfumes. This consumption by no means indicated passivity or lack of agency on their part. Consumption, which de Certeau (1984:31–32) translates into the notion of use, is a powerful act of claiming and making. Women, here as every-

---

34. Consumption is particularly critical in the case of working-class women. As Haug points out, capitalism harnesses working-class people not only as sellers of labor power but also as buyers and consumers, which he calls "secondary exploitation" (1986:103; see also Marx 1981:745; Mouffe 1988).

where, made their own history, even if they may not have done it exactly as they pleased.

More importantly, however, the process of constructing women's language—in its critical articulation with the emergent discourses of nation, race, and class, as well as with those of culture and tradition—opened up a new discursive space (a metapragmatic discursive space) where the cultural meanings of women are produced, processed, and turned into a concrete object that is knowable, transparent, and readily available for social—not to mention self—control. This is precisely the condition under which indexing gender itself is possible and thinkable and under which statements such as "Women speak more politely than men" or ontological questions such as "Why do men and women speak differently?" make sense. Paradoxically, however, this new space also simultaneously allows for strategic appropriation and subversion of dominant projects. A utopian speech community constructed in the readers' column in girls' and young women's magazines is proof of this point.

By outlining the genealogy of Japanese women's language, I aim at a historical narrative that problematizes what is claimed to be natural and obvious in the present. The stability of Japanese women's language as a discourse is commonly believed to derive precisely from its supposedly ancient origin and its continuity and linearity up to the present. The approach here puts that historical narrative into methodological question. I search, not for the evolutionary origins of an essence with a natural history, but, as noted, for a genealogy. A genealogy historicizes the past, and by doing so, the present is problematized (Scott 1996) in a way that makes visible the potential existence of heterogeneous temporalities, spaces, and experiences. By locating the emergence of what has been essentialized as women's language in real historical context, and by treating it as one of the historically contingent (yet powerful) events that objectify the relationship between femaleness and language, I recognize diverse linguistic experiences as they are situated in and refracted by class and other parameters of social force. The point is not, however, simply to celebrate subaltern voices and resistance, but to recognize the ways in which women's linguistic experiences are shaped by the larger processes of the real social and historical social world, in which access to women's language is as unevenly distributed as other forms of capital—of both the cultural and the more familiar kind (Bourdieu 1977, 1991).

In this chapter, I have also sought to demonstrate the social power of the indexicality of language. A focus on indexing forces one to think historically, and historicizing the practice of indexing, as I have outlined here, echoes a larger and growing concern in linguistic anthropology to bring political economy (social power and its orchestrating and organizing potentialities) into linguistic analysis (Friedrich 1989; Gal 1989; Irvine 1989). A metapragmatic category such as "women's language" is never pregiven, but is contingent on historically specific social arrangements in which linguistic forms are motivated and regimented to become indexes as they are mediated through the broader political and economic processes of things bringing themselves into being.

Often, language does not wait until the category it refers to or indexes is "out there." In addressing the case of the development of women's language, I show that indexical practice was involved with the construction of modern Japanese women right from its inception. Indexicality constitutes reality, not by naming and pointing to a preexisting object, but by inverting the order of the indexed and indexing as if the indexed preceded the indexing. Finally, a focus on indexing forces one to think critically and counterfactually because the process by which a particular speech form is selected or negotiated out of multiple competing voices and interpretations to become an institutionally discrete index of femaleness is an inescapably political process. The index is inherently unstable and more a process than a thing, and its reproduction is a perennially political matter of self-naturalization. It is, however, precisely this processual and productive nature of indexicality that allows one to see how much any established structure of linguistic rules in a rule-governed context is in fact saturated with individual strategizing, cultural remaking, politics, and historicity.

CHAPTER 3

From Schoolgirl Speech to Women's Language

Consuming Indexicality in Women's Magazines, 1890–1930

The schoolgirl's voice was reified as teyo-dawa speech and was excluded from the public sphere of the print media as self-representing speech. At the same time, it proliferated and propagated in the print media through incessant and endless circulation and citation in the public sphere of print commodities as represented speech. The iterability of the schoolgirl's voice-as-sign, however, inevitably produces unruly excess and contingency, and potentially leads to transformation and, possibly, subversion (Butler 1990, 1997; Derrida 1977). Likewise, in spite of intellectuals and educators deploring teyo-dawa speech, its indexical meaning simultaneously *failed* to be faithfully iterated in the endless circuit of dislocating. The inherent performativity of the indexicality of teyo-dawa speech eventually led to its being disintegrated and resignified, if not subverted, as the sign of the Japanese female modern and of all that the female national citizen would be disciplined to desire. By the 1930s, teyo-dawa speech had appeared as an "unmarked" women's voice in the print media. With a syntactic compounding with auxiliary verbs such as *desu* and *masu* and honorifics to mark explicit politeness and deference, teyo-dawa speech appeared in etiquette books, for example, in which it was displayed as an essential linguistic component of model dialogues appropriate for various imaginary social events and speech situations for urban middle-class women. Teyo-dawa speech came to be elevated as part of the essential linguistic habitus, along with ideal bodily movements and postures in walking, bowing, and eating, associated with the urban middle-class

Japanese woman, and it increasingly came to be claimed by young women—their actual speech being a different matter—as they came to be socialized to desire things, ideas, and images that teyo-dawa speech indexed in the print media.

If the schoolgirl's voice was objectified and rationalized as it was by the male intellectual, and if it hailed him—as an auditory double that mirrored his fear and anxiety—then the question remains: How did women, including schoolgirls, hear the schoolgirl's voice? What were their encounters with teyo-dawa speech? A handful of privileged schoolgirls in the 1880s could have claimed it as their own language and themselves as its original speakers. But such conscious awareness of a particular set of speech forms would have been possible only after it had been objectified *as the other,* in the citational loop of appropriation, mimicry, and identification (and possibly disidentification). The relentless displacement and circulation did not allow anyone to encounter it as self, but only as alterity. As Taussig succinctly puts it, "The ability to mime, and mime well, . . . is the capacity to Other" (1993:19).

The resignification of teyo-dawa speech took place because the conditions of discourse, which governed the narrating voices that quoted and cited teyo-dawa speech, and the forms's relationship with the quoted voice of teyo-dawa speech eventually shifted, as simultaneously competing and complicit modernizing social forces and institutions necessitated and thus constructed the cultural category of the modern Japanese woman. The most significant and critical modernizing force was located in the rapidly expanding network of capitalist markets and the life space that it carved out as commodity experience. Just as the state discovered the schoolgirl's body onto which ideologies of the gendered national citizen were to be inscribed and thus constructed the subjectivity of the schoolgirl, markets similarly discovered her as a consumer and thus constructed her as a consuming subject. And just as the commodity acquired the enigmatic quality of self-animation (Marx), the resignification of teyo-dawa speech in the realm of commodity consumption entailed the acquisition of an automaton-like quality, so that it sounds like the trace of the real speech of the real living speaker.

This chapter will trace the process by which teyo-dawa speech came to be resignified and to be animated, and how that process was connected with the gender-specific and class-specific way in which women experienced modernity and thus were constituted as modern subjects. I will focus on one of the most important sites where young women overheard— just as male intellectuals overheard schoolgirls speaking on the street—and experienced teyo-dawa speech and where its indexical meaning was dramatically shifting: young women's magazines published and circulated from the late 1890s to the 1930s. Those three decades marked a significant transition and an ultimate transformation of magazine publishing as it attempted to target the expanding population of the new middle-class women, and, later, to reach out to working-class women. Not only were these magazines one of the first readily available consumer goods for young women, they were also one of the first *media* of commercial goods by virtue of carrying print advertisements.

The magazine, through its unique format, effectively socialized literate middle-class readers to be desiring gendered bourgeois-citizen-consumers. Consumption opened up a new space for the citational practice of schoolgirl speech, and for its resignification. In what ways, then, did the magazines, in their specific graphic and textual organization, contribute to such a resignification process? I will argue that reading the mass-circulated young women's magazines was one of the most critical experiences of (gendered) modernity for literate young women and that it is in such magazines where one can observe the most dynamic resignification process of teyo-dawa speech. To put it differently, encountering teyo-dawa speech in the magazine was part and parcel of essential commodity experience. I will discuss the extent to which schoolgirl speech came to be transformed into modern Japanese women's language in and through the realm of consumption, and, in turn, how this productive process of consuming the indexicality of schoolgirl speech in print-commodity form, as a critical modern experience, socialized female readers into gendered consumer subjects, in short, the subject position of the modern Japanese woman.

Schoolgirl speech was multiply displaced and shunned as other. It was the voice that belonged neither to male intellectuals nor to their vision of modernity. It was also the "other" of nationalist female educators, who attempted to turn young women into docile national subjects through disciplining their language use. Even socialist feminists did not approve of it, for it symbolized to them the bourgeois gender sociality of "good wife and wise mother" and apolitical consumerism. It was also the voice of alterity for modern standard Japanese, by which schoolgirl speech was simply to be quoted. It was, however, embraced by some of the most commercially successful girls' magazines and their readers as a linguistic marker of and device for their counterpublic sphere. In these magazines, schoolgirl speech was no longer reported speech, but reporting speech, as if girls spoke directly to reader "friends." Readers wrote to the letters' columns, using precisely the speech style that adults condemned and the magazines published. It was also used in various representational genres in the magazines, including dialogues in serial novels, paratexual commentaries in advertisements and portraits, reportage, and testimonial essays.

The material will be analyzed to demonstrate how readers experienced schoolgirl's speech as consumers and spectators, and how certain speech forms associated with women's language came to index commodities in advertisements, portraits of daughters of upper-class families, authors of letters in readers' columns and reportage, and characters in play scripts and diaries. While women's language was paradoxically positioned as the alterity of standard Japanese language (which interpellates the universal subject as fundamentally male and modern), it made semiotically possible a sense of girls' modernity—a gendered (mass) modernity. The striking phenomenon in some of the commercially successful magazines is that teyo-dawa speech was embraced not only by writers of serialized domestic novels, as was seen in chapter 2, but also by advertisers, editors, and, most importantly, readers themselves. Moreover, we can observe the emergence of new textual and paratextual genres that identify the structural subject position "I" with a young woman (a schoolgirl), so that one could read as if she had been speaking to, or addressing directly, the magazine reader without the formal mediation of a quoting voice. These genres include advertisements organized by dialogues and testimonials, reportage, paratexts attached to photographic portraits, and, most importantly, readers' columns, which published letters from readers using teyo-dawa speech. In these genres, teyo-dawa speech was no longer a *quoted* but a *quoting* voice, a self-representing and self-organizing metalanguage. In other words, the magazine created a space where these genres structurally produced the effect of making teyo-dawa speech look and sound like a metalanguage, by rendering the real quoting voice of publishers and advertisers formally invisible. Women appeared to be "speaking"—as opposed to being "spoken"—in the magazine.[1]

The formal suspension of the (male modern) quoting voice and the

---

1. It is important to note that the oral quality of schoolgirl speech and the accompanying experience of "hearing a voice" in writing should not be taken as "natural." That schoolgirl speech is real speech spoken by real people and that schoolgirl speech in writing is the more or less faithful representation of actual speech are precisely the ideological premises that make the idea of schoolgirl speech possible. The functionalist dichotomy between orality and writing and the idea that the former precedes the latter provides the fantasy that schoolgirl speech originates from real human bodies. What needs to be explored here is a set of metacommunicative signals that insist that schoolgirl speech is a language spoken by real speakers and that we are "hearing" the speaking voice in letters and other text.

subsequent functioning of teyo-dawa speech as a metalanguage in the new textual genres also corresponded with the increasing commercialization of young women's magazines in terms of a gradual shift in editorial policies toward being mass-oriented with an emphasis on expanding readership and selling advertising space. Advertisements, in pursuit of persuasive power, began to employ a testimonial style of copywriting with extensive use of teyo-dawa speech along with lithographic or collotype portraits and illustrations of schoolgirls and other modern young women as if they were directly addressing readers.

The emergence of teyo-dawa speech as metalanguage also marks a specific way in which a public space is created in the print media. It simulates a face-to-face oral community in which voices are embodied and cannot be sustained without the (imaginary) presence of the speaking body. As I have discussed in previous chapters, it was precisely such a mode of publics and language that the male elite eventually rejected as a suitable textually mediated public of the national community and its operational language (gembun'itchi). The modern Japanese bourgeois public sphere, made up of rational citizens whose rational voices were instantiated through the modern standard Japanese, circumvents the physical presence of localized and particularized individual bodies. It is in this sense that some of the women's magazines facilitated "counterpublics," whose members were often disenfranchised from the official political public space of national citizens—women, after all, could not vote—and were, instead, embraced by the industrial-commercial space as sovereign consumers.

To bring out the critical linkage of the historical construction of the idea of women's language to the historically specific social formation that I call "modernity," I will use a specific strategy in the analysis of the magazines. Central to my analysis is an understanding of the relationship among teyo-dawa speech, the emergence of the new textual genres, and the materiality of the magazine as both a print medium and a commodity, on the one hand, and of its linkage with the broader context of modernizing Japan, particularly the new mode of sociality and sensory experience, under which the magazine was produced, circulated, and consumed, on the other hand. This means that I treat the magazines not only as a collection of texts and images produced, circulated, and read at the particular historical juncture of the late nineteenth century through the interwar period but, more importantly, as a social space (of modernity) that is extended from the other loci sharing the same space of that particular historical moment. It is shared by and linked to other sites and their experience of social communication newly available in that time, including city streets, department stores, the railroads, and, later, movie theaters. What traverses these sites is a shared mode of perceptual experience of fragmentation and distraction, which is closely associated with modernity (Benjamin 1999). This is the fundamental historical condition under which the magazine was consumed.

The magazine format requires a way of "reading" radically different from the way a book, and especially a novel, is read. The mélange of texts and images and the graphic ordering specific and unique to a magazine format do not allow a linear reading, but force the reading to be distracted and fragmented. A text is disrupted by a graphic image or another text, or it skips one page because of an intervening advertisement. Or a "sidebar" article is inserted within a text. An advertisement is on the corner of a page of text from a serialized novel, or a cooking recipe appears juxtaposed with a graduation photograph of schoolgirls. This material structure of the magazine format, I would argue, facilitates a critical unruly intertextual environment in which teyo-dawa speech came to be resignified.[2] It constitutes the semiotic condition in which readers engaged in the "indexical labor" of following teyo-dawa speech as indexical arrows pointing to scattered and fragmented images, ideas, and things in the magazine. "Indexical labor" necessitated and was necessitated precisely by the material organization of the magazine format, which defies a linear and hermeneutic mode of "reading." Thus, by situating magazine reading in a broader historical context, I argue in this chapter that it is *only* in this historical linkage that we can understand how teyo-dawa speech came to be resignified, and, ultimately, how language came to be a critical cultural knowledge and space, particularly for women, in their experiences of and responses to the broader social formation, that is, modernity.[3]

The monumental shift in the indexical meaning of schoolgirl speech

---

2. It is for this reason that "reading" cannot be equated with "analyzing" the magazine, because each medium requires its own historically specific mode of reading. It is thus critical to develop an analytical method for media studies by taking into consideration historicity and corporeality. Hall's (1993) coding/decoding model is in this sense somewhat ahistorical and abstract.

3. For the specific purpose of this chapter, I am less concerned with delineating, again, in Hall's terms, "the dominant reading" of the underlying ideological functions and workings of a particular text. Nor am I concerned with the hermeneutic search for the true essence of the text or the history of reading, the phenomenological reconstruction of how the magazine was actually read by historical readers, which would be, to use Hall's terms, "negotiated" and "oppositional" readings. If, for example, some historical materials such as a personal diary, autobiography, or a memoir, were available, or if one could interview people for their recollection of reading experience in the past, one might see how an actual historical reader interpreted or decoded a particular text or image from a particular social and

meant that for the first time, it came to be a pure *gender marker:* it lost its ability to index a historically and economically specific group of women, that is, daughters of privileged families. Schoolgirl speech, or "women's language," lost its semiotic function to mark (material) differences among women. And instead it was now subsumed by the ahistorical binary of "maleness" and "femaleness," abjecting other structural and material differences such as class and region, and marking ahistorical, universal modern femaleness, envisioned variously by the state, the market, and the civil society. And it is this historical moment—when women's language came to be purified as a gender marker of the ideal modern Japanese woman— that the nation inaugurates as its *origin.*

Young Women's Magazines

In this chapter, I will mainly examine two women's magazines, *Jogaku sekai* (Women's learning world, 1901–25) and *Fujin sekai* (Ladies' world, 1906– 33).[4] These were the first commercially successful women's magazines and, at the same time, the first women's magazines in which schoolgirl speech started to appear in the form of *quoting* language. While the full-fledged commercialization and mass circulation of women's magazines did not emerge until the interwar period, these magazines, which stretched from the late Meiji (1900s) to the threshold of the heyday of Taisho mass culture of the 1930s, illustrate the dynamics of changes in editorial policies over content and layout that were a response to the shift in the demography of the readership, as well as to the socioeconomic changes that shaped the readership, and that marked their transformation into mass magazines. This movement toward the mass magazine, which was in a way inevitable to gain wider readership and thus to remain profitable in an increasingly

---

political location, and thus appreciate the openness and vulnerability of any text or image to multiple interpretations and recover ethnographic truths about reading practice. But still, these are not the condition, but rather the effects that the condition made possible. Throughout this book, I aim to describe and analyze the underlying political, economic, and cultural conditions under which the idea of "women's language" came into being.

4. As I have sketched out in the previous section, my focus is on the analysis of the format of and the genres in the magazines. For a pioneering work on Japanese women's magazines in prewar Japan and their construction of diverse images of modern Japanese women, see B. H. Sato 2003. There have also been interesting reception studies examining letter columns in prewar women's magazines, in an effort to understand how these magazines were actually read by the readers (Kawamura 1993; Kimura 1992; Sato R. S. 1996).

competitive print capitalism, gave rise to the new textual and paratextual genres in which schoolgirl speech took the subject position "I."

Modern forms of women's magazines had been around since the late nineteenth century, or the mid-Meiji period. Between 1894 and 1898, a total of ten such magazines were published (Nakajima 1989:7). As "women" emerged as a national issue in the wake of modernization movements, these magazines addressed the question of how women should be enlightened and reformed to make them a productive constituent of modernizing Japan. While they all shared the mission of educating women, each magazine was founded on its own modernizing ideology, including Western liberal democratic Enlightenment thought; Christianity; and a reactionary nationalist reinvention of "traditional" Japanese womanhood—and each variously attempted to create a corresponding vision of Japanese womanhood. In addition, a number of bulletins of various women's religious-based organizations, including Christian and Buddhist, occupational newsletters such as those for midwives and school teachers, and class lectures for those who could not attend girls' high schools, had been published since 1877.[5] It was to such magazines that educators and intellectuals contributed essays and articles about the linguistic corruption of schoolgirls.

---

5. These printed materials also functioned to promote and sustain newly consolidated national and regional communities of women's organizations, such as what was called *jogakukai* (the world of women's education), by educating readers about current news and events. Although their readership was strictly limited to the elite, such earlier enlightenment magazines for women attracted both men and women as readers, for, in the context of building a modern civilized nation, "women" emerged as a target of "reform" *(kairyō)* and of nationalizing. One of the most representative magazines published in this period was *Jogaku zasshi* (Journal of women's learning, 1885–1900). Founded by the educator Iwamoto Yoshiharu (1863–1942), who advocated women's education based on Christian ethics, the magazine dealt with a wide range of social issues related to women's rights and enlightenment, including moral reform and the abolition of prostitution. Recognizing the diversifying needs and interests of readers and the growing gap between what the magazine provided and what the readers were perceived to want, however, Iwamoto split *Jogaku zasshi* into two separate issues in 1892 and alternatively published them under the same magazine title: one for young male and female readers interested in editorials on current domestic and international affairs and the other for older women, including housewives, who might benefit more from topics such childrearing and household management (Nakajima 1986:8). Another notable magazine published during this period is *Jokan* (The paragon of womanhood, 1891–1909), which, as citations in the previous chapter showed, frequently carried essays and articles on schoolgirls' linguistic corruption. Against the newly imported idea of women's equality and independence informed by Western liberal thought and Christianity, *Jokan* led the reactionary nationalist line, and (re)invented the "traditional" Japanese woman. Equating the ideal Japanese woman with the ideal national and imperial subject, *Jokan* consistently offered the view that a woman's virtue—which is the virtue of a

These magazines were eventually replaced by a new set that appeared in the late Meiji period. Between 1899 and 1912, or the end of Meiji, a total of 106 different magazines targeting women were published and circulated (Nakajima 1989:7), some of which became the first commercial successes in the publishing of women's magazines. Both *Jogaku sekai* and *Fujin sekai* were launched during this period.[6] The surge of women's magazines at this time was triggered partly by the anticipation of an increase in the female reading population.[7] Girls' enrollment in compulsory education had been steadily increasing, and the 1899 Directive on Girls' High Schools, stipulating the mandatory establishment of girls' high schools, resulted in a significant "demographic" expansion of schoolgirls and of those who graduated from being schoolgirls to become housewives and the emerging segment of working women *(shokugyō fujin)*. The infrastructure for print capitalism had also been gradually consolidated after the Russo-Japanese War, as Japan's economic, social, and political structure came into maturity as a modern industrial nation-state. Technologies for both printing and a nationwide distribution sys-

---

(gendered) imperial subject—is to be found in obedience to her husband and dedication to motherhood. The magazines published in this period commonly exhibited a simple magazine layout in which reading materials—often pedantic and didactic—are placed linearly with few illustrations or graphic images. The readership was strictly limited to the elite segment of the society. See Miki (1986:167–219) for a comprehensive chronology of women's magazines from 1877 to 1944.

6. A sales survey for women's magazines in major bookstores in the City of Tokyo in 1911 (*Asahi Shimbun,* April 12, 1911) shows that *Fujin sekai* and *Jogaku sekai* rank first and second, respectively (cited from Nakajima 1986:56). *Fujin sekai* sold seventy to eighty thousand copies, whereas most women's magazines sold two to three thousand on average and seven to ten thousand maximum; *Fujin sekai* claimed sales of four hundred thousand copies at its peak (Ogawa 1962).

7. The commercial expansion of the magazine market for female readerships at the turn of the century accompanied its internal segmentation. As a result, the first decade of the 1900s also witnessed a flurry of publications of girls' magazines *(shōjo zasshi)*. This was prompted by the anticipation of the increasingly literate female population as the enrollments of elementary schools and higher grades steadily rose. While their readership could partially overlap with young women's magazines, this age-specific carving out of the female population, a transient and fleeting period between childhood and adulthood, came to be significant unit of culture, "girls' culture" *(shōjo bunka),* around which the social identity of *shōjo* was distinctively constructed. Some of the representative magazines include *Shōjo kai* (Girls' world, 1902–13), *Shōjo sekai* (Girls' world, 1906–31), and *Shōjo no tomo* (Girls' friend, 1908–55). Sato Rika Sakuma (1996) estimates that 80–90 percent of the readers were older than twelve but younger than fifteen, inferring from the age indicated for the readers who were prizewinners for quizzes and who contributed their poems (haiku and waka) and compositions to *Shōjo no tomo*. This category of *shōjo* still holds significance in girls' subculture, including comic magazines, novels, and others.

tem via the postal service were also ready for mass circulation of magazines (see Nagamine 1997).

By the late 1910s, the huge commercial success of women's magazines such as *Shufu no tomo* (Housewife's friend, founded 1917)and *Fujin kurabu* (Ladies' club, 1920–88) marked the massification of magazine publication for women by addressing the steadily growing market of urban new middle-class women *(shinchūkansō)*, including wives of the new wage workers who had migrated from rural areas. Editorial contents reflected what the capitalist, gendered division of labor prescribed as "women's interests and needs." Visually spectacular and textually accessible, by the 1920s, these magazines had also incorporated into their readership working-class women, including factory girls, maids (Nagamine 1977: 201–2), and rural women.[8]

Eventually, *Jogaku sekai* and *Fujin sekai* got lost in the fierce competition with magazines such as *Shufu no tomo* and *Fujin kurabu*. In a sense, *Jogaku sekai* and *Fujin sekai* came at this interstitial period between the earliest pedantic enlightenment magazines and the full-grown commercial publication of women's magazines for the masses in the 1920s and 1930s. What sets them apart from magazines published before 1899 has to do with the degree to which they discovered the increasing female reading population as a new niche of *consumers* as opposed to a population to be didactically enlightened and discussed. Although both magazines initially pledged their determined commitment to the advancement of the state's "good wife and wise mother" policy and continued to carry pedantic essays on the topic and articles contributed by well-known educators and intellectuals, their editorial policies clearly shifted toward the expansion of more practical and entertaining content with more advertisements, graphics, and visually appealing layouts. Editorial policies, for both the quality and the quantity of graphic and illustrative materials, the sheer volume of advertisements, and the way they were placed in the editorials pages, underwent a significant transformation over the years to keep up with the shifting demographic configuration of female readerships. And this transformation runs precisely and clearly parallel with the process by which schoolgirl speech came to be resignified in the increasingly commercialized, mass-oriented, and commodified textual and graphic contexts of the magazine.

Jogaku sekai (*JS,* henceforth) launched its first issue in 1901 with its

8. Garon (1993:22) notes that by 1935 magazines such as *Shufu no tomo* were widely read by women in rural areas.

mission to educate the reader to be "a good wife and wise mother." It was published by Hakubunkan, one of the largest publishing companies at that time. The July issue in 1901 (1 [7]:207) announced its new and improved editorial policy, promising more practical content for household management, from cooking and childrearing to home economics, in addition to aiming at serving as a guide to women's learning. *Fujin sekai* (*FS*, henceforth) started publication in 1906 at Jitsugōno tomo sha, another large publishing company. Like *JS*, *FS* put "good wife and wise mother" to the fore as editorial policy, which, against the background of the recent victory in the Russo-Japanese War, held a strong nationalist tone and characterized the wife/mother role explicitly as women's social, national, and imperial duty.[9] And like *JS*, it promised to reflect upon a wide variety of content from self-discipline *(shūyō)* to cooking and childrearing. *FS*'s nationalist line differentiated it from *JS*. Many of *FS*'s frequent contributors were ardent nationalists, and it often carried essays and commentaries criticizing schoolgirls' language use, whereas *JS* had almost no critical commentary directly on schoolgirl speech.[10]

Both magazines carried commissioned didactic essays and commentaries contributed by prominent educators, writers, politicians, journalists, and aristocrats, whose signed texts carried authority. As noted, in *FS*, schoolgirls' linguistic corruption was one of the popular topics such authorities wrote about. Another attraction was color illustrations (often as foldouts) by famous illustrators such as Takehisa Yumeji (1884–1934). These generally depicted schoolgirls, landscapes, or birds and flowers. In addition to the didactic essays and commentaries and illustrations, typical content initially included photographs and portraits (of schoolgirls or of women from famous families), model literary works (calligraphy, haiku, and epistles), editorials, articles and essays on homemaking and home management (cooking, making and repairing clothes, how to use maids, how to be frugal, hygiene), etiquette, ethics, fashion, biographies (of famous women both in Japan and overseas), lectures by educators, anthropological reports

---

9. The inaugural issue promised *FS*'s commitment to the nationalist cause and thus to educating readers to be imperial-national citizens, expecting women "in view of the advancement of the empire entering the arena of fierce world competition, to aspire first to reform the family, along with promoting the welfare of the nation-society, by recognizing one's responsibilities for the family, the nation, and the society, and cooperating with men" (cited in Nakajima 1986:126).

10. One of the few articles that mentioned schoolgirl speech simply noted that its prevalence was an uncontestable "fact" since there were so many schoolgirls using it (Takada Mineko, "Jisei ni houmuraruru onna" [A woman buried in the current of the times], *Jogaku sekai*, 1908:940).

on women in "primitive" cultures, current affairs in both Japan and the West, interviews with women in high society, domestic novels, miscellaneous news, readers' literary works, and readers' columns.

The editorial policy of both *JS* and *FS* shifted, not necessarily consistently but clearly, in a direction toward the more practical and the mass-oriented. This meant, for example, an expansion of space for serial novels, practical advice, and visual content. It also meant an incorporation of what was imagined as the reader's point of view. We can observe an increase in unsigned or anonymous texts or pen-named authors, whose author function is textually constituted as a nonauthority, an "ordinary" person, just like a reader. These essays and commentaries capture the world not from an authority's or specialist's standpoint, but from that of someone with whom a reader can identify herself. The construction of this ordinary woman's viewpoint gave rise to textual genres in which the subject position "I" is identified as an ordinary "she," often epitomized as an anonymous schoolgirl. Such authors contributed regular essays and commentaries, but also diaries and epistles, readers' letters, advertisements, and some eclectic genres whose whole function was to display the "real" voice of "real" schoolgirls to be "heard" in the written text. This is the textual condition in which schoolgirl speech appeared in the form of self-representing language.

From Quoted Voice to Quoting Voice

The realist technique of direct reported speech developed in the literary movement, and the schoolgirl speech that it made possible, crossed over into more commercial textual and semitextual genres as mass-produced print commodities, such as newspapers and magazines, proliferated. As in the domestic novels in general in the early twentieth century, novels that appeared serialized in women's magazines used schoolgirl speech extensively in dialogue, including utterance-ending forms *yo* (*yo, te-yo, no-yo, wa-yo, koto-yo*), or with the polite auxiliary verb *desu* inserted, such as *desu-no-yo, desu-wa-yo*), *wa* (*wa, da-wa, desu-wa*), *no* (*no, no-yo, desu-no-yo*), *-chatta, -te, -mono,* and *-kashira*. Readers who contributed prizewinning short stories to the magazine's literary contest also emulated schoolgirl speech in their dialogues. There schoolgirl speech not only further disseminated itself, but also came to represent itself as subject-metalanguage, as opposed to language that is merely object-represented and reported. With the formal level of the male-national-modern quoting voice temporarily vanished from the pages of the magazine, schoolgirl speech literally shot into the reader's ears without third-party mediation and was given linguistic agency as the structural and discursive subject who spoke it was made knowable and concrete in the same pages. It is the voice of a particularized individual, diametrically opposed to the voice of the transcendental subjectivity of modern Japan achieved through the standard Japanese of the gembun'itchi movement. And this particularized individual, this "I," figures in the composite of the modern woman socially imaginable from the photographs, illustrations, domestic novels, and advertisements, where she is directly talking to the reader in schoolgirl speech.

Although its formal marking is invisible, the quoting voice is still present, of course. In fact, it is the authorial quoting voice, which mimes schoolgirl speech and resolves the boundary between the reporting voice and that of the reported, as if "she" were speaking, not "he." This schoolgirl speech without the quoting voice—the strategic disintegration of the double voice—approximates what Voloshinov (1973:120–21) calls "pictorial" reporting, in which

> the verbal dominant may shift to the reported speech, which in that case becomes more forceful and more active than the authorial context framing it. This time the reported speech begins to resolve, as it were, the reporting context, instead of the other way around. The authorial context loses the greater objectivity it normally commands in comparison with reported speech. It begins to perceive itself—and even recognizes itself—as subjective, "other person's" speech. (121)

What we can add to Voloshinov's discussion is the specific relationship between the pictorial reporting style and the condition of production of art forms under capitalism and the new technologies that produced and (mass-)reproduced them. In other words, the proliferation of the pictorial style under the imperative of mass print capitalism cannot be separated from the process of commodification of literary forms. "Other people's speech" in this case is for and of the emerging mass readership. There is, however, more to it. First, just as workers in general lost control over production, writers enmeshed in capitalist social relations became "proletarian," working for salaries by producing in quantity (Buck-Morss 1989:138). Benjamin thus observes the proliferation of dialogue-based prose as a result of factorylike mass production of literary works: "Fees for *feuilletons* went as high as two francs per line. Authors would often write as much dialogue as possible so as to benefit from the blank spaces in the lines" (1999:586 [U9a, 1]). The transformation of literary forms into commodities was also accompanied by a "massive melting-down process of literary forms" (Benjamin 1978:231; cited in Buck-Morss 1989:140). Particularly critical is the role of writing and its medium in bestowing the commodity with "value," the ultimate example of which would be advertising copy. Benjamin provides a vivid image of the function and location of writing drastically displaced in modern industrial space: "Printing, having found in the book a refuge in which to lead an autonomous existence, is pitilessly dragged out onto the street by advertisements and subjected to the brutal heteronomies of economic chaos. This is the hard schooling of its new form" (1978:77). The commodification of literary forms thus meant they crossed over into, and gave rise to, various commercial literary genres and styles, such as serial novels, paratext to the photographic images, and advertising copy, in which pictorial style in the form of direct reported speech increasingly appeared. As Buck-Morss aptly puts it, "Under capitalist relations, style adapted to the exigencies of the medium" (1989:139). This illustrative language also works in tandem with commodity display, by perfecting the aesthetic illusion of its quality and features, and offering authentic testimonies and endorsements. As I will show below, the pictorial reporting style increasingly appeared in advertisement copy.

THE SUBJECT OF DIALOGUE-BASED PROSE

Women's magazines carried play scripts and short stories with only direct reported speech dialogues, in which schoolgirl speech was used as the voice of girls' and women's characters.[11] For example, a play script titled "The First Ball" (Hatsu no butōkai) appeared in *JS* in 1904. The play develops around two seventeen- or eighteen-year-old schoolgirls, who are cousins, preparing for their first ball.[12] It was translated from German and modified to be suitable for the Japanese setting by Iwaya Sazanami (1870–1933), a well-known writer of juvenile literature. He notes that this play was often performed in girls' schools and homes in Germany and that it would be fun for the readers to try to perform it on occasions such as a school reunion (1904:173). Another example can be drawn from a text titled "What Kind of Fashion is in Vogue in Tokyo Today?—Hairstyle, Collar, Coat,

---

11. Such dialogue-style prose appears more frequently in girls' magazines.
12. In the play (Iwaya 1904), the two characters are quite opposite in personality, one being bookish with little interest in her appearance or adornments such as clothes, hairstyle, accessories, and makeup. The other is precisely the opposite. The play depicts their preparation for the upcoming ball.

Obi?" which appeared in *JS* in 1911.¹³ The text is entirely a dialogue between two girls, one of whom has just come back from a visit to Tokyo and is telling another girl about what kind of things (kimonos, hairstyles, and so on) were in vogue in Tokyo, and what she took to be authentically "haikara." The contrast between Tokyo and the rest of the country (including the colonies) is a trope in the women's magazines in late Meiji and Taisho. Essays such as "About Women in Osaka from the Point of View of a Woman from Tokyo" or "My First Trip to Tokyo" frequently appeared during this time.

THE SUBJECT OF CONFESSION: EPISTLE- AND DIARY-STYLE GENRES OF BOURGEOIS INTERIORITY

In both girls' and women's magazines, schoolgirl speech in the dialogue of novels was emulated and transported into new textual genres. In these genres, schoolgirl speech itself became a quoting voice, and "she" became both the object and the subject of the text. What is also notable is that these genres allow an individual's inner thoughts to be represented in schoolgirl speech. Here, schoolgirl speech works as the linguistic technology instrumental to the construction of "bourgeois interiority" (Foucault 1978), or the psychological depth and inner truth of the modern subject with the attendant studied indifference to politics and history.

While in modern prose the gembun'itchi style is the language of the modern reflective self, it is noteworthy that schoolgirl speech also started representing the reflective inner state of the modern gendered individual, through genres that can be loosely identified as the diary and the epistle. This was a confessional style in which "I" is incited to reveal herself and produce truth, and it takes the form of bringing the intimate details of her private thoughts and experience into the public (display and spectacle). And what is displayed is the everyday private world of the imagined bourgeoisie.

Let me draw on one example of epistolary-style prose from a text titled "A schoolgirl's letter reporting the real state of affairs in the life of a girls' school," which appeared in *JS* in 1909.¹⁴ With the pen name Wakaba (Verdure) attached to it, the text constructs the identity of the narrator "I" and the narrated "me" as a schoolgirl who had just come to Tokyo

---

13. "Tokyo dewa kono setsu donna fū ga hayari masuka: kami no katachi, eri, kōto, obi," *Jogaku sekai* 1911, 11 (1):130–38.
14. "Jogaku seikatsu no naijō o hōzuru jogakusei no tegami," *Jogaku sekai* 1909, 9 (7):78–81.

from a rural area and entered a Tokyo girls' high school. As has been noted, the contrast between Tokyo and the rest of Japan as rural *(inaka)* is a recurrent theme in the magazines in late Meiji, an essential trope of modernity through which Japan was imagined as a unified modern nation-state with a center and peripheries (see Williams 1973). On a nice Sunday morning, when her dorm-mates have all gone out, she is left alone in her room and is writing to her hometown friend. Using schoolgirl speech, "I" tells her friend about how her classmates, who are all from wealthy and noble families, are well dressed and refined like princesses. "I" describes to her friend the details of the spectacular commodities, such as clothes, accessories, and cosmetics, her wealthy dorm-mates adorn themselves with and of how they look like "a daughter of Earl such and such, or a sister of Lord such and such, which we used to see together in the frontispiece of the magazine." She then reveals the "truth" of this new world that she now inhabits: she tells her friend, with surprise and disgust, about how little those wealthy classmates of hers care about their schoolwork, and that, instead, all they care about is "to marry into money" *(tama no koshi)*. "I" is someone who used to imagine the daughters and wives of the wealthy and noble families in Tokyo by looking at the pictures of aristocrats in the magazine, just like the readers do. The readers see themselves in what "I" does, witnesses, and thinks, and it is all done through the narrative voice constructed by schoolgirl speech.

 Some texts can also be identified as a diary style, in which "I" writes about her intimate everyday life, using schoolgirl speech. One example can be drawn from "Lady's Diary," which appeared in *JS* in 1908, under the pen name Kinsenka (Calendula).[15] The diarist is constructed as the twenty-year-old daughter of an obviously wealthy family and details her everyday experiences and thoughts. "I" contemplates her prospects for future marriage. While her old classmates have married one by one, she still is single. To her frustration and surprise, some of her old classmates, of whom she never would have expected it, managed to marry into wealthy families and become the wives of earls or viscounts, while her own future is unknown. But she thinks that being proposed to merely on account of one's image in a photograph is the same as being a geisha: she would be nothing but a temporary toy.

 "I" also details the design of her kimono, her ruby ring (and she never fails to mention that her diamond ring is put aside for a special occasion), her hairstyle, her *koto* (Japanese harp) practice (although she confesses that

---

15. "Reijō nikki," *Jogaku sekai*, 1908, 8 (9):50–58.

she prefers playing the piano), letter writing, sewing, and reading novels. Common to such a diary-style text is its spectacular visuality that allows the reader not only to "see" what the text describes, but also to imagine the social relations that grow out of the goods that surround "I." Such visuality in texts rehearses the commodity display of the department store and exhibitions, in which goods displayed for visual consumption organize social relations.

These genres share some elements of the speech act of "confession," "a ritual of discourse in which the speaking subject is also the subject of the statement" (Foucault 1978:61), and it is a powerful technique of producing truth and knowledge. It is critical to note here that in women's magazines, such a practice of confession and thus of constructing and displaying bourgeois interiority was carried out through schoolgirl speech. Furthermore, this "truth" is not limited to the psychological, but includes the veracity of the spectacular world of the commodity and novelty that saturated the City of Tokyo and of its new wealthy residents who had access to that world.

In short, schoolgirl speech produced the gendered subject "to confess." As Foucault explains (61–62), confession is also a speech act that entails power relations, in that it is made to institutional authorities such as priests and judges. In the magazine, "confession" in epistle- and diary-style genres is made to the readers, and *power is thus accorded to the readers,* which contrasts with the pedantic essays and commentaries contributed *by* recognized authorities that both *JS* and *FS* originally boasted as their selling point. In confession, the "agency of domination does not reside in the one who speaks . . . but in the one who listens and says nothing" (62).[16] As the women's magazines entered into Japanese consumer society of the 1920s and 1930s, and attempted to gain a wider readership in an increasingly fierce competition, confessional genres became more popular and, in a way, more elaborate. This period can be marked by magazines starting to solicit widely for essays and notes from the readers about their "real experience."[17]

---

16. Karatani also identifies "confession" as a system to produce modern Japanese subjecthood, and thus notes, "It was the literary form of the confession—confession as a system—that produced the interiority that confessed, the 'true self'" (1993:77). In fact, "confession" as an autobiographical narrative style was a crucial part of the history of modern Japanese literature in the first two decades of the twentieth century, and it developed into a distinctive genre: *shishōsetsu,* or the "I-novel." See Suzuki 1996 for the literary history of the I-novel and its critical linkage with the constitution of the modern Japanese self.

17. The increasing presence of "confession" as a public genre in magazines is illustrated in Robertson's (1999) study of lesbian confessions of suicide attempts in 1930s Japan.

THE SUBJECT OF COUNTERPUBLICS:
READERS' COLUMNS

Perhaps no other genre so verisimilarly constructed the presence of the living, speaking body of schoolgirl speech than the readers' letters column. And no other genre was so saturated with schoolgirl speech as these letters. Appropriating, or re-citing schoolgirl speech from the dialogue of the novel and the epistle and diary styles in the magazine, readers started writing in schoolgirl speech to the magazine, and thus claiming it as *their* language, by which they collectively engaged in personal and intimate, yet virtual, relationships with the anonymous others whom they never met but *knew* existed. It is an act of approximating and identifying with the enunciation—the individual utterance—the "I" of schoolgirl speech, and thereby of becoming its subject. The readers' correspondence column thus offered readers a new mode of belonging and of defining who they were. The process was both oppositional to and co-opted by the existing categories for identity and affiliation, such as family, class, and nation-state. And it was with schoolgirl speech that readers were identified, addressed, and organized. Thus was a new public brought into reality.

For a modern reader living in the twenty-first century, the letters printed in the women's magazine are simply "dated": they are too flowery, sugary, sentimental, romantic, and, above all, what contemporary Japanese would describe as *otome-chikku*. *Otome* refers to a maiden or the figure of a female with her purity intact, someone who lives in a romantic dream world, a world she reads about in a novel or a magazine (see also Robertson 1998b); *chikku* is a suffix meaning "-like," which came from "tic" in the English word "roman*tic*." In fact, it was the ethos of otome that characterized the world that the readers' correspondence column instantiated (Kawamura 1993). This ethos is the aspiration to the bourgeois family and to the role of the urban middle-class housewife. It takes various forms, beginning with aspiration to the ownership of commodities advertised in the magazines. It is also realistically visualized in the form of, for example, portraits of women from wealthy noble families. It is textualized in serial novels, diaries, and letters. Practical advice on household management would provide readers with tangible ways to fulfill their aspirations. It is this ultimate ideal of the modern Japanese woman—the urban middle-class housewife—that readers crafted in the space they were given by the competing forces that meant to subject them, including the state, the market, and the patriarchal family. Accordingly, schoolgirl speech, once deplored as vulgar and common, came actively to index the ethos of otome.

JS started its readers' column, called "Shiyū Kurabu" (The magazine's friends club) in 1909. It also had a separate correspondence column, called "Jogakusei tsūshin" (Schoolgirls' correspondence), where schoolgirls and ex-schoolgirls wrote about their school life, past or present. Other magazines, including girls' magazines, created similar spaces. The letters were addressed to the editors, the writers, the magazine itself by anthropomorphizing it, or to peer readers as "sisters."[18] They came not only from all over the country, but from Japan's colonies, and diasporic Japanese in places such as the United States and Canada.

The space for the readers' participation in the magazine had existed prior to *FS* and *JS*. A magazine would commonly offer a space for the readers to interact with it through, for example, organizing competitions for literary works. What was new in the girls' and women's magazines in the late Meiji was the emergence of the reader's *reflexive* community, where readers made metacommunicative and metamedial comments in the form of letters about the magazine and its contents, and the readers' literary works and the "community"—the public—the readers created in the magazine. This is a remarkable social effect. Printedness has social meanings (Warner 1990). The same text would carry different meaning and significance if it was simply handwritten than if it was printed in a publication. The mere fact that a particular text is printed and circulated accords it prestige and authority, and at one time only authoritative texts by authorities could get to be printed and circulated. In this sense, the readers' column marks a significant transformation of the social meaning of printedness and the critical moment of the rise of the print-mediated public sphere: the print media are no longer simply for communication by authorities to laypeople but include communication from laypeople to laypeople. This new public space appropriates the talk of ordinary people's self-representation of their private thoughts, feelings, desires, and experiences—things that had not been included in the official public sphere—in schoolgirl speech, the linguistic register that had been considered utterly unsuitable for public communication.

Ordinary readers get to see their own writing printed and circulated, and, furthermore, get to be seen by the newly emerging public of people

---

18. For example, readers' letters in *FS* addressed themselves to "Fuseko," a girl's name invented by putting together the first syllables of *Fujin* and *sekai*, and adding *-ko*, a typical ending of a girl's name.

just like themselves. Even if one does not write a letter to the editor, seeing letters from ordinary individuals printed is part and parcel of the way individuals participate in a public sphere. It is this reflexivity that is the critical foundation of the public sphere and of the sense of a community. And it was here, in this reflexive space and practice, that readers started "chatting" in schoolgirl speech in their letters. With no formal or visible authority quoting it, schoolgirl speech came to be the self-representing and self-understanding language, expressing the readers' bourgeois interiority. The reader's act of identifying her enunciation with the "I" of schoolgirl speech was thus "animated," as if she were its origin and initiator and as if it were the outcome of her practice of "write as you speak."

This public space and its accompanying public mode of communication that emerged in the readers' columns represent a new mode and function of the public sphere, consistent with the notion of "counterpublics" elaborated by Hansen (1991, 1993) and Negt and Kluge (1993). A counterpublic is constituted by "particularized individuals" and their interests and experiences situated in their concrete material situations. This stands in contrast with the bourgeois public sphere theorized by Habermas, which is made up of abstract "universalized individuals" who share the universal language of instrumental rationality and the privilege of self-representation. In spite of its claimed principle of liberal democracy, however, those who could actually participate in the bourgeois public sphere were (male) property owners, or agents of commodity exchange (Habermas 1989:109–10), thus inevitably excluding from the public sphere working-class people, whose lives were commodities in the form of alienated labor power, and other disenfranchised people, including women and ethnic minorities, and their situated interests, needs, and experiences.[19]

The public developed in the readers' correspondence column in particular and the women's magazines in general is grounded precisely in this

---

19. Coming from the Marxist tradition, Negt and Kluge (1993:28–32) develop a critical concept of a public sphere that accounts for the material condition of people, or what they term the "context of living," as the ontological basis of people's experience. They thus attempt to restore the concrete experience of those who were excluded to the concept of public, as well as the domains of life the bourgeois public sphere excluded as "the private sphere" (property owners are not supposed to be concerned with their individual material needs and interests in formulating *public* disclosure or in assuming a *public* subjectivity). What transpires is the possibility of multiple and overlapping publics based on particularities and specificities of the needs, experiences, and interests of people who are not served well by the abstract universal subject of capitalism and liberal democracy. Such plural publics became all the more relevant as the consumer culture developed because it is precisely "particularized individuals" that the market welcomes (or exploits) as consumers. Taking a cue

type of counterpublicity. It is substantiated by the public display of the private or the public communication of particularized interests and experiences specific to, or considered by the market to be specific to, "women," a newly discovered niche that the market calibrated. It is no coincidence that schoolgirl speech, this gullible, chatty, excessively emotive, present-tense speech, flourished and played the central constitutive role in organizing young women's counterpublics.

The readers' correspondence column as a counterpublic operates through a culturally and historically specific linguistic register and communicative mode. In addition to utterance-ending forms such as *teyo, dawa, noyo,* the linguistic register of the correspondence column consists of significant display of diacritics of excessive affect such as exclamation marks, interjections ("Oh"), and graphic traces of what exceeds speech (breath, sighs, groaning), frequent use of English words, and formulaic poetic phrases.

We don't know if the letters and their authors' identities are "authentic," nor do we know that the content of the letters is "true." They could be editorially exaggerated or simply written by the editorial staff. We also don't know how the letters were selected, however "fair" the process might have been. But this is beside the point, for what we understand as something like "identity" and "community" in the print media is first and foremost the textual effects or metacommunicative functions that such genres as "a letters column" produce by signaling the cue that it should be recognized as such. It is imperative to recognize the constitutive power of printedness and its mediation. Once the letters were printed and circulated in the magazine, and thus acquired the new value of publicity,

---

from Negt and Kluge, Hansen elaborates a framework she calls "industrial-commercial publicity" for late capitalist and postmodern forms of publicity, in particular, through consumption. She observes (1993: xxix–xxx) that such forms of publicity, including the mass media, inherently entail a contradiction between appropriating the legitimacy of the liberal bourgeois sphere, with its exclusionary principle and pursuit of class interests, and maximizing private profit. It is in the face of this contradiction that new functions and modes of publicity came to be available for traditionally disenfranchised people: "Founded with the explicit purpose of making a profit, these public spheres voraciously absorb, as their 'raw material,' areas of human life previously bracketed from representation—if only to appropriate, commodify, and desubstantiate that material. Likewise, they often cater to social constituencies that had not been considered before as a public—if only to integrate them into the community of consumers. Thus, in their structural dynamic, Negt and Kluge contend, industrial-commercial forms of publicity bring into view a substantially different function of the public sphere: that of a 'horizon of experience,' a discourse grounded in the context of everyday life, in material, psychic, and social (re-)production" (xxx).

they were irreducible to any original intention, individual identity, or authorship. And it is equally important to recognize the *textuality* of the readers' column as a genre, which simulates face-to-face communication and produces real effects on the readers' participation—*imagined* though it may be—in the magazine community. Text does not necessarily owe itself to "reality." It is the genre and the textuality that the genre produces that create the *effect* of reality

Kawamura astutely characterizes such a mode of communication as "narrative communication" *(monogatari teki komyunikēshon)*. It constructs a utopian world that is neither fictional nor "real" and that defies any realist assumption or skepticism. Letters are written and read in a logic other than truth/falsity or authentic/inauthentic. Referring to Anderson's "imagined community," Kawamura notes that the world the readers collectively construct in the readers' column is not derived from somewhere else, but is "the world of 'narrative communication,' crafted by the faith that readers share 'the same dream' and 'the same heart'" (1993:53). What is shared is, again, the ethos of otome. Although as we have seen, a dictionary definition suggests that the otome is young and unmarried, a demographically limited category, in the world of the otome community of the magazine, it is a "pan"-identity; regardless of one's age or social or regional background, anyone can be an otome as long as she shares its ethos. Accordingly, it is irrelevant to the readers whether or not schoolgirl speech, which they extensively use in their letters, is written or spoken language or whether they actually "speak" it in their daily lives (36–38). Accordingly, schoolgirl speech as the index of otome identity is a translocal and transtemporal linguistic register: it erases any linguistic trace of age, class, or regional difference. It can be best understood as the shared linguistic code and indexical network readers appropriate to construct "the world that does not exist anywhere" (53). It is a quintessentially virtual community.

Schoolgirl speech, then, is the language that is not ("actually") spoken anywhere but, paradoxically, is indexical of the corporeal and physical presence of those who share the otome identity. As I have discussed in chapter 2, it was such particularized and spatiotemporally specific corporeality that the gembun'itchi movement eventually eliminated from its vision of modern standard Japanese. Oral performance style—*desu* and *masu*—therefore failed to be a candidate for the modern novel, for it explicitly encodes the performer-narrator's material presence of "here" and "now." The (male) modern subject constructed in and by modern Japanese language, as the linguistic register of the bourgeois public sphere, must speak from nowhere, and its language indexes no body. Contrastively, otome, the ideal form of address for the young women's magazine readers, "spoke" and was "heard" in precisely the register that the literay gembun'itchi dismissed as nonserious (see chapter 2). Indexing the ephemeral "here" and "now" in the present tense, the overexposure of the speaking body grounded the counterpublics of the otome community.

THE SUBJECT OF PHOTOGRAPHY: PARATEXT TO IMAGES

Schoolgirl speech also started to appear as a paratext to photographic images of renowned families with their daughters and wives, including those of aristocrats, college professors, medical doctors, politicians, military officers, and wealthy businessmen. As Barthes succinctly put it, the photograph "is a message without a code" (1977:17). Its denotational force and literalness are so overwhelming that it does not allow a viewer to interpret and thus to generate a second-order meaning (connotation) without an attached linguistic message to "anchor" the photograph's meaning (38–40), or what it is supposed to mean.

The earliest captions for photographs (either illustrating content or "gratuitous" to content) in *FS*, for example, were strictly denotational in nature, simply identifying the photographed—her name, her father's name and title, for example—in compact noun phrases. Or if there was any full-sentence caption, it would be in classical Japanese with utterance-ending forms such as *nari*. By the 1910s, full-sentence captions with modern colloquial polite utterance-ending forms such as *desu* and *masu* had begun to appear. Such captions, increasingly more narrative and illustrative, function to bring forth the corporality and presentness of the caption's authorship. In other words, they are indexical not only of the photograph, but also of the physical presence of the caption's narrator or the imaginary spatiotemporal congruence between the caption and the photograph, as if the third-person narrator had stood right next to the subject of the portrait, introducing her to and sharing the "here and now" moment of viewing with the reader. Captions were now "speaking" to the reader on behalf of the subject(s) of the photograph.

The major shift came around the end of the 1920s, when schoolgirl speech began appearing in captions in the form of direct reported speech—as the imputed literal voice of the daughters and wives of the bourgeois family. Some took the form of the caption-narrator directly quoting the speech of the photographed. Others, which gradually replaced the former, were characterized by the entire caption in schoolgirl speech, without any quoting voice: the photograph itself is now "speaking" directly to the reader in schoolgirl speech. The caption in plate 1, a photograph of the painter Kosugi Misei and his daughter, Yuriko, reads:

> "My father travels almost half of the year-**desu-no**. This time he *traveled* to China, stopped at Kyushu on his way back, and has just come home-**desu-no**," says Yuriko-sama in a manner that still retains schoolgirl-like buoyancy. Because of her father's influence, Yuriko-sama indeed has a lot of hobbies, including violin, tennis, and literature, which seems to be her brother's influence, too. This photograph was taken with her father, when he came out of his atelier.

(Note that "women's language" utterance-ending forms used in the original text are included in boldface in the examples in this chapter. Verbs in the form of honorifics in the original text are in italic. Note also that I omit marking other co-occurrent sociolinguistic features such as specific pronouns and lexicons, the omission of copulas, and syntactic inversion, which would be of interest to linguists. My goals here is to represent speech forms and functions that are meaningful for historical actors.)

Here, the narrator incorporates into her/his narrative Yuriko's speech in the form of direct reported speech. She is quoted as using the characteristic utterance-ending form of schoolgirl speech, *desu-no*. This is a shift from a "linear" reporting style to that of the "pictorial" par excellence: not only the caption's referentiality but also its pragmatic faculty of "all the linguistic peculiarities of its verbal implementation" (Voloshinov 1973:121) is mobilized to anchor the photographic meaning. The indexical relationship between the text (the caption) and the image also shifts: no longer being external to the photographed body, a caption is now *internal* to and immanent in it as her voice. The caption is now an organic part of the imagined body, functional to the expression of her consciousness and inner thoughts. Acquiring a body and the physical (metonymical) connection to it, the caption is thus bestowed with the quality of "speech" and accords its speaking body immediacy and pure self-presence.

This shift parallels a change in the way the social identity of the photographed is defined. Unlike the traditional caption, which simply identified the woman in the portrait by her father's status, a schoolgirl-speech caption narrativizes her social identity by illustrating in detail her bourgeois "lifestyle." Here we have "a unitary set of distinctive preferences which expresses the same expressive intention in the specific logic of each of the symbolic sub-spaces, furniture, clothing, language or bodily hexis"

――小杉未醒氏と令嬢――　　美術家と令嬢

「父は一年のうち半年ぐらゐは、旅行ですの。今度も、支那の方へまゐりまして、帰りに、九州の方をまはつて、やつと歸りましたばかりですの」
小杉未醒畫伯の、愛孃百合子様は、女學生らしさのまだぬけきれぬ快活なお話ぶりです。藝術家のお父様の御趣味も、ヴァイオリンに、テニスに、文學に、――これはお兄様の御感化もありさうですが――ほんとに、多方面の御趣味でいらつしやいます。アトリエから出ていらしたお父様と御一緒にお願ひしてとらしていただきました。

PLATE 1. "Bijutsuka to Reijō" (Artist and his daughter), *Fujin sekai*, 1930, 25 (10):6.

(Bourdieu 1984:173). By virtue of being the very medium by which the ideal bourgeois class habitus is narrated and displayed, schoolgirl speech in turn acquires symbolic value that is homologically transposed onto other properties of the bourgeois lifestyle it narrates and displays. As Bourdieu describes it, "Each dimension of life-style 'symbolizes with' the others . . . and symbolizes them."

By the 1930s, schoolgirl speech had found other photographic bodies, such as film and theater actresses and fashion models. Of particular significance was *moga*, or the Modern Girl. Moga represents the image of a young urban unmarried woman who enjoys sexual and economic freedom (B. H. Sato 2003; Silverberg 1991b). Magazines such as *FS* frequently carried photographic images of moga with captions in schoolgirl speech in the 1930s. These captions garrulously speak in detail about her choices, tastes, and preferences, not only concerning consumer goods but also sexual partners. Plate 2 is a photograph of a moga with her imaginary speech in the caption.

> Nuts! Did you say that I don't know the taste of love? Sorry! I am a fool who has long abandoned virginity in another world. I am a twice-convicted heartbreaker-**desu-wa**. Yes, I am. I am a rotten red snapper. But even if it is rotten, it attracts flies, "rubashka" flies and "red tie high-collar [haikara] with kid shoes" flies. Gathering around the tangle of Eros under the romance of the red light, living in fun and nonconformity, and bravely and candidly enjoying the value of reality. That's my philosophy of life. Did you say chastity-**desu-tte**? Such a joke is no longer in fashion nowadays-**teyo**.

Plate 3 is another image of a moga, whose caption, again, in the form of schoolgirl speech, represents her as an avid consumer. The repeated assertion of "I like" is an expression of the consumer self who has learned to have and express distinct personal desires and "style," and thus to define her social position through her relationship with the commodity.

> This is a new-style dress that I just bought yesterday-**nano**. I really like the collar, cuffs, and I particularly like the right shoulder part-**noyo**. The brooch has moved up here-**wa**. This is my favorite watch-**nano**. It has a small, oval-shaped gold frame and a pitch-black band! These shoes are simple, but are made of cream-colored kid leather, and I like their light and smart style-**nano**. How wonderful it would be to walk in the early summer on the street in such a style-**kashira**.

Her verbal "display" of the consumer objects—why and how she likes and chooses them—takes on a particular semiotic quality, or "sign value"

モダーンガールの姿態その六

チエ、私が恋の味なんか知らないだらうつて？憚りさま、とつくにヴァージニティーを彼世に捨てて來た痴者ですわ、どうせ破れた恋の前科者ですわ、どうせ破れた恋ですよ、腐つた鯛でも蠅が集る、ルパシカ服、キツト靴、赤ネクタイのハイカラ蠅が、赤い灯の情緒に、つどひよる官能の交錯に、面白可笑しく落ちて、勇敢に率直に現實の價値を甜めるのが私の哲學と人生觀、貞操ですつて、そんな洒落は今時流行なくつてよ。

PLATE 2. "Modāngāru no shitai sono roku" (The pose of a modern girl, act 6), *Fujin sekai*, 1930, 25 (1):6.

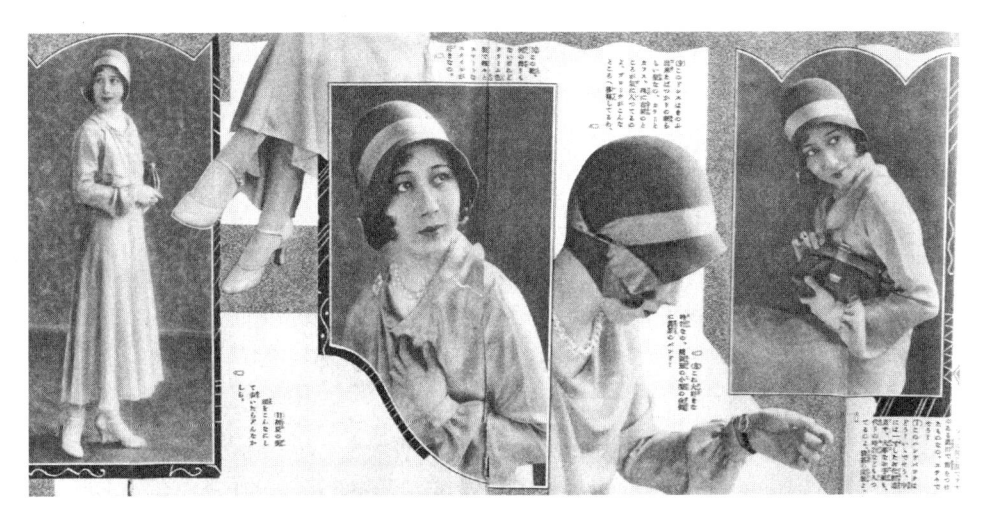

PLATE 3. Untitled image of a moga, *Fujin sekai*, 1931, 26 (5), unpaginated.

(Baudrillard 1981), which signifies her identity as a moga, a hyperconsuming and hypersexual body.

THE SUBJECT OF CONSUMPTION:
VOICES OF ADWOMEN

The indexical relationship between commodities and schoolgirl speech—and the constitution of the consumer body as an effect of this relationship—is perfected in advertisement. A commodity does not have any intrinsic value; value is acquired in the commodity's "social" relationships with other commodities within the system of the market and the logic of exchange. Valorization is external to the commodity and autonomous from its thingness, and value is fabricated in such a way that it convinces the buyer of its excess over the values of other products as well as of why one needs to desire and to posses the specific good to which the value is attached. The linguistic agent "I" of schoolgirl speech now speaks to the reader, performing the speech acts of testifying, persuading, seducing, and creating value.

While initially the majority of the advertisements carried in *JS* and *FS* were for the books and other magazines their publishers also produced, other kinds of advertisements, for kimonos, traditional scented hair oil, medicine for "women's diseases," and other items, also appeared. In addition, one would regularly find spectacular advertising displays of bourgeois feminine commodities, including Western luxuries, novelties, beauty products, and domestic goods, such as jewelry, perfume, face powder, lotion, menstrual garments, soap, skin-whitening cream, and toothpaste. The unrelenting visual and textual reference to whiteness, social hygiene, Tokyo, and the West shared among these advertisements is veneered onto the surface of things and mystically stimulated people's "empathy with inorganic things" (Benjamin 1973:55), an essential process of turning readers into modern consumers.

In the Meiji and early Taisho periods, at the center of such new referents was the image of a schoolgirl—the modern Japanese woman—and the referents were inscribed onto her imaginary body, marked by her hairstyle (called *tabanegami*), maroon-colored hakama (*ebicha-bakama*), lace-up boots (*amiagegutsu*), and book-reading. The image of a schoolgirl was most frequently used in advertisements for cosmetics and skin-care and hair-care products. Such commodities are indexically connected with the image of a schoolgirl in mainly two ways. One way is exhibited in plate 4, an advertisement by a store selling Western luxury goods. Here, the schoolgirl's image is inserted in a way that is physically detached from the commodities advertised and yet symbolically connected with them through the shared cultural code of the modern. As I have noted, the "schoolgirl" had been a semiotic being of the gendered modern, representing the modern and thereby often caricatured as a brazen consumer of the novel and the Western.

In contrast to this metaphorical presence of the woman and her relationship with the product, there also emerged the image of a woman in physical contact with the commodity, holding, pointing to, or touching the product. Plate 5 is an advertisement for a towel. It is held by a woman, thereby marking her temporal and spatial copresence not only with the product but also with the reader. She is metonymically present and contiguous with the product, as its owner, user, seeker, or recommender, so that the product is "illustrated" as a concrete part of the ideal gendered modern lifestyle, in contrast to the early situation where the connection needed to be described to the reader in the advertising copy. By virtue of physical contiguity, the same spatiotemporality and thus immediacy—here and now—is shared not only between the adwoman and the product but also between them and the viewer.

In some of the earlier advertisements, the schoolgirl's role is to point her finger directly at the product (see plate 6). She herself is thus emptied of any symbolic meaning and is turned into a "pure index" (Peirce 1931, 2:306). She functions as a *deictic,* like an arrow: "Look! At the end of my fingertip (or of my glance), there is a product worth looking at!"

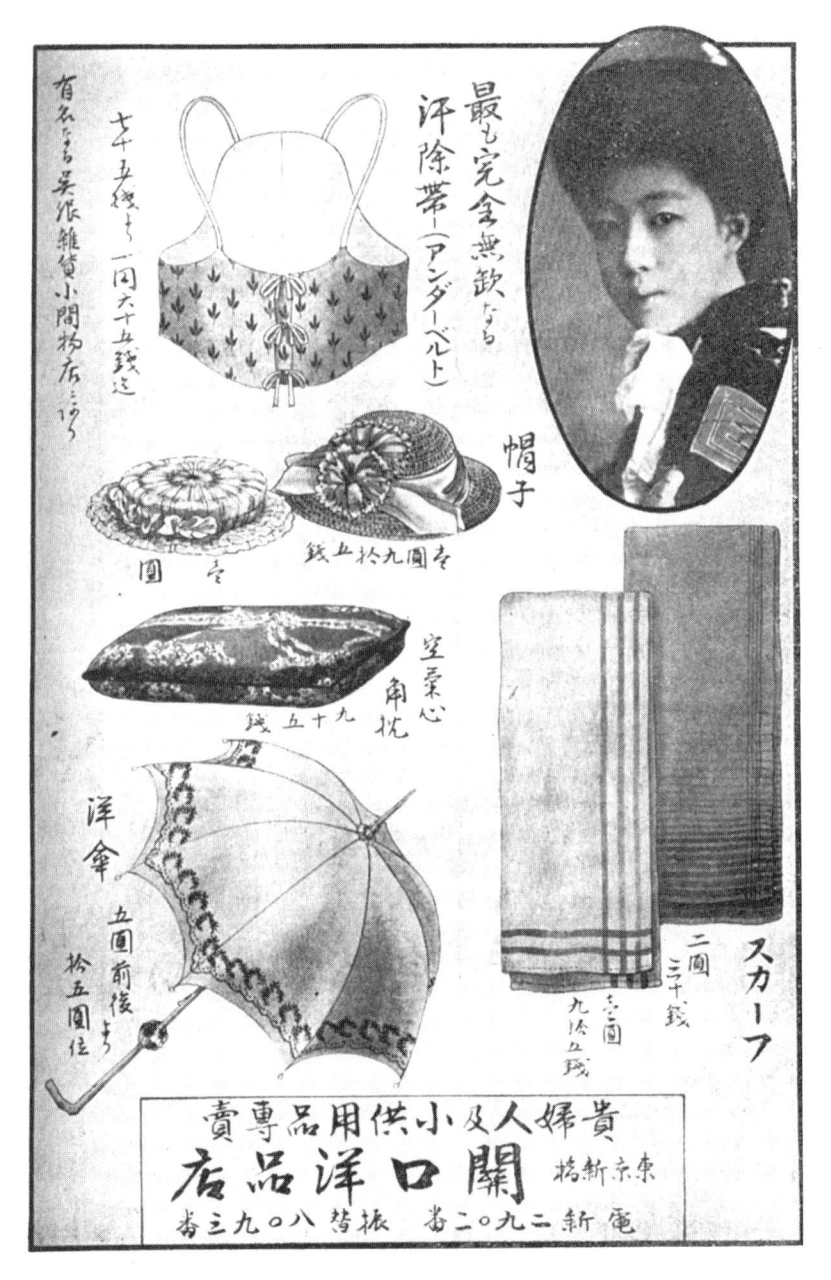

PLATE 4. Advertisement by Sekiguchi Yōhinten (Sekiguchi Costume Store), *Fujin sekai*, 1911, 6 (7), unpaginated.

PLATE 5. Advertisement for Bigan Taoru (Beautiful Face Towel) by Itō Shōten (Ito Company), *Fujin sekai*, 1909, 4 (10), unpaginated.

FROM SCHOOLGIRL SPEECH TO WOMEN'S LANGUAGE 139

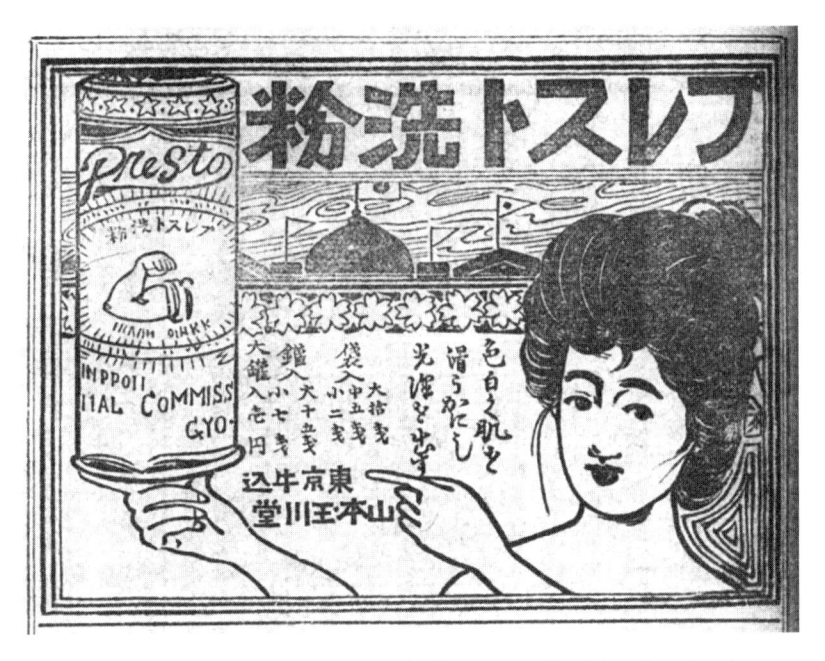

PLATE 6. Advertisement for Puresuto Araiko (Presto Washing Powder) by Yamamototamagawadō, *Jogaku sekai*, 1907, 7 (6): jin no ichi [the traditional page numbering].

Like the captions attached to the photographic portrait of the modern Japanese woman, advertising copy followed a similar historical trajectory. Earlier advertisements used written literary Japanese styles, including the epistolary style *(sōrōbun)* and a mix of classical Chinese and Japanese *(wakan-kankōbun)*. The voice from nowhere speaks to the viewer-reader over the shoulder of the image of the schoolgirl. This was followed by colloquial gembun'itchi styles—*desu* and *masu,* and their honorific form, *gozaimasu*. By the late 1900s and early 1910s, schoolgirl speech started appearing in advertising copy, as if the adwoman was speaking directly to the reader, thus taking a role in establishing spatiotemporal contiguity between the image of a woman and the advertised product.

The advertisement in plate 7 is for Pearl Paste Hair Oil, and the copy takes the form of a testimonial in schoolgirl speech.

> I used to have very frizzy hair, and was really troubled-**desu-no**. I have tried all kinds of remedies and oils and did my best, but could not possibly do my hair in a chignon *[mage]*. So I wondered what to do. Then my husband

told me that Pearl Paste Hair Oil has a reputation for being good for hair, and that I should try it. So I gave it a try. Good Heavens, before I knew it, I was able to do my hair chignon beautifully like this-**no**. Besides having a really nice fragrance, Pearl Paste Hair Oil makes your hair miraculously beautiful-**desu-noyo**.[20]

Schoolgirl speech in this advertisement is double-voiced (Bakhtin 1981). It indexes the commodity, performing a series of potential speech acts, including pointing, describing, testifying, and persuading, and, at the same time, it indexes the adwoman who speaks it, signaling who she is. It is in this sense that schoolgirl speech was a crucial linguistic strategy of what Marchand calls "social tableaux," in which "persons are depicted in such a way as to suggest their relationships to each other or to a larger social structure" (1985:165). Semiotically speaking, it is based on an "indexical icon" (Silverstein 2000:117–18), a sign relation to the social world by virtue of similarity (icon) and at the same time by virtue of contiguity (index). A social tableau shows a "slice of life," which includes the product as well as the social context to which it is claimed to belong. This social context in the Japanese period under consideration meant increasingly a class context, inciting the desire and aspirations of the nascent new middle class. Along with other visual and graphic strategies, schoolgirl speech was steadily incorporated into the politics of capitalist aesthetics as a marker of social distinction in an everyday drama the advertisement presented.

The appearance of schoolgirl speech in advertising as the metalanguage—the voice of the adwoman—has much to do with the unique nature of advertisement as a genre. Unlike other genres, successful modern advertising needs to hide its generic identity as a manipulative and agenda-bearing message and, at the same time, to achieve its instrumental goal of selling the product. In other words, advertising must suppress its explicit metacommunicative function to signal that it is an advertisement and yet must still function as an advertisement. This inherent predicament is resolved by what I call "intertextual disguise." For example, by the early twentieth century, one would frequently find advertisements that mimic regular editorial pages of reportage in graphic and typographic layout, which is called an "advertorial." Until one reads it to the end, there is no way to tell that it is an advertisement for a skin-care

---

20. Note that the spatiotemporal coexistence of the adwoman and the reader is also marked by deictics such as *this* and *here*.

PLATE 7. Advertisement for Pāru Nerikōyu (Pearl Paste Perfumed Hair Oil) by Hirao Senya Shōten (Hirao Senya Company), *Jogaku sekai*, 1912, 12 (15), unpaginated.

product. This kind of reportage might tell a story about an unfortunate woman who eventually overcame hardship and improved her life, but the advertisement adds to this plot that it was the lotion that made her skin white and thus brought her success in life. The parasitic nature of advertisement appropriates the new genres I have described in this chapter in which schoolgirl speech constitutes "I" as the subject of the metalanguage, including dialogues in novels, confessional stories, letters, and drama scripts, and turns the speech into the voice of adwomen and so intertextually turns novel characters, heroines of confession, letter writers, and actresses themselves into adwomen.

Accordingly, schoolgirl speech flexibly inhabits diverse emerging new bodies of the female modern as an adwoman, including urban middle-class housewives, moga, film actresses, and white-collar working women. The earliest examples also show that schoolgirl speech was accorded not only to the image of a schoolgirl but also to geisha and geisha apprentices. This is particularly the case with advertisements for cosmetics and other beauty products, for their availability was limited traditionally to women in the pleasure quarters and upper-class women. Plate 8 is an advertisement for milk lotion with the image of a geisha. The advertisement copy reads: "Oh my goodness, look, nēsan, what a beautiful flower? It is as beautiful and fragrant as when you put on makeup with 'Lait-**teyo**.'"[21]

Advertisement copy with excessive use of exclamation marks also indicates a direct quoting of schoolgirl speech, which emulates the voice in the letters in the readers' column and dialogues in domestic novels.[22] Plate 9 is another advertisement for Lait Cosmetics. Here we see the image of a schoolgirl dozing while reading and daydreaming.

> Dream? Reality? Dreams are fleeting!!! Reality is everlasting!!!
> A splendid dream which disappears when awakened!
> I dream a beautiful dream of joyful dancing and excellent makeup.
> Using "Lait," which makes you beautiful, may I keep the beauty of reality
>   forever.

By the 1920s and through the 1930s, the advertising bodies that schoolgirl speech inhabits diversified. For one thing, the image of the

---

21. *Nēsan* means a "big sister," an older female sibling. In the world of geisha and geisha apprentices, it is used by an apprentice to address a geisha. The use of a question format is in the original.

22. An incomplete utterance-ending in ellipsis marks (. . .) is another characteristic of schoolgirl speech in advertising copy, adopted from dialogue in novels, readers' letters, and play scripts.

PLATE 8. Advertisement with geisha for Rēto Nyūhaku Keshōsui (Lait Milk Lotion) by Hirao Sanpei Shōten (Hirao Sanpei Company), *Jogaku sekai*, 1909, 9 (12), unpaginated.

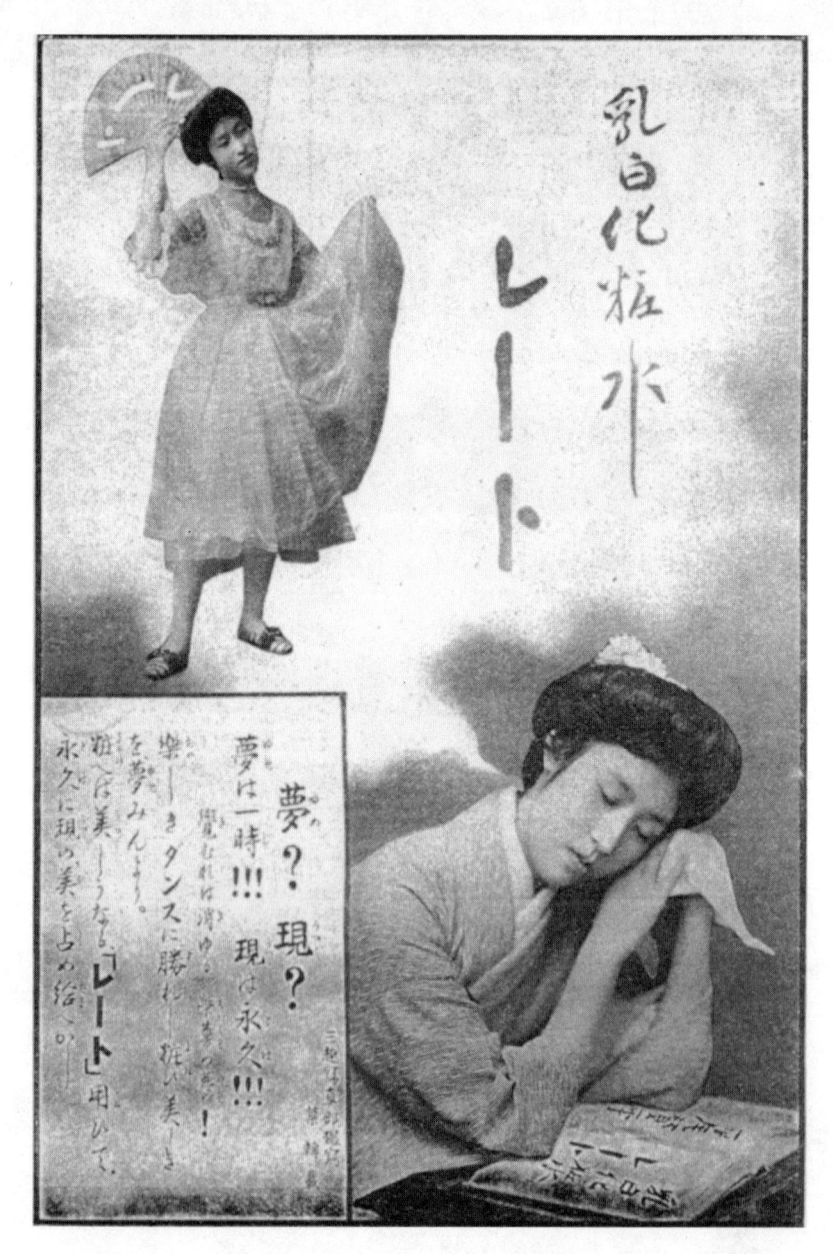

PLATE 9. Advertisement with schoolgirl for Rēto Nyūhaku Keshōsui, *Fujin sekai*, 1909, 4 (10), unpaginated.

schoolgirl had lost its semiotic attraction as the symbol of the gendered modern and of novelty and luxury, although the geisha continued to be a favorite advertising body for cosmetics. Instead, schoolgirl speech found new modern female bodies, as a new type of modern Japanese woman took the place of the schoolgirl in interpellating the readers into gendered consumers.[23] Accordingly, the products that schoolgirl speech made a pitch for also diversified, though still limited to female-related commodities. Plate 10 is an advertisement for a menstrual garment called Victoria. The copy takes the form of a conversation between two sisters, a "slice of life," to which the menstrual garment metonymically belongs:

Sonoko: Sister, you kindly *invited* me to the karuta game, but I . . . I can't make it tomorrow-**noyo**.
Older Sister: Oh, how come?
Sonoko: But . . . but, I have been in the moon disease all day-**nano**.
Older Sister: Period? . . . Sono-chan, don't you know about a menstrual garment called Victoria? If you wear it, you will not have to worry at all for hours-**wa**.
Sonoko: Ah, my friends are actually all *using* Victoria-**desu**-**wa**. Why didn't I think about that! Sister, I will go home right away and will definitely *visit* you tomorrow-**teyo**.
Older Sister: Oh my, you suddenly look all cheered up-**none**.

The image of the product is placed inconspicuously in the upper-left-hand corner of the advertisement (recall that Japanese is read from right to left), and the conversation between Sonoko and her older sister and their visual image are centrally placed. This is an exemplary "social tableau" format of advertising, but it features not so much an image as language to mark the social (class) position of the adwomen and, by extension, the product in broader social relations and class structure.

One of the most prominent forms of adwomen in print advertisement during this period was film actresses appearing in so-called tie-in advertising campaigns, where the product sponsor and the film company mutually benefit from popular actresses' product endorsements.[24] By the

---

23. See Silverberg 1995 for her critical analysis of the visual imagination of modern female bodies in prewar Japanese advertising from the 1920s through the 1940s.
24. Hirao Sanpei Shōten, the manufacturer of the Lait brand of cosmetics and beauty products, for example, used geisha and beautiful women in its ads until 1920, after which it started using popular film actresses. It contracted with the Shōchiku Film Studio and developed tie-in ad campaigns (Hirao 1929:339–40; Sakamoto 1951:418, 452–54).

PLATE 10. Advertisement for Bikutoria Gekkeitai (Victoria Menstrual Garment) by Yamato Gomu Seisakusho (Yamato Rubber Manufacturing Company), *Fujin sekai*, 1925, 20 (1):333.

1920s, actresses were readily praising, endorsing, and giving unrestrained testimonies for products in schoolgirl speech. Plate 11 is an advertisement for Misono Mizuoshiroi (Misono Liquid White Powder). It successfully masquerades as a "round-table" *(zadankai)* interview and features the popular film actresses Tanaka Kinuyo and Yakumo Emiko, who endorse the product and offer testimonials. The product and its company identification are placed at the lower-left-hand corner in a small box as if it were a separate advertisement inserted into regular magazine content, an increasingly common practice in the late 1920s and early 1930s. By making the insertion look like an advertisement, the rest of the advertisement—the faux round-table interview—appears as reportage and not advertising.

In addition to film actresses, schoolgirl speech was ventriloquized through the multiple imaginary bodies of the female modern, including moga, flappers, and working women such as typists, office and sales clerks, schoolteachers, telephone operators, and café waitresses. In turn, the metapragmatic reference to schoolgirl speech as *teyo-dawa kotoba* or *jogakusei kotoba* disappeared from the public discourse. This marks the decisive moment when a set of speech forms ideologically associated with "schoolgirl speech" erased from the national and cultural memory its derisive origin in "vulgarity" and its geographical and class specificity, and inaugurated itself as the universal "Japanese women's language." For the first time, schoolgirl speech started functioning as a "gender marker," signifying the universal abstract idea of "femaleness" and foreclosing the trace of everything else that historically constituted the genealogy of "women's language," including race, class, nation, and modernity, and expunging the trace of everyone else who does not have access to "women's language" as habitus, including working-class women, peasants, and regional dialect speakers from national peripheries.

Regardless of the specificity of the female body that emits women's language, its job is to describe and to index commodity goods and to create desire and the subject of desire. It is this moment when women's language becomes commensurable and exchangeable with commodity goods and when women's language successfully invokes the desire for them and thus interpellates the reader into a capitalist consumer-subject, endowed with "appropriate" sociality, affect, taste, and habitus. And it is this moment when women's language becomes truly the universal (urban middle-class) woman's voice in the modern industrial nation. And *that* is the (absent) origin of Japanese women's language that the nation remembers and memorializes.

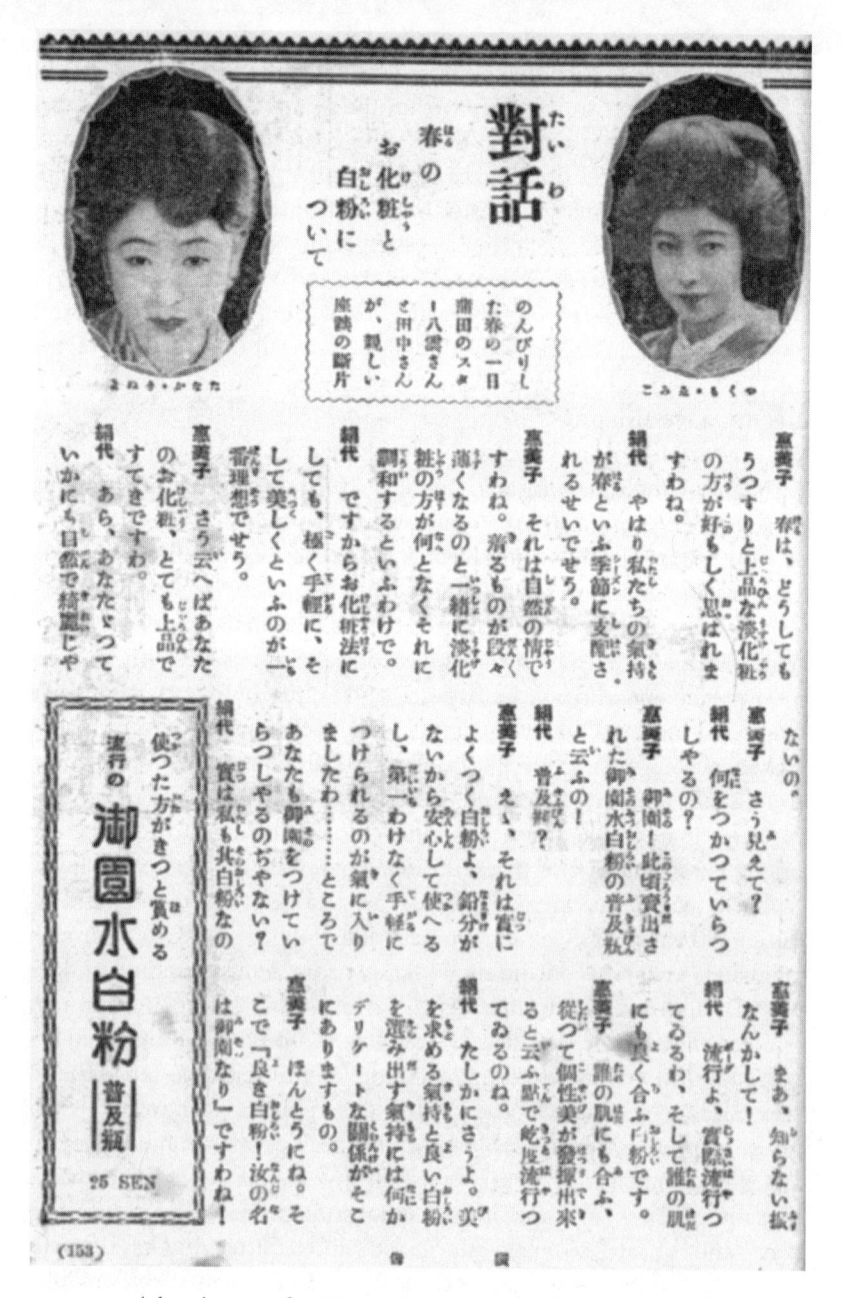

PLATE 11. Advertisement for Misono Mizuoshiroi (Misono Liquid White Powder) by Higashi Kochōen, *Fujin sekai*, 1929, 24 (4):153.

"Good Wife and Wise Mother" as Commodity Spectacle: Intertextuality and the Nationalization of Female Magazine Readers

Texts and images bounded by the genres I have described above are, however, never self-contained. As noted, the nature of the magazine format essentially discourages readers from reading linearly and, instead, socializes them into a habit of distracted and fragmented reading, in which one begins with any page or any passage and even looks at multiple texts and images at the same time. This results in an extremely volatile intertextual environment, where the ground of interpretation transcends a generic boundary and loses its metacommunicative ability to provide "meaning" with its text and image. Rather, the text and image become each other's context and code, informing and transforming one another in the magazine format that mandates the contingency of the juxtaposition of texts and images and the reader's promiscuous page flipping and thus keeps their meaning infinitely unstable and undecidable. Thus, the magazine's intertextuality is critically bound up with socializing the reader's bodily and kinetic tactics into those of a modern consumer/spectator.

Intertextuality is a general characteristic of any text that attests to the impossibility of its autonomy and to the necessary connection with other, temporally prior texts.[25] The possibility of intertextual connection unique to the magazine format derives not only from the text's relationship to those temporally prior to it, but more importantly from its physically contingent juxtaposition with other texts and images that are copresent in the magazine. To put it differently, it is not a metaphorical connection, in which text is associated with another text beyond immediate time and space, but that of the metonymic, in which text engages in mutual indexing with other texts that are physically contiguous to it.[26]

This specific media environment of the magazine makes the indexicality of schoolgirl speech highly mobile. The heroine's schoolgirl speech in the novel dialogue would index the portrait of an aristocratic daughter on the next page or an advertised lotion at the corner of the page. Or the

---

25. See Kristeva 1980 for one of the original discussions on intertextuality. For a programmatic article in linguistic anthropology on intertextuality, see Briggs and Bauman 1992.
26. Some of the advertisements in the late 1920s and early 1930s take advantage of such juxtaposition on facing pages. For example, a medicine advertisement, facing a color illustration of women showing the latest fashion of kimono patterns, uses the same illustrator and carries an identical image of a woman (*Fujin sekai*, 1929, 24 [6]).

voices of confession in schoolgirl speech in letters to the editor and in the adwoman's sales pitch might mutually index one another. This unstable textual juxtaposition unique to the magazine format requires the reader to engage in "indexical labor" in order to contour the composite of the modern Japanese woman and her voice.

Intertextuality bound up with indexical contingency and the semiotic mobility of schoolgirl speech that it enables also serve to resolve the tension between politics and consumption and between the state and the market in such a way that gendered citizenship was articulated through the mediation of the state's fantasy of nationalism and the reader's fantasy of consumption (Carter 1984; de Grazia 1996; Kawamura 1993:210–12). From their first issues, both *JS* and *FS* avowed their national mission to propagate the government's gender policy of "good wife and wise mother." At the same time, however, the editorial pages were equally devoted to novels and other reading matter that both explicitly and implicitly cultivated the reader's consumer desire. One could, for example, find a pedantic essay deploring the linguistic corruption of schoolgirls in the same issue in which the letters column was saturated with precisely the language the essay condemned. Or the magazine would occasionally carry a list of voguish vocabulary among schoolgirls and thus positively display schoolgirl speech.[27] Although not specifically engaging the issue of gender, Silverberg, who discusses the extent to which consumer subjects in prewar Japan were simultaneously imperial subjects, poses important questions: "To what extent was the dashing crown prince being used to peddle commodities? Or alternatively, to what extent was the media a medium for the state? Did it serve to illustrate the ideologically freighted 'Imperial Rescript on Education,' which was recited by every school child?" (1991a:76).

Although gradually replaced by serial novels, confessional stories, and other "practical" or "popular" reading matter, in the 1920s and 1930s pedantic essays by educators and renowned figures were still centrally featured in women's magazines, directly speaking about the virtue of womanhood in the roles of wife, mother, and imperial subject *(kōmin)*. Yet the complicity of women's magazines in nationalizing women, if there is any, lies not so much simply in their instrumentality as a medium to mechanically disseminate such ideological messages as in their mediation— in a true sense of medium—of such ideological messages by virtue of their

27. See, for example, "Modern Schoolgirls Vocabulary" (Gendai jogakusei yōgoshū), *Jogaku sekai*, 1921, 21 (1):123.

specific intertextual environment. To put it differently, the centrality of women's magazines in nationalizing women and in normalizing their (voluntary) subjection to the state ideology of "good wife and wise mother" had to do with their capacity to transform the message into an object of visual and textual consumption by the bourgeois family through contingent intertextual connections with concrete commodity goods and concrete images such as heroines in the novel and portraits of princesses and daughters of aristocrats and wealthy families.

This linkage between nationalism and commodity fetishism, in which "things" express the ideology of "good wife and wise mother" and vice versa, just as social relations of production are expressed through things and vice versa, is compellingly argued by McClintock in her critical engagement with Anderson's (1983) notion of "imagined community." McClintock takes issue with Anderson's "imagined community" forged in and through print capitalism, which is to say, the novel and the newspaper, whose accessibility inevitably limits the readership and therefore the "people" who can belong to only the literate; she argues instead that "the singular power of nationalism since the late nineteenth century . . . has been its capacity to organize a sense of popular, collective unity through the management of mass national *commodity spectacle*" (1993:374; emphasis in original). McClintock lists fetish objects of (Western) nationalism, such as "flags, uniforms, airplane logos, maps, anthems, national flowers, national cuisines and architecture," all of which are symbolically associated with nationalism. What could be added here from the Japanese case of the relationship between nationalism and commodity fetishism is a type of connection by contingent intertextual contiguity enabled by the magazine format, which exceeds the confines of metaphoric associations that rely on preexisting symbolic convention.

Plate 12 shows facing pages from the July 1915 issue of *Fujin sekai*. The page on the right (b) carries photographs titled "Patriotic Women's Association's [Aikoku Fujinkai] General Meeting and Their Royal Highnesses." The caption reads:

> The Patriotic Women's Association's general meeting was held on June 4 at Hibiya Park, Tokyo. In the right-hand photograph, at the center is Her Royal Highness Princess Wakanomiya Keiko, representing Her Majesty, the Empress. On the left is the [association] president, Her Royal Highness Princess Kan'innomiya, who is reading an address. On the right are Her Royal Highness Princess Higashifushiminomiya, and Her Royal Highness Princess Nashimotonomiya. The left-hand photograph of the stage is taken from the members' seats.

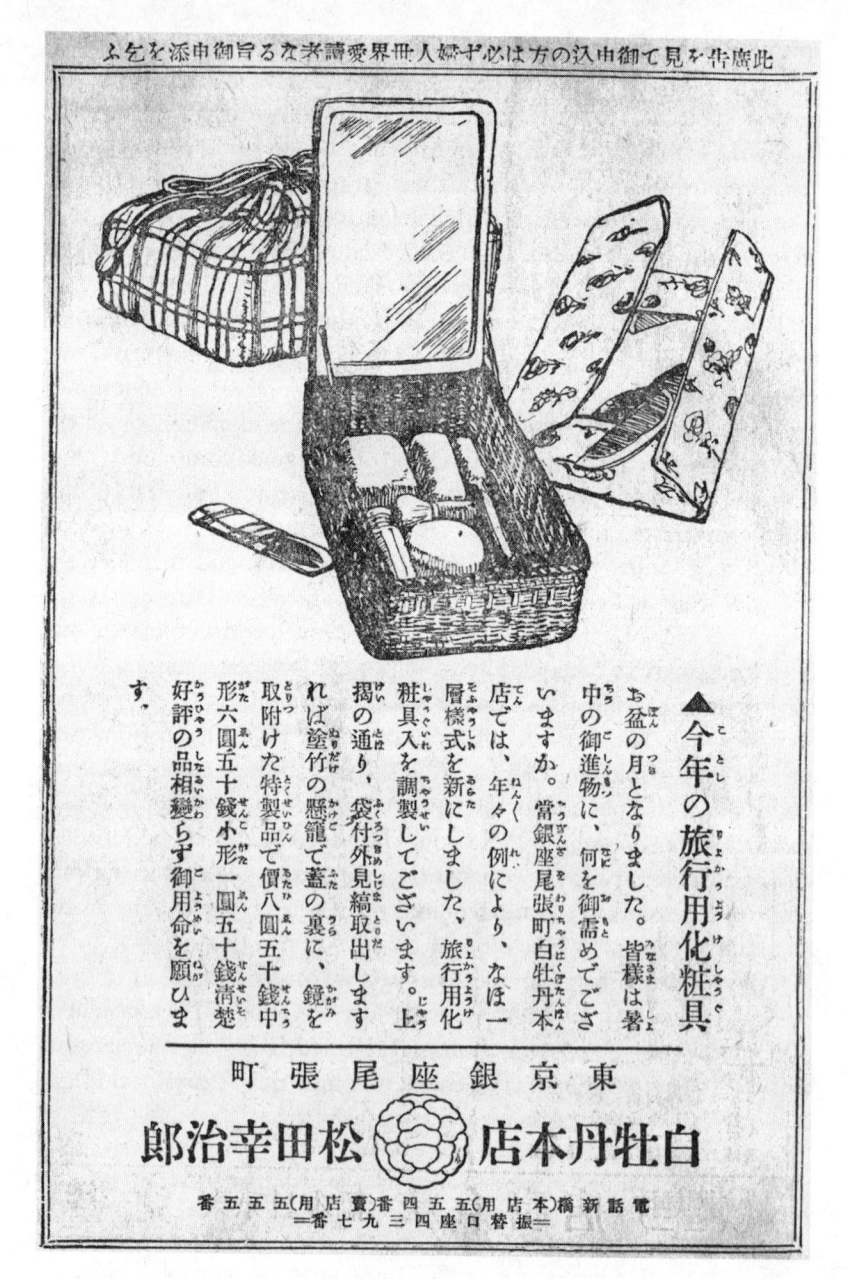

PLATE 12. Facing pages in *Fujin sekai*, 1915, 10 (8), unpaginated. (a) Advertisement for travel cosmetics cases by Shirobotan Honten, Matsuda Kojiro (White Original Peony Store, Matsuda Kojiro, owner). (b, opposite) Photographs from the general meeting of the Patriotic Women's Association's (Aikoku Fujinkai).

The Patriotic Women's Association was founded in 1901 by Okumura Ioko, a nationalist activist whose mission was to support soldiers and military life. Backed by Konoe Atsumaro, an aristocratic politician, it was run as a charity by wives and daughters of the peerage, famous nationalist women educators, and other upper-class women. Its complicity with the state policy on women, imperialism, and nationalism was self-evident. The 1904–5 Russo-Japanese War gave it a tremendous opportunity to increase its membership, which rose to 460,000. The association played a significant role not only in mobilizing women in the war effort—comforting soldiers, sending personal supplies to the front, and aiding those bereaved in war—but also in propagating the state ideology of "good wife and wise mother" through a sense of national obligation (see also Nolte and Hastings 1991:159–63).

The left-hand page (b) is an advertisement from a variety store called Shirobotan for a new travel cosmetics case.

> This year's cosmetics for travel. The month of the Bon festival [August] has come. What are you getting for summer gifts? Here in Ginza Owaricho Hakubotan Honten, as is customary, we have procured a travel cosmetics case in a new, refined style. As shown above, it is a specialty item.

Taken out of its cloth sack, there is a lacquered bamboo box, and the mirror is installed at the back of its top. . . . It is a neat and popular item. As always, may we have the opportunity to serve you?

The political spectacle on the right-hand page and the commodity spectacle on the left intertextually articulate an ambiguous complicity. Beyond the photographic meaning delimited by the caption in plate 12(b), would it not be possible to imagine a reader's eyes becoming fixed on the Western dress and hats the royal princesses on the stage are wearing? Would it not be possible that the reader, glancing distractedly at the travel cosmetics case on the left-hand page, would imagine that such goods might be owned and used by the princesses on the right-hand page? Such intertextual connection by virtue of spatial and temporal contiguity of the images constitutes a montage, bringing together visual and narrative pieces beyond the generic and layout boundary and compositely organizing a "social tableau" of the imaginary modern Japanese woman and her bourgeois family. The aestheticization of the commodity—which is to say, advertising (Haug 1986)—goes hand in hand with the aestheticization of politics (Benjamin 1968), and both are predicated upon the perceptual alienation endemic to people's modern experience as spectators. The commodity fetishism in these images of Western hats and dresses in the photographs of the Patriotic Women's Association and of the travel cosmetics case on the facing page thus promotes the desirability of nationalism, and the political pageant normalizes imperialist and nationalist desire into consumer desire. Imagining the nation and a (gendered) way of belonging to the national community through commodity goods is, of course, neither the only nor the dominant way of consuming these images. Yet the magazine's unique intertextual horizon tends in the direction of such contingent and promiscuous reading of the montage that it creates.

The nationalization of women thus undergoes this necessary detour of commodification and commodity fetishism, in which the surface of concrete things and images takes on meaning as indexical of the bourgeois family. Shifting the ground of expression from the national to the domestic, and from politics to consumption, the commodification of "good wife and wise mother" rearticulates its ideological agenda as the class distinction and habitus of the urban middle class, and recasts women's subjection to the state, patriarchy, and the market as the concern for consumption, taste, affect, and self.

Schoolgirl speech, or now "women's language," was once the nation's, the state's, and Japanese male modernity's other, but became increasingly identified as the voice of the adwoman and the consumer whom women's language addressed. The mutual aestheticization and normalization of consumption and nationalism were enabling conditions in which women's language came full circle to be connected with "good wife and wise mother" and thus to be rearticulated as the ideal language of the female national citizen through the mediation of commodity fetishism.

The (New) Origin of Women's Language

By the 1930s, what was formerly called "schoolgirl speech" had come explicitly to be recognized as the model linguistic style for the bourgeois woman.[28] Plate 13 is the cover page from a *furoku*, or supplement, to a regular issue of *Fujin kurabu* (1921–88), one of a number of commercially successful women's magazines launched in the 1920s.[29] Properly titled "The Collection of Women's Model Language Use: Daily Reception and Greetings of Various Etiquettes (Fujin no kotobazukaimohanshūu: nichijō no ōtai sho reishiki no aisatsu), it sets up the scenario of a young woman, Kimiko, visiting her friend Kikue's house. Covering all the possible speech events involved in "a visit to a friend's house," it displays model linguistic exchanges for each context. Each context also demands the proper way of controlling one's body, which is shown in photographs. From greeting at the entrance, walking, sitting, serving and receiving tea and sweets, complimenting ornaments in the alcove, serving and receiving lunch, holding chopsticks and soup bowl, and chatting to departing guests, it presents the meticulous coordination of the linguistic and the corporeal, the habitus of the bourgeoisie.

Plate 14 shows a page where Kimiko and Kikue are chatting in the garden of Kikue's Western-style house. The narration and dialogue read:[30]

---

28. The semiotic process in which the re-citation of teyo-dawa speech in other genres in women's magazines and beyond transformed it into "women's language" parallels the valorization process of "Received Pronunciation," the prestigious variation of British English, during the eighteenth and nineteenth centuries, in which, as Agha (2003) argues, the value of Received Pronunciation valorization was predicated upon its recirculation in other genres such as drama, the novel, the etiquette book, and the like.

29. *Furoku* is a supplement to a regular issue of the magazine that focuses on a particular—often practical—topics ranging from cooking, sewing, or letter writing to etiquette. Such supplements became increasingly "thick" and elaborate as the top commercially successful women's magazines saw them as a featured item with which to compete with their rivals.

30. Although the sense of the "conversation" suggests that the first speaker here is Kikue,

PLATE 13. The cover page of "The Collection of Women's Model Language Use," supplement to *Fujin kurabu*, August 1932.

No end of conversation, and upon a cool breeze blowing in the garden and the rustle of leaves whispering,

Kikue: Would you be interested in going out to the garden?
Kimiko: Yes.
Kikue: The other day, I *saw* the picture of you *rowing* a boat-**teyo**. You seemed to be enjoying it.
Kimiko: Oh, it's embarrassing to show my being a tomboy. [gentle laughter]
Kikue: Not at all, you *photographed* very well-**koto-yo**.

Gold fish, emerging beside the water lilies, are beautiful.

Such utterance-endings, once called "vulgar," are now centrally anchored in the semiotic circuit of things, images, and embodiments that are associated with the bourgeoisie. Photographs thus show peripheral but critical information about the imaginary lifestyle of the "Japanese" bourgeoisie, including the woman in the kimono on the cover of the supplement wearing a (Western) ring, the Western-style mansion with traditional Japanese rooms inside, the automobile waiting outside the house when Kimiko in her kimono departs, not to mention the little advertisements for cosmetics, the British black tea *(kōcha),* lotion, face cream, hair lotion, hair remover, and soy sauce inserted into the corners of the pages, capitalizing on the textual and visual imaginary of the ideal lifestyle.

I have discussed the shift of schoolgirl speech from the quoted voice to the quoting voice in women's magazines in the context of Japan's accelerated development of industrial capitalism and its attendant formation of the new social space of consumption. This process entailed the dramatic shift in the indexical meaning of schoolgirl speech from vulgar street speech to the speech of the universal modern Japanese woman. I have argued that the birth of "women's language" was enabled by gendered print capitalism and consumer culture in the early twentieth century and after. The "I" in schoolgirl speech as metalanguage in new genres in the magazines is the subject position of the modern Japanese woman. In particular, schoolgirl speech was mobilized by advertising, which intertextually borrowed those genres and created the "I" of the consumer subject.

The readers of the magazines "heard" schoolgirl speech in the novel, in the letters, in confessions, and in advertising as if an actual speaker had directly addressed the readers. What animated schoolgirl speech to the extent of giving voice to inanimate and inorganic things and images and

---

in the original text, it is not clear which utterances belong to Kikue, the hostess, and which to Kimiko, the visitor.

Plate 14. Kimiko and Kikue chatting in the garden, in "The Collection of Women's Model Language Use," supplement to *Fujin kurabu*, August 1932, 6.

to the extent of creating a temporal and spatial co-presence of the character in the magazine and the reader and of the virtual community the magazine readers belonged to? Perhaps schoolgirl speech shares the enigma that Marx (1976:165) attributes to commodity fetishism, which turns an object into a subject, taking on its own life and animating itself, independent of the social relations of labor that produced it. The auto-animated quality of the commodity is described by Marx in the following way: "The form of wood, for instance, is altered if a table is made out of it. Nevertheless the table continues to be wood, an ordinary, sensuous thing. But as soon as it emerges as a commodity, it changes into a thing which transcends sensuousness. It not only stands with its feet on the ground, but, in relation to all other commodities, it stands on its head, and evolves out of its wooden brain grotesque ideas, far more wonderful than if it were to begin dancing of its own free will" (163–64). When schoolgirl speech was mobilized into the semiotic economy of commodity aesthetics to turn the inorganic into the organic, as Marx describes, commodity fetishism gave it life and the breath, the whisper, the voice, and the language of the advertising and advertised modern Japanese woman. And it was through commodity fetishism hollowing out its original meaning, history, and politics that the (new) origin of women's language—the language of the ideal "modern" "Japanese" "woman"—was inaugurated and its modern myth was born.

PART TWO

The Nation's Temporality and the Death of Women's Language

CHAPTER 4

Capitalist Modernity, the Responsibilized Speaking Body, and the Public Mourning of the Death of Women's Language

> Although, with the Equal Employment Opportunity Law established, gender equity in the workplace has taken one step forward, still it must be a tough situation for working women where they are not allowed to take equity for granted. But when it comes to "language use," gender equity has already been advanced, and women's language has died out. In fact, female students are using far more vulgar and *sugē* ["kick-ass"][1] language than male students.
>
> "Advanced? 'Gender Equality' in Language Use,"
> *Nihon Keizai Shimbun*, June 17, 1985

A century after the Meiji intellectuals deplored the vulgarity of schoolgirls' speech, there was a resurgence of the practice of citing women's language in the public sphere in the late 1980s and the early 1990s, again deploring the vulgarity of schoolgirls' speech in particular and women's language use in general. In this chapter, I will first examine rituals marking the loss or death of women's language through various metapragmatic citational practices in the public sphere, including readers' columns in newspapers and public opinion surveys, and will then examine how these technologies produce the truth of women's language by way of citing. I will also consider how this emerged at a particular political-economic conjuncture.

Rituals of citing the loss of women's language in public texts identify

---

1. *Sugē* (kick-ass) is playfully used here to represent schoolgirls' "vulgar" language use and to suggest this is the kind of language that they use nowadays.

the origin of linguistic corruption solely in women's own bodies and souls and so produce women as what we can call *responsibilized subjects* (Dean 1999), or self-governing selves. This kind of modern subject has clear linkages to a Japanese version of the neoliberal subject, displaying *jikosekinin*—self-responsibility or self-accountability—a term that has appeared in the Japanese public sphere since the end of the bubble economy, which "popped" in 1991. At the same time, however, it is through this responsibilized subject body that the public hopes to bring the putatively deceased women's language back to life. The attempt at the resurrection of women's language through the self-regulating body also took the form of a flurry of self-help literature describing "how to speak in a feminine fashion" and promising success in the workplace and in upward class mobility.

Mourning the loss of women's language thus underwrites a relentless normalization both of the idea of women's language and of women as its subject. By the 1930s, "vulgar" schoolgirl speech had been transformed into the salient sociolinguistic markers of the ideal urban middle-class housewife. "Women's language" is thus an *emergent norm* (not in the statistical, but in the Foucauldian, sense), and it requires a normalizing discipline deployed by a range of cultural agents (writers, teachers, scholars—and, of course, reflexive, norm-conscious readers, speakers, and listeners) to institute and maintain it as a norm, even if not as a statistical pattern. The power of the norm is not its ability to compel behavior "externally," but its relentless imposition of a self-examining, self-governing gaze. Such self-governmental techniques always involve the discursive marginalization of the extranormal; discipline presupposes the identification of the "deviant" for purposes of excluding it, marginalizing it, or otherwise marking it as the abject.[2]

Finally, I will describe how the scholarly production of knowledges of women's language during the 1980s through the early 1990s authorized and disseminated the idea that women's language was passing out of existence, and how this played a critical role in setting the terms of the government's national language policy regarding gender difference in language use. The normalization of women's language involves scholarly institutions creating a national narrative of the history of women's language by linking all its historically disparate manifestations up to the

---

2. I recognize that *governmentality* and *discipline* may be distinguished for some purposes, but this is a case in which the concepts interpenetrate and reinforce each other, as Foucault suggested they might. See Dean 1999; Foucault 1991; and Rose 1999.

present in a single time line, presenting women's language as a continuous essence of Japanese culture and tradition.[3] Claims that women's language originated in premodern times and was passed down faithfully (traditionally) to the present—except for the instances of its "corruption," which may actually be the statistical norm—is thus a technology for rooting the modern nation in the "soil" and in time immemorial. The nation's temporality—the uninterrupted past flowing seamlessly into the essence of the modern nation—gets coded in the imaginary continuity of women speaking women's language.[4]

Mourning the death of women's language is a way to maintain and normalize the ontology of women's language in its purest form by pointing out its absence in the present and its presence in the past, insisting that today's "corrupted" language use by women is a historical consequence of women's continuously and collectively failing to preserve a unique Japanese cultural trait. This charge recurs throughout the history of the modern Japanese nation-state. It has existed since the birth of women's language, since the latter's ontology can be guaranteed only by claiming in compulsive repetition that it is degenerating and vanishing. As long as people continue to mourn the loss of women's language, such statements as "there is a gender difference in speech in Japanese language" are admissible as "truth."

The social life of women's language is temporalized by and, in turn, temporalizes Japan's national-capitalist modernity. Obituaries of women's language, in complex refraction, operate as a cultural terrain where modernity's forward/backward-looking linear temporality of progress and/in unity is experienced and reproduced in a way that is intensely affective and interpersonal. Here it is imperative to understand the historical relationship between the discourse of women's linguistic corruption and Japan's political economy in the late 1980s through the early 1990s. In particular, it is important to situate and read the commentaries, debates, and opinion polls about women's linguistic corruption in the broader historical and political context of the ambivalence and contradiction between modernity and nationalism on one hand, and between modernity and tradition on the other.

---

3. Hill's (1998) discussion of the discourse of "nostalgia" among speakers of Mexicano provides a lucid analysis of the way "pastness" is imagined and constructed in the present through metapragmatic discourse (and its contestations).

4. Claims for ancient origins and continuity also presuppose one speech community, where all women have equal access to women's language and where women are all (middle-class urban) standard-Japanese speakers. Claims for historical continuity and the search for origins thus necessarily result in an exclusionary practice.

The Temporality of Capitalist Modernity and Women's Language

As I have discussed in part 1, women's language, since its birth, has been discursively linked to the cultural and historical negotiation of the meaning of modernization and modernity in Japan. Japanese modernization, like modernization everywhere, has involved the contradictions of continued poverty and powerlessness in the face of wealth and power and of increasing inequality in the face of expanding freedoms. Capitalist development is inherently uneven and continuously produces and reinforces social inequalities. But this "universal" characteristic of the capitalist world-system aside, the particular contradictions of capitalist modernization in Japan—shared with other non-Western countries—lie in the tension between modernization, which always threatens to take the form of *Westernization*, and nationalism, which may seem to require autonomy from the West or even from modernity itself (Chatterjee 1993). On the one hand, the importation of Western technology, rational bureaucracy, and liberal democracy advanced Japan and helped to forge it into a modern nation-state. On the other hand, in the process, Japan became incorporated into the geopolitics of Western cultural and political-economic hegemony, within a modern world-system in which Japan has always been decentered and marginal to the Euro-American center—even at the height of its global economic power (Harootunian 1988; Sakai 1988). This contradiction of the non-Western location in Japan's modernity demands narrative resolution for the Japanese citizen-subject.

Japan as an industrialized, modern nation has relied ideologically on a linear and progressivist narrative of its own history "from feudalism to modernity," and this inexorably entails a profound temporal bifurcation between the past and the present, often understood as a contrast between tradition and modernity. Modern linear temporality requires two forms of cultural work that create spatial unity and cultural idioms for social order for both poles of the bifurcation. One involves the imagination of an authentic Japanese culture, an essential Japanese self, and a racial boundary from "Western" people, the consequence of which was historically increasing interest on the part of Japanese intellectuals, cultural critics, and state cultural officials in the search for the essence of Japaneseness, known as *Nihonjinron*.[5]

---

5. *Nihonjinron* (the theory of the Japanese) engages in a relentless search for cultural identity and puts under self-reflexive scrutiny all aspects of Japanese social life: mind, self, psy-

The other kind of cultural work involves a universalizing (and normalizing) definition of the modern Japanese family as middle class—thus making other class positions somehow less legitimate, or, more precisely, invisible. The "completion" of modernization—in the sense of becoming the undeniable economic challenger of the Western industrial powers—and its spectacular material achievements linked larger numbers of Japanese families and individuals to both national and global political and cultural economies. *Middle class* as a postwar discourse of social order informs people of the benefits of modernity and economic growth, and the concept levels or denies the distinctions between haves and have-nots, urban and rural, men and women, and, at least in terms of standard of living, Japan and the West.[6]

Mediating and mediated by such cultural idioms was the idea of women's language. It was in fact in the 1960s and 1970s, during the fruition of Japan's postwar modernization, that scholarly interest in women's language reemerged. This was the period of unprecedented economic expansion and widespread innovation and advancement in technology, communication, and transportation. The nationwide urbanization saw an explosion of wage earners surpassing the number of family business owners and farmers, the widespread replacement of the extended family by the nuclear family, and the full-scale differentiation between the roles of salaried husband and housewife (see Ueno 1987a, 1987b:79–80). During this period, a substantial body of literature and reprints of previously published works on women's language appeared.[7] Scholars looked for "women's language"—in both spoken and written texts, in both the present and the past. Disparate and highly localized cases from the records of various historical periods, including the use of terms exclusively by sequestered groups such as court ladies, Buddhist nuns, and women in the pleasure quarters, were set into an imaginary and continuous time line from the ancient past to the present. "Women's language" thus was brought into being as a self-evident scholarly object.[8]

---

chotherapy, child-rearing, social structure and social relations, business practices and labor relations, the emperorship, and so on. Characterizations are commonly constituted in sharp contrast with the West. See Befu 2001 for further discussion of the politics of Nihonjinron.

6. For a historical and ethnographic discussion of the idea of middle class *(chūryū)* as a *cultural* idiom in postwar Japan, see Gordon 2002; Ivy 1995; and Kelly 1986, 2002.

7. See Terada's (1993) comprehensive bibliographic survey of the history of studies of Japanese women's language.

8. Thus, intellectuals struggled with the dilemma of asserting women's language as symptomatic of Japan's uniqueness from the West *without* relegating their culture to the category

As McClintock points out, however, such linear temporalities of modernity have an anomaly regarding the past, an anomaly that is resolved in gendered terms: "The temporal anomaly within nationalism—veering between nostalgia for the past and the impatient, progressive sloughing off of the past—is typically resolved by figuring the contradiction in the representation of *time* as a natural division of *gender*" (1995:358–59; emphasis in original). The temporal rupture underwrites an acute sense of urgency to collect, memorialize, and preserve what is perceived to be "lost," including the authentic feminine, in this case embodied in feminine language. This national crisis of preservation in Japan is recurrently resolved—or at least a futile attempt is made to resolve it—by mobilizing discourses of "women's language," through which the public mourns "the corruption" of women's language use and the loss of an imagined pristine feminine language.

It is also important to recognize that the fetishization of women's voices, be it called "schoolgirl speech," "women's language," or something else, articulates one fundamental way in which the discourse of *nationalism* is gendered. Women's language as a fetish approximates McClintock's "impassioned object":

> The fetish marks a crisis in social meaning as the embodiment of an impossible irresolution. The contradiction is displaced onto and embodied in the fetish object, which is thus destined to recur with compulsive repetition. Hence the apparent power of the fetish to enchant the fetishist. By displacing power onto the fetish, then manipulating the fetish, the individual gains symbolic control over what might otherwise be terrifying ambiguities. For this reason, the fetish can be called an impassioned object. (184)

The recurrent Japanese nation-tradition crisis is thus displaced onto women's language (and its corruption) in the context of the unattainable symbolic resolution of cultural ambivalence and contradiction.

The nation's temporal estrangement from its imagined authentic past was articulated and managed by citing women's language through its "cor-

---

of "premodern," "primitive," or "uncivilized." Kindaichi Haruhiko (1988:36–39), a prominent linguist, for example, drew on the case of "women's language" in an American Indian language in order to point out the rarity of "women's language" in the world, and yet carefully (and defensively) asserted that the affinity with American Indian languages did not mean that Japanese women's language was "primitive" or "uncivilized": the very fact that Japanese women's language is the language of *civilized* people and still culturally rare makes it all the more unique and valuable.

ruption." As I have discussed in chapter 1, schoolgirls' language use drew intense public attention as "linguistic corruption," which, by extension, was also "moral corruption." While a century separates the two dramatically different political-economic contexts described in chapter 1 and in this chapter, socioeconomic "progress" was similarly translated into women's linguistic "regression" in both moments. And, similarly, in both periods "women's language" was given its ontological a priori and its imaginary origin, so as to claim that "there was once a pure women's language." In both historical instances, this was done by temporalizing the indexical order of "women's language" in such a way as to uphold the nation's temporal order of capitalist progress.[9]

"Corruption" of women's speech was viewed as the result of *historical change* in the language, a change directly linked in the prevailing view to wider social changes stimulated by modernization. In the late nineteenth century, the source of women's linguistic contamination—the foundational order of indexicality—was *spatially* sought in class and regional peripheries. Teyo-dawa speech was rationalized as the bad influence of low-class neighborhoods and of the (rural or regional) hinterland. In the late twentieth century, it was sought *temporally* as the consequence of degeneration from the imagined first-order indexicality, or the archaic, pristine, feminine speech of the past. From the standpoint of this interpretive framework, examples of contemporary women's speech that did not fit the norm of women's language were seen, not as diversity, but as cases of *degradation from a norm* that was believed to have been more respected in the past. Thus was synchronic diversity converted into historical corruption—normalized, in Foucault's sense—and understood as the "tragic" consequence of change in society away from all that was traditionally Japanese. Claim for the historical continuity of women's language and anxiety over the loss of gender difference in speech invoked the imagined past in which there was once a pure women's language, spoken by all or most women (or by women who *mattered* and

---

9. The common metapragmatic explanation of "women's language" teleologically presupposes that a speech form such as *dawa* sounds "feminine" because it sounds "soft" and "elegant." Semiotically speaking, this means that the foundational ground of its indexicality is claimed—or, better, tacitly assumed—to be anchored in the "natural" gendered human traits of women, such as "gentleness." Women's language is then rationalized as the natural outcome of women's intrinsic nature: because women's nature is such, they prefer, or are socialized, to use feminine speech. Again, the indexical order is inverted; as I have discussed earlier, speech forms such as *teyo* and *dawa* had no established denotational origin. Or "morally" they had "questionable" (by modern standards) origins at best. Their indexical meaning was far from "softness" and "gentleness" as modern "feminine" characteristics.

held the essence of Japaneseness, even if they were few in number). The concept of "corruption" from a historic norm thus preserves and valorizes a very concrete ideal of Japanese women's language even when Japanese women do not speak it. It thus preserves the idea of fundamental male-female speech difference by storing it in the past. Moreover, it preserves the idea of the immortal essence of Japanese culture by storing it in the past—because gender difference upholds national (historical) unity (McClintock 1995:353).

It is critical to note that the ontology of women's language—and, by extension, national unity and purity—has to be presented as its *bankruptcy* in the present, rather than as its successful preservation. In the linear temporality of national history, women are mobilized by what Duara (1998) calls the "regime of authenticity," which posits them as the unchanging subject of history, the guardian of the authenticity of the nation. Women must not change. Women's language must not change. But precisely because it must not change, its failure in changing, or its submission to change, creates a spectacle and works in fact as a centripetal force to draw people into the nation as a community of affect.[10]

Gender and Political Economy in Japan in the Late 1980s and Early 1990s

The public debates about women's linguistic corruption in the late 1980s and early 1990s took place at the height of Japan's "bubble" economy, a period of formidable economic growth and inflated stock and real estate prices, during which new capital was invested and business expanded. This was accompanied by both an explosion of new consumer goods and services and a labor shortage, which put demand pressures upon the "reserve army" of female workers stored as wives and daughters in Japanese households (as well as creating a demand for foreign workers). The number of working women significantly increased, but most were hired as contingent workers who straddled work and home and thus could be put back into "storage" at the end of their contracts, depending on business con-

---

10. With respect to the way in which the tension between linear temporality and the regime of authenticity gets played out, Duara makes the following insightful observation: "The hegemony of linear time accompanying the transforming drive of capitalism necessitates the repeated constitution of an unchanging subject of history—a regime which stands outside time—precisely because this very combination of capital and linear time erodes it and simultaneously exposes the spectacle of this erosion" (1998:294).

ditions.[11] Nevertheless, it was politically unacceptable for this flexible mobilization of female labor to appear to be purely a cost-benefit calculation by corporations, without any social responsibility implied.

Coinciding with the unprecedented economic boom, the Equal Employment Opportunity Law (EEOL) was enacted in 1986 and phased into implementation.[12] Although the EEOL had virtually no effect in changing discriminatory business practice, it was promoted nationally by the government and symbolically made gender-at-work and the idea of *danjo*

11. The labor shortage was serious. Female part-time workers—contingent, low-waged, and without benefits packages—were in great demand, particularly in tertiary service sectors where women's employment had been rapidly increasing since the mid-1970s. The proportion of women employed increased by 11 percent between 1975 and 1991, and the absolute number of female workers in public or private employment rose by 33 percent during the same period. The proportion of working women in the tertiary sectors rose from 55.7 percent in 1975 to 63.8 percent in 1991, besting the proportion of male workers in those sectors, 55.2 percent. In 1991, 29.3 of all female workers were part-time, a 68 percent increase in the proportion from 1975 (Statistics Bureau, Management and Coordination Agency, various years). For background on Japan's bubble economy and the "post-bubble" long-term economic recession, see Itoh 1994; Kerr 2002; Y. Noguchi 1994; and Yamamura 1997.

12. The EEOL included provisions concerning vocational training, fringe benefits, compulsory retirement age, retirement, and dismissal; identified *kinshi-kitei*, or "prohibited" company practices; and provided for court enforcement of violations. These provisions did not, however, allow for financial penalties for companies in violation. What is more, the critical areas of recruitment and hiring, job assignment, and promotion were designated as *doryoku-kitei*, or (merely) "exhortation." Employers were expected to endeavor to live up to the stipulations, but they were not legally accountable for any violation. It was precisely in these evaluative aspects of labor management practice that women needed the most protection. The EEOL thus authorized legal intervention only in the case of discriminatory entitlement among employees—vocational training, fringe benefits, compulsory retirement age, retirement, and dismissal—in which biological sex was the criterion of discriminatory practice. The labor management aspects involving *evaluation*—recruitment and hiring, and assignment and promotion—in which it was hoped by activists that sociocultural gender would be brought into focus, were not cognizable by this law. It was here, in these procedures, that gender inequality was systematically—if insidiously—reproduced and naturalized into a "structured" labor market, both internally within the company, and within the labor market at large. Brinton (1993) explicates the cultural specificity of the system of human capital development that constitutes gender stratification in the Japanese economy. She focuses on the linkage among social institutions, namely, family (or the socialization process), the education system, labor markets, and recruitment practices. The EEOL, working in tandem with the Temporary Work Act, left completely untouched the underlying issue of women's exclusive responsibilities for domestic (and reproductive) labor, and thus left in place a fundamental disadvantage in their nondomestic labor force participation. In stark contrast to its real limitations, the law claimed an intent to "achieve harmony between [women's] working life and family life." The EEOL thus proclaimed its basic principles: "In view of the fact that women workers contribute to the development of the economy and society and at the same time play an important role as members of families raising children—who will be a mainstay of the future—the basic objectives of the improvement

byōdō (gender equality) into social issues. Large companies also took advantage of the public awareness promoted by the law as an opportunity for corporate public relations work and attracted media attention by appointing women to managerial positions and implementing programs to promote women's status in the workplace.

In reality, however, the government's promotion of women's (re)entry into the labor market within the context of the limitations imposed by the broader social role expectations of women assumed in the EEOL resulted in consolidating women as a reserve contingent workforce that could be called up or furloughed as needed.[13] Employers recruited women under an employment status (part-time) different from men's, which not only secured the continuous provision of cheap (but skilled) labor, but also avoided direct violation of any of the stipulations in the EEOL. This move was further helped by two less visible legal reforms implemented around the same time as the EEOL. One was the Temporary Work Act (Haken Rōdōhō), which legalized and regulated temporary workers dispatched by third-party firms to offices and companies. The idea was to give employers legally legitimate security and flexibility with the work-

---

of the welfare of women workers as set forth in this Law were to enable them to achieve a full working life by making effective use of their abilities, with due respect for their maternal role, but without discriminatory treatment on the basis of sex, and *to achieve harmony between their working life and family life*" (the Equal Employment Opportunity Law, Chapter 1, Article 2. Basic Principles; emphasis added). See Lam (1992:89–116) for a critical and comprehensive introduction to the EEOL. See also Molony 1995; Omori 1993.

13. The job market for female labor was also talked about as if women were free agents with likes and dislikes, very much like *consumers*. In the seminars and symposia for employers that I attended, the key word for companies in terms of job design was "flexibility" (*furekishiburu*). Potential employers, job-hunting magazines, think-tank organizations, and government agencies presented part-time employment as a viable and legitimate career choice that could satisfy a woman's professional aspirations and net returns on educational investments, and promise financial autonomy without compromising a future "return" to the traditional role of a married housewife. Lecturers and panelists emphasized the urgency of the immediate labor shortage, the collapse of the "traditional" work ethic that had sustained loyalty to one's company as well as company commitment to "lifetime employment," and the divergence of lifestyles and values. In one seminar I attended in 1991 on female labor force management, the lecturer addressed an employer audience, composed of personnel staff from various companies, and emphasized the importance of facilitating various career tracks for women and thus giving them "choice" so that they could make home and work compatible. This was, of course, based on the assumption that the female labor force would be useful only as contingent workers. A restaurant menu was, for example, used as an analogy to make a point: the more variety a restaurant has in its menu, the more it can attract customers. Likewise, the more the employer provides potential recruits options in employment style, the more the firm can attract good (part-time) workers.

force and to give part-time workers legally protected rights and security as contingent workers. The other was the revision of the Labor Standards Law, which gave employers greater latitude on setting work hours.

But it was not just a matter of women working. The consumer market also rediscovered women as avid agents of consumption. Through consumption, women were said to be "empowered" by having "equal"—or, better, their "own"—access to the previously male-exclusive (as well as class-exclusive) world of upscale commodities—from tobacco and beer to golf club membership and overseas travel. Both the labor market and the consumer market thus celebrated the new "women's era." With their increasing disposable incomes—which might, in fact, support them "independently" for a time (which meant, in the home of their parents)—women were said to be more selective regarding their future spouses and to demand "three highs" *(san-kō)* in a prospective husband—high stature (tall), high education (graduate of a university), and high income.[14] The increasing presence of women in the labor market as well as in consumption inevitably led to the reconfiguration of the traditional gendered division of labor and, more importantly, to a crisis of moral order that gender difference upholds.

In ways paralleling the situation a century earlier, this revamping of "women's role" was potentially disruptive of settled gender relations in particular and of social order in general. The public seemed to be scandalized that women might "shop around" and study the features of potential husbands, as one would weigh the pros and cons of a purchase. The media featured the first female division manager, the first company executive, the first female government cabinet member, and so on. The term *josei kanrishokusha*, or "woman managers," incited the public's imagination of "female company executives," anticipating the remaking of the social and economic hierarchy marked by gender. During the period of the mid-1980s to early 1990s, such ambivalent images of the "progress" of women—and all that this meant for the men caught up in the apparently revolutionary changes—prompted anxious narrative accountings.

14. The term *san-kō* circulated widely in popular media discourses on contemporary young women during the height of Japan's recent bubble economy. The implication was that the increase in women's participation in work created more economic independence for women and thus more of a buyer's market for husbands as women's expectations for a marriage partner became higher and they could now enjoy the privilege of "choosing" their future spouse, rather than being chosen by men. For young men, it was said that competition in the marriage market was becoming increasingly stiff. It was already the case that men outnumbered women, and the inflation of female expectations made things even more difficult for unmarried men. Or so it was described in the popular media.

The terms of moral crisis came to rest on women's linguistic "corruption." Metapragmatic statements—such as "women's language and men's language have been mixing *[majiriau]*"; "women are now speaking like men, and men are now speaking like women"; or "women have recently come to speak roughly"—were widely heard and read in the media, as well as in the scholarly literature. Opinion polls and letters to the editor in magazines and newspapers actively cited women's language use, particularly that of young women, as rough, loud, and vulgar. Not unlike the unhinged Meiji intellectuals who overheard and cited schoolgirls' "vulgar" speech, the late-twentieth-century critics, concerned citizens, and the statistically constituted public "heard" the spectacular bankruptcy of Japanese authenticity in the imputed speaking voice of women.

Readers' Columns in the Newspaper

The readers' column is a key microtechnology of the public sphere (its "lowbrow" form making it all the more powerful in reproducing the taken-for-granted) that produces the reflexive image of the nation's citizens from diverse backgrounds and statuses, freely and rationally expressing their opinions about national issues. The capitalist public sphere displays its diversity in unity by juxtaposing opinions and comments authored by citizens from different backgrounds. Letters normally indicate the author's occupation, gender, age, and place of residence. Here, as in earlier discussions of letter columns in women's magazines, I will examine readers' columns as a *genre*. Instead of assuming the authenticity of letters and their authors' identities (which we can never know), I focus on how the formal organization of the readers' column as a genre produces a text that looks like a series of letters contributed and authored by a range of real people with real identities. A man could write a letter by taking on a female identity. The moment that a letter is selected, recontexualized, circulated, and consumed, its author's intention and authenticity lose relevance in terms of how it is read, by its public(s). We should, therefore, look at how this particular genre in its specific semiotic structure produces the knowledge of women's language.

Critically, readers' letters defy the scholarly attempt to define women's language formally and functionally and, instead, show the diverse ways in which it is defined and understood in an everyday sense. For those who mourn the death of women's language, citing women's language is a task of saying something about that which no longer exists, for its pure identity is located in the fantastic national past. It is not unlike trying to speak of a ghost. The strategy in readers' letters is then loquaciously to lament what women's language is *not,* out of which "women's language" emerges negatively or in ghostly form as an object of discourse. In the readers' column, women's language is discursively identified by a list of what it is *not:* "rough language," "vulgar language," "men's language," "speaking in a loud voice," "language that hurts others' feelings," "ungrammatical language," "peer language," "the language of bad upbringing," and "language that lacks in humanity."

Women's linguistic corruption is a perennial topic in the readers' column. In the late 1980s and early 1990s, letters on women's language use mourned the loss of pure women's language as people perceived the law (the EEOL) and the economy (the bubble economic boom) to be transforming the nature of the culture (gender difference) toward the idea of gender equality.[15] The connection between language and the perceived new legal and economic condition of women could not be any clearer to the commentators. Concerned parents sought advice on how to discipline a daughter who "speaks like a boy" or complained of their children's young female teacher "speaking like a man." Schoolteachers deplored the fact that girls' voices were significantly louder lately, marking the loss of women's "gentle" voice. A corporate manager reported being appalled by the ignorance and inability of young workers—particularly female workers—to use the proper honorifics in the workplace.

In May 1991 a series of exchanges took place in the readers' column in *Asahi Shimbun,* one of the national daily newspapers in Japan, about the corruption of women's language use. The following debate started with two letters that appeared on May 1, describing recent experiences with young women's "rough language":

> *Letter 1: "Disillusioned by a woman in a wedding gown using vulgar language" (a forty-seven-year-old housewife in Yokohama)*
>
> "Hey, this is not the kind of place where you guys can hang around!" *[Chottoo koko wa **anta**tachi no kuru tokoro ja nain**dayo**.]* [This is what I heard] when

---

15. The loss of femininity is inseparable from the loss of women's language in the prevailing assumption. Such a consensus is often performatively constructed in the public sphere through opinion polls. *Yomiuri Shimbun,* one of the major nationally circulated newspapers, for example, conducted a public opinion survey in 1995 regarding femininity and masculinity. To the question "Do you think today's women are losing their femininity?" 63.8 percent of the respondents answered affirmatively. And 55.6 percent agreed that the loss of femininity was evidenced by women's "bad" language use.

I attended a wedding ceremony as an official matchmaker. To my surprise, this was what the bride herself said to her brothers who had just entered the dressing room at the wedding hall. It is so disillusioning to hear a bride dressed beautifully in a wedding gown and makeup speak this way. In the train, I hear ladies *[redī tachi]* dressed in the latest fashions speak in men's language. I wonder if this is because they are not brought up well by adults. In the kindergarten where my son went, a teacher *[hobo-san]* used very polite language. Her polite language must have relaxed the feelings of my child—his physical strength considerably improved. When I was a child and traveled in Kyoto for the first time, *jochū-san* [a female employee at an inn] gave us a warm welcome by saying, *"Oideyasu"* [welcome]. Though I was a child, I was touched and thought what beautiful language it was. I know that many women have high *san-kō* [three highs] expectations for a husband, but when they use such vulgar language, I wonder if they really deserve such a man?

Letter 2: *"What vulgar language for a woman of a marriageable age [myōrei no josei] to use!"* (a thirty-one-year-old salaried man in Chiba City)

When yet another crush of passengers got into the already jam-packed morning rush-hour train, a woman was pushed and bumped against a man who was standing near the door. At that moment, she [shouted], *"Ouch! How dare you! You, filthy lecherous man!" [Itai-wane. Nani sun-noyo, kono dosukebe!]* The man was taken aback and struck speechless. Another day, as the train lurched with a jerk, a woman who was walking in the aisle, which had begun to empty out, stomped on the toe of a man who was standing near her with her high heel as hard as she could. The next moment [she shouted], *"Don't just stand there, you idiot!" [Nani bosatto tsuttaten-noyo, kono usura-boke!]*. The man was so dumbfounded that he even forgot about the pain. Both of the women were young and good-looking in their own way. They looked pretty smart in their suits. I just don't understand how such vulgar words could come out of their mouths. I wonder if for young women today, guys [like me] having little in the way of *san-kō* are simply nothing but beings they foul-mouthedly abuse and instinctively dislike. By the way, it was me who was almost accused of being a *chikan*.[16]

In letter 1, the correspondent's reconstruction of the bride's vulgar speech concentrates on the second pronoun, *anta* (in bold in the text above), which is considered informal when used by a woman (Ide 1979:43), and the final particle, *n[o]dayo* (again, in bold above), considered a male speech form (Okamoto and Sato 1992:481). In the second letter, the vulgarity of young women's speech is located particularly in curs-

---

16. *Chikan* is a groper who "cops a feel" on a crowded train.

ing phrases such as *do-sukebe* (filthy lecherous man) and *usura-boke* (idiot), and, probably most importantly, in the act of humiliating a man publicly by accusing him of being a *chikan* in front of people, and allegedly of causing him physical pain by stomping on his toe with high heels.[17]

While those letters are explicitly concerned with young women's speech, they in fact engage with a larger public discourse on gender relations and social change, which entails the view that contemporary Japanese young women have been socioeconomically empowered by the law and other forms of modern social change and that, as a result, they have become undisciplined and even (unfemininely) calculating. Both letters end with reference to the "three highs" in the expectations of young women looking for husbands. Both correspondents also criticize women for being materialistic or worldly-minded by alluding to the gap between their much-invested appearance and the poverty of character disclosed by their manner of speaking.

A week later, on May 9, three responses to the above letters appeared in *Asahi Shimbun*. One letter, entitled "Empty Head," was from a seventy-one-year-old male in the literary profession. He shares the anger of the unfortunate man who had his toes stomped on by a woman and develops a similar, yet more scornful, commentary about women's moral corruption by attacking their allegedly vulgar speech.

> When I read "What vulgar language for a woman of a marriageable age to use," it angered me. If I had been him, I would have immediately turned her in [to the police] for committing an act of contempt, according to section 231 of the criminal code. If, in particular, he had had his foot stomped on by the woman and been injured, she could have been arrested for the crime of inflicting injuries. I just can't help but feel that since the Equal Employment Opportunity Law was enacted, I don't know who women think they are, but they have started acting big and bossy these days, while men have become cowering. Since, by the EEOL, women are now treated equally to men, they should abide by the nation's laws, and should be severely cracked down on just like men if they commit a crime. Today's women are preoccupied with appearance, and their brains are empty. That's why they blurt out such violent *[bōgen]* words. While being attentive to their appearance, they should also care about learning. If they have money to buy clothes, I would like to see them buy books, too. I think studying law is important as well as socializing with others, and studying

17. Note that the bride is actually quoted as using speech forms identified as "women's language," such as *wane* ("Ouch-wane!") and *noyo* ("How dare you-noyo?"). The pragmatic effect of "vulgarity" and "rudeness" in the level of speech act, namely, cursing and abusing, overrides that of "femaleness" in the level of utterance-ending.

how to use the Japanese language correctly is also basic to becoming "rich" [*ricchi*]. One can be "rich" only with learning.

This author also attributes women's "vulgar" language and "big" attitude to their economic and legal advancement. Women's moral corruption and questionable marriageability could certainly be discussed without referring to their speech. One could simply and directly denigrate women by pointing out that they are preoccupied with crass consumption and superficial appearance and that they expect their marriage partners to be more ideal than they are or than they are entitled to. Why is criticizing a woman's manner of speaking apparently so important and so commonly practiced in criticizing women? The answer lies in the fact that language and gender have been historically sedimented so as to become an enabling discursive space where being female is delimited, disciplined, governmentalized, and channeled—and thus continuously challenged, negotiated, denied, and reproduced. In other words, given the particular history of the evolution of Japanese modernity since Meiji times, language and linguistic ideology have always (and already) been at the center of the construction of gender: gender cannot be talked about—in any register—without also talking about language.

Two other responses in the May 9 readers' column were from young women, challenging the two letters printed the previous week and defending the use of "vulgar" speech by the young women in question. One was entitled "For Self-Assertion," by a twenty-eight-year-old woman from Omiya, who was currently out of work, and the other, entitled "Understandable under the Present Conditions," was by an eighteen-year-old student from Kawagoe preparing for a college entrance exam (*jukensei*). They first point out the present deplorable sexism that confronts women. The twenty-eight year-old writes:

> I cannot help but sympathize with the contributor who was called names by a young woman in the train and deplored her language use. But I want men to remember how they normally treat women. I was working in America until recently, and what depressed me every time when I came back to Japan was the rude behavior of the "corporate warriors." Particularly in the train, they board by shoving people in their way, they never help when someone is trying to put his/her heavy load onto the overhead rack, they spread open newspapers with indecent material, and on top of that, a man in a business suit who does not look base engages in groping in a nonchalant manner. I suspect that he must slight women in the workplace too. The woman [in the letter] tried to assert herself by using rough language. I think that the only effective language in that situation is the language used in the male society. When I was teaching in a so-called low-ride high school, I

had no choice but to use rough language in order to teach male students. I don't intend to affirm rough language use. On the contrary, what I hope for today's Japan is caring for each other and beautiful language. But this has nothing to do with whether one is a woman or a man.

Similarly, the letter by the eighteen-year-old female student points out:

I understand how it raises eyebrows when a young woman is heard using rough language. But I think it is understandable why such a woman exists. In the train, one never fails to find advertisements for obscene magazines dangling from the ceiling and guys reading magazines and sports newspapers that contain pornographic comics and photographs. Who wouldn't feel agitated if you are a woman and witness such a disdain for women, to say nothing of the experience of sexual harassment in the workplace? Isn't it that those two women mentioned in the letters dated May 1 used vulgar speech because they had grievances about their situations and thought that they would be taken for fools by men if they kept to using polite language? It seems to me that the women in question railed, not against the guys who don't measure up to the three highs, but against sexism. As long as the present attitude of leniency toward male sexism continues, I think women like them will not disappear.

A week later, on May 16, three more letters appeared in the readers' column, responding to the growing debate among readers regarding women's rough speech. All three were from women. The first, from a twenty-three-year-old female college student from Tokyo, expressed regret toward the letter entitled "Empty Head," seeing it as overly generalizing about women and their speech. She notes: "Even if it is a trend observed among some young women, he should recognize that there are quite a few young women out there who strive to enrich themselves through art and learning, rather than merely decorating their appearance, and behave with good manners and good Japanese language use."

The second letter, from a forty-three-year-old housewife from Omiya, raises an objection to the letters of May 9, which attributed women's vulgar speech described in the first two letters, respectively, to their self-assertion in the male-dominant society and to the concerns with being underestimated by men. She suggests that the women in question must have grown up without having been taught or disciplined to use language differently and correctly, according to the context:

Isn't it likely that the young women who burst into vulgar words on the train have grown up addressing people, *"hey you!" [temee!]*, and shouting things like *"You idiot!" [bakkayarō!]* since their childhood? [I can see it] because my daughter and her friends also talk in a similar manner. I told my daughter many times to correct her speech. She would argue with me and say, "I'll be shunned from the group! And even teachers speak like this." In the end, we compromised and came to an agreement. I said to her, "Polite and graceful speech is not something that you can acquire in a single day after you are grown up. So start using language differently according to the context *[tsukaiwakenasai]*. Don't use 'vulgar' language to people other than your school friends." She did her best to do so as a child and has become a [well-spoken] junior high school student. Isn't it the case that those young women have grown up only with peer language?

The third letter, from a twenty-two-year-old female college student from Tokyo majoring in women's studies, like the one above, objected to the idea that young women's vulgar speech is a function of struggling with sexism. Rather, she argues that the issue here is not the level of speech, but one's character as a human being *(ningensei)*.

I was surprised to read the readers' column dated May 9. To say that in a sexist society some women will inevitably use abusive language in reaction, is, I recognized, a line of argument too vested in the viewpoint that it is women's social condition that is at issue. I major in women's studies, but the issue of language use discussed here does not belong to the level of language use as such, but to the question of the person's character. I know someone who looks very sophisticated and classy, but she pulls no punches in using expressions like "I will go piss." No matter how much we grimace at her, she is nonchalant, saying "Don't worry; I wouldn't speak like that in front of men." The thing is that from her sophisticated appearance, one could not imagine her using such language. In short, the point is not that those women who started this debate deliberately use vulgar language toward men (to assert themselves), but that they simply lack character. To put it more clearly, it has more to do with whether an environment [home, family] exists where character is nurtured. Therefore, I don't want anyone to rationalize young women's bad language use as women's rebellion.

Variously arguing against the sociological explanation that it is sexism that makes women speak roughly, these three letters seek to localize the issue of linguistic corruption, insisting that the women in question are deviant cases. By doing so, the innocence and the normativity of the rest of the female population can be protected from attack. The first of the May 16 letters claims that most of the women out there are decent and behave with good manners and use good language. The second letter, drawing on the case of the writer's daughter, explains the vulgar speech of some young women as a result of the lack of discipline and parental guidance. Likewise, the third letter sees women's speech as a function of the quality of a specific individual's character and the specific home environments where it is, or is not, nurtured.

Both the above series of recontextualizations and re-citations of the original letters and the discourse of women's language in general show the extent to which the repeatability of the statement in diverse enunciations is in fact limited and normalized in the public sphere facilitated by print capitalism, in this case in the form of a national newspaper. In spite of the seemingly diverse standpoints represented, the readers' column as a genre is, after all, an institution whose network of relations with other institutions constitutes a discursive field that enables everyone to speak but does not enable everything to be spoken. Given the historical formation of the discourse of women's language discussed in part 1, we can now stand at its threshold and see what is *not* spoken and *not* thinkable.

The letters with mutually opposing opinions collectively manage to keep the ontology of women's language intact. In other words, anyone can speak so long as *the object of discourse itself* is not questioned. This is done by, first of all, leaving the linear temporality of women's linguistic corruption unquestioned or positively reproduced. A common letter-text, for example, is authored by a mother whose daughter(s) speak(s) "roughly." Linguistic "regression" imagined to be taking place intergenerationally guarantees the premise that women "used to" use more polite and beautiful language in the past.

It would also make no sense in the public discussion of women's linguistic corruption to mention women in dialect-speaking communities and those of the working class because they do not fit into the singular linear temporality of women's language presumed in the discourse. In dialect-speaking communities, it is the younger generation that is more susceptible to the integrating force of the national linguistic market privileging standard Japanese and designating local dialects as unsophisticated and backward. And it is the older generation's language that is more often said to be "rough," "crude," and " genderless," precisely the reverse temporality of the discourse of women's language. Similarly the figure of working-class women cannot enter into the public discussion of women's language use, since their linguistic image—also said to be "rough," "crude," and " genderless"—is predicated upon its contrast with the middle-class housewife.

The discursive condition that reproduces the ontology of women's language also construes women as responsibilized subjects, rational, enterprising citizens who can regulate, discipline, and govern themselves, by which the location of accountability and responsibility is squarely centered in the individual and her body and self (see, for example, Foucault 1991; and Rose 1999). The two responses following the initial letters attributed women's rough language to sexism and attempted to relocate the source of the problem from women to men and the society they control. The readers' column, however, successfully undercut such a critical reading by trumping it with the last three letters, which recentered responsibility back in the sovereign individual. So when the first of the final set of letters argues that not all women, but only some, use rough language, corruption is reduced to a matter of the individual's "choice," and the responsible citizen does choose to speak politely. The locus of the problem, for the author of the second letter, is in the domain of individual's self-discipline, and the third suggests that it is a matter of "character." All three of these letters, of course, ignore both history and social power. Transcending historically grounded differences marked by gender and class and strangely resonating with the image of the unproblematic citizen in democracy and of the consumer/worker in the free market, they declare that it is not the social context but specific (deviant) women themselves that are responsible for their linguistic corruption and the loss of women's language. As I will show, it is this responsibilized subject-body of women that public opinion surveys on women's linguistic corruption discursively create as the sovereign agent who is either destroying or capable of saving women's language.

Public Opinion Surveys on Language Awareness *(Kotoba Ishiki)*

A public opinion survey is another powerful technology for constituting knowledge of the (imagined) community. But knowledge must be understood here as *productive,* and rather than merely reflecting existing beliefs, opinion surveys insert and secure a particular fragment of knowledge into the "common sense" and "truth" of "the people" themselves. Statistics are never merely the transparent representation of reality, as no form of representation is unmediated. A survey is one of the technologies of truth by which the modern nation-state constitutes its subject and knowledge, turning particular statements into measurable, countable, and citable information for administrative or other governmental purposes (see, for example, Urla 1993). Accordingly, the opinion survey on women's language to be discussed here is not a set of epistemologically innocent questions and answers, but one of the diffused *sites of the production of knowledge* on Japanese women's language, knowledge that is (re)inserted into "the population" by that act of conducting and reporting the survey.

The survey represents reality in a peculiar way, through a series of binaries of question-and-answer. The questionnaire is straightforward, familiar, and simple to answer. It is designed to pose questions that everyone has heard before, spoken about, or thought about: "Polling gives to the questions which 'everyone asks themselves' . . . rapid, simple, and quantitative answers, in appearance easy to understand and to comment on" (Bourdieu 1990:168). The survey relies on the respondents' ability to contextualize questions in the current social context. In other words, respondents are expected to understand why they are asked *these* particular questions *now*. These simple and simplified questions and the answers they elicit thus break reality down into bite-sized (or, increasingly, byte-sized) pieces, which are then summed as an authentic picture of a reality imagined to be independent of the survey.[18] In this mode of communication, the act of "speaking" is reduced to the act of *selecting* among what are given as "options." It constitutes a particular mode of narrating the nation, organized by a self-contained circularity, in which the questions provide answers. Within such circularity disguised as an extension of a face-to-face dialogue, the function of public opinion as an institution keeps intact the nation's story about women's language and its temporality.

This particular mode of communication and of representing reality is closely connected with imagining the national community. Quantitative methods and representations materialize the sense of the nation as an organic, variegated whole, and authorize the survey as the voice of the citizenry, *a subject* that is beyond the mere amalgamation of individuals. We do not know, and these surveys do not ask, exactly what respondents' perceptions are based upon. Does one's perception that there is less gender difference in speech come from his/her immediate experience at home, school, the workplace, from the scripted dialogues in TV dramas, or from the debates in the media about women's linguistic corruption? The sources and grounds for respondents' evaluations are obscured, and it is this strategic ambiguity that blurs the boundary between the local and

---

18. Thus Baudrillard observes, "Today, the object is no longer 'functional' in the traditional meaning of the word; it no longer serves you, it tests you. . . . Both objects and information result already from a selection, a montage, from a point-of-view. They have already tested 'reality,' and have asked only questions that 'answered back' to them. They have broken down reality into simple elements that they have reassembled into scenarios of regulated oppositions, exactly in the same way that the photographer imposes his contrasts, lights, angles on his object" (1983:120).

the national, the personal and the public, and the message and the medium, and creates the voice of the nation, the organic voice that transcends the particularities.

"Language awareness" *(kotoba ishiki)* is one of the established themes of public opinion surveys in Japan. The impetus for constructing the national knowledge of language awareness is accounted for in part by the extent to which "language use" *(kotobazukai)* is both a site and a means by which the self is disciplined and fashioned. The persistent language ideology that holds that language use is a reflection of a deeply ingrained, integrated part of the individual's inner state (frequently invoked as an important criterion to measure or evaluate people, like upbringing, personality, ability, and other psychological and acquired qualities) generates not only individual narratives of self (see chapters 5 and 6), but also, as in nationwide opinion polls, collective narratives about the nation's self as "the Japanese." The question of how the people as a nation, as "the public," think about the Japanese language, its use, and its future has therefore been a vexing one, regularly studied, surveyed, measured, and reflected upon in the form of public opinion polls *(yoron chōsa)* conducted by government agencies, including the National Language Research Institute, the National Language Council (Kokugo Shingikai), and the Japan Broadcasting Corporation (NHK), as well as private research and academic institutions. Among the various questions within the linguistic awareness survey genre are frequent and regular items regarding women's language and its corruption.[19]

I will now examine such a narrative produced by the survey as a technology of truth and knowledge. When the EEOL was implemented in 1986, NHK conducted a survey titled "Women and Language." It was administered to 363 working women in the Tokyo Metropolitan Area, aged twenty and older (figures 4 and 5). Limiting the sample to respon-

---

19. Topics in the survey include the use of loan words, honorifics, certain address terms, Japanese spoken by foreigners, the English proficiency of Japanese, orthography, and standard Japanese and dialects. Other types of survey question are designed to look at the correlation between the answer and the respondent's sex. These are not directly about "women's language," but differential distribution of answers across sex difference would be expected, for which interpretations are provided. Questions include, for example, "Do you think honorifics should be more simplified in the future?" or "Which do you think is more important, dialect education or standard language education?" Another type of question consists of perception tests in which sample sentences are given and the respondents are prompted to choose which one they would actually use. This type of question concerns particularly the use, and perception, of speech level and honorifics to ascertain how they differ across gender and generation. The expected result would be that women choose more polite forms than men and that older respondents choose more polite forms than younger respondents.

dents within the Tokyo Metropolitan Area reflected the cultural assumption that its residents are speakers of more or less standard Japanese and therefore could adequately speak women's language (if they wanted to). Some questions, as will be seen below, ask about the respondent's view of specific speech forms associated with women's language. These would be significantly irrelevant to dialect speakers, for whom such forms are not available in daily sociolinguistic repertoire.[20] The Tokyo Metropolitan Area thus represents the place of the white collar, the middle class, and the speaker of standard Japanese, in spite of the undeniable existence of social stratification and the constant influx of migrants from the regional areas. It is also assumed that what happens in the Tokyo Metropolitan Area will happen in the rest of the nation, with some time lag. Reflecting the growing social awareness of gender equality as an "issue," the survey targeted middle-class white-collar working women, based on the assumption that, with the increasing entry of women into the public domain, understanding the shifting linguistic awareness of working women would best represent the current status of women's language use and would best forecast its future.

As figures 4 and 5 show, the majority of the respondents either agree or more or less agree that women's language has recently become more masculine and that characteristically feminine speech forms have disappeared. The majority also prefer to have some distinctive difference in language use between men and women. Opinions are, however, almost evenly split on whether the forms of women's language should be preserved and whether women can capitalize on their position as women if they speak women's language.

While the results of the survey generate a range of narratives whose possibilities are both limited and enabled by the broader discourse of women's socioeconomic progress and moral regress within the immediate context

---

20. In this nationwide survey, in order to make the issue of women's language nationally relevant, instead of asking about the respondents' views of concrete speech forms, questions were posed about the level of speech acts and about whether women perform them to demonstrate certain socially expected feminine attributes through their way of speaking. For example, regardless of the regional dialect one speaks, a woman can speak in a way considered "polite," "deferential," "reserved," and "gentle," and this can be accomplished in multiple levels of language use, from tone of voice to interactional styles such as not interrupting the interlocutor or more frequent back channeling. As Austin's speech act theory would have it, the matter is about social behavior that takes the form of linguistic behavior. Talk of women's linguistic corruption is therefore ultimately about social and, particularly, moral corruption. Surveys and opinion polls on women's language use in fact measure the nation's perception of women's social behavior.

FIGURE 4. NHK "Women and Language" survey of Japanese women (1986).

(1) Some people say that recently women's language use has become more masculine *(danseika)*. What do you think about such a view?

Agree	30%
More or less agree	46
More or less disagree	6
Disagree	6
Undecided	13

(2) Some people say that utterance-endings *(gobi)* such as *-shita-wa, -dawa, -ne, -nano, -koto* have ceased to be used in women's language. What do you think about this view?

Agree	23%
More or less agree	41
More or less disagree	11
Disagree	15
Undecided	9

(3) Do you think we should preserve such woman-specific utterance-endings?

Agree	16%
More or less agree	30
More or less disagree	11
Disagree	26
Undecided	17

(4) Do you think women can better capitalize on their position as women if they speak women's language?

Agree	13%
More or less agree	22
More or less disagree	17
Disagree	25
Can't say	23

(5) What do you think about difference in language use between men and women?

Prefer distinctive difference	8%
Prefer some difference	67
Prefer not so much difference	16
Prefer no difference	1
Undecided	8

SOURCE: Mogami Katsuya. 1986. *The NHK Monthly Report on Broadcast Research*. November, 14–28.

FIGURE 5. Selected NHK survey responses by age, marriage status, and education (1986).

	Age[1]				Marriage status		Education	
	20s	30s	40s	50s	single	married	college grads	high school grads
(1) "Women's language use has become more masculine."								
Agree	22%		50%		27%	36%	33%	49%
More or less agree	52%							
(2) "Characteristically feminine utterance-endings have ceased to be used."								
Agree	22%	17%	34%	31%			69%	59%
(3) "We should preserve such woman-specific utterance-endings."								
Agree/More or less agree	50%	47%	40%	28%	51%	42%	43%	54%
Disagree/More or less disagree	28%	42%	55%	52%	31%	39%	37%	31%
(4) "Women can capitalize on their position as women if they speak women's language."								
Agree	35%			39%			26%	39%
Disagree	40%			50%			36%	50%
(5) "There should be a difference in language use between men and women."								
More or less agree	70%		58%				60%	71%

SOURCE: Mogami Katsuya. 1986. *The NHK Monthly Report on Broadcast Research*. November, 14–28. (The original statistics are not available; these numbers are mentioned in Mogami's analysis.)

[1] The women interviewed ranged from 20 to 60; responses are grouped by decades.

of the EEOL enactment, what is more significant is the very fact that the questions asked are even possible and make sense. What kind of story do these questions collectively narrate? We can see how they perform a self-contained narrative of women's language, which goes like this:

> Some people say that women's language has become more like men's language lately, because women no longer use feminine speech forms such as *wa, dawa, ne, nano,* and *koto*. Should or shouldn't we as a nation preserve women's language? With more women entering the previously male-dominated public arena, where women have to compete with men, women might find it disadvantageous to act like women and useless to use women's language. Can women capitalize on being women and speaking women's language even in the male-dominated world? And if not, is that why women's language is dying? Should there even be differences in language use between men and women?

Public opinion—as registered by the survey—is by its own epistemological claims (only) a summation of an already existing social reality. In liberal democratic theory, it mediates the state and the civil society. As an essential medium of the public sphere, it is a reflexive display of the voice of the citizenry, who put aside their personal interests and rationally and objectively reflect upon their community by responding to neutrally formulated questions concerning pressing social issues. My point, however, is that public opinion is also always productive of social reality, because its intelligibility—for research subjects, analysts, and readers of survey results—presumes the existence of a collective citizenry, of a corporate public that has specific, definable characteristics. The members of a citizenry or a public become aware of themselves as such a group with such and such characteristics through, among other things, the technology of public opinion itself. This is not just an "instrument effect," but the implantation of a group-imaginary. In this particular case, the survey questions on "women and language" are *a narrative* that retells and, thus, re-cites the foundational myth that the *original* national speech community had gender difference in language use and that it has been lost. However one chooses to answer public opinion poll survey questions, one can "speak" only within the limits of a self-fulfilling prophecy, "regulated oppositions" (Baudrillard 1983:120), which do not give one the option of questioning the question itself. Bourdieu (1990: 222) presents three premises implicit in the game of public opinion polls. First, everyone is equally entitled to and capable of having an opinion. Second, all opinions are to be equally valued. Third, opinion polls entail the hypothesis that there is an agreement that the questions asked deserve to be answered. Putting these into the context of the survey on "women's language," *the questions themselves disseminate the conviction that there exists distinct sex difference in speech,* with which respondents engage through giving answers. My point is not to critique public opinion polls by arguing the distorting consequences of "instrument effect," but, as I suggested above, to read public opinion polls as technologies that *implant, solidify, and rationalize particular public opinions.*

This particular mode of representing the public sphere is a good example of "discourse" (Foucault 1972) that regulates what can or cannot be said and what makes or does not make sense. Accordingly, the survey questions and their pre-scripted answers are "statements" in the Foucauldian sense. They have a fixed subject position, "I," who utters the statement, "Do you think there should be difference in language use between men and women?" What is more, the "I" who responds to that question, "Yes, I prefer some difference to exist," is the *subject* of those questionnaire statements, not of the respondent's own speech or thought, if there is any. The respondent's act of selecting an answer from the provided options, however, renders itself into the citizen's sovereign act of expressing her opinions, which thus constitutes her as the subject of democracy. The role of the respondent is to activate the answer selected from among the options provided, transforming it from a statement ("what is uttered") into an enunciation ("the act of uttering"), as if it were an utterance spoken at a particular time and place by a particular individual.[21] By doing so, the respondent fills the subject position provided by the selected answer, so as to appear as if she would have formulated that answer by herself. But this very process, in turn, transforms the respondent into the subject of the statement, of the survey as a discourse, and, by extension, of women's language as a discourse.[22]

As in the case of the readers' column discussed above, this subject constructed in the survey is closely connected with the neoliberal notion of a self-regulating, self-responsibilizing actor (Dean 1999), capable of fulfilling *jikosekinin* (self-responsibility or self-accountability). The statement that the preservation of women's language depends on women's self-awareness of their responsibility compulsively repeats itself in the public discussion of women's language. Figure 6 depicts part of an NHK linguistic

---

21. See Lacan (1977:138–40) for his discussion on the difference between statement and enunciation.

22. The question remains of the possibility of the survey result having any subsequent impact on the discourse itself and of the social location of the respondent's "will" in the form of responding to the survey. My point is that the survey itself does not have much performative force, until it gets cited, dislocated, and circulated. That is where the possibility of producing a counternarrative lies.

FIGURE 6. NHK "Linguistic Awareness" survey (1989).

(1) What are things that concern you regarding people's recent language use? Choose answers from the following (multiple answers allowed).

    (a) Use of honorifics has become corrupted.   68%
    (b) Women's language has become rough.   60
    (c) There have been more unintelligible loan words and foreign words.   55
    (d) There have been more strange manners of speaking and words in vogue.   53

(2) For those who chose the answer (b), what are the particular points about it that give you that impression (multiple answers allowed)?

    (a) It is particularly young women's language that has become rough.   75% (71%)*
    (b) There are more women who use rough language, such as "Konoyarō" ("You bastard").   45 (68)
    (c) There are more women who use men's language, such as "Oi omae" ("Hey, you") or "Yaruzo!" ("Let's do it!").   44 (57)
    (d) Women have ceased to use honorifics.   38 (23)
    (e) Not only women's language but men's language is becoming gender-neutral.   37 (25)
    (f) There are more women who enter (public) society.   28 (23)
    (g) Women's language, such as "sō-na-noyo" ("that is right-noyo") and "iya-dawa" ("I don't like it-dawa"), has ceased to be used.   24 (34)
    (i) Gender equality has been advanced.   22 (14)

(3) What do you think about the difference between men's and women's language becoming extinct?

(a) Not desirable.	Total	42%
	Female	45
	Male	39
(b) Can't help it, the course of nature.	Total	31
	Female	30
	Male	33
(c) Don't care.	Total	14
	Female	14
	Male	15
(d) The loss of language difference by gender should not happen.	Total	6
	Female	6
	Male	6
(e) Desirable.	Total	5
	Female	4
	Male	6

SOURCE: *The NHK Monthly Report on Broadcast Research*. 1990. July, August, and September.

*The numbers in parentheses show the result for the group of female respondents from sixteen to twenty-four years old.

awareness survey conducted in 1989, in which a set of questions systematically asked about women's language use. Again, the sample, this time consisting of eighteen hundred men and women aged sixteen and above, was restricted to residents of the Tokyo Metropolitan Area. For the first two questions, multiple answers were offered and the choices ranked by frequency. One analysis of this survey (Ishino and Yasuhira 1991) concludes that people are significantly concerned with women's language use. It makes special reference to the results for question 2, which asks the respondent to identify what he/she means by "women's language use becoming rough." The analysis of the survey draws the reader's attention to the most frequent answer (75 percent), which specifically identifies young women's language use as having become rough. The analysis then considers the group of sixteen- to twenty-four-year-olds who chose this answer(71 percent). Interpreting these results, Ishino and Yasuhira note "the perception that women's language use has become rough represents young women's self-judgment" (98). It suggests, in other words, that women are themselves aware of their language becoming rough, and are therefore responsible for it *as if* it were they—real historical women—who were the origin of women's language.

Regarding question 3, Ishino and Yasuhira again focus attention on the female respondents and point out that women are more likely than men to support the continuing existence of women's language. They thus observe: "although, with this percentage of women supporting gender difference in language use it might be not be possible to prevent women's language use from coming closer to that of men, this probably serves as a breakwater against the complete extinction of gender difference in language" (101). They also cite data from the national survey conducted in 1986, which indicates that more women than men are interested in learning honorifics usage and note that "from this result as well, the chance of women's language becoming completely assimilated into men's language in the near future would seem to be very small."

Disciplining Women: From the Didactic to the Scientific

Texts on women's language as a scholarly *object* begin to appear at least as early as the 1920s (for example, see Kikuzawa 1929), while, as I discussed in chapter 1, didactic essays on schoolgirls' linguistic corruption appeared as early as the 1880s. The pre–World War II essays and books on women's language can be characterized by their deliberate conflation of the pedagogic and the pedantic, and of scholarly discipline and scholarly disciplining. The purpose of such work was for the author-educators to teach the "correct" way women should speak. The pedagogic and disciplining tone has been much less explicit in postwar scholarship, and, indeed, contemporary sociolinguistic studies of women's language avow a clear break with prescriptivism and insist upon their purely descriptive commitment to objectivity and science. But the discipline-disciplining elements of the discourse have not completely disappeared. Informed by empiricism and objectivity, the new system of knowledge developed in a context of different socioeconomic conditions, gender relations, and cultural politics, and (re)iterated statements that avow the ontological existence of women's language, which was thus reproduced and renewed.

The characteristic scholarly production of women's language in the late 1980s and early 1990s was also managed by the nation's linear temporality, which necessitated the representation of the urban middle class as the generic "Japanese" and of gender difference as the original and normative state of Japanese language. Almost without exception, informants for the major sociolinguistic studies of women's language have been drawn from the urban middle-class white-collar population. In empirical studies, researchers are expected by their scholarly peers to attest that their informants are native speakers of "standard (Tokyo) Japanese." This designation of this (particular) population as generic significantly influenced empirical research design, as it literally became one of the prerequisites for legitimate empirical research, on a par with attention to sample size, statistical significance, and so on. Sociolinguistic studies therefore often contain mandatory assurances of minimum "contamination" of informants by nonstandard linguistic variations (dialects) and by nonstandard social status (non–white collar). For example, in their study of sex difference in the perception of honorifics, Ide and colleagues insert this proviso: "They [the subjects] were chosen as a sample representing typical middle-class men and women in contemporary Japanese society" (1986:26). Choosing Mitaka, a suburb of Tokyo, as a research site, Shibamoto also describes her sample population as "composed primarily of middle-class white-collar workers and their families," and assures her readers that all the subjects were verified as native speakers of "standard Japanese" and that blue-collar and merchant residents were not included in the study (1987:69).

Closely citing and cited by the public discussion of women's linguistic corruption in public opinion polls, readers' letters, and other lay forms, major sociolinguistic studies of language and gender in the late 1980s and early 1990s were as tied up with the perceived socioeconomic and sociocultural change and its supposed effect upon gender relations as were the lay forms. Two major tropes, which substituted for an explicitly judgmental term, "corruption," developed in the academic realm: *majiriai* (blending in) and *tayōka* (diversification). *Majiriai* is the label for a sociolinguistic diagnosis in which women's and men's language use are *"mutually* approximating each other" *(ayumiyoru).* The point is that it is not just women's language use that is becoming more like men's, but also that men's language use is becoming closer to women's. To make this argument it is necessary, of course, to premise that there "originally" was clear and systematic gender difference in language use. Remarkably echoing "diversification" and "diversity" in the consumer market (niches in style, taste, and value), the term *tayōka* also frequently appeared during this period to suggest that women's language use is (and is expected to be and should be) more diverse and heterogeneous, particularly as more ("diverse") women enter into the public domains of work, media, and commodity consumption.

For example, based on survey data, Kawaguchi (1987) examined the variation of the utterance "Are you going?" based on the assumptions that the structural availability of the various speech levels and registers potentially allows multiple ways of making the utterance and that a certain pattern of distribution according to gender and occupation would emerge. The survey was administered to both male and female professionals between the ages of twenty-two and fifty-five in the publishing and broadcasting industries. For comparative purposes, the study also drew on another study in which the same survey items were administered to housewives in the same age range. The results show that a significant range of variation in uttering "Are you going?" is shared by both men and women professionals (except for some registers exclusively associated with either feminine or masculine), from which it is concluded that male and female language use are "blending in" with each other. Kawaguchi further observes that, compared with the range of varieties evidenced in the housewife data, language use by female professionals is "closer" to that of men, implying that it is not some innate quality of femaleness that makes women speak a certain way, but that it is with a change in social role—from housewife to professional—that women's language use changes. Takasaki (1988:39) also notes that "gender blending in language use" is characterized by "an increase in the number of words and expressions that are naturally selected by both men and women as a result of an increase in the number of situations where language is used regardless of gender." With more traditionally male occupations and social roles opened up by the gender equity law and social change, these studies anticipate that women's language use will become more diverse and heterogeneous with time.

The emergence of tropes such as blending and diversity accompanied the shift in the subject of study from urban middle-class housewives to urban middle-class professionals. The new knowledge produced by such studies of professionals was then identified as evidence of "historical change" in women's language. In other words, a social differentiation that had always existed (even before the bubble economy)—housewives and women in the labor market—was first ignored, then discovered, and the new data interpreted as evidence of a new phenomenon (working women). What we can call the (contemporaneous) social *spatiality* of women's labor—its partitioning into waged and unwaged sectors in the public and private spheres, respectively—was read *temporally* as change over time, moving forward in a progressive line. This, of course, reiterated and recapitulated the temporality of national modernity with the cultural complexities and ambiguities of Japanese modernity. With respect to women, this move, of course, elides the question of when women's language use has *not* been heterogeneous or when "women's role" (understood in all its variations across Japan) was ever radically limited to "housewife."

Another significant development in the study of women's language in the 1980s and early 1990s has to do with more Japanese native sociolinguists writing and speaking to international audiences. During this period, Japanese sociolinguistics gained significant presence in English-language journals. There, women's language as a scholarly object came to be recast as "culture," something essentially positive (and depoliticized) and unique to Japanese language and society, which works as an antithesis of the Western theoretical model that treats gender difference as a sign of the oppression of women. Ide and McGloin, for example, express their skepticism about approaching the issue of Japanese women's language in terms of sexism and social power. In their judgment, feminism was never well received in Japan, because "Japanese women prefer a complementary vision of status and role differences, giving them equal dignity, despite differences in form" (1990:ii). Based on her observation that women speak more politely than men, Ide maintains that women's frequent use of more polite language is "not just to defer to the interlocutor and to lower herself, but also to demonstrate her own (high social) status and dignity" (1993:7).

Such narratives could be readily viewed as self-orientalization and cultural nationalism. But it is important to put them into the context of contesting Euro-American hegemony over knowledge production, in which the West offers theories and models—such as "gender difference = sexism"—and the undifferentiated "rest" offers itself up as data to be interpreted and spoken of. The Western feminist critique has been received as compelling in many quarters, academic and popular, in Japan and is commonly recognized as having something to say about "Japanese women" and their oppression; gender differences in language have been part of this narrative. But the additional message conveyed clearly in the Western feminist analysis of Japanese women is that Japanese women are more oppressed than—(temporally) "behind"—Western women, a measure of the "holes" in Japanese modernity. Thus, the indigenous assertion of women's language as "culture" is a way of refusing, on the part of Japanese scholars, simply to be a time-lagged copy of the West and of asserting Japan's co-evality with the West.

The "indigenous" expert linguistic knowledge of Japanese women's language responds, then, to the temporal paradox of Japan's modernity. As we have seen, modernity perennially threatens to make Japan seem like a "follower" of the West and, at the same time, "less Japanese" because of the increasing remoteness of "modern" Japan from the essence of Japan stored in its imagined archaic past as it moves temporally along the track of national progress. But the indigenous discourse, that of *gender* in particular, can make this assertion of the Japanese past in the present—and of the uniqueness of *Japanese* modernity—only by converting the temporal paradox into a spatial paradox: the urban middle-class standard—a very *provincial* standard, we might say, after Chakrabarty (2000)—becomes "standard Japanese," with all the impressive elisions and exclusions entailed. What is postulated is one homogenous national space in which one class of women represents all Japan, and the language they allegedly speak is "women's language." Digressions from this are "the breakdown of women's language" or even "resistance to women's language," but the point is that both degeneration and resistance are made possible and regulated by the discourse of women's language that postulates the uniformity of the standard to begin with. None of this would be possible without the abjection of all nonstandard linguistic practices and experiences that would endanger the imputed homogeneity from the start.

But in the end, this spatial temporal move cannot resolve the temporal paradox of Japanese national progress, and the digressions from the norm are, as we have seen, both legion and highly publicized, even if they are not theorized by indigenous linguists other than as breakdown or resistance. A process of abjection takes place in the temporal mode, just as it does in the spatial mode described above. The presumed inevitable regression of things perceived as uniquely Japanese in the face of "progress" in economic growth and modernization, however, silences alternative temporal regimes of modernity, particularly those rooted in the regional peripheries, where the increasing prevalence of "standard Japanese," at least in public contexts, registers a linear narrative not of regression, but of "progress" from speaking regional dialects to standard Japanese, from the vulgar and unsophisticated to the sophisticated and the cosmopolitan. The metropolitan knowledge of women's language is thus utterly oblivious to the linguistic experience of women dialect speakers as well as working-class women whose linguistic habitus—and the temporality of its change—cannot be represented by the middle-class standard Japanese language. The vector of modernity in the regional peripheries thus precisely contradicts that of the metropolitan and the national. It is in this sense that the scholarly production of the knowledge of women's language is disciplining by presuming a *particular* Japanese women's linguistic experience—that of the urban middle-class standard-Japanese speakers—as the norm, the proximity to which is functional to the national disciplining of women linguistically. Even for women who do not, and never will, produce women's language, their own metalinguistic narratives of their own speech can never be external to the dominant discourse.

The National Language Council

The mode of knowledge produced by the technique of public opinion surveys such as those by NHK is cited and used for official language policies. For example, in December 2000, after seven years of deliberations on the topic "On National Language Policy Suitable for the New Era," the National Language Council submitted to the government a final report titled "Deferential Expressions in Modern [Japanese] Society."[23] Designating *keii hyōgen*, or deferential expressions, as key to normative pub-

---

23. The preface of the report reads: "The National Language Council proposes 'deferential expression' as an important concept in thinking about how language should be used in contemporary society. Deferential expression refers to a way of language use in communication in which one chooses expressions differently by taking into consideration the interlocutor and the context, based on the spirit of mutual respect. A speaker, in respecting the personality and role of the interlocutor, chooses as his/her self-expression an appropriate form from a variety of expressions, including honorifics and others. The National Lan-

lic language communication in modern Japanese society, the report devotes one subsection to gender difference in language use.

As can be seen from figure 7, the report cites a survey conducted in 1995 by the Agency for Cultural Affairs, which indicates that the majority of people prefer gender difference in language use. In its perfected bureaucratic language, the report communicates little, or is strategically equivocal, to say the least. This is the government's eulogy to women's language. The critical statements that organize the national narrative of women's linguistic corruption we have seen in the public opinion polls and readers' letters reappear here clearly, not as hidden intention, but right on the surface: (1) the original and normative state of national language is characterized by gender difference, and (2) gender difference in language use is vanishing in the face of the prevailing movement for gender equity. The National Language Council's guidelines tacitly but resolutely reproduce the singular linear temporality that underwrites simultaneously Japan's progress *and* women's language's regression.

Moreover, it is noteworthy that, in the process of drafting the final report, at least some members of the council promoted the view that valorizes "women's language" as a "positive" identity marker. For example, the minutes of the council's meeting on April 17, 1998, include comments and discussions around the passage in the draft of the report that touches upon the issue of gender difference in language use among the council members. For example: "Gender difference in language use is a matter of identity," and "Women's language is used as an expression of one's identity even if women are equal to men." "It should be positively worded," one comment on the planned report stated, "such as 'women show pride as women by using women's language.' The intention of this passage is in conjunction with language use in the workplace. The National Language Council's judgment on the issue of gender difference would be so critical that our credibility would be doubted *[kanae no keichō ga towareru]* if we mishandled it." One member also commented, "When I hear fem-

---

guage Council hereby submits the report entitled 'Deferential Expressions in Modern [Japanese] Society,' for the general theme, 'On National Language Policy Suitable for the New Era,' which the minister of education commissioned in 1993. We came to the judgment in our deliberations that it would be important to make recommendations as to how language should be used on the basis of an appreciation for the multiple dimensions of language use in contemporary society. Specifically, the council recognizes that the core of language use in contemporary society is deferential expression, which works to facilitate communication, and accordingly has drafted guidelines for language use, centering around deferential expression" (Kokugo Shingikai 2000).

FIGURE 7. The passage from the section titled "Gender Difference in Language Use" in "Deferential Expressions in Modern [Japanese] Society."

In Japanese, there exist vocabulary and usages that are characteristic of each sex, and it is conventionally maintained that there is a difference in language use between the sexes. Recently, there has been increasing awareness of the issue of gender equality, and various efforts are being made toward the realization of a gender-equal society. In such a social conjuncture, difference in language use by gender has been diminishing by both sexes' language use coming closer to each other. Regarding the existence of difference in language use by gender, there is a variety of opinions, including the opinion which views such gender difference in language positively, that which thinks it can't be helped, and that which thinks it better not to have gender difference in language use, although the latter is not the majority's view.* Basically, whichever gender one belongs to, the issue is to choose an appropriate expression that is satisfactory as self-expression, onto which each person projects his/her own personality, and that furthermore is appropriate for the interlocutor and the context. This is one dimension of language use as deferential expression.

*According to the public opinion survey administered by the Agency for Cultural Affairs in April 1995, there were the following responses to "Although it is said that difference in language use between men and women is becoming the thing of the past, select the response that is closest to your view."

Prefer gender difference in language use.	44.1%
The loss of gender difference is a natural course of things, and cannot be helped.	41.2
Prefer no gender difference in language use.	9.8

SOURCE: Kokugo Shingikai, 2000.

inine language use, I feel gentleness and richness and feel pleased. If men and women speak in the same way, it would feel disconsolate and empty. Nonetheless, the main thing is that we should not impose [upon women the use of feminine language]."

The guidelines thus ask people to *choose* ways of speaking appropriate for the context as mutually respectful citizens responsible for normative communication identified by the guidelines as "deferential expressions." When it comes to gender difference, the officials' sense of "appropriateness" is insinuated into public consciousness by the public opinion poll it cites. The guidelines do not tell people how they should speak. Instead, they ask citizens to act "appropriately" and normatively through their (rational) free choice without government intervention, and thus to fashion themselves into self-regulating subjects. Women's language, stripped of its history and politics, is now reduced to one style of choice available to the subject as an interpersonal linguistic expression.

Help Yourself and Fake It: Women's Language Speaking though the Responsibilized Body

The market welcomes neoliberal subjects as consumers and workers, for such buyers and sellers readily and predictably respond to products, ideas, services, and employment opportunities that promise to help them improve and reinvent themselves. Bookstore shelves that were already saturated with self-help volumes were further crowded with books on language use, targeting in particular working women during the 1980s and 1990s. Titles such as *Desirable Manners of Speaking for Office Ladies* (Kanai 1987), *Attractive Women Are Raconteurs* (Nagasaki 1986), and *Beautiful Speaking Manners for Women That Make You Charming* (Suzuki K. 1989) promise to teach the reader the proper ways of speaking in situations and contexts relevant to young working women, including workplace interactions with bosses, customers, and peers, dating scenes and courtship, formal speeches at a colleague's wedding, and so on.

The books are clear in their emphases: the importance of correct and proper honorific use, of choosing proper linguistic style according to the context *(tukaiwakeru)*, of listening (much more important than speaking), of language use sensitive to others' feelings, of unlearning peer language, and of using a soft and gentle voice, along with proper bodily movements. Without exception, sample dialogues use women's language in its most stereotypical sense, with universal use of utterance-endings such as *noyo, dawa, wane, kashira,* and others. These concrete speech forms of women's language thus take on the indexical burden of grounding the import of speech acts, such as "sensitivity to others' feelings" or "being a good listener," which these books promise will make the reader a "talk beauty" *(hanashi bijin)*.

Of course, the modern discourse of self-help on language use for women in these books is not new. It has been around since the early 1900s, when educators deplored schoolgirl speech and lectured on how to speak womanly. As was seen in chapter 3, women's magazines in circulation as early as the 1930s had already developed women's language into a commodity form as a body of knowledge for sale. Unlike the prewar period, when there was less movement between social strata, the postwar political economy enabled and demanded belief that "you can move up if you work hard"—and part of that work had to do with "appropriate" (gendered) language use. What was new in the late 1980s and early 1990s was that faith in class mobility was remobilized in powerful ways by the increasing semiotic capacity of consumption by which the commodity communicates and stands for something other than itself (Baudrillard 1981; Bourdieu 1984). In the context of extreme economic optimism, the commodity signifies "moving up," or a shift in social relations, if not necessarily moving one "up" materially. A euphoric sense of abundance and of the accessibility of luxurious commodities spread across the class system during the bubble economy. This extreme economic optimism, which after all brought about the dramatic economic boom and its equally dramatic aftermath, made people feel that they could own Louis Vuitton and Prada, join Club Med, and dine in exclusive restaurants, thereby communicating that they belonged to what an "authentic" Louis Vuitton owner belongs to.[24] The sign value inhering in commodities incites a fantasy of class mobility for everybody, and this at precisely the time when the economic disparity between the elite class and the lower class was growing faster than at any other time, even more than during the prewar period (Sato T. 2000).[25]

It is in this context that the idea of "moving up" started referring not so much to actual material social relations between classes, *but to itself* as a sign of a sign without reality, and that women's language, in the specific speech forms stereotypically associated with it, resurfaced not only as a commodity, but also as linguistic capital for *class* distinction—this commodity/capital was purportedly purchasable/accountable and "available" for *everyone*. This specific sense of women's language demands a diligent neoliberal body which is prepared to improve, modify, and transform its own body, language, and psyche, and to invest in itself for maximum return, and which,

24. One of my acquaintances working in downtown Tokyo noted that the popularity of so-called gourmet guide magazines such as *Pia* during the bubble economy resulted in disrupting the invisible class boundaries of the space of consumption: now that information about "exclusive" restaurants previously monopolized by wealthy people was widely circulated by such magazines, the "masses" were invading these restaurants, their class distinctions were lost, and the "real connoisseur" stopped frequenting them.

25. Sato Toshiki (2000) argues that while the 1980s intergenerational upward mobility was increasing, by the late 1980s and the beginning of the 1990s, the chance of the sons and daughters of lower-white-collar and blue-collar families climbing "up" the class ladder was significantly reduced. At the same time, the elite became more successful in social reproduction, by passing down their social and economic privilege to their children. According to Sato, while the bubble economy provided the masses with euphoria about their perceived opportunities for upward mobility through consumption, the credibility of the "everyone-is-in-the-middle-class" conviction had long ago collapsed. It is the collapse of the belief that one can move up if he/she works hard that appeared with the collapse of the bubble economy. Along with Sato's work, a series of studies were published in the late 1990s through the early 2000s that created a public debate among intellectuals about the disappearance of the middle class. See Chuō Kōron Henshūbu 2001.

thus, would cite the law of woman's language and "own" it. While the loss of women's language is mourned in the public sphere, its ghost discovers this enterprising body, through which it attempts to speak.

The status of women's language in the age of the neoliberal economy and culture—and the collapse of the distinction between them—can be summed up by the circulation of the term *ojō-sama*. *Ojō-sama* refers to a daughter from a decent family, and, in this particular context, a daughter from a wealthy upper-class family, who was brought up with tender care in isolation from the cruelties of the real world. Women's magazines frequently feature "ojō-sama fashion," or actual young women identified as ojō-sama, and display their hobbies, places they eat, cars they drive, music they listen to, and clothes and accessories they wear. Just as "moving up" became hyperreal, "upper class" in this context does not necessarily refer to any material social relations. In this image cultivated in the mass media, the ojō-sama marks the ultimate female figure of upward mobility that consumption promises. While class background is beyond one's control, the mass consumption fueled by the economic boom tells consumers that they can at least buy what an ojō-sama has, and that they can then at least look like an ojō-sama by possessing what she has and what she wears, going where she goes, eating what she eats, and *speaking the way she speaks*. Critically, ojō-sama is posited as mastering the pure women's language as habitus.

The book *Ojō-sama Language Quick Study Course* (Kato E. 2000), which walks a fine line between self-help literature and its parody, teaches how to speak like an ojō-sama. The foreword explains that the idea of this book came from a group of women editors who "wanted to act haughty in (upscale) restaurants and boutiques" (3). The book's lessons are a strikingly faithful replication of the prewar model conversation for the middle-class housewife in terms of the use of stereotypical female utterance-endings, elaborate honorifics, and polite greetings (see chapter 3). But it also gives the reader tongue-in-cheek instruction on subtle uses of women's language. Openly manipulative and calculating, the book parodies "feminine" ways of speaking by offering practical advice on how to carry out certain speech acts that are the least "ladylike" by using the most "ladylike" language. Advice includes, for example, how to "trash" someone in women's language.

What distinguishes this from its prewar counterpart lies in its open admission that there is only so much one can do cover up one's not-so-classy upbringing, and that one will never be an authentic ojō-sama. But this is okay, the book says, since most people do not have a classy background. Kato gives this final tongue-in-cheek advice to the reader, in best ojō-sama language:

Finally, I hope you will confidently use what you have learned in this book without being bashful. If you only put into practice the first three or four points, most people will think that you are an ojō-sama and a polite lady. There will be little possibility, as little as 20 percent, of your real upbringing coming out, because it is likely that your interlocutor is not a real ojō-sama either. Not unlike you, most of them are simply faking it. But don't be intimidated. Keep the grin off your face, or fake identity will be detected. Act like an ojō-sama with your head held high, and use what you have learned in this book. Good luck. (115–16)

Such cynicism implies less the irrevocable disjuncture between the authentic and the inauthentic than the cancellation of the distinction itself in the late-capitalist historical moment. The experience of class—at least in the Japanese metropole—has come increasingly to take the form of signs and not social relations. "Social reality" is, it appears, really only about individual manipulation, consumption, and trafficking in signs (of class). What matters, it seems, is not authenticity, but the *idea* of authenticity and its sign value. To put it differently, through performing ojō-sama language, what the neoliberal body cites is not the reality of women's language, but its hyperreality, the myth of women's language.

The lost and dead women's language is thus resurrected as a self-conscious *fake*. Not unlike Butler's drag, which *"implicitly reveals the imitative structure of gender itself"* (1990:134–39; emphasis in original), however, "faking," as an inauthentic and illegitimate citation of the original, exposes the hidden quotation marks around women's language. This trace of citation shows that it does not originally or naturally belong to the person who speaks it. It thus dramatizes the extent to which the inner essence or unity of women's language is fabricated on the mere surfaces of the body.

With varying degrees, however, "faking" is the general condition for any self-fashioning project, and its parodic nature is constitutive of that condition. Self-help literature offers a site where the dead women's language is brought back to life through its "hyper" correct citations by subjects engaged in self-improvement in a mode shaped by Japan's late-capitalist political-economic adventure. At the same time, however, it is precisely the site where excessive imitation inadvertently exposes the original absence of pure women's language and thus undermines its ontology as "fake." While public opinion purifies women's language by claiming its death, its commodified form as self-help literature, which equally intends to resurrect ideal women's language, ends up displacing the attempt.

PART THREE

Re-Citing Women's Language in Late Modern Japan

Introduction

Women and Men at May Japan Limited, Inc.

This brief section will provide background information about May Japan Limited, Inc. (MJL; a pseudonym), where I conducted ethnographic fieldwork from April 1991 through August 1993, working with the women whom I will describe in chapters 5 and 6. These women worked at the headquarters of MJL, located in one of the central business districts of downtown Tokyo. Its seven-story 1970s Japanese modernist building looked rather like a matchbox stood on one end, and it faced a busy street leading to one of the imperial palaces. This is a neighborhood whose name is celebrated in popular songs and is known to virtually everyone in Japan.

My field research at MJL was arranged by my former undergraduate advisor, who had connections with several managers in the personnel division.[1] I was contracted as a fixed-term part-time worker *(pāto)* in three different offices over a period of two and one-half years, for twelve months

---

1. Rohlen (1977) describes in the introduction to his ethnography of a Tokyo bank, Uedagin, how the degree of one's freedom as a researcher and the territory where one can move around depends upon the managerial level of one's corporate hosts in the company. My entry into MJL through the personnel department secured my initial "neutrality" as a researcher. I waited for a job to become available just as other women do, without receiving any privileged arrangements. Between my three fixed-term contracts, I waited an average of three months to be rehired. Introduction to the president and other upper-level executives—for the purpose of discussing my research—was made after I entered the company, through the supervisors I was directly working for in my section.

of cumulative work. During the term of each contract, I worked full days and full weeks. In each office, I worked for periods of two to six months. My responsibilities ranged from skilled work—operating both English and Japanese word processors—to unskilled work such as making and pouring tea, photocopying, collecting and distributing mail, ordering stationery, doing data entry, and other clerical tasks. These were all considered to be women's jobs—and these were the jobs that were done by the majority of female workers, both part-time and full-time, at MJL.[2]

MJL no longer exists. By the time I had finished doing my fieldwork, the rumor was spreading about a major *risutora,* or organizational "restructuring," which has become all too familiar a term today in Japan. First the weaker divisions in the company got severed and made into independent companies; then the most profitable division merged with one of its rival companies. The existing workforce was drastically pruned. People were demoted or "encouraged" to retire or to resign, and many people I worked with, both women and men, were transferred to the newly merged or severed companies. In addition, young female workers, to whom I became close, also left the company, one by one. Some got jobs elsewhere. A couple of them got married.

Formed in 1966, MJL was a subsidiary of a foreign multinational; as of February 1993 it had 2,670 employees (including its affiliated companies) in Japan, dealing in the production, import and export, sale, and research and development of pharmaceuticals and other chemicals. It had nine branches in major Japanese cities, as well as forty-three sales offices, two production facilities, four research and development facilities outside of Tokyo, and two affiliated companies with seven joint-stock corporations.

MJL, as a foreign-affiliated firm, was referred to as *gaishi(-kei)* (foreign-capital affiliate). The mass media and popular literature often represent the gaishi as dream workplaces, particularly for aspiring female college graduates, although for many male workers, working for gaishi often means that they have not been able to get jobs in prestigious large Japanese corporations. Popular cultural images of foreign-affiliated firms, often conjured up by reference to Euro-American multinationals such as IBM, Coca Cola, or Xerox, involve scenes of modern spacious offices with desks individually partitioned, and sophisticated bilingual Japanese businessmen and busi-

---

2. For excellent sociological works on gender and work in Japan, see Brinton 1991, 1993 for the mid-1980s and Ogasawara 1998 for the early 1990s. See also Allison's (1994) ethnographic work on night clubs, which describes the reproduction of patriarchy in the elite salaried men's interaction with club hostesses.

nesswomen interacting on equal terms with each other and with their Western colleagues and bosses. The persistent popular belief in the basic differences between working conditions in foreign-affiliated and Japanese firms holds that Japanese firms enforce traditional management practices such as lifetime employment *(shūshin koyō)* and the seniority system *(nenkō)*, and that foreign affiliates operate on "modern" (read Western, as a Japanese popular category) rational management, with a thoroughgoing entrepreneurial merit system *(jitsuryokushugi)* for promotion, pay, and benefits.

The idea of a merit system appeals particularly to aspiring female college graduates because it supposedly promises gender equity in job assignments, pay, and promotion. Many young MJL female workers—as well as some male workers—told me that they chose to apply for a job at MJL because it was a foreign-affiliated firm, and that they had expected that the company would appreciate and respect their abilities and aspirations. They also told me, however, that they were surprised and disappointed by how "Japanese" MJL turned out to be. The original admiration of female college graduates for MJL as a dream employer makes an interesting contrast with the reluctance, compromise, and sense of anomaly that some male employees in their mid to late forties claimed to have felt at the time of entry into MJL during the 1970s, the formative period of MJL in the heyday of postwar Japanese economic growth.

Men and women were both vertically and horizontally segregated at MJL, through both hiring practices and occupational segregation: in terms of organizational rank and career grade, women were consistently found in the lower strata of the hierarchy, and they were systematically confined to support, or "indoor jobs," as opposed to line, or "outdoor jobs," within the company. Sales work in particular was an area where women were excluded. Thus, these practices shaped a specific—and limited—career path for women (see table 1).

All male workers were full-time except for a handful of contractors *(shokutaku)* hired to fill specific—and less prestigious—job assignments, such as clerical work or warehouse security. Part-time workers were all female and represented 22 percent of the female workforce at MJL. Like most Japanese white-collar organizations, MJL preferred to hire predominantly men at the time of their university graduation for the core of the workforce (primary labor force). The EEOL in no way prevented this practice, which was outwardly discriminatory both in intent and in effect. Male recruits were largely baccalaureate graduates, although some in research and development facilities had master's or doctoral degrees, and some in the manufacturing facilities and other specific offices and facilities were

TABLE 1. Demography and Rank System at MJL

Rank	Foreign delegates[1]	Male workers	Female workers
CEO	1	0	0
Unit manager	3	2	0
Division manager	3	7	0
Department head	8	47	0
Deputy manager	3	88	1
Section chief *(kachō)*	0	299	8
Kakarichō[2]	0	511	69
Rank-and-file workers *(hira-shain)*	0	731	620[3]

[1]Foreign delegates are all male.
[2]*Kakarichō* at MJL refers to the rank title given to those senior to regular workers in terms of age and work experience. Informally, they are expected to train younger and newer employees in their subsection of the department, but they have no formal managerial responsibility and are not considered managers.
[3]Full-time: 467; part-time: 153.

only high school, vocational school, or junior college graduates. In the late 1960s and 1970s, a number of high school graduates had been recruited for the primary sector because the company was not large or prestigious enough to attract university graduates; by the 1990s they had risen to lower-managerial positions. New college graduates created a relatively egalitarian cohort in terms of age (or the year of entry) and education level. Overall men were thus organized into a larger, rigorously graded age hierarchy in the primary sector (see table 2).

Women were recruited at three different educational levels: high school, two-year junior college (or two-year vocational school), and university. Hiring female university graduates was a relatively new practice at MJL. No female university graduate was hired until the late 1970s in its pharmaceutical division or the general administration division, when a couple of women were hired for the public relations office as well as several female licensed pharmacists who had passed the national certification examination. In its chemical division, there were no female graduates until 1989, when three were hired for clerical work. These hirings were ostensibly a voluntary compliance with the EEOL in pursuit of equal opportunity for women.

The recruitment of male college graduates was a systematically and tightly crafted annual event. The MJL personnel staff visited various cam-

TABLE 2. Job Allocation for Newly Graduating MJL Recruits, 1993

Unit	Occupation	Male	Female
Pharmaceutical unit	Sales	44 (U)[1]	3 (U)
	Marketing		17 (U)
	Clerical	0	1 (JC)
	Research	2 (U)	3 (U)
		7 (MA)	3 (MA)
Synthetic materials unit	Sales and marketing	7 (U)	0
		2 (MA)	
		1 (JC)	0
	Clerical	0	0
Advanced technology and research unit	Sales and marketing	1 (U)	0
		1 (H)	0
	Clerical	0	0
	Research	2 (Ph.D.)	2 (MA)
Administration	Clerical	1 (U)	2 (U)
		1 (JC)	
Personnel and general affairs	Clerical	0	0
Other	Clerical	1 (U)	2 (U)

H: high school graduates; JC: junior college graduates; U: university graduates; MA: master's degree holders; Ph.D.: Ph.D. holders.
[1]These males did both sales and marketing work.

puses and held a series of seminars for selected candidates, which were followed by the first interview with aptitude and essays tests and further screening through one or two more interviews and finally a health checkup. Successful candidates received an informal job offer, usually by November or December, and joined the company the following April, right after their March graduation. The recruitment of female graduates (particularly college graduates) was, on the other hand, highly contingent upon the immediate personnel needs and the degree to which the company was pressured to comply by the larger social climate with the ideal of equal employment and opportunity for women.

For women what is called *chyūto saiyō,* or mid-career employment, was the major path of entry into MJL. With two exceptions, all the women I will describe in the following two chapters joined MJL through chyūto saiyō. This is an irregular form of recruitment in contrast to the strict age-based system in which primary-sector recruits entered the company as a cohort immediately upon graduation. During my fieldwork, thirty-two new female college graduates were hired in 1993. Forty-two mid-career women were hired in 1992 and 1993. One of the reasons women were available for mid-career hires became obvious in interviews. Many were ambitious, career-oriented women who had taken their first jobs in large Japanese companies immediately after they graduated from college. They quit, however, because they saw no chance of promotion or upward career development, given the internal gender-organized labor markets in Japanese corporations. They joined MJL because it was *gaishi*, hoping that it would give them more opportunities.

Mid-career hiring thus undermined hierarchy among female workers and constituted them as more or less an undifferentiated aggregate, despite their various backgrounds and experience. Most women recruited through mid-career hires were in the secondary low-paid, low-security, low-authority segment of the labor force and so were marginal to the company hierarchy anyway.[3] While the strict regular recruitment system with its age cohorts ensured that a male supervisor would outrank a junior male colleague not only in organizational rank within the company but also in career grade, experience, salary, and age, women workers recruited through the mid-career system were a less rank-ordered group. One female employee might be a twenty-seven-year-old junior college graduate who had been with MJL for six years, and her female colleague at the desk across from her might be a twenty-five-year-old graduate of a "good" university who had just been hired. One interesting consequence of such an ambiguity of any potential hierarchy was that women were often very aware of questions of speech level in speaking to one another. They had to figure out which factor—age, length of service, rank, or part-time versus full-time—should be the basis of level of speech style they would use to each other.

In 1986, in response to the enactment of EEOL, MJL reformed its pay system to abolish gender difference and equalize men's and women's base salaries *(kihonkyū)* among cohorts with the same education level. In this scheme, a female four-year-college graduate, for example, would receive the same base salary as her male counterpart hired in the same year, with the same academic credentials. This equal-pay system, however, applied only in the first five years of service. After that, the pay system incorporated discriminations based on gender as well as rank, age, occupation, education, and "ability." The salary difference between men and women in the same cohort with the same education was estimated to be about 40,000

---

3. As has already been mentioned, women also had relatively short tenures—six years on average—at MJL, no matter how they were hired. This also ensured that women would seldom be in a position to form any hierarchy among themselves, since no woman was likely to accumulate any appreciable power within the company.

yen (about $400) per month. On top of that, male workers in sales divisions would receive merit-based pay, which heavily influenced one's total pay. The salary gender gap inevitably grew, since sales jobs were available only for male workers, and women were engaged mostly in clerical work.

As described, recruits fresh from college created a relatively homogeneous age cohort; they were within an extremely narrow range of age at the time of entry to the company—between twenty-three and twenty-five for university graduates. Recruits would be twenty-eight to thirty years old at the end of the first five years of service. This was a critical stage for both men and women. For men, it was the point when workers who joined MJL in the same year began to be gradually differentiated within the company hierarchy. For women, this was the point at which many of them quit—for marriage and child care or for another job.

Toward Performative Histories of Women's Language

I started out my field research examining how certain speech acts routinized in the white-collar workplace are differently carried out by men and women, and, more concretely, how women in managerial positions execute the same linguistic tasks performed by their male counterparts. I was initially interested in coming up with a taxonomy of speech acts according to contexts, events, and tasks that routinely take place in the workplace. With the permission of the people in the office, I tape-recorded the conversations taking place on the office floor.

A week or so after I started running the tape recorder in the second office in which I was placed, some coworkers began talking directly to it when I momentarily stepped out to go on errands on other floors and in other offices. They used the recorder like voice mail, leaving me a message about whom I should interview for my research, simply saying hello, or other messages whose content was less important than the fact of leaving a message for me. At first I found this quaintly amusing, but later it became a theoretical challenge and eventually caused me to shift my research focus.

Researchers engaged in the study of language often limit legitimate linguistic data to the category they call "naturally occurring conversation." "Natural" in this case means that speakers are not conscious of the tape recorder in a way that affects speech, and that the technology for recording data pretends to be invisible and silently listens in on slices of people's everyday life like the proverbial "fly on the wall." The messages left on my tape recorder are thus traditionally considered the least legitimate of "linguistic data" because those who left the messages not only were fully aware of the machine, but even consciously "used" it in a way that it was not supposed to be used by informants in data collection (after all, it was not meant to be the researcher's answering machine). In the middle of my research, those playful messages, however, came to insist on this question: On what grounds can one say that one kind of speech is "natural" and others not? The fact is that the messages were uttered in real time and space. What is this, if not "naturally occurring conversation"?

A tape recorder is the ultimate metalanguage. It purports to represent reality in a most pure and faithful manner, and turns subjects of whatever it records into its objects with no trace of this process of mediation and objectification. Whatever is recorded—speech, interviews, and events—had its subject when it was executed. Once recorded, however, the subject loses its ability to represent itself. The tape recorder does not allow speakers to explain how they frame and interpret their utterances. It mechanically takes the speaker's voice sound, and it mechanically excludes her metalanguage, because it is the tape recorder (and ultimately the researcher's interpretation) that is the metalanguage.

The messages deliberately left on my tape recorder were theoretically disturbing to me, not because they compromised the otherwise "uncontaminated" data, but because they made me think about the politics of the supposed distinction between naturally occurring data and non–naturally occurring data, and allowed me to appreciate this binary as part of the technique of "truth" production in linguistic research, which reproduces the hierarchy between researchers as agents of metalanguage (theory), and speakers as agents of language (data). The messages left on my cassette tape exposed the very material existence of the tape recorder and its pretence of invisibility and transparency. When my coworkers "used" it to leave me messages, they demonstrated that they were conscious of the simple fact that the tape recorder as a thing shared time and space with the real and "natural" ongoing situation in which they spoke. It is like waving a hand at the surveillance camera at the mall—"You think I am not aware of you looking at me, but I am. If you look at me, I look at you, too!"

What I had missed earlier in my research was the dense layers of metalanguages that people themselves provide to frame their linguistic production, in the form of commentaries, theories, narratives, and strategies. I started paying attention not only to how people speak but also, and more importantly, as this book argues, to how people speak about how people speak, how people interpret their own speech and that of others. But such everyday commentaries on language use cannot be "elicited" by asking people "so, tell me what you think about how you speak." Narratives about language use are surreptitiously embedded in narratives about things other than language, and vice versa. Narratives about life, aspirations, the past and the future, the world, and so on draw upon the semiotic order and upon the coherence that narratives about language provide, to the extent that they are mutually imbricated in nondissociable ways.

Such narratives are central to my analysis in the next two chapters. Because language accumulates the history of its use, metapragmatic narratives are sites where, and means by which, people historicize and temporalize their lives, social relationships, and such social things as male and female, race and nation. Citing the law of Japanese women's language, however, in and through such local and contingent historicizations of language and self inevitably brings out moments of its displacement. Iteration is repetition *in difference* by virtue of the fact that every new iteration takes place in a new, different context, and language—and the social things it helps sediment—has a history. This recognition of the openness of discursive grounds thus formulates my question for the next two chapters: If the discourse of women's language is temporalized by that of Japan's national modernity, then how do women as historical actors linguistically and metalinguistically perform this temporality and, thereby, potentially disclose its paradox and contradiction? I describe several ethnographic moments when women diversely perform "women's language" as their radical alterity both to distance and to mimic, thereby invoking various cultural boundaries and social differentiations that cannot be contained by the binary of gender. Thus is women's language *defamiliarized* by showing it to be not about gender.

Through both their linguistic and their metalingusitic performances in everyday workplace contexts, women's metapragmatic accounts approximate what Bhabha calls "the performative," whose contingent, diverse, and repetitious enunciations of the sign intervene in the pedagogical narrative of the nation by "introduc[ing] a temporality of the 'in-between' through the 'gap' or 'emptiness' of the signifier that punctuates linguistic difference" (1990a:297, 299). The differences these women mark through performing "women's language" cannot be assimilated into the other designated in the discourse of women's language; they thus expose the ambivalence and contradiction in the discourse and undermine its fundamental stability, which is based on the tacit assumption of "Japanese" spatial and temporal homogeneity. What is at stake here is both the presumption that "women's language" is about women, and that "Japan" is a compelling cultural, linguistic whole either historically or geographically. How do the female workers at MJL rewrite the temporality that informs the discourse of women's language and its linkage with that of national modernity through their everyday citational practice of women's language, citational practices that are constitutively bound to fail?

I focus in the following chapters not only on how these women actually spoke but also on how they heard themselves speaking and made sense of their linguistic experience in the workplace and beyond in narratives that encompassed the past, the present, and the future. Talk about one's linguistic experience cannot be separated from talk about one's work experience and life history. The kinds of linguistic units, categories, and rules to which users' reflexive consciousness has access become discursive resources for them to make sense of, and thus to historicize, their arcs of life and work, and, in turn, to historicize their language use in life and work. I will describe diverse points of articulation between the social and the linguistic in intensely local and situated contexts of women at May Japan Limited. The rupture they create between the performative and the pedagogical radically historicizes and particularizes the idea of women's language and, thereby, disrupts its tacit yet stubborn linkage with national modernity and its temporality.

CHAPTER 5

"Just Stay in the Middle"
The Story of a Woman Manager

This chapter is about Yoshida Kiwako, one of the nine women managers at MJL. Interestingly, Yoshida-san did not use any of the utterance-ending forms associated with women's language in any context, which complicates and even obscures the mode by which and the location in which her citational practice constitutes her as a subject of women's language. Born and raised in Kansai in western Japan, she was not a speaker of standard Japanese until she moved to Tokyo. The speech forms typically associated with women's language, which would be readily available to standard-Japanese speakers, were not necessarily available to her unless she consciously chose to acquire and adopt them. What, of course, equally complicates the situation is her professional responsibility as a corporate manager, which has tensions with, and demands creative negotiations with, the ideology of gender and women's language. As I will show in this chapter, her linguistic strategy as a woman manager is ambiguous, to say the least. She represents a case that allows us to understand how the discourse of women's language is lived (and thus cited) by a historical actor who has no access to, or has made a conscious decision not to use, its most saliently associated speech forms, but who nonetheless speaks within its discourse.

Since they were so few in number, the women managers at MJL were highly visible. Among them, Yoshida-san appeared the least "spectacular," with no bright-colored business suits and no bright makeup. She was someone whom many Japanese would describe as *jimi,* modest or quiet. The other women managers were also more audible with their high-heeled shoes. Footsteps in high heels are the vibrant sound of the presence of female workers in the office, loudly announcing their entry and departure. I even learned to tell who was entering the office just by listening to the footsteps. But Yoshida-san always wore low heels. One of my coworkers jokingly said to me once that Yoshida-san would be right next to you or right behind you before you knew it because you did not hear her quiet footsteps in her low heels.

Although her reserved manner tended to make her appear inconspicuous, she was well known by many people—both men and women—at MJL as one of the *dekiru josei,* or "capable women." At the time of my research, Yoshida-san was the section chief of the Facility Management Section. I met her initially through my own part-time work, which required me to visit her section at least once every day. Later, I was introduced to her as a researcher through Okada-san, another woman manager, with whom I was working. She said to me, "Why don't you talk to her? She looks quiet, but she will burst forth with words if you ask the right questions. She has a lot to say because she is someone who 'knows her own mind' and is self-consciously an individualist" (*jibun o motteiru*; literally, has her own self).[1] After the formal introduction through Okada-san, I had more opportunities to have informal chats with Yoshida-san at work, sometimes in her office and at other times in the corner of the hallway, on the stairs, or in the elevator.

One day, she took me to her favorite *kissaten,* or a tea parlor, near the office, located in the fancy underground shopping and restaurant area at one of the busiest subway stations in downtown Tokyo. Passing by all the fancy restaurants, shops, and tea parlors, we got to the very end of a rather dreary blind alley, and there was her favorite tea house—a dimly lit, almost deserted *jimi* (modest) tea house—looking as if time had stopped around that spot in the 1970s. Looking around, I realized that we were

---

1. *Jibun o motteiru,* or *jibun ga aru,* is a frequently used idiomatic phrase in daily conversation. The oppositional phrase is *jibun o motteinai* or *jibun ga nai* ("not having self" or "lacking a self"). This idiom is often studied by psychological anthropologists who have sought to identify characteristics of the Japanese self. Lebra (1976:156), for example, in her reference to Doi Takeo's seminal book *The Structure of Amae* (1971), describes *jibun o motteiru* as "an individual's awareness of some independence from the group he belongs to, while *jibun ga nai* refers to the individual's total involvement in the group. Indeed, Japanese often take pride in the freedom of *jibun* and its power to resist social pressure." Distancing from the group is not necessarily enacted explicitly in one's opinions or behavior as being "different," "independent," or "resistant." This is particularly the case with Yoshida-san. As will be described shortly, her narratives emphasize her active compliance with her surroundings. Nonetheless, she can be said to have *jibun* because she can be independent even from herself, seeing and locating herself in relation to the surrounding world. See Rosenberger 1992 for a comprehensive overview of studies of the Japanese self; the collected articles in Bachnik and Quinn 1994; and Rosenberger 1992 for the range of studies done in this field.

the only women there. In the absence of fancy OLs (office ladies) or housewives, tables were occupied by worn-out salaried men with no company to talk with over tea or coffee. They all sat by themselves, reading or simply staring into space. Yoshida-san said that it was her secret place to come and relax because there she knew that she would never run into anyone she knew from work. In her secret place, she told me her "secrets," "things I don't normally talk about to people," as she put it.

She did not mean secrets in a sense that their exposure would embarrass her. She meant that they were not for "public consumption" as some kind of sharable and commensurable "recipes" for the making of a successful professional woman. While she—as well as the other women managers—was often invited to give talks about her experience as a woman manager both within MJL and beyond, she never accepted any of these invitations. She would say with humility, "I have nothing special to talk about." But I took it as a quiet but firm resistance to the commodification of her work experience, and as a quiet but firm request to me that I honor her stance. Her "theory" about language, work, and life, which she developed over the years, cannot be "canned" or commercialized into a "how to" program. Instead, she generously shared her philosophy with young female workers as an informal mentor.

Her narratives, which she carefully framed and protected as "things I don't normally talk about to people" were her "theories" that came out of intensive intellectual and critical reflection and soul-searching. Her responsibility as a manager and her visibility as a female manager forced her to monitor, think out, rationalize, and comment on how she spoke or should speak as a "woman manager." It is in this reflexive linguistic practice, in its incessant feeding to/from the actual production of speech, that Yoshida-san concretely—if only pragmatically and situationally—intertwined language use and structure, on one hand, and her social life, on the other hand, and developed specific and concrete configurations of indexical relations between the linguistic and the social. Narratives about her managerial work or her relationships with her subordinates were laid out in terms of how she thought she spoke as a manager or how she spoke to her subordinates. The distinction between them is creatively blurred in the everyday world of this woman manager.[2] It was at this gloomy jimi tea house, her favorite tea house, that I "rediscovered" this jimi woman

2. The semiotic condition that enables talk about language use to offer a template for talk about social connections has to do with a speaker's selective attention to some aspects of language that are referential, segmentable, and presupposing, the most readily available to their conscious use of language (Silverstein 1981). When people talk about language, at-

as a remarkable, even spectacular individual—articulate, intelligent, and perceptive—who knows who she is, where she is, what she has gone through, what she wants, and how she speaks.

Yoshida-san shared the material ground of knowledge and experience with women employees at MJL and with women workers in Japanese society at large. As I discussed in the introduction to part 3, it is standard operating procedure for companies systematically to assign different jobs to men and women (both vertically and horizontally). Women are located almost consistently in the domestic ("indoor") divisions—providing support for line employees or, in the lower strata, working for male superiors. Career development for women is contingent upon both the company's immediate personnel needs and the specific female opportunity structure regarding life choices (marriage, childbirth, and other expected domestic roles and responsibilities).

My goal in this chapter is to do justice to the ethnographic fullness of the work life of Yoshida-san—as I observed it and as I participated in office life with her, and as she thought about and explained that life to me. The complexity, diversity, and creativity inherent in her local linguistic practice—the richness, spontaneity, and social embeddedness of her speech and ideas about speech—overflow the idea of women's language and complicate the facile conflation of speaking and agency. Far from being "representative," but also not a mere "outlier," her case embodies one of the creative ways of being and speaking within the constraints and opportunities inherent in the material situation shared by women in the company and beyond that is connected to larger political-economic arrangements in mediated ways. Just as Ortner recognized that actors may "embody" class even if they do not "articulate it" (1991:184), so Yoshida-san embodies the discourse of Japanese women's language without articulating it.

Yoshida-san's Work at MJL

The Facility Management Office was one of three sections in the General Affairs and Facility Management Office at MJL. This office, in turn, was

---

tention tends to go to units of language that are bounded, such as lexicons and, in the case of Japanese, utterance-ending forms. It is this segmentability, referentiality, and pragmatic saliency of some aspects of language, such as a speech-level system, that enables linguistic actors to render their lives and selves, which are otherwise fragmented and partial, through reflexive accounts of language use into coherent and bounded "experience."

CHART 1. The location of Yoshida-san's Facility Management Office within the Personnel and General Affairs Unit.

```
Personnel and General Affairs Unit
├── Personnel Affairs Division
│   ├── Training
│   ├── Personnel I
│   └── Personnel II
├── Personnel Development and Planning Division
│   ├── Project Office
│   └── Personnel Department
│       ├── Recruiting Section I
│       └── Recruiting Section II
└── General Affairs and Facility Management Office
    ├── Facility Management Office
    ├── Housing Office
    └── Operation Section
```

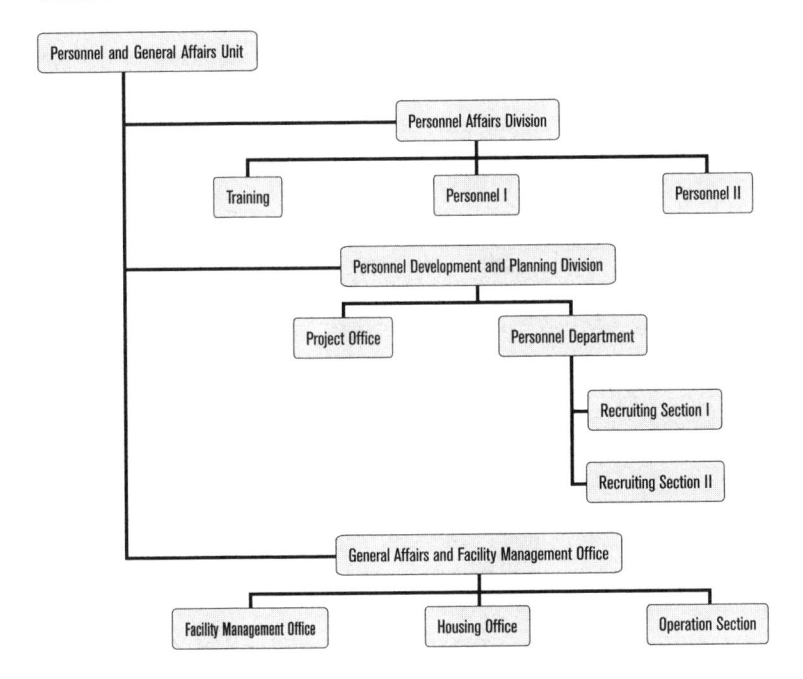

located in the Personnel and General Affairs Unit, along with the Personnel Affairs Division and the Personnel Development and Planning Division. The Personnel and General Affairs Unit was considered an "indoor," or *naikin,* domain of work in the unit level, which is contrasted with the three sales—"outdoor," or *gaikin*—units. Chart 1 locates Yoshida-san's section in the larger unit.

At the divisional level, the General Affairs and Facility Management Office can be characterized as the "indoor of the indoor" at MJL. The two other divisions—the Personnel Affairs Division and the Personnel Development and Planning Division—enjoyed a certain influence and authority over major corporate affairs; the former dealt with the management of the pay system, benefits, personnel training programs, and other matters directly related to individual employees, and the latter controlled recruitment activities. The General Affairs and Facility Management Office, on the other hand, had little influence in larger corporate affairs.

The Facility Management Office, headed by Yoshida-san, specialized in the most "domestic" of the support—therefore the most female-associated—services within the company.[3] These included ordering office supplies and stationery, tea leaves, employees' business cards, *hanko,* and *obento;* scheduling conference and reception rooms; receiving and distributing telexes from overseas; administering the company library; staffing the visitors' information and reception desk; assigning office space; arranging for building repair and maintenance; and stocking supplies for emergencies (such as an earthquake), to name a few.[4]

The Facility Management Office took a modest share of office space on the first floor, only as much as required for eight steel desks (two rows of four desks) pushed together to create a rectangular section. But the small size is misleading, since this office had one of the highest volumes of personnel traffic in the company. Yoshida-san's desk was placed across the aisle from the two rows of desks in order to command a full view of the eight workers. Her desk and chair were distinguished from those of regular workers: her desk was slightly bigger, with drawers on both sides instead of only one side, and her chair had armrests.[5] The section was cordoned off from the neighboring section by a modular partition, only slightly higher than the height of the average woman. The work environment was always noisy, with many incoming phone calls, visitors, and ambient noise from neighboring sections.

The eight staff members working under Yoshida-san's supervision were all women, whose ages ranged from twenty-three to thirty-nine years; Yoshida-san herself was forty-one. The women's desks and shelves were filled with a variety of colorful "Post-Its" with meticulously noted phone numbers, memos, and instructions for repetitive tasks. This color and clut-

---

3. Within the General Affairs and Facility Management Office, the Operation Section was MJL's post office, as it were, where mail was collected and delivered; the Housing Section was in charge of housing and housing allowances for employees and of relocating foreign executive delegates.

4. *Hanko* is a personalized seal used in place of one's signature in endorsing Japanese legal and other documents; all adults have such a personalized seal. At MJL, the size of a hanko normally corresponded with rank: the higher one's rank, the bigger the hanko. It also marked gender difference in that women's hanko were smaller and slimmer than those of men. *Obento* is a boxed lunch with rice, some side dishes, and miso soup. MJL provided this lunch free from a catering service as part of standard welfare benefits because of the company's location in a neighborhood where few eating places were to be found, and those few were very expensive.

5. When someone was promoted to a managerial position, he/she was provided with a new desk with drawers on both sides and a chair with armrests. Sometimes this modest privilege was sarcastically or jokingly mentioned by middle managers to make the point that, as one of the male section chiefs put it, "there is nothing good about being a manager. You have to work as hard as ever. After all, there is not much difference between *hira* [rank and file] and *kanrishoku* [manager]. The only difference is you've got a bigger desk and a nicer chair."

ter on their desks contrasted with Yoshida-san's desk, on which there was almost nothing but a telephone. While seven of her staff were full-time workers, one was a temp receptionist.[6] Yoshida-san also supervised two other workers (one male and one female) who worked in the company's library.

The most frequent visitors and (phone) callers to Yoshida-san's office were women clerical workers who performed similar tasks in their own sections. That is the capacity in which I visited or phoned Yoshida-san and those working under her. I used to stop at her office every day, for example, to pick up telexes or to bring order forms for office supplies and other minor support tasks. Visitors to Yoshida-san's office also came from outside the company: vendors who delivered office supplies, for example, and plumbers and electricians, dispatched from companies under service contracts with MJL. These people could be seen coming in and out of Yoshida-san's office. Very often she personally walked with the contractors around the building to discuss repairs, remodeling, and alterations of office space.

Yoshida-san's office was organized on a horizontal structure. Everyone in the section—except Yoshida-san—had equal responsibility and authority. Each employee was assigned all functions associated with a substantive task, so that one person would follow a project or problem through from start to finish. For example, if someone was in charge of ordering obento, she took orders from throughout the company, called any departments that neglected to place an order, totaled the orders, placed the total order with an outside vendor, checked the statement of delivery and payment, and stocked extra obento in case of unexpected need or emergency. Such an arrangement encouraged the decentralization of information, authority, and responsibilities attached to these jobs. In contrast, in the sales divisions, a low-level employee would merely record orders, which would then be filled by higher-ranking personnel.

This work arrangement was not, however, consciously developed by Yoshida-san. That is, the more "egalitarian" work structure was not a result of the fact that the head was a woman, but predated Yoshida-san's appearance on the scene. In fact, before the Facility Management Office was established, several of its functions had been assigned to various sections under male section chiefs. Even with male section chiefs, however,

---

6. It is common for companies to hire specialist temp receptionists such as this woman, whose professionalism as a receptionist was reflected by her bright red uniform jacket, good looks, polished makeup, and flawless use of elaborate honorifics for visitors.

the sections were nonhierarchically organized because of the particular functions involved. For example, when Yoshida-san first joined MJL—before the Facility Management Office existed—she was placed in the procurement department. This department handled all the support work for general affairs, including facility management–related tasks. Here, Yoshida-san found herself typing next to male coworkers who were also typing:

> There were no tasks that I had to do under someone's instruction or supervision. All the tasks were organized "horizontally."[7] So we, both men and women, were all doing the same work and we were all typing. So I did not have to feel a sense of discrimination because everyone, regardless of being a man or a woman, had a task with as much responsibility as everyone else's. It had a school-like atmosphere.

But even if a woman manager did not create this egalitarianism in the company, it is not a coincidence that a more egalitarian division of labor was found in a section headed by a woman, and that a woman was in charge of a section with a less prestigious role in the company. It may be that the kind of work the section did is most efficiently organized in a nonhierarchal way, or it may be that because there is so little power and prestige involved here, there is, in effect, nothing for people to form hierarchies over. In either case the "flat" line of authority—in effect, *no* line of authority—within the section resonated strongly with the general lack of power, authority, and prestige of this section headed by a woman.

The egalitarian structure was further enhanced by the members rotating the tasks on a regular basis. A monthly schedule arranged who did which job in which week(s) of the month. The job-rotation plan also assigned each member a secondary task to support the main person in charge. For example, the person in charge of obento was always backed up by someone else who could perform her task in case she happened to step out. They also made a "shadow" rotation table, as it were, for emergencies, when someone could not come to work or was on vacation. The monthly job-rotation plan allowed everyone to perform every job, and the section was able to perform every necessary task every day, regardless of individual absences. Furthermore, a complete manual for each task was available, which made it possible to incorporate a newcomer readily into

---

7. Yoshida-san used the term *tatewari* to refer to the horizontal division of labor. *Tatewari* literally means "vertically divided," in the sense that the individual worker is responsible for a particular task throughout the whole "vertical" process from start to finish. I here translate *tatewari* into "horizontally organized" to avoid the confusion the English term "vertical" might cause by conjuring up images of vertical hierarchy.

the workforce and standardize job quality, efficiency, and accuracy. These manuals often took the form of flow charts that illustrated the whole procedure in question, from start to finish. Whoever was assigned a particular task—whether she was experienced or someone who had just started—the outcome was expected to be the same assured quality.

This organization of tasks had the effect of minimizing Yoshida-san's daily interactions with—or, more specifically, daily authority over—staff members, particularly in the form of formal instruction or orders. Staff members only consulted her for the purpose of double-checking, final approval, and the occasional unexpected problem. Most of the problems and questions from the younger members and part-time workers could be solved by the senior and more experienced staff members, including Watanabe-san, the only *kakarichō* in the section.[8] The youngest and newest member, Nishiyama-san, who had just graduated from college and joined MJL a year before, for example, had few reasons to go directly to Yoshida-san's desk for consultation or help.

Besides her regular supervisory duties, Yoshida-san also had her own "production" job to do—just like her staff. This was the case with most of the middle managers in any section in the company. In the sales section, for example, a section chief managed the total profit goal and the marketing strategy, but he was also one of the salespersons who had his own customer accounts and had to contribute to bringing in profit. One male sales section chief explained to me, using military terms: "A section chief is like a commander at the front *[zensen-butai no taichō]*. You command and take responsibility for your unit. But you can't just sit back and order people around. You yourself also have to fight at the front." This responsibility to produce as well as to supervise was often described by managers as an indication of how petty was the power and authority a section chief could enjoy as a manager.[9]

Previously, when the company was rapidly expanding, Yoshida-san had worked on several projects, including standardizing company policy on air travel and arranging housing allowances and company housing. She

---

8. *Kakarichō*, as explained in table 1 of the introduction to part 3, is an official rank for senior employees without any substantial managerial authority or responsibilities. While it is not a managerial appointment with official supervisory duties, a kakarichō assumes more informal, but nonetheless required, day-to-day responsibility to give on-the-job-training to junior employees.

9. Some senior managers reminisced about this difficult situation of being a section chief as the most exciting and challenging aspect of their career—when they were young and the company was rapidly growing.

also handled large-scale procurement of office equipment. In each of these projects, she organized an ad hoc project team with selected—senior—staff members. In each, Yoshida-san was delegated formidable authority to execute plans and to contract with suppliers. She told me how much she enjoyed the air travel policy project in particular: "To make a regulation, you have to do a lot of research, and you can learn a lot. And once you make a regulation, it will persist, and people will rely on it. It feels great to see that something you worked very hard on is used and functions in the company."

Yoshida-san was quite articulate about how to manage her *buka* (subordinates): "My way is simple. All I do is to assign this person a job and leave it completely to her/him *[makaseru]*, and offer to care *[keaa suru]* but never to cut in." By "care," Yoshida-san meant an unobtrusive guidance that respects the autonomy and creativity of her buka and their ability (not "treating them like children") and that provided them with a sense of security that comes from awareness of support. Yoshida-san continues:

> I want to be someone who is always there, available for my buka whenever they need help. I do not teach them how to do their job by "holding their hands and feet" *[te-tori ashi-tori]*. I do not do that because it would be like treating them as if they were children, I think. But I also want to give them a sense of security that I am always behind them and support them.

In fact, makaseru is widely recognized in the business world as an ideal managerial style by both managers and their subordinates. When, in the winter of 1992, MJL's newsletter reported the results of a survey conducted by its Public Relations Office on the communication and perception gap between supervisors *(jōshi)* and subordinates, makaseru was listed by bosses as one of the ideal manager's attitudes toward subordinates.[10] But, in comparison to Yoshida-san's situation, makaseru was often difficult to execute for managers and often caused resentment on the part of subordinates. This was particularly the case where jobs were organized on a vertical, sequential model. In the sales section, for example, complex jobs were divided into sequential tasks and assigned to different people who each contributed their part in sequence. In this vertical organization of

---

10. The survey, entitled "Between Bosses and Subordinates" (Jōshi to buka no aida ni wa), was administered to two hundred MJL employees. The purpose of the survey was to examine how personnel in the positions of supervisor and subordinate felt about each other. The supervisor-subordinate dyad was the essential unit of the hierarchal culture of the company. Both the joys and the bitterness of company life for employees were often linked in discourse to this dyadic relationship, particularly from the point of view of subordinates.

tasks, reminiscent of a factory assembly line, makaseru often resulted in the roles for these cooperative, sequential tasks being annoyingly ambiguous.[11] A manager who failed to direct and assign specific responsibilities in an unambiguous way could only cause difficulties for his subordinates. There was constant negotiation—as well as contestation—between the section chief and his staff over who should do what job. Who should, for example, work on a set of handouts for a unit-level meeting? The actual operation of a word processor might be a rank-and-file employee's job. But who would work on the content? Who was going to collect and organize the data and other material? Who would get the credit when the presentation at the meeting went very well and received compliments from the unit manager? In such a context, makaseru could easily be interpreted, from the point of subordinates, as being irresponsible, abusive, and manipulative.

In fact, makaseru was also frequently mentioned as one of the managerial skills that women managers purportedly tended to lack. When I attended a seminar for women managers sponsored by the Japanese Ministry of Labor and its affiliated organization, the Institute of Women's Employment, for example, one of the lecturers pointed out the inability "to makaseru," or to delegate tasks to one's subordinates, as being typical of women managers and a critical drawback for them (obviously, makaseru means more than simply delegating authority, as seen in the text above, but the shorthand translation will suffice for present purposes). The lecturer said, "While men have no problem with this, women have tremendous difficulties in delegating tasks to their subordinates because women don't have a role model and rarely have an opportunity to see what it is like to manage an entire office. Makaseru is the first step to assuming a managerial position."[12]

In Yoshida-san's case, makaseru was a more feasible style because of the horizontal work arrangement. Because each job was followed from

---

11. The lack of a concrete job description was often characterized as "Japanese" or "traditional" by MJL employees. During my research, the company underwent a series of reforms in the job assessment system, which was intended to reorganize the existing seniority-based and gender-based promotion and pay systems, ultimately toward a more merit-based system. One of the changes under this reform was to describe explicitly the responsibilities attached to each job.

12. See Lebra (1992:403), who captures this view of women as lacking the ability to makaseru in her interview with a woman entrepreneur: "Mrs. C wants to promote a woman to departmental chief, a position now monopolized by male staff, but not until the female managerial candidate learns to delegate some tasks to her subordinates instead of trying to do everything herself."

start to finish by one person, it made sense to leave that person to use her own best judgment throughout the task. This is not to deny tension or conflicts in her office deriving from the ranking between her and her staff and between junior and senior staff members, but people were aware of the difference between her makaseru style and unsuccessful attempts at it in the sales division. Yoshida-san described her (support) work—in comparison with that of male colleagues—as *komakai,* or detailed and minute, and claimed a natural connection between even such komakai work and the essential characteristics of women.[13]

During the late 1980s and early 1990s, "female management style" was imagined, celebrated, and anticipated, by both women themselves and the society in general, as a more nurturing and enlightened alternative to the "male management style." This essentialized female management style included many of the things that Yoshida-san talked about as her (female) style, and it was pointedly different from what male managers actually did or could do in the company. The point is, however, that it was different not because of essential male/female alterity, but because of (gendered)

---

13. See Ong (1987:152–53) on factory owners and investors valorizing the "biological" aptitude of young (Asian) women for semiskilled assembly line work that requires detailed manual dexterity. Such a discourse can be found even in reference to recent highly skilled jobs that are increasingly available to women in Japan, such as computer system engineer, which also tend to be characterized as requiring the quality of *kime-komakai,* and, therefore, as being suitable more for women than men. *Kime-komakai* is almost synonymous with *komakai,* except that the former intensifies the degree of meticulousness with the additional word *kime* (texture), "meticulous, detailed, careful." During the late 1980s and into the early 1990s, when women's labor was in high demand, large corporations cultivated their progressive image in terms of gender-equal employment opportunity by opening new offices and programs staffed by women only. In such promotions, the essential advantage of femaleness in business was claimed through such ideas as the quality of *kime-komakai.* One example is a company that was featured by one of the national newspapers for its "women-friendly" recruitment and management program. Mitsui Marine System Development Co., a subsidiary fully owned by Mitsui Marine Insurance Co., was reported to recruit exclusively women and to provide generous benefit packages acknowledging maternity needs. The head of the General Affairs Department explained why they exclusively hired women: "Computer system development requires creativity and the quality of *kime-komakai,* and women have a remarkable aptitude for it" (*Nihon Keizai Shimbun,* October 24, 1994).

Yoshida-san's claim for gender essentialism is complex. It is a subtle but decisive response to the prevailing Japanese (and, of course, Western) evolutionary imaginary in which the ongoing social and economic change in Japan will eventually make Japanese women look like and act like Western women. The image of women managers in Japan—well educated, economically independent, assertive, and feminist—is one that is considered particularly "American." Yoshida-san's affirmation of gender essentialism is expressed through her critique of what she imagined as American women fighting for equality and aggressively leveling gender difference (inequality). "I think that America is going to extremes a bit. It is unreasonable to try to eliminate the difference between men and women because they are structural constraints and opportunities: Yoshida-san was able to be egalitarian and unobtrusive because of the specific work arrangements and functions in her office. If this had been a sales section, things might have been very different. If there was anything like a "female management style," it did not come from some biological aptitude or even gender habitus, but from the concrete social conditions under which women's managerial work has been gendered and associated with a less hierarchical organization and greater distance from the site of profit-making.

Yoshida-san's Life History

Yoshida-san joined MJL in 1976 through the mid-career employment program. She was in her mid-twenties at the time of hiring. She had married in 1973, immediately after graduating from a four-year college in Kansai, and her husband worked for a Tokyo-based bank. Upon her husband's transfer to the Tokyo headquarters, they moved to Tokyo from Osaka. For the first three years of her marriage, Yoshida-san stayed home as a housewife. Such a leisurely or slow *(yukkurishita)* life, as she put it, however, did not suit her: "I grew up in the countryside, and my mother was always working out in the fields. She was such a hard worker. I helped her a lot with housekeeping when I was a child. And seeing my mother working outside, it was just a matter of fact *[atarimae]* that I should work outside the home. When I first got married, I was restless. I could not possibly enjoy staying home at leisure."

One day Yoshida-san happened to see an MJL job advertisement in the subway, which eventually brought her to the company. She was hired on the condition that she would go to an English-language typing

---

physiologically different. It might work in America, but not in Japan. We don't have to imitate America. The best way is to be true to *shizentai* [natural posture]; rather than competing with men, women should cherish their own innately given abilities, and men should also cherish their own innately given abilities, and that's how men and women can complement each other. That's what society is about. It is a division of labor. In the company, too, there are certain jobs that women have higher aptitude for, and there are other jobs that men are much more suited for. Indeed, work is sometimes hard, and I have gone through various hardships because I am a woman. But there is always some room in the company, or in the society, where women can excel." Gender essentialism in contemporary Japan, whether understood as an effect of social structure or as innate difference, in feminist or nonfeminist terms, is a markedly *Japanese* one, and thus inseparably upholds the essentialism of the Japanese race, nation, and culture as against "the West."

school at her own expense. In the next six months, she diligently learned how to type. This, however, should not be understood as a sign of commitment and enthusiasm, as she cautioned me: "Originally I intended to work for just three months. I just wanted to feel 'the breeze outside' *[soto no kaze]*. At that time, I never assumed that I would stay for this long a time."

After her first three months, when Yoshida-san was ready to quit as she had planned, she was approached by her boss, who asked her to stay until a replacement was found:

> So I thought, "I am going to work for another three months, for the time being, until the end of the year. Then I will quit." But all the women who had just been hired quit, one after another. The work was hard, and the workload was enormous. Sometimes we had to come to work on Saturdays, without even being paid overtime.[14] As a result, no one lasted more than six months, and I kept missing the chance to quit. But every day I kept saying to myself, "OK, I will quit tomorrow."

She said that what made her stay in the company was not income that might buy financial stability or independence from her husband, but the idea that she would never again be able to work outside the home once she quit. Yoshida-san explained:

> Most of the women, you know, were young and unmarried, and they quit for good reasons; they weren't well-paid, their benefits were not good, or they were assigned to a type of job that they had not expected or wanted. If you are married, these would not be sufficient reasons for quitting your job. I think I could not find any legitimate reason for quitting. It did not matter much to me how much I got paid, because I was married. I wanted to quit, but I knew somewhere in my mind that the fact that the work was hard was not enough of a reason for me to quit my job. In the first three years, I used to make long phone calls, or write long letters, to my mother, exploring the question of whether or not I should quit. My mother never suggested that I should quit, but said, "be responsible for whatever you decide to do." I never complained about my job in front of my husband because I knew he would say, "I have never asked you to go out to work! If you want to quit, just do it!" And once I quit, I would not be able to get another job because I knew my husband would never let me.

In those days, for a woman to change jobs *(tenshoku)* was out of the

---

14. MJL had always had a five-day week, officially. In the early days of which Yoshida-san was speaking, however, a five-day week was still extremely rare and considered a business practice associated with *gaishi,* foreign-invested firms.

question, she said. Within the first ten years, she wrote her resignation letter about every three years, every time she became ill and could not go to work. And as she handed it to her boss, he would tell her, "You can think about it when you get well." When she got well and went back to work, she found herself all the more inclined toward staying in the company. Soon after Yoshida-san wrote her third resignation letter, she received an offer of promotion to kakarichō, the first step to the managerial track. Ordinarily a promotion is not made as an offer, but because she is a woman, her supervisors thought it best to find out if she wanted the added responsibility before they gave it to her. She was thirty-four years old. Yoshida-san recollected: "I was not prepared for that at all. I had no idea what it meant to be promoted to kakarichō. Besides, I did not even want to be promoted. I just wanted to work without much responsibility *[kiraku-ni]*. But my boss said to me, 'We don't need anyone who is getting senior but wants to remain a *hira* [rank-and-file, nontitled employee].' So I had no choice." It took her more than a year to make up her mind to accept the offer. The final decision came, however, when she learned that she was infertile. She said, "If I could have become pregnant, I would never have accepted that promotion." Yoshida-san's self-described career history is characterized by her subdued ambition, stressing that she did not aggressively pursue career advancement, but as she describes in her narrative, took more responsibility within the company as an afterthought on the part of a married woman who clearly had other priorities.[15]

In 1985, Yoshida-san accepted the promotion to kakarichō in the section she had started in at MJL. In 1987, during a company reorganization, she was promoted to *kachō* (section chief) of this new unit, the Pur-

---

15. Yoshida-san's presentational style for her life history stressed the degree to which her agency was not involved with the course of events. In other words, whatever came to her, she presented herself, not as the agent who made it happen, but as someone who simply accepted the outcome. This seemingly passive reconstruction of agency was in fact shared by almost every woman manager I interviewed. Any career success or achievement was presented in such a way that the narrator did not actively seek it, but merely fell into it. In her studies on Japanese female entrepreneurs, Lebra notes a similar pattern: "What surprises me is that launching an enterprise, which would seem to call for great commitment, is also recalled and presented in such a self-suppressing style" (1992:386). While recognizing this more as a generally observable (Japanese) "cultural style" that basically characterizes both men and women, Lebra continues: "The inconspicuous status accorded to self may characterize both female and male Japanese autobiographies as a matter of cultural style, but the same principle is likely to be more rigidly applicable to women, who need extra justification for launching an unfeminine career to protect themselves from looking selfish."

chasing Section in the Procurement Department.[16] She became a manager over ten subordinates (eight female and two male). The transition to the position of kachō was, according to Yoshida-san, smooth; her boss was promoted to an upper managerial position, and his position was offered to her, the oldest of the possible kakarichō candidates, and she became his successor. The functions of her new section were similar to those of her previous one. No new skills were necessary on her part, but Yoshida-san recollected: "For the first time, I was responsible not only for my job, but for my buka, what they do, and even their families." In 1990, after a short appointment to an ad hoc taskforce committee, Yoshida-san was transferred back to the Administration Unit and was assigned to head the Facility Management Office.

"Staying in the Middle": Yoshida-San's Metapragmatic Accounts

Just as she had a clear idea about the way she managed her office, Yoshida-san had a reflexive account of how she spoke in the workplace. One time she told me, "When I was younger and was just one of the rank-and-file employees *[hira-shain]*, I did not really care about how I spoke. I think I used to say just what I liked and spoke in the way I liked. But now, I am much more conscious of how I speak." Yoshida-san's attention to language use specifically centered around the polite utterance-endings *desu* and *masu*. On several occasions, she told me how the use of *desu* and *masu* was critically linked with her position as a woman manager:

> In order to make things go smoothly, I think *kotobazukai* [language use] is very important. Now, I am not an expert, and I think you know much better than I do because you are an expert. But, well, this is just my idea from my own experience, but I think I make it a rule to speak in *desu/masu [desu masu de hanasu]*, whoever the person is, whether this person is a vendor or top management. You know, men really do not like a woman to stand out. If you stand out, if you are in a certain kind of position, such as being a woman and a manager at the same time, you are all the more resisted and pressured. You need to learn how to evade it. The best way is to become neither plus *[purasu]* nor minus *[mainasu]*, neither the head nor the tail,

---

16. MJL underwent several reorganizations. The Purchasing Section was established by integrating several domestic-related offices and dealt with most of the functions the Facility Management Office performed at the time of my fieldwork, when Yoshida-san supervised the latter.

just to stay in the middle, not too polite, not too rude, not to go too far ahead or too far behind, not to stand out, but not to be ignored either. This is my stance [*kore ga watashi no sutansu nandesu yo*]. So I stay in the middle in the manner of speaking, too.

Grammatically speaking, *desu* and *masu* are what are called "polite" auxiliary verbs placed at the end of an utterance and may be joined with verbs, adjectives, or nouns. As part of the broader sense of honorifics, they mark politeness or deference to the person addressed. *Desu* and *masu* are used as the most normative—and therefore almost unmarked—speaking style in public institutional settings, including the white-collar workplace. Insofar as these forms are "polite," Yoshida-san does not violate the norm of women's language, that is, being "polite." But using *desu* and *masu* regardless of the context and the interlocutor could be seen as ambiguous, as possibly violating the norm, for the ideal way of speaking as a mature adult is often said to entail flexibly shifting speech styles according to the context and the interlocutor. In this style of speaking, one is expected to use honorifics when one speaks to someone senior or of higher social status. In other words, such code-switching is expected and idealized for reproducing the existing social order and hierarchy. Thus, given such a prevailing linguistic-social norm, the consistent and universal use of *desu* and *masu* might not always or necessarily be the unmarked strategy.

In fact, Yoshida-san's speech style was "flat." This flatness or genericness was best explained by one of the young female workers who was known to be the best impersonator in the company. She told me, "I can impersonate most of the people in the company, including the (male) senior executives. But Yoshida-san is the hardest to impersonate, because she has no *kuse* [characteristics] in her manner of speaking." Her "stay-in-the-middle" strategy kept her linguistic style-shifting to a minimum, regardless of her interlocutor. Even with those junior to her in terms of age, rank, or business relationship, Yoshida-san usually maintained a polite speech style, as shown in examples 1 and 2. She also often avoided utterance-ending forms, so that her speech did not entail any social marking other than the basic civility of being polite. This was particularly the case with some close subordinates and colleagues with whom she has had a long working relationship.

Yoshida-san's metapragmatic account—staying in the middle—embodied an intensely local configuration of language use and structure, on one hand, and relevant aspects of her (company) life, shaped by gender and corporate hierarchy, on the other hand. When she emphatically

EXAMPLE 1. An exchange between Yoshida-san and a male vendor (age 27).

(1) V: (kon'nichi)wa::   itsumo   osewani   natte **ma**::**su**
                                                                                                        be-POLITE
(2) Y: ha::i   gokuroosama**de**::**su**
                                                                                                               be-POLITE
      aa Tanaka-san moosugu   modotteki**masu**   kara
                                                                return-POLITE
(3) V: a ... ( )
(4) Y: chotto   matte**kudasai**-ne::
                 wait-POLITE
(5) V: ( )

Translation

(1) V: (Hello) Thank you (for using our service). [formulaic expression]
(2) Y: Hello thank you (for your trouble) [formulaic expression]. Oh, Ms. Tanaka will be back soon,
(3) V: (I see . . .)
(4) Y: so please wait for a moment.
(5) V: ( )

   Transcription conventions from Gumperz 1992 and Shibatani 1990 (for Japanese glosses). Indented lines show speech overlapping with line above.
      . . .   pause
      ::   lengthened segment
      ( )   unintelligible speech (which may be filled in if it can be surmised)
     POLITE polite style
   Y: Yoshida-san; V: vendor

stated, "this is my stance," it is clear in the context that the discourse can hardly be reduced to mere language use or her identity as a woman manager abstracted from language use. Language use and position as a manager were inextricably intertwined. It is in this sense that her metapragmatic configuration of "just stay in the middle" was not accidental, nor was it permanent or an essentialized part of her as a consistent subject or agent. It was rather developmental, situational, historical, and political: it emerged at a specific moment of her life under specific conditions. Yoshida-san began to become aware of the "problem" of kotobazukai when she was promoted to kakarichō and kachō. Given the prevailing assumptions about women's language, it might be thought that the problem emerged directly out of her need to find an appropriate way to supervise subordinates—as a woman. This was not, however, the source of the concrete problem she encountered. First of all, the work in her section was routinized and horizontally organized so that she had few occasions on which she had to supervise directly or issue instructions. Her duties as a section chief were far from authoritative, and therefore in no way made her status as a woman, or her language, problematic.[17]

Rather than her supervisory responsibilities in her own section, it was her interactions initially with male colleagues of section-chief rank and higher from other divisions and units that created the situation in which "gender" emerged as a social category in conflict with the role of manager, and "language use" appeared both as a practice and as an object of contemplation to resolve the tension between them. As Yoshida-san put it, "I never realized or even thought about what it meant for a woman to be a manager until I went outside of my own office." She told me, on separate occasions, about her awakening experiences outside of her office, which unfolded through a series of events connected with her promotion to managerial positions. These opportunities to interact with (male) managers outside her section, she believed, allowed her to shape her own knowledge of kotobazukai, which she explained as her "stay-in-the-middle strategy." The spatial metaphor was apt for describing her attempt to find her social "place" as a woman manager both in the realm of language and in the corporate organization. Yoshida-san recollected: "I distinctly remember when I first started seriously thinking about my own kotobazukai." It was when she attended *shinnin kakarichō kenshū* (the workshop for newly appointed kakarichō). This was a collective four-day in-house training workshop held at MJL's seminar house, located in a resort area outside of Tokyo, for those who had just been promoted to kakarichō. The workshop was designed to provide basic skills in the areas of leadership, goal-setting and achievement, and personnel management. The seminar emphasized the development of self-awareness and understanding of others in order to be a good communicator. Seminar participants were asked, for example, to describe their jobs objectively and explain them to their group members. Transactional analysis was also introduced, by which the manager could reach a "scientific" and "objective" understanding of himself or herself in a network of social relations. The participants took part in work simulations where group members collaborated to solve a

---

17. Some of the women managers I interviewed outside of MJL also told me that the self-awareness of being a manager does not come so much from the exercise of power and authority in their daily (vertical) interactions with their subordinates, but from the sense of relatedness to, or involvement with, larger corporate affairs.

EXAMPLE 2. An exchange between Yoshida-san and Sasaki-san, a younger male worker (age 28), over the parking fee.

(1) S: de chuusharyoo wa mata betsu ni . . . . **haratten-no** -**kana**?
                                              pay-PLAIN   I wonder-FP (informal)

(2) Y: kore betsu ni ( ) ee   ( ) kara **desu**
                                         be-POLITE

(3) S: shanai de kariru toki wa doo **suru-no**   -**kana**,   chuusharyoo
                                    do-PLAIN   I wonder-FP (informal)

(4) Y: anone   **itadaite-masu**   ano eekan no chika no ( ) ano nakaniwa ni natteru tokoro   **desu** ne
                charge-HON   be-POLITE

(5) S: ha:: un

(6) Y: soko wa muryoo **desu**
                     be-POLITE

(7) S: a soo   **desu** ka
               be-POLITE

(8) Y: anoo senyoo suru baai wa   yuuryoo **desu**
                                           be-POLITE

(9) S: un . . . yuuryoo donokurai **desu** ka?
                                                           be-POLITE

(10) Y: sanman hassen en

(11) S: sanman hassen en   **desu** ka
                                    be-POLITE

Translation

(1) S: So have we been paying a parking fee separately?
(2) Y: We (charge) this, yes, from ( )

(3) S: How does this work within the company?
(4) Y: Well, we charge a fee. You know, that place in the basement of "A"-Building ( ) in the courtyard.
(5) S: Yes, yes.
(6) Y: Those areas are free of charge.
(7) S: I see.
(8) Y: Well, it is charged if it is for exclusive use.
(9) S: How much is it?
(10) Y: 38,000 yen.
(11) S: I see, it is 38,000 yen.

Transcription conventions from Gumperz 1992 and Shibatani 1990 (for Japanese glosses). Indented lines show speech overlapping with line above.

…   pause
::   lengthened segment
( )   unintelligible speech (which may be filled in if it can be surmised)
FP   final particle
HON   honorific
PLAIN   plain style
POLITE   polite style

Y: Yoshida-san; S: Sasaki-san

hypothetical problem—which had no bearing on their actual daily work—from designing a timetable to making presentations to the other groups about how and what they did.[18]

Yoshida-san was one of the three women participants; the remainder—about forty-eight—were all men. The participants were divided into groups consisting of five or six people each. The three women were spread among the different groups. Yoshida-san was in a group with five or six male colleagues. Her recollection of the seminar concentrated on the awkwardness she initially felt in the group discussion:

> The group discussion was quite something. Well, I used a lot of *ki [ki o tukatta]*.[19] Everyone in the group was kakarichō, of course, so our rank was the same, and everyone was equal. But, here is the problem. First of all, they were all men except for me. This made me wonder how I should participate in the group discussion and how I could fit in. Should I just keep quiet? Or am I expected to play a different role? You can't just sit there and say nothing. It is a discussion, so you have to say something. Then, another problem was that we were of all ages![20] Some were nearly in their late forties, and others, late twenties. So I decided to wait and see for a while.

Interaction with male workers equal to her in rank was nothing particularly new for Yosida-san. The difference between the regular work context and group discussion at the seminar was that while the ordinary work context would position men (because the nature of her office is a support

---

18. The training seminar also aimed at both formal and informal exchanges among kakarichō across the divisions and units. Ordinarily, these managers would have no opportunity to get to know one another, but collegial interaction in the seminar aroused a sense of solidarity and professional competence, as well as professional rivalry. In general, collective in-house training seminars, from the freshman seminar to those for specific managerial ranks, allowed participants to have a sense of connectedness with or belonging to the larger corporate organization. This was particularly the case for those who worked in regional branch offices.

19. *Ki* is described by Rosenberger as "the basic energy of the human being—mind and body" (1989:94). There are a variety of idioms in which *ki* is combined with other verbs and nouns to refer to emotions and actions. "To use *ki*" *(ki o tsukau)*, therefore, refers to the act or the state of being attentive and accommodating to others: their feelings, needs, and expectations. Situations when one might have to use his/her *ki* include, for example, social relationships with strangers; interactions with people senior in status to oneself, such as a teacher, a supervisor at work, or in-laws; and interactions with others potentially involving a degree of tension and uncertainty.

20. The age when (male) workers were promoted to kakarichō varied to a greater extent at the time Yoshida-san described. The company was still not large enough to attract new college graduates and had to rely heavily on the mid-career employment program. Age, as well as previous work experience and educational background, therefore, varied among employees at their point of entry into the company.

role) as her "customers," the situation of group discussion required her—as well as the male members—to talk and to work together on a totally equal basis without relying on a regular work relationship. The rule in this training game was that rank—equal status—trumped other differences such as age, job description, and, most of all, gender. As the group discussion proceeded, she began to notice a pattern of interaction among the (male) participants: some specific men were constantly talking, and some others persistently kept silent. Describing her discovery, Yoshida-san said, "There are various kinds of male workers. When they are taken out of the regular work environment, they really show what kind of personality they have." The course of the discussion and the subsequent decision making were in the hands of particular people, while others, including Yoshida-san, were silenced. Then she thought about her role, or how she could contribute to the discussion:

> I wanted to do something to change the atmosphere of the group discussion so that those quiet people could also participate in the discussion. So I started speaking politely by using *desu/masu*. If you use *desu/masu*, it is neither too polite, nor aggressive or intimidating, is it? You know, it worked very well! I don't remember what I actually said, but after I started speaking, the quiet members gradually started speaking. I made them more comfortable about speaking by nodding and saying, "*Sō desu nē*" [It is, isn't it?], or "*Dō desu ka, naninani-san*" [How about you, Mr. So-and-so?]. I think that, because I am a woman, speaking consistently with *desu/masu* broke the high-tension atmosphere in the discussion.

Soon after Yoshida-san was promoted to kakarichō, she worked on setting up an office for a newly established division, which required her to work closely with a male division manager in his late fifties, senior to her both in rank and age. In close consultation with him, Yoshida-san made a large-scale purchase of furniture and office supplies, and arranged for interior finishing. She recalled: "I consciously avoided using honorifics to him; whenever and for whatever reason I had to talk to him, I remained on the same level with *desu/masu*, being neither too familiar nor too distant."

Later, back in her office, Yoshida-san was further assured of the benefits of her "just-stay-in-the-middle" strategy. As I have previously described, when Yoshida-san was first promoted to section chief, she supervised ten subordinates, two of whom were male workers. The two male subordinates soon became a concern not for her, but for her supervisors. One of the male workers was kakarichō, only two years junior to Yoshida-san, and the other was a freshman. Yoshida-san was directed by her superiors to let the male kakarichō take care of the male freshman through OJT (on-the-job-training). Her supervisors decided that it would be difficult for someone like Yoshida-san, who had just been promoted to section chief, to train a male freshman, and that it would more beneficial for him to receive his first training from a male senior member, rather than a woman, even if she was higher in status.

As a rule, during OJT, an informal and close hierarchical relationship is established among section members, between a junior staff member and a senior. In this particular case of two male subordinates, however, Yoshida-san's supervisors had decided that the fact that they were the only male members made it all the more crucial for Yoshida-san to completely leave the freshman's OJT to the male kakarichō. This way, the male kakarichō, whose title otherwise had almost no substantial formal authority, could create a small-scale hierarchy and experience exercising authority through the process of "teaching" and "guiding" the freshman. More importantly, this was aimed at evading the male kakarichō's sense of possible indignation at working under a woman's supervision.

The arrangement, however, did not work. Yoshida-san found that these male workers did not get along with each other. Even though the male freshman expressed his wish to be placed under Yoshida-san's supervision, this never happened, and he subsequently quit his job. Yoshida-san analyzed this mismatch, and her analysis took the form of a subtle critique of how some male workers were obsessed with the ideal of work sustained by the masculinity-hierarchy association. She said to me,

> The male kakarichō had various ideals in his head, theories of "ought-to's" *[bekiron]*, as it were, like how men should be, how the work should be done, how a man should behave as an "organization man" *[soshikijin]*. So the issue was how that young freshman could fit into his ideal picture, not how he could understand who he was and what he was thinking about. As a result, that male kakarichō became really frustrated with the young guy, because he did not "grow up" in the way the male kakarichō taught him to. Work is not something that you do with abstract ideals. One must first look with cool eyes *[sameta me de]* at what you are expected to do in the given workplace, and then act upon it.

Then Yoshida-san referred to the kotobazukai of the male kakarichō as part of his problematic idealism and reflected upon hers as a lesson:

> His kotobazukai was overly polite and obsequious to people in higher status, using honorifics, and he spoke in very casual and bossy tones to people junior to him, particularly to that male freshman. The gap between when

he was polite and when he was casual was huge. I think he thought that's how he "ought to" speak in the workplace. Maybe he was intentionally authoritarian and preachy to the freshman in order to train him to be a full-fledged businessman. That male kakarichō was my lesson. From the point of view of people under me, particularly male subordinates, I think they want me to be a stable, reliable, and always accessible person, so that there is no need to ask, "Oh, do I have to *gokigen ukagai* [to feel out how someone is doing, or if he/she is in a good mood or not] her?" or "Do I need to *ki o tsukau* [use *ki*] when I talk to her?" That's why it is important to control yourself and your kotobazukai. If I am constant with my kotobazukai, always staying in the middle, using *desu/masu*, they do not have to worry about such things. I think they expect me to be someone they feel free and comfortable with coming up and talking to anytime, whenever I am there. Then, what happens is that you get more information from people.

For Yoshida-san, "staying in the middle" embodies the linguistic topography of affect and of corporate hierarchy in which "the middle"—emotionally neutral and hierarchically (socially) medial—is the "place" she self-consciously identified: accessible from and available to people from the top to the bottom. Given the particular history of her work experience, which I detailed above, this position and strategy were irrefutably a gendered topos shaped and enabled by the gendered structural arrangement in the corporate organization as well as in Japanese society in general.

Taking the Middle Road: Managerial Position, Gender, and Class

As I mentioned in the beginning, Yoshida-san does not use the speech forms associated with women's language. Example 3 gives part of a conversation between Yoshida-san and her closest female manager colleague, Kimura-san. It shows a contrast in which Kimura-san uses feminine utterance-ending forms, while such forms are absent in Yoshida-san's speech.

The way Yoshida-san reiterates the norm of "women's language" does not involve the familiar cultural imaginary of gender marking by the speech forms stereotypically associated with "women's language," whose historical development and dissemination as an ideology I have described in previous chapters. It entails a different semiotic mode, whose effect, if elusively, displaces its regime of normalization. Yoshida-san's citational practice of women's language is located at a different level, has a different

EXAMPLE 3. An exchange between Yoshida-san and Kimura-san, another woman manager, part of a conversation that took place when Yoshida-san gave Kimura-san a pair of crystal wine glasses with a respected brand name for her fortieth birthday.

(1) K: [while opening the present] WA:: KORE:: (BAKARA)JANA::I

(2) Y: kyonen issho ni mini itta toki sokono ga iitte   yutteta-**desho**
                                                                                                             be-POLITE

(3) K: HE:: yoku oboetete kureta -**wa**::   takai   -**no**yo::   kore::
                             FP(feminine)   *FP(feminine)*

(4) Y: kotoshiwa   ne   Kimura-san mo oodai dakara [laugh] . . . funpatsu shite to   ***omotte*** . . . [laugh]
                  FP(neutral)   *think-GER*

(5) K: ma:: honto ni::?

(6) Y: dezain wari to   ii-**deshoo**?
                      be good-POLITE

(7) K: ureshii   -**wa**::?   ARA:: wain made tsukete   kureta-no::?
              FP(feminine)   *get-PLAIN*

Translation

(1) K: Oh my goodness, isn't this (Baccarat)?
(2) Y: Last year when we were looking together, you were saying that you had wanted the one from that brand, weren't you?
(3) K: Oh my goodness! How nice of you to remember that! This really IS expensive.
(4) Y: Because you have finally made it to the forties this year . . . I decided to dish out for you, so . . .
(5) K: Oh dear, you really?
(6) Y: The design is not so bad, is it?
(7) K: I really like it. Oh, you even got me wine, too?

Transcription conventions from Gumperz 1992 and Shibatani 1990 (for Japanese glosses). Words in all caps in the transcription indicate extra emphasis.

. . .	pause
::	lengthened segment
( )	unintelligible speech (which may be filled in if it can be surmised)
?	final rise
FP	final particle
GER	gerund, verb + *te* form
PLAIN	plain style
POLITE	polite style

Y: Yoshida-san; K: Kimura-san.

logic and different tensions than the kind of linguistic constraints and possibilities associated with women's language. In other words, her being constituted as the subject of women's language involved a specific semiotic venue and terrain.

Her awareness of language use—developed from her historically contingent and situated standpoint—did not concern matters that have been identified as the "female" speech style—specific final particles, elaborate honorifics, and other co-occurring speech forms. Rather, her attention to language use—her citational practice of women's language—revolves around the polite utterance-ending forms *desu* and *masu*, which have *no fixed or direct indexical association with specific gender*. *Desu* and *masu* are, in principle, gender-neutral. They can mark femaleness only in a *relative* sense, conceivably when she uses *desu/masu* while the interlocutor does not reciprocate, in which case the asymmetrical exchange makes her "more polite" than the other and thus compliant with the norm of women's language use, that is, "be deferential and polite." But such a mode of marking that relies on the contingency of the context is ambiguous, if not unviable.

In her "stay-in-the-middle" strategy, the significance is not the use of *desu/masu*, or its indexical marking of "being polite" per se. What is more crucial is the polite utterance-ending's *paradigmatic relation* with other classes of linguistic alternants, or its relative positioning within this pragmatic system, which iconically produces the meaning of "the middle," and "staying in the middle" as Yoshida-san eloquently expressed it. It is this semiotic mapping of speech level that is at stake and where the regulatory ideal of women's language hails her. Apart from the scholarly classification of speech styles, the everyday sense of speech level identifies three classes: the plain style, the polite style, and honorifics. *Desu/masu* is considered to be in the category of polite style, the middle category.[21] It is common for Japanese speakers to gloss its style as *desu/masu de hanasu* (speaking with/in *desu/masu*).[22]

---

21. The difference between *desu* and *masu* is morpho-syntactic, rather than stylistic. *Masu* is attached mainly to the adverbial inflection of a verb, while *desu* is attached to auxiliary verbs, adverbs, adjectives, and nouns (and nominalized forms):

(a) ka-ki *masu*
write- ADVERBIAL + *masu*
"(I) write."
(b) ringo *desu*
apple- NOUN + *desu*
"(It) is an apple."

22. In a more scholarly glossing, it is often called *teinei-go* (polite language or speech). The formal category of teinei-go does not, however, perfectly correspond with the folk glossing

The polite style is contrasted with honorifics *(keigo)*, which entail two classes of speech level: "respect language" *(sonkei-go)* and "humbling language" *(kenjō-go)*.[23] In a simple sense, use of *keigo* marks a higher level of politeness or deference than the polite style. The polite style, *desu/masu*, is further contrasted with plain utterance-ending forms, which are those without *desu/masu* auxiliary verbs or honorifics. The following shows the contrast between utterances with a plain utterance-ending form.

(a) Messēji ga *aru*. (plain form)
    aru- PLAIN VERB
    "There is a message (for you)."

(b) Messēji ga *ari-masu*. (polite form)
    ari- PLAIN VERB + *masu*- POLITE AUXILIARY VERB
    "There is a message (for you)."

It is commonly observed that speakers of Japanese organize such different utterance-ending forms as three distinctive classes of speech style—the plain style, the polite style, and honorifics—and recognize a paradigmatic relationship on a continuum of degree of politeness or deference. Honorifics and plain forms are at the poles of the continuum, and polite language is in the middle. The location of the *desu/masu* form in its relation with other classes of speech style, rather than its own indexical value as a politeness or deference marker, is central to Yoshida-san's metaprag-

---

"speaking with *desu/masu*." Both scholarly and more popularized literature, including self-help "how-to" books on honorifics, include in the category of teinei-go another verb-ending form, *de-gozai-masu*. Ordinary people, however, clearly differentiate *de-gozai-masu* from *desu/masu* in terms of degree of politeness, or deference, and formality: *de-gozai-masu* is perceived to be far more polite than *desu/masu*. Thus in the following utterances (b), with the verb-ending form *de-gozai-masu*, would be perceived as much more polite than (a), with *desu*.

(a) Hai, May Japan *desu*.
"Yes, this is May Japan Ltd."
(b) Hai, May Japan *de-gozai-masu*.
"Yes, this is May Japan Ltd."

23. In a broader definition, however, the polite style is included as part of the honorific system, which is composed of three speech levels. They are, in order of degree of deference, *kenjō-go* (humbling language), *sonkei-go* (respect language), and, at the lowest level, *desu/masu* style, or *teinei-go* (polite language) or *teinei-tai* (polite style). But the narrow definition of honorifics is more prevalent in its popular classification: *keigo* refers only to respect language and humbling language. Furthermore, *desu/masu* is distinguished from the narrow definition of honorifics in terms of the orientation of deference: *desu/masu* is oriented toward the addressee, while honorifics (respect language and humbling language) are oriented toward the referent (see, for example, Shibatani 1990). For a comprehensive discussion of the various theories and classification systems of honorifics, see Wetzel 2004.

matic account. The spatial or iconic location of the polite utterance-ending forms—what Yoshida-san understands as "the middle"—enables her to define her social and affective positionality. She regiments her linguistic practice through her concrete experience in the workplace and likewise regiments her life in the workplace by mapping it onto the indexical order of the paradigmatic relation of the three speech styles and thus by "staying in the middle," both in the actual social world and in that of the linguistic. And if there is any sense of agency on her part, it emerges not so much through the indexical practice of pointing to and mediating some contextual features, such as gender or class, as through the iconic practice of positioning in the realm of linguistic structure.

"Staying in the middle" was the situated knowledge through experience over the years in which Yoshida-san learned to become a manager. Beyond this local process, however, the "middle" also indexes Yoshida-san's topos within the broader society in both class and cultural terms. This "middle" location within the realm of the linguistic also marks the *cultural* term of "middle-ness" in class relations—to which she aspired to belong.[24] As has been mentioned in chapter 2, the *desu* and *masu* polite utterance-ending forms were the products of the gembun'itchi movement and the government's promotion of language standardization. In postwar Japan, it came to be designated as the desirable linguistic style of new, democratic civil society, not unlike the norm of public politeness reflected in the term "civility" in the United States. In 1952, the final year of the American Occupation, the National Language Council, an advisory body of the Ministry of Education, issued a proposal titled *The Future of Honorifics* (Korekara no keigo). This proposal illustrates the state's official language policy in postwar Japanese society, promoting its vision of the direction people's use of honorifics should go—toward more plain and simple forms—and listing the speech forms and styles that the government designated as "desirable." Whereas in prewar Japan, use of elaborate honorifics was encouraged to mark social hierarchy in the society, in postwar Japan, a self-consciously "democratic" country, the basic manner of interaction in civil society should exclude explicit linguistic markings of social hierarchy.

In this statement, *desu* and *masu* are officially recommended as the basic style of public conversation:

> Generally speaking, the conversation of adults in society is one of mutual equality, and yet it must contain respect. On this point, language use be-

---

24. I thank Michael Silverstein for encouraging me to develop this point.

tween, for example, public servants and the public, or all the various workers in a workplace, should take *desu, masu,* as fundamental, [because of its] being of a form that is kind and polite. After the war, clerks and the authorities had already put such language into practice along these lines, but from now on it is to be desired that this tendency achieve even more universality. (*Korekara no keigo,* 1952, translated in Wetzel 2004:117–22)

They thus constitute a "linguistic utopia" (Pratt 1987), in which anonymous citizens of the new postwar democratic Japanese society, marked neither as male nor female, neither high status nor low status, speak with civility, mutual respect, and rationality. The social location that this utopian language indexes is equally a utopian topos of "the middle class," in which people are formally equal, homogeneous in democratic values, and equally well off. This is a class position that Yoshida-san has aspired to achieve, not only in political-economic terms, but also in cultural terms that accord her cultural citizenship as an unmarked citizen. "Staying in the middle" in the domain of affect and that of corporate hierarchy is then linked up with a middle-class position and sociality.

But understanding this middle-class position needs to take into account the specificity of Japan's cultural hierarchy and disjuncture. The pervasive cultural and economic boundary between "Tokyo" and the undifferentiated rest, which relegates the rest of the country simply to the category of "regions," or *chihō,* is often translated into the terms of a spatial disjuncture and temporal lag that informs binaries such as the sophisticated and the backward, the advanced and underdeveloped, the urban and the countryside, and other associated hierarchicalized pairs. The mass-mediated Japanese cultural imaginary of Tokyo is of a middle-class space filled with salaried men and housewives and with cosmopolitan citizens, whereas "the rest" is imagined to be trying in vain to catch up with the former. In the domain of language use, this internal cultural hierarchy between the center and the rest is saliently mapped onto the imagined difference between standard Japanese, presumably spoken in Tokyo and its metropolitan region, and "dialects," or *hōgen,* presumably spoken in "the rest."

Coming from a region in the western part of Japan, as a dialect speaker, Yoshida-san was put in a position that required conscious adjustment, not so much economically as culturally, in her transition to Tokyo and to a professional (managerial) career. For her, being "professional" is in part being able to display the Tokyo middle-class habitus, including language use. As shown above, she did not use speech forms explicitly associated with "women's language." Because utterance-ending forms are contextually open to indexing social meanings such as gender, region, class, age, and other differences, by not learning to use them, or by simply avoiding them, she marks no linguistic trace of the social, be it gender, region, class, or even social relationship. "Staying in the middle" was her culturally mediated class strategy.

The Enigmatic Subject of Women's Language

Yoshida-san's linguistic strategy is, however, neither new nor exclusive to women. Let me draw out Mr. Fujita's case for the purpose of comparison. Fujita Tetsuo was one of the sales section chiefs—a line manager—in a sales department of the Synthetic Materials Unit, where I worked for six months. Fujita-san was in his mid-forties, and his demeanor was often described by his colleagues and people under him as soft-spoken and gentle. One day, when seven or eight workers from the same division, including Fujita-san and myself, were eating our obento lunch together, Fujita-san asked me how my research was going and if I had discovered anything interesting; this prompted an interesting lunch-time conversation topic for that day. We started talking about who spoke in what manner, who spoke the most polite language, who spoke the most feminine language, and who was the worst communicator in the company (which quickly generated a list of people who were all senior managers). The conversation proceeded through both entertaining impersonation and serious contemplation of how to use language in the workplace. Would linguistic skill in terms of how to use honorifics help one to be promoted? Would skill as a speaker be as important as job performance in advancement? Would self-help books and business etiquette workshops for newly hired employees really help?

The following exchange took place when I asked Fujita-san for his thoughts. He began it by saying

> I think I always try "to narrow the range of kotobazukai" *[kotobazukai no haba o sebameru]*, to speak with *desu/masu* to everyone, whether this person is above me or below me, because that way, I can suppress emotion. Some managers show emotion at work, don't they? They raise their voice or say things loud without much thinking. That's not professional. When you are doing your job *[shigoto]*, you have to remain calm and keep the same state of mind at all times, everywhere and with everyone, and even if you are in a bad mood or worried about your personal problems. *That's* professional.

Then Yamaguchi Keiko, a twenty-six-year-old female worker who worked under Fujita-san, said to him, "I think you are always soft-spoken and polite *[teinei]*." Fujita-san replied, "Well, it is not that. It is not 'polite.' I think, if you use only *desu/masu* consistently, you treat everyone with equality, which means sincerity. I think that is what it takes to do business." Because he was normally quiet and seemed to prefer to take the role of listening rather than speaking even at lunch time, it was a rare occasion for many of the workers at this lunch, including myself, to hear him passionately and eloquently talking about his philosophy of professionalism. One of the workers at the lunch later said to me, "I did not know that he had such deep thoughts!"

It is not surprising that Yoshida-san and Fujita-san arrived at the same apparent strategy for and theory about language use and its relationship with professionalism, since the *desu/masu* form is recognized as a salient and normative linguistic form in institutional and public interactions. Both of them displayed their understanding of the paradigmatic relationship of the speech forms system as three hierarchically organized, distinctive classes—the plain, polite, and honorific styles—a hierarchy regimented by the social idiom of politeness and deference, and situated themselves and their linguistic strategy in the middle. Based on their different work and life experiences, shaped by the company as well as the society at large, they narrativized it differently. Fujita-san turned the indexical meaning of politeness and deference into the matter of self-discipline and the emotional state of the inner self, through which he expressed his ideas about leadership and professionalism. For Yoshida-san, the consistent and universal use of *desu/masu* was metaphorically aligned with neutrality and unmarkedness that—she strategized and hoped—could override gender and organizational stratification, so that she could "treat everyone in the same way," and would not "stand out."

Such difference in the cultural rationalization of *desu/masu* is, however, not directly connected or reducible to gender difference. What is most critical, but least visible, is the fact that this seemingly similar practice and strategy of using *desu/masu* are regulated and rendered viable by different regimes of discourse, by which Yoshida-san and Fujita-san are hailed as and into different subjects of gender. In other words, the practice of "stay in the middle," which they are compelled to repeat, seemingly as knowing subjects, is a forced act of citational practice by which they are mobilized into different fields of subject formation. For Yoshida-san, "staying in the middle" belongs to the discourse of women's language as a linguistic practice to cite its law, however elusive and dislocating it is.

Just like her appearance, demeanor, and her favorite tea house, her linguistic strategy of "staying in the middle" seems *jimi*, or modest, passive, and even conservative, but is a resilient one precisely because its effect is ambiguous. This elusiveness accounts for the fact that she speaks from a position that the discourse fails to name. She does not use women's language in an overt sense. Yet she does not speak against women's language, or outside its regime, either. In her use of *desu/masu*, she speaks within the discourse of women's language, citing its regulatory ideal and responding to its call with no sign of disobedience. Her strategy, and the semiotic position that it creates as "the middle," ambiguously circumvents all the possible positions and names that the discourse designates as *external, oppositional,* or *deviant:* she speaks neither like a man nor like those women whom the public debate charged with corrupting women's language, as we saw in chapter 4. Her strategy also approximates neither the cultural imaginary of bossy and aggressive women in authoritative positions nor that of urban upper-middle-class housewives, confined to the domestic space and adorned with excessive honorifics. It also eludes the sexist innuendo, as in the survey question we saw in chapter 4, that women calculatingly attempt to make an advantage of their femininity by using women's language for their career promotion.

What transpires is an enigmatic trace of a doer, or an enunciator, who leaves very little trace of the singularity and contingency of her deeds and who appears to be loyal to the law of the discourse. By virtue of minimizing the disjuncture between the discourse and the body that cites it, however, its effect produces her appearance as a sovereign, self-knowing doer who originates the discourse and her identity through language use.

Her citational practice refuses to identify itself with the subject position the discourse hails her into. Instead, it points to a position of the abject *within* the discourse of women's language, the position that it fails to name. In other words, her "staying in the middle," while being regulated by the discourse, nonetheless resulted in dislocating the terrain and in shifting the terms in which the law of women's language is to be cited. It is the effect of this regulated misplacement or decentering that makes her its enigmatic subject and her linguistic strategy effectively elusive.

Yoshida-san's case complicates our understanding of the act of speaking. The term *choice,* as assumed to be universally available to everyone according to the National Language Council, does not constitute her linguistic-gendered agency. As someone from a regional area, her original encounter with women's language was the "authentic" copy, overpoweringly mediated by the cultural imaginary of femininity and femaleness constituted by Japan's national modernity. For them, women's language is not a viable linguistic "choice" in the same way that it is for those with generational and habitual access to it. The temporality of their transition to the nation's cultural, economic, and linguistic center inverts that of the national narrative of women's language, in which it claims to originate in the actual bodies of female speakers. More importantly, this temporal inversion entails the visceral and estranged experience of its culturally and historically dense layers of meanings that makes untenable the assertion of women's language simply and only as a gender marker. Yoshida-san also shows us that agency cannot be directly identified either with the sovereign act of speaking or with the intersubjective exchange and construction of the signs, for what is at stake for her is the iconic *positioning* within what she construes as the system of speech level. What is highlighted here concerns the possibility of agency in the *impossibility* of choice (Butler 1993a:124) or the (im)possibility that arises from within the very regime of discourse that attempts, in repetition, to repudiate it and to erase the trace that it repudiated. This is the general condition for any project of linguistic agency.

CHAPTER 6

Defamiliarizing Japanese Women's Language
Strategies and Tactics of Female Office Workers

In this chapter, I will introduce some of the female workers at MJL with whom I worked as a peer. Although different in age and in the types of work they did at MJL, they were all hardworking, intelligent, and fun-loving women, and I came to be fond of them as we worked together. Their linguistic practice and experience vis-à-vis the discourse of women's language show remarkable diversity and mark different kinds of social differentiations and tensions, as well as meaning-making, that are central to their sense of who they are and who they want to be. For them, "women's language" is already objectified as the voice of the other, and they perform women's language only in the act of citing it. Citing and quoting are simultaneously acts of evaluation (Voloshinov 1973). We can see how "women's language" emerges as an aftereffect of their performing and can therefore evaluate it in historically contingent contexts.

These women invoked the idea of women's language to claim social positions that are, paradoxically, unintelligible within the discourse of women's language and the temporality it creates. It is those moments when women's language is invoked to mark unrepresentable locations and identities within its discourse that radically expose the internal contradiction of the very idea of Japanese women's language, and thus destabilize its normativity and familiarity. Observing the ways in which Japanese women's language is inevitably vulnerable to multiple cultural enactments by different individuals according to their social locations and the ways in which such evaluations have material consequences for individuals allows us to destabilize its identity and to see how it is embedded in social relations inherently saturated with power and inequality.

Tanabe-san and Ikegami-san

Tanabe-san and Ikegami-san were twenty-five-year-old female workers at MJL. I became friends with them initially through my placement in the same business unit (the Synthetic Materials Unit). Upon my introducing myself to them, they showed their curiosity about my research. Using their formidable personal network in the office, they took the role of my "consultants," providing me with the latest stock of gossip in the company and telling me whom I should interview and how I should approach prospects.

Tanabe-san was born and raised in Kanagawa, south of Tokyo but within the metropolitan region, and Ikegami-san was from Tokyo proper. Both were daughters of middle-class salaried-man families. Majoring in economics, both of them graduated from one of the well-known private universities in Tokyo in 1989 and joined MJL the same year. Along with two other women, they were the first female four-year university graduates ever hired and placed in the Synthetic Materials Unit, which many MJL workers described to me as the most conservative business unit in the company when it came to the treatment of female employees. This was part of MJL's voluntary compliance with the prevailing national politics at that time—a liberal commitment to equal employment opportunity for women. In the year that Tanabe-san and Ikegami-san joined MJL, new female employees were allowed to take a one-week English-language program that previously had been exclusively for new male members. And for the first time, new female employees were allowed to carry *meishi*, a business card, whereas previously the company made business cards only for male employees.

When it came to job assignment, however, "equality" was not necessarily the case. While their male counterparts were assigned to marketing and sales, Tanabe-san and Ikegami-san were placed in "indoor" work. Tanabe-san's job was to handle orders by phone and fax and to manage stock control of products, while Ikegami-san worked at compiling and analyzing sales performance data. This kind of work was equally shared by other young female workers who were only junior college or vocational school graduates. Not satisfied simply with the given tasks, they made various attempts to expand their range of work more toward sales planning and to improve the efficiency of their workplaces. The commitment and ambition they demonstrated went well beyond that of their male supervisors.

Dressed with casual sophistication in the latest fashions and impeccably yet naturally made up, they were what I had imagined young female workers at a foreign-invested company would be like. Quick, cheerful, and affable, they were also very popular among young male coworkers. When we went out for drinks, I used to be amused by a handful of young male coworkers who were shy and quiet at work but who, with a little help from beer and sake, would desperately try to impress them. Unlike their male counterparts, who would worry about too long an absence from the office, Tanabe-san and Ikegami-san did not hesitate to use up all their paid leaves as a matter of *right,* enjoying overseas travel on vacation. At the same time, they were well-respected by both male and female colleagues of their cohort and beyond for their professional competence: they were bright, capable, fluent in English, and articulate. Ikegami-san once said to me that her motto was "Yoku asonde, yoku nonde, yoku hataraku," meaning "Play hard, drink hard, and work hard."

I was first intrigued by their language use, which reflected their persona as young female professionals on equal footing with their male counterparts and thus to be differentiated from mere "office ladies." For example, they called each other by their last name, a common practice among male workers, while women customarily address each other by their first name or surname + *san* in the workplace. Women are customarily addressed by their surname and *san* (as I do here) by men and women of all ranks, and they are also expected to address both men and women by their surname and *san*.[1] Tanabe-san and Ikegami-san also called some male workers junior to them by their surname plus an address term, *kun*. When it is used by a woman to address a man, *kun* is often perceived as impertinent because an asymmetrical exchange of *kun* often marks a sharp status and age difference. A familiar context in which a man is addressed with *kun* by a woman is a school setting, in which a (female) teacher addresses a (male) student. In anticipation of the presence of more female managers, the popular media in the late 1980s and early 1990s often carried images of male workers humiliated by being called *kun* by a female manager.

The women's language use was also characterized by a consistent absence of any speech form identified as feminine in private conversations between Tanabe-san and Ikegami-san or between them and their male peers. This speaking style is often referred to as *tomodachi-kotoba,* literally meaning "the language of peers," and self-help books for women normally caution them to refrain from using it in the workplace. The most strik-

1. In some sections and divisions, particularly in sales divisions, where the organization rested on a rigid and sharp hierarchy, managers were addressed by their surnames plus their managerial titles. It was, however, the company's tradition (still relatively new at the time I did my fieldwork) through the initiative of the CEO, who was not Japanese, that all employees, regardless of rank, should be addressed by their surname plus *san*.

ing aspects of the two women's linguistic practice in the workplace was, however, the skillful, and even thrilling, swift and perfect *code-switching* between their gender-neutral and informal speech style and an elaborate and flawless use of honorifics when answering business phone calls. I often observed moments of swift code-switching, such as in example 4.

The conversation between Tanabe-san and Ikegami-san was not only informal but also characteristically gender-neutral. In fact, some of the utterance-endings they used, such as *dayo* and *yo,* could even be identified as "masculine" forms (see, for example, Okamoto 1995). As soon as Tanabe-san picked up the phone, ready to talk to a customer, however, she swiftly code-switched to an elaborate honorific style: deference was demonstrated first by correctly and appropriately using the honorific term of address *sama* for an outside call with Mr. Asada ("Asada-*sama*") and honorific verbs, and correctly and appropriately using humbling language, not only with reference to herself but also to MJL's Mr. Shinoda, by which he would not be referred to with any polite term of address, but simply be called "Shinoda." Also, her code-switching entailed equally appropriate and measured pitch and speed: she deliberately slowed down and increased pitch on the outside call, whereas with her coworkers she spoke much lower in pitch and much faster. Furthermore, Tanabe-san demonstrated her mastery of professional phone manners by controlling an ideal sequence, efficiency, and information exchange (Wetzel and Inoue 1996). For example, in Japanese business-manners workshops, it is commonly stressed that when one takes a phone message, one should not give details about why an absent person is not available (just say "out of the room"), and that one should always double-check the name of the caller before hanging up. Tanabe-san executed such practices flawlessly

Tanabe-san also successfully demonstrated conformity to the norm of women's language in its broad contours, since her practiced honorifics use is gendered on multiple levels. First, it satisfied the idea of women's language in that women (should) speak politely. Second, it demonstrated her linguistic capital marking her "good upbringing." Third, not unlike a telephone operator, it is women's job in the office, on account of the clerical nature of their work and their nontitled rank, to answer the phone and to transfer to whomever the caller requests. Because initial business phone calls from customers and business partners are expected to be handled by women, the honorifics use expected in such phone calls is also gendered.

What is significant, however, is not so much Tanabe-san's ability to handle business calls with consistent and skillful honorifics use, but her flexible and swift switching back and forth between polite language with

EXAMPLE 4. An exchange between Tanabe-san and Ikegami-san, interrupted by a customer's phone call.

(1) T: hora   koko-**dayo**,   kore:::
       Look,   here is-FP (informal, gender neutral) this

(2) I: aaa   kore-**ka**::
       ahhh   this is-FP (informal, gender neutral)

(3) T: soo   koko kara   zure-chatte-run-**jan**
       right   from here   out of alignment be-PLAIN

(4) I: aaa
       ahhh

(5) T: ichidan   ageru ga ii-**yo**.
       by one row   better to move it up-FP (informal, gender-neutral)

(6) I: koko o   so::**ka**
       here   so-FP (informal)
       aaa
       ahhh

(7) T: chotto   originaru . . .
       for a moment   original

[The phone rings; Tanabe answers.]

(8) T: hai   MJL kagakuhin bu   de **gozai-masu**.
       hello   MJL Chemicals Section   it be-HON

   a   mooshiwake-**gozaimasen**,   Shinoda   wa   tadaima   a   seki o   hazushite-**ori-mashi-te**
       sorry   be-HON   Shinoda   is   now   seat   step out-HON

       hai   sugu   modotte-kuru to   omoi-**masu**   ga . . .   itsumo osewa ninatte-**ori-masu**.
       yes   soon   return   I think-POLITE   but   always   be indebted-HON

       hai . . . hai . . . a   sayoo de **gozai-masu-ka** . . .   soredewa   a   modori-**mashi-tara**   hai
       yes   yes   be so-HON   then   when return-POLITE   yes

       orikaeshi   odenwa   sasemasu . . .   hai . . . a   sayoo de **gozai-masu-ka** . . . .   de-**gozai-masu-ne**
       by return   phone call   make him   yes   be so-HON   be-HON

       shoochi-**itashi-mashi-ta** . . .   hai Kurihara kemikaru no   Asada-sama   mooshiwake-**gozai-masen-deshita**
       yes understand-HON   yes Kurihara Chemical   Mr. Asada   be sorry-HON,

       hai shoochi **itashi-mashi-ta**   hai . . .   taihen
       yes understand-HON   yes,   very much

       hai hai . . . shitsurei-**itashi-masu**.
       yes yes   excuse-me-HON

[Tanabe-san hangs up the phone]

(9) T: originaru   mitemina-yo.
       original   *look at-FP (informal, gender neutral)*

Translation

(1) T: Look, here it is, this one.
(2) I: Ahh, this—
(3) T: Right. It is from here that things are out of alignment.
(4) I: Ahhh—
(5) T: You should move it up by one row right here
(6) I: Oh, I see.
(7) T: The original—
(8) T: Hello, This is MJL Chemicals Section. [Formulaic phrase for greeting customers, meaning something like "We are always indebted to you."]

I am very sorry, but Shinoda has stepped out right now and, yes, I think he will be back soon, but, yes, yes, I see. Then, as soon as he returns, I will have him call you. Yes, I see, yes, I understand. Is your name Mr. Asada from Kurihara Chemical? I see. Yes, I am very sorry [that Shinoda was not available]. Yes, yes, Good bye.

(9) T: Why don't you look at the original?

Transcription conventions from Gumperz 1992 and Shibatani 1990 (for Japanese glosses).

. . .	pause
::	lengthened segment
( )	unintelligible speech (which may be filled in if it can be surmised
FP	final particle
HON	honorific
PLAIN	plain style
POLITE	polite style

T: Tanabe-san; I: Ikegami-san

outsiders and plain language with Ikegami-san. In a stark contrast with her persona of playing a lot and drinking a lot and with their college student–like playfulness between themselves even on the job, when it came to taking care of business, Tanabe-san did it perfectly in a professional (and feminine) manner.

Tanabe-san, Ikegami-san, and I occasionally went out for drinks after work. Conversation often came around to the recurrent and pressing topic of "marriage or work." Both Tanabe-san and Ikegami-san were determined to quit their jobs for marriage and child-bearing—or in order to do something else. They did not make this a secret at work. Although they were hired with a great deal of fanfare and expectation as the first female employees promised company treatment equal to that of their male counterparts, and although they claimed that they were quite happy with their pay, benefits, and work assignments, they presented themselves as having no interest in permanent careers with the company. They got used to my habitually saying *"mottainai"* (a waste [of talent]) every time we got into a conversation about their eventual resignations. And every time, my mottainai met with their gentle smile, as if they wanted to say to me how hollow it sounded and how little I understood what constituted happiness for them.

One time after they had told me that they enjoyed working at MJL, I asked why they were not interested in pursuing their careers. Ikegami-san said:

> I think both I and Tanabe—well, I am going to involve Tanabe because we have been talking about this a lot these days [Tanabe-san was nodding and smiling]—we are talking about our work situation over, let's say, the next ten or fifteen years. Would you like to be one of those worn-out "middle-aged men" *[ojisan]* who go to work simply by inertia and live their life for no purpose other than receiving their monthly salary? They have no will to try to make their office a better place, no will to nurture or train *[sodateru]* their subordinates. I do have sympathy for such middle-aged men. I think that women can have a choice, and men can't. But you have only one life to live. We don't think we want to become like them.

Tanabe-san jumped in and continued:

> We have no desire to be promoted to higher ranks *[eraku naritai to wa omowanai]*, right? [asking Ikegami-san, who nodded in agreement]. If I have to use my time, I would like to spend it on my own child. Even if you spend your time for the company and work hard for the company, it will not do anything for you in the end.

Their disappointment with their ojisan male superiors who, perhaps jealously, quashed their every attempt to do more and better in their jobs is obvious. Equally obvious was their liberating idea of "choice" in that life is in one's sovereign control in a series of choices one chooses to make.

The conflicting forces among the availability of college education for women, the increasing market for educated female labor (at the time), and the ideal middle-class woman's role as a domestic reproducer in the nuclear family of industrial capitalism provided middle-class, college-educated young women with a structure of opportunity in which paid work is one of the options, but not necessarily an essential or preferable one for long-term survival. But, at the same time, their educations and the then-new "culture" of gender equality made it difficult for young women like Ikegami-san and Tanabe-san to identify with their housewife mothers. In fact, they took pains to differentiate themselves from their mothers. Ikegami-san jumped in and continued: "But, it is not that we want to be like our mothers' generation, staying home and sacrificing everything for their children and husbands. The deal would be [laugh] to be able to do something for myself and by myself, without sacrificing my family." Tanabe-san added: "Right, I just don't want to get old and become a mere old woman [obasan] living in a small and isolated world. I would like to maintain contact with society, whatever form it might take, and to continue to learn things."

The generational distancing, the alienation from and rejection of the housewife role, symbolized for them by their mothers' generation, heavily shaped the ways Tanabe-san and Ikegami-san located themselves vis-à-vis "women's language." For them, it was the language of their mothers' generation. On one occasion when we went for a drink, the conversation concentrated on "how not to end up being an 'ordinary old woman' [futsū no obasan]." Tanabe-san, after emptying a glass of beer in one gulp, said to me:

> Inoue-san, I swear! Even when I get to thirty or forty, or more, even when I become a mother, I will *never* be speaking like a middle-aged woman. I don't know how I will be speaking, but this is for sure: I will never be saying such-and-such *desu-wa*, or such-and-such *desu-noyo*. They just sound so archaic, and . . . I don't know how I can say it, but they just don't sound like me. However old I get, I would like to be like myself *[jibun wa jibun rashiku aritai]*, regardless of the expectations out there. Ten or twenty years from now, you can come back and check to see if I am speaking like an *obasan*.

Referring to speech forms associated with women's language, *wa* and *noyo* compounded with the polite auxiliary verb *desu*, Tanabe-san presents them as the language of alterity, with which she passionately dis-identified herself. "Women's language" here emerges as the language of their housewife mothers, who did not have any choice but staying home and raising children. Having grown up in the standard–Japanese speech community and endowed with social, educational, and linguistic capital, Tanabe-san and Ikegami-san were in close proximity to the prevailing image of the daughters of the canonical speakers of women's language, urban middle-class housewives. And their social, economic, and linguistic position epitomized the image of young women in the media who have "corrupted" women's language (chapter 4), imagined as the direct descendants of original women's language speakers who failed to preserve the nation's treasure: urban educated white-collar professional women who gain economic and social independence and lose women's language. But it is important to understand that, in their acts of "resistance" to women's language, Tanabe-san and Ikegami-san re-cited its law in such a way that it reproduced itself, since it was their purposive disruption of the intergenerational lineage (from mother to daughter) of women's language that, in the breach, nevertheless asserts the temporality of women's language, in which the ancient existence of women's language's original purity comes to be "corrupted" as the nation progresses and a younger generation "fails" to abide by "tradition." Furthermore, while feminine speech forms were not in their habitual sociolinguistic repertoire, Tanabe-san did conform to the idea of women's language in that she was perfectly capable of elaborate honorifics use, but not in the more continuous, reflexive way her mother would speak, since Tanabe-san's conformity to women's language was meant to mark her *professionalism*. And more importantly, although she swore that she would never speak like an "old" woman, the facts are that she had access, as habitus, to the sociolinguistic resources of elaborate honorifics and "feminine" utterance-endings, and other extra-linguistic and discourse-level encodings of femininity, and drew regularly on that valuable linguistic capital.

It is therefore their conscious choice not to use such speech forms, as an index of generational difference. Code-switching indexically aligns with the sense of "choice" in life opportunities. Just like Tanabe-san's verbal display, which showed her flexible ability to code-switch between informal, gender-neutral talk and "professional" honorifics use, she could "choose" her life course (within, of course, a structure of opportunity). If she wanted to be a housewife, she could, by her own choice. If she wanted to work, which she never questioned as inconsistent with the former as a life course, she could, but would not become like those uninspiring male managers, and would choose to work in her own way. And just as they could "work" if they want to (but they would not), Tanabe-san and Ikegami-san could "speak" women's language if they want to (but they would not).

As they had predicted, both of them left the company soon after I came back to the United States. After she took some time off, traveling overseas on her retirement savings, Ikegami-san got married. Tanabe-san studied English in the United States and came back to Japan to become an English instructor. I promised that I would contact them in twenty years to check on how they are speaking.

Performing Okusama-Kotoba: The Speech of "Leisure-Class Housewives"

The second case involves three women in their forties: Fujiwara-san, a forty-five-year-old female worker at MJL, and two female coworkers, Sugimoto-san (forty-two years old) and Toda-san (forty years old). They were all senior secretaries for male executive managers. Being close in age and having worked together for a long period of time, they were not only coworkers but also good friends, always joking and teasing each other and sharing sweets their bosses received from clients with each other when the bosses were not around. I got to know these women through my job delivering files and documents to their offices. On some lucky days, when I went to their office at the time of their little tea gathering with sweets, I was kindly asked to stay for a few minutes for chocolate and cookies.

One of their joking rituals involved the mocking of "women's language." I often observed female workers engage in such mocking by performing hyperfeminine speech, but these three women's mockery always entailed subtle yet edgy commentaries as part of the performance's effects. One day, when I was about to wrap up an interview with Fujiwara-san, Sugimoto-san and Toda-san came in. When Sugimoto-san asked Toda-san what she had been doing lately on weekends, she started complaining about how much she had to do to take care of her house and how much she felt sick and tired of living alone. Sugimoto-san then said to her, "But in the worst case, you can still go back to your parents' home *[jikka]* and live with your family. Didn't you have a brother living with your parents?" Toda-san said, "Yes, but I am not going to live with them. I can't get along with my sister-in-law. She is terrible. Speaking on the phone to her even for a minute gets on my nerves. I would rather live alone than live under the same roof with her!" Fujiwara-san and Sugimoto-san started jokingly admonishing Toda-san by shifting to a highly "feminine" speech style, accompanied by exaggerated body movements also meant to parody (example 5). Toda-san laughed and asked for my agreement—"Kono futari kara iwareruto sewa naiwayonee"—indicating that they were in no position to "preach" to her about the need to respect her family as a proper woman should.

A shift in "footing" (Goffman 1981) took place in this exchange between Fujiwara-san and Sugimoto-san. This segment of the exchange was marked off from what went before by the intensive use of some quintessential speech forms associated with women's language and co-occurring elaborate honorifics. Utterance-endings used in this conversation such as *koto-yo, wa-yo,* and *desu-mono,* honorific forms such as *asobase,* and the excessive beautification prefix, *o* in *o-kuchi* (mouth), accompanied by a sharply rising intonation, are strongly and exclusively associated with the stereotypical "women's language." This "hyper" women's language—in particular the utterance-ending *koto-yo* and the honorific form *asobase*—is often glossed by native speakers as *okusama kotoba* (the speech of the leisure-class housewife). Often these forms are characterized as too "archaic" to be used any longer in daily conversation, and they are caricatured in the media as being used by women of the leisure class or those who are snobbish and stuck-up.

In the workplace, I occasionally observed female workers engaged in such a playful mockery of women's language by using quintessential feminine speech forms. For example, in the morning, when female workers who are close friends greet, they check each other's clothes and makeup, and give and receive compliments in a mockery of women's language. For example, one would say, "Kyoono omeshimono suteki *desu-koto*" ("Your dress today is lovely"), and the other might reply, "Anatano omeshimono mo suteki *desu-wa-yo*" ("It is yours that is lovely"). Comments on skin condition and makeup also tended to be delivered by mocking women's language. For example, someone jokingly and teasingly might say, "Reiko-san, saikin okeshoo nori yoroshiku naku-*tte yo*" (Reiko, your makeup does not sit well on your face lately"). Or someone could say, "Kyoowa ohada no chooshi zekkochoo *desu-no*" ("My skin today is in the best condition"). Such mockery performance often ends with a farewell, "Gomen *asobase*" ("Good-bye"). These utterances are normally accompanied by exaggerated high pitch and prolonged utterance-ending, as well as "feminine" body gestures, such as putting hands on cheeks or to the mouth (to cover it), or bending the knees and tilting the body sideways like a little bow.

EXAMPLE 5. An exchange between Sugimoto-san and Fujiwara-san.

S:	maa sonna koto	**osshacchaa**	ikemasen	**koto-yo?**::
		say-HON	*should not-POLITE*	*FP(feminine)*

	go-kazoku	wa daiji ni	**nasaranakuchaa** nee [turning to Fujiwara-san for agreement]
	family-HON		*should do-HON*

F:	soo **desu-wayo?**::		kekkyoku saigo wa kazoku	**nan-desu-mono**::
	be so-POLITE + FP(feminine)			*be-POLITE + FP(feminine)*

	sukoshi	**o-kuchi** wo	**o-tsutsumi** . . . **o-tsutsumi** . . . **o-tsutsushimi asobasee?**:::
		mouth-HON	*m-m-mind-HON*

Translation

S: Oh, you should not say such a thing. You must respect your family. Don't you agree?
F: That's right. After all, it is your family you can rely on. You should m-m-mind your language.

Transcription conventions from Gumperz 1992 and Shibatani 1990 (for Japanese glosses).

::   lengthened segment
?   final rise
FP   final particle
HON   honorific
PLAIN   plain style
POLITE   polite style
S: Sugimoto-san; F: Fujiwara-san

The hyperbole saturating such exchanges works as a "contextualization cue" (Gumperz 1982) to signal that the speakers are "quoting" or "citing" women's language as the *other's* voice and to make it clear that it is *not their speech*.[2] This exaggerated and parodied feminine speech style—framed as the speech of a "leisure-class" woman—and the accompanying exaggerated intonation rise and body movements also signal that the speech is "play," and that the women are not seriously commenting on and critiquing each other's skin condition or fashion. Mocking is constituted by the linguistically perfect citation of women's language accompanied by the perfect topics that are stereotypically associated with it, that is, those extremely domestic and "superficial" matters, such as makeup and clothes. And yet, doing it a bit in excess radically displaces its intended performative effect and produces disobedience. Performed by working women, the most "feminine" topics in the most "feminine" language create defamiliarizing effects that allow the performers to assert their difference and distance from those they mock. It is also a mockery of the society that (unreasonably) expects women to assume domestic roles and to isolate themselves from the society, minding only their appearance.

A "leisure-class" woman does not have to work, and she can afford to care only about her clothes and skin condition. Likewise, in the above exchange between Sugimoto-san and Fujiwara-san, the former was not seriously scolding the latter for her "disrespectful" remark toward her sister-in-law. On the contrary, by using the mock women's language in an exaggerated fashion, and therefore by invoking the image of traditionally ideal, but unrealistic, women and their expected roles and dispositions, Sugimoto-san and Fujiwara-san successfully reversed the meaning of what they said. The statements "you must respect your family," "after all, it is your family you can rely on," and "you should mind your language," were turned into a powerful critique of the ideology of family and gender.

Particularly notable is Fujiwara-san's stuttering or repair when she said "*o-tsutumi . . . o-tsutumi . . . o-tsutsushimi asobasee*" ("You should m-m-mind your language"), which was the highlight of this speech play. The honorific verb *asobase* is considered an archaic form and is imagined to be part of the speech style of "upper-class" women. Coupled with the phonological fact that the verb *tsutsushimu* (mind one's language) contains a se-

2. Such implicit metapragmatic activities are differentiated from more explicit ones (Lucy 1993). Explicit metapragmatic activities include directly commenting on, critiquing, explaining, interpreting, and evaluating the language use of self and others. Implicit activities, or virtual metapragmatics (Silverstein 1993), as in this case, entail contextualization cues in an ongoing conversation to signal how the interaction should be appropriately interpreted.

ries of africated (/tsu/) and palatalized (/shi/) consonants, it is all the more difficult to pronounce when it is conjugated with the honorific verb *asobase* and with the co-occurring beautification prefix *o-*.

Although Fujiwara-san's stuttering could have been real, she skillfully took advantage of it to improvise another contextualization cue to signal that it was "play." Given the fact that "you should mind your language" is a fairly serious reprimand, she needed to make an extra effort to signal play. In addition to a mischievous smile, her repair, "m-m-mind your language," involved an exaggerated mouth movement, suggesting how hard on the tongue it is to say "o-tsutsushimi asobase." By displaying the difficulty of handling such elaborate honorifics, Fujiwara-san indicated that she—as well as Toda-san and Sugimoto-san—did not have the luxury of speaking such elaborate language and that they did not belong to a group of women who do. In other words, through stuttering, it was made clear that they were not the kind of women who could stay home and assume housewife roles.

Fujiwara-san was a working mother, and the other two women were not married, which was considered "unusual" for their age. All three were economically independent working women who were fully able to support themselves. The sarcasm lay in the fact of one economically independent working woman preaching to another about the importance of respect for the family as a source of financial and moral support. These women did not follow the expected life course for women and had had to confront their families at some point about the choices they made. Toda-san would not be able, and would not want, to go home, for a woman far beyond "marriageable age" who remains unmarried and at home is stigmatized, and she had a tense relationship with her sister-in-law, who lives with Toda-san's parents.

Performing women's language as the voice of "leisure-class" women drew a boundary for them between "us" as working women and "them"— housewives construed as both economically and socially dependent upon the institution of the family. The boundary thus involved distancing from the familial and gender ideology that these working women had been struggling against. And at the same time it embodied the complex negotiation on the part of these professional working women over their sense of gender identity, which is differentiated from that which the notion of domesticity guarantees.

What these women show us in their mocking performance of women's language attests to the structural possibility of "misfire" that is constitutive of the performative. Note that they did not refuse to cite the law of women's language. They did not speak against it. To the contrary, they (re)cite it *so* correctly and *so* perfectly—in fact, *too* correctly and *too* perfectly. This excess produced the effect that dislocates the origin and ontology of women's language. Thus, Butler notes:

> Where the uniformity of the subject is expected, where the behavioral conformity of the subject is commanded, there might be produced the refusal of the law in the form of the parodic inhabiting of conformity that subtly calls into question the legitimacy of the command, a repetition of the law into hyperbole, a rearticulation of the law against the authority of the one who delivers it. (1993a:122)

Citing women's language is a constitutive act of imagining, identifying, and presupposing its "original," which then is to be copied. And in its temporal inversion, *only after* it is copied, is its original brought into existence. The women I have described above create and dislocate its original *as* the language of leisure-class housewives, thus turning it into a critique of the subject of women's language, into which they were hailed.

Mocking is a subtle but powerful metapragmatic act to render maximally visible the trace of citing, and thus the disjuncture between the cited and the citing, by which one's (quoted) utterance is framed by another layer of (quoting) utterance that alienates and contradicts the former. This chasm momentarily allows the subject of enunciation—a person who mocks—to remain the subject within the discourse of women's language, resisting its hailing and becoming its object.

Kashira no Sawada-san (Ms. *Kashira* Sawada)

Sawada Junko was a twenty-eight-year-old female office worker at MJL. She joined the company through the mid-career employment program after teaching high school in Tokyo for five years. Fluent in German and English, she worked as a secretary for a division manager who was one of the foreign delegates. I became friends with her through my work in the same unit, and later through hiking together with her and other coworkers on a weekend outing.

Initially, however, it was several of the young female coworkers who directed my attention to Sawada-san, including Tanabe-san and Ikegami-san. On separate occasions, they each suggested to me that I should interview Sawada-san; they singled her out as a speaker of authentic women's language and referred to her as "someone whose language use is quite 'feminine' *[onna rashii]* and 'beautiful' *[kotobazukai ga kirei na hito]*." Although feminine speech in the workplace was often negatively associated by young female workers with being "archaic," "conceited," and "pretentious," those who mentioned Sawada-san to me positively distinguished her "feminine" speech from such negative associations. One of them, a twenty-five-year-old female worker, told me: "I think Sawada-san's speech is feminine but without sounding conceited. You know what I mean? She does not excessively use honorifics or 'feminine speech style' *[onnappoi hanashikata]*. That would sound affected *[iyami ni kikoeru]*, wouldn't it? But hers is not like that. I don't know what it is, but somehow, she sounds pleasantly feminine. And she speaks that way to everyone, to us and to men, too. Anyway, she is my model."

Sawada-san's colleagues fondly referred her as "*kashira no* Sawada-san," or "Ms. *kashira* Sawada." *Kashira* is a final particle quintessentially associated with feminine speech form. It is attached to the end of an utterance (predicate) to make the statement less assertive.[3] An English translation would be "I wonder . . ." This nickname, "*kashira no* Sawada-san," derived from both the literal and figurative senses; it came out of the perception of her colleagues that she frequently and even hypercorrectly used *kashira*. In a more symbolic manner, however, *kashira*, because of its exclusive association with the female speech form, also symbolized the extent to which Sawada-san's speech style was perceived as "feminine" by her colleagues. Example 6 presents examples of Sawada-san's use of *kashira*. It should be noted that, as both parts (a) and (b) show, Sawada-san often used *kashira* with polite auxiliary verbs such as *desu* and *masu*, which made her sound all the more feminine.

One day when I had a chance to have lunch with her alone, I told her that some of her female colleagues, including myself, admired her speech style. Self-consciously smiling, Sawada-san said to me, "Did you know that I am from Tohoku?" In surprise, I said, "No." Tohoku is in northern Japan and is associated with distinctive regional dialects that are often caricatured and mocked in the national media as "backward" and "unsophisticated," like other regional Japanese dialects. Sawada-san's confession that she was from Tohoku and my denial of any prior knowledge of her origin—suggesting that I did not find any trace of her origin from her speech—set the course of our conversation. How and why had she

---

3. Whether *kashira* should be categorized as a final particle or more loosely as a utterance-ending form is not definite among the linguists of Japanese. See Shibamoto Smith 1992 for a detailed account of *kashira* as part of the continuum of modalities for evidentials.

EXAMPLE 6. Examples of Sawada-san's use of *kashira*.

(1) *Situation*: Sawada-san's office had developed a new product and had distributed flyers throughout the entire company, advertising a contest for a name for the new product. Sawada-san stopped at our office and asked me if the flyer had already been passed around in our office. Showing the flyer to me, Sawada-san asked:

kore	moo	kochira ni	mawatte	ki-mashita-kashira
this	already	here-POLITE	pass	come-POLITE + I-wonder-FP(feminine)

"I wonder if this has already come to be passed around in your office?"

(2) *Situation*: In one interview, Sawada-san contrasted her previous job (high school teacher) with her current one (secretary for a manager) and explained to me why she preferred her current job. My initial question, which ultimately prompted the following answer, was if she would be interested in becoming a manager.

sanjuunin no	kodomo no	mendoo wo mirori	hitori no	hito ga	
thirty	children	rather than taking care of	one	person	
nani o	shite hoshii noka	sono shite hoshiikotoni	awaseteno	hoo ga
what	wants me to do	those things [he] wants me to do	adjusts to	better
jibunniwa	atterun-desu-kashira ne,	kekkyokuwaa		
to me	suit-POLITE + I-wonder-FP (feminine)	after all		

"Rather than taking care of thirty children, I wonder, after all, if focusing on what one single person wants me to do and adjusting myself to his needs better suits my nature."

Transcription conventions from Gumperz 1992 and Shibatani 1990 (for Japanese glosses).

FP   final particle
POLITE polite style

mastered such a "feminine," and what her colleagues described as "beautiful" *(kireina)*, speech style?

Sawada-san represents a successful upwardly mobile migrant from a rural regional area to cosmopolitan Tokyo. Her life history is one of geographical and socioeconomic displacements and discontinuities—with movement from the cultural and economic periphery to the center. In Sawada-san's autobiographical narrative, this movement paralleled the changes through which she adopted and acquired "feminine" speech—or what she identified as "the speech of women in Tokyo." Just as she moved toward the center to gain access to seemingly better life opportunities, she actively sought access to a "feminine" speech style.

Sawada-san was born and grew up in a small town, where "people spoke 'rough' *[ranbō]*." When she passed the entrance exam for one of the top regional high schools, she started commuting to a nearby city:

> Up until I was in junior high school, I used to refer to myself with *ore* or *ora*. You wouldn't believe this, would you? That's how we all used to refer to ourselves. There was no male-female difference. Looking back now, I just can't believe it. Then, I went to the city for the first time to go to high school. My high school was in Kosaka-shi [a pseudonym]. It is a big city in my prefecture. It was a different world from where I grew up. There, I noticed that girls did not use *ore* or *ora,* but they said *watashi* or *atashi*. I thought to myself, "Wow, how beautiful *[kirei]* their speech is!"

From the perspective of standard Japanese usage, *ore* is considered one of the male-exclusive first-person pronouns, understood to be "crude" (see, for example, Ide 1979:39, 1982:358). *Ora* is not even included in "standard colloquial Japanese," but is registered as a dialectal (nonstandard) first-person pronoun.

Straight from the top regional high school, Sawada-san passed the competitive entrance exam and moved to one of the prestigious national universities in Tokyo as the first in her family to go to college. The displacement in Sawada-san's life, the geographic and class mobility, was closely tracked by—and no doubt partly enabled by—the change in her speech: "Since I came to Tokyo, I have learned to speak more beautiful *[kireina]* speech. I thought coming to Tokyo was a good opportunity for me to correct my speech. I wanted to correct the part of my speech that would be inappropriate for a woman to use *[ippanteki ni josei ga tsukattara okashii kotobazukai o naoshitakatta]*." She continued:

> When I first came to Tokyo, I thought to myself, "how elegantly women speak in Tokyo!" For example, I had a good impression when I first heard them saying things like "such-and-such *kashira,*" "such-and-such *desu-tte,*"

or "such-and-such *noyo*." It sounded very elegant and somewhat like the speech of a big sister *[onee-san-kotoba]*.

When I asked her to clarify what "the speech of a big sister" meant, she continued:

> It felt like the speech of someone senior *[toshiue no hito]*. I think urban people are mentally more experienced and mature than those in the countryside. For example, *desu-tte* is not the speech of a child, but that of a social adult *[shakaijin]*. The child would say *da-tte*. In my high school days, I used to say "such-and-such *da-tte*."

The utterance-endings—*kashira, noyo,* and *desu-tte*—that impressed Sawada-san so much are well documented in sociolinguistics as properties of women's speech (see, for example, Okamoto and Sato 1992:480–81).[4] For Sawada-san, to become a standard speaker or to become a generic speaker of Tokyo was not simply to acquire "standard Japanese" or "the Tokyo accent," but to become a speaker of "feminine" speech capable of using the perceived "feminine" speech forms and accompanying demeanor that are associated selectively with the idealized image of the urban middle-class woman.

Like many people who migrated from the regions to the city, Sawada-san led a bidialectal life, in which the variations indexed her split worlds: the hometown and the city, childhood and adulthood, and work and family. I asked her, "Do you have or have you had any sense of estrangement *[iwakan]* about speaking standard Japanese?" "No, not at all," she said and continued:

> When I go back to my rural hometown *[inaka]*, I now feel that their speech sounds rough and crude. And, of course, if you speak like this [referring to her "Tokyo" speech style] over there, you would be ostracized *[mura-hachibu]*! But, whenever I go home and, as when I speak with my friends from junior high school, I speak like this [referring to her "Tokyo" speech style]. I can't help it. If I try to break into [the dialect] *[muri ni kuzusu to]*, I feel like even my personality *[jinkaku]* would change. "What I am" in standard Japanese is now more natural for me *["kyōtsūgo no jibun" no hō ga shizen nandesu, imawa]*.

---

4. *Desu-tte* is the combination of a polite auxiliary verb, *desu*, and a quotative particle, *-tte*. An example would be "Kyō wa ame *desu-tte*" ("It is said that it is going to be raining today"). Its association with "femininity," at least in Sawada-san's understanding, seems to derive from its polite auxiliary verb and its contrast—as she herself pointed out—with its plain, and far more common, form, *da-tte*.

Sawada-san's enthusiasm for adopting standard (i.e., feminine) language contrasted starkly with the attitude of most of the male workers transferred from the branch offices in Kansai, in western Japan, who resisted speaking standard Japanese or the speech associated with Tokyo, and continued to speak a Kansai dialect *(kansai-ben)*.[5] As Sawada-san was concerned with the possible damage to her personality by shifting back to her original dialect, the male workers from Kansai maintained their dialect for exactly the same reason—concern with damaging their personality. One of them told me: "I am just too lazy [to try to learn standard Japanese]. But I am also afraid of being a double personality if I speak standard language at work and in Tokyo and the speech over there [Kansai] at home." The perception of the linguistic assimilation into the center as both a symbol and a material means of socioeconomic mobility is often gendered. And it has to do with the cultural and historical configuration of language and gender, not unique to, but specific to Japan.[6]

In the process by which Sawada-san was displaced into the national center, she crossed layers of culturally meaningful boundaries understood as the urban vs. the countryside, Tokyo vs. regions *(chihō)*, the adult vs. the child, the standard language vs. the dialect, and gendered vs. genderless language use. For Sawada-san, this move took place against the background of a reconfigured national economy and evolving class tensions both within the Tokyo metropolis and between it and the undifferentiated regional satellites. It was in these cultural divides that "Japanese women's language" emerged for Sawada-san. To become a "feminine" speaker, which she valorized in aesthetic terms such as "beautiful" *(kirei)* and "elegant" *(ereganto)*, was to cross the boundary of those oppositions: from her hometown village to the city and Tokyo, from being a child to a (social) adult, and from being a dialect (rough speech) speaker to a standard (beautiful speech) speaker.

Sawada-san's linguistic history, as she moved though national space from periphery to center, also embodies the *temporality of regional modernity,* in which becoming modern entails regional language becoming more "beautiful" as dialects are gradually and evolutionarily replaced by standard Japanese. Sawada-san could afford neither to refuse to speak women's language like Tanabe-san and Ikegami-san nor to mock it like

---

5. See Sturtz Sreetharan 2004a, 2004b for a sociolinguistic analysis of male speech in Kansai dialect.

6. See Haig 1990. Such a metaphorical displacement between dialect/standard and men/women has also been amply reported in cases in the United States, Britain, and other countries by variational sociolinguists. See, for example, Labov 1972; Trudgill 1972, 1974.

Fujiwara-san and Sugimoto-san. "Women's language" is not even a matter of choice for her. For Sawada-san, "beautiful" language, which women's language represented, was connected with regional economic development and urbanization (the countryside becoming more like the metropole by a process of diffusion) and with—as in her case—urban migration; in both instances, better life opportunities were directly associated with women's language. The temporality that such a regional modernity presents directly contradicts that of metropolitan modernity, in which women's language, as we have seen, is *corrupted* as Japan becomes more modern. For dialect speakers, "women's language" both symbolically and instrumentally promises national female citizenship, which is accompanied by translocal anonymity for a regional migrant who lives in Tokyo, as well as an upward and centering mobility and a metropolitan, even cosmopolitan, identity.

It is noteworthy to point out the contrast between Sawada-san and Yoshida-san, the woman manager described in the previous chapter. Both women were originally dialect speakers. But the transition to the center and the attainment of cultural citizenship in the center take different linguistic strategies in conjunction particularly with indexing gender. While for Yoshida-san, managerial identity and cultural citizenship as a generic Japanese middle-class woman revolved around *not* marking gender in an explicit way through use of the speech forms associated women's language, for Sawada-san, a parallel sense of gendered citizenship is sought through active use of and valorization of women's language.[7]

Sawada-san's story about her linguistic encounter with the center parallels my childhood experience, described in the introduction, of hearing women's language for the first time in Tokyo. Many years later, however, when my dissertation research brought me to Tokyo, instead of TV-like standard Japanese and perfect women's language, this time my ears picked up more heterogeneous and fluctuating accents produced by people at construction sites, vendors, taxi drivers, women at kiosks, janitors, and sandwich-men. And—my most surprising discovery—my aunt, who had

---

7. The difference between Yoshida-san and Sawada-san also has to do with the differential "value" of their original dialects. Kansai, where Yoshida-san came from, is the second-largest region of the country. Tohoku, on the other hand, has historically been one of the most economically deprived regions, whose dialects were severely stigmatized and had been the target of "dialect reform" since the language standardization movement in Meiji. Although it is beyond the scope of my analysis, the relative political-economic status of the Kansai and Tohoku regions within the nation clearly underlies the differential value of their dialects, and, accordingly, the differential orientations toward women's language between Yoshida-san and Sawada-san.

impressed me so much when I was a child with her Liz Taylor–like women's language, had not in fact used any of its linguistic features when I met her as a child. She was a speaker of Shitamachi-kotoba, "the language of the Low City," a characteristic speech style associated with parts of old Tokyo, inhabited traditionally by merchants, workers, and artisans (Bestor 1998; Kondo 1990). My childhood ears must have been so spellbound by my aunt's standard-Japanese-accented speech, which sounded just like what I heard on TV and was so eager to hear, that I simply assumed it was women's language because she was a woman. Perhaps it is such a passionate gaze, or in this case such passionate "ears" from the periphery, that creates and maintains the fiction of the center as the place of the original and the authentic, even when the center is empty and holds nothing.

The Transnational Displacement of Japanese Women's Language

I will now move out from the context of MJL to make a further point about diverse performative histories of women's language. We have so far examined the ways in which women on various social and cultural boundaries (re)cite women's language and thereby locally (re)write its pedagogical history. The above cases show how the metapragmatic construction and the linguistic properties of women's language are divergently experienced by differentially situated actors. Their diverse modes of performative excess, in turn, dislocate and defamiliarize its indexicality of universal femaleness.

Restricting the site of citational practices of women's language only to Japanese women and Japan still succumbs to the normalizing power of discourse and fails to examine the full range of ways in which discursive power has effects—not to mention a range of modes of contestation and contradiction.[8] Women's language "travels."[9] It crosses national and racial boundaries, and it affects people who cross them. It then produces multiple and unintended effects contingent upon the historical and ideolog-

---

8. Although beyond the scope of this book, the powerful critique of the reified equation of Japanese women with Japanese women's language has been made by recent studies that bring the issue of sexuality to the fore. See Shibamoto 1987, chapter 6, and Ogawa and Shibamoto Smith 1997 for the male appropriation of Japanese women's language. See also Lunsing and Maree 2004, and Maree 1997, which compellingly argue how heterosexual normativity is reproduced in the discourse and practice of "Japanese women's language."

9. See Appadurai 1996; Clifford 1992; Gupta and Ferguson 1997; Kaplan 1987.

ical configuration specific to the place and the people in question, and thus exposes other forms of tension and contradiction within the presumed unity of the discourse of women's language. Siegal's study of Western (upper-middle-class) women studying Japanese language in Hiroshima, for example, presents a compelling example of how women's language is a problematic and ambivalent resource for the construction of their identity when they speak Japanese. She quotes from one of her informants: "I don't think I've found my Japanese persona yet, who I am when I am speaking Japanese—I was listening to this lady speaking on the telephone in a little squeaky voice [imitates voice] it's like no, I don't think I can do that, it's not for me—um—I don't know . . ." (1994:642).

For these women, "Japanese" women's language includes the dimension of national and racial particularity and difference, and becomes a site for the (re)construction of, and tension of, gender identity in the context of race and nation—who are "Japanese women" and who are "we" (Western women)? And, who am I who speaks Japanese? These questions are necessarily brought to the fore when a Westerner selectively acquires gendered (or nongendered) Japanese speech forms. Siegal's work thus shows us another imaginative subject position from which the normative understanding about Japanese women's language is defamilarized.

My final example draws on the context of Japanese language learning in the United States. For Japanese language learners (Japanese) women's language is problematic and ambivalent because of prevailing American racial and gender stereotypes of Japanese women. What does it mean, from the point of view of an American college student, to learn or speak (Japanese) women's language? For native Japanese teachers, many of whom are Japanese women living for longer or shorter periods in the United States, this tension in the classroom highlights not the gendered specificities of women's language, but *the Japanese* specificities—that is, the way Japan is perceived as an other by the West—with the resulting understandable desire on the part of Japanese teachers to "explain Japanese culture" with authority, including all those things about gender that do not translate easily into American culture. One of my Japanese acquaintances who teaches Japanese in an American university once explained to me: "Some students studying Japanese claimed that female speech is a reflection of discrimination towards women in Japanese society, and they don't want to be forced to use it. Even some TAs insisted that students have freedom in choosing which style to use. I didn't like their ideas, but I also didn't know how to explain things in a convincing way."

Such overt resistance in the U.S. classroom to learning female speech style in Japanese is generated out of a long-standing American concern with "sexist language" and American imaginaries of Asian sexism. The way out of the difficulty for the American student is then sought by invoking the liberal notion of "choice," to use it or not, as if it were one of the styles available equally to everyone, oppressive equally for everyone. Such a view, of course, leaves no room for the case of Sawada-san, for example, for whom Japanese women's language was a source of empowerment and to acquire it was not simply a matter of choice out of a range of options of equal economic and cultural value, but was of significance in terms of her life opportunities. It is also worth remembering that the constitution of Japanese women's language was occasioned by the literary demand for representing *white women's speech* in modern Japanese (chapter 2).

By being displaced from its familiar place (Japan) and its familiar speaker (Japanese women) and being relocated into a different political context, women's language travels transnationally and is reterritorialized in different political narratives, such as U.S. feminisms. In such a transnational displacement, the discourse of women's language gets rearticulated and opens up unprecedented linguistic strategies where "race" (and its political history) inescapably figures in, which would be contained by the (national) gender binary in Japan. The point is not simply how Japanese women's language is re-cited and dislocated by American women (or men for that matter). It is equally critical to see how it gets re-cited and dislocated by Japanese women who teach in American classrooms. What is foregrounded for them is the racialized gaze of the West, not necessarily or not only the situation of women. And what they feel compelled to do, while standing in the middle of the dense web of historical and political relations of powerful institutions and social forces that mobilize the category of gender, is a complicated task of presenting women's language as "Japanese culture" and a distinctive marker of "the differences between the East and the West," in a way that resists the Orientalist impulse to name women's language according to the West's temporality and idioms of gender and language. In saying "I didn't like their ideas, but I also didn't know how to explain things in a convincing way," my acquaintance, in this expression of her confusion and frustration, is in fact eloquently and pointedly telling us that *there is no nameable place from where she can speak about women's language*. It attests to a moment when the enunciator looks for the speaking position *within* the discourse (of women's language), but contingency fails to provide any fixed subject position for the radically estranged enunciator. It is just such a void of the speaking subject position within the discourse that we can turn into a critical standpoint.

Diverse and contingent locations where women's language is cited, and the equally diverse and contingent effects it produces, compel us to ask about *historical* interconnections among them, rather than treating each enactment as its own isolated incident. What is the connection or relevance between a Japanese woman who actively acquires women's language and American women who refuse to learn it? What is the relationship between them and Japanese women who seemingly share the same strategy not to use women's language? What are the connections among them—not in the abstract sense that they are all women, but in the historical and material sense? In other words, again, we need to *historicize* these connections. That then allows us to see how women's lives, experience, and subjectivities are differently constructed by the multiple axes of social forces intersecting gender—including class, nation, and race. Mohanty's critique of relativism and cultural and historical plurality is critically relevant here:

> How do we negotiate between my history and yours? How would it be possible for us to recover our commonality, not the ambiguous imperial-humanist myth of our shared human attributes, which are supposed to distinguish us all from animals, but, more significantly, the imbrication of our various pasts and presents, the ineluctable relationships of shared and contested meanings, values, material resources? It is necessary to assert our dense particularities, our lived and imagined differences. But could we afford to leave untheorized the question of how our differences are intertwined and indeed hierarchically organized? Could we, in other words, really afford to have *entirely* different histories, to see ourselves as living—and having lived—in entirely heterogeneous and discrete spaces? (1989:13, emphasis in original)

I have described multiple positionings and strategies vis-à-vis Japanese women's language. The women I have described here cross or negotiate culturally meaningful boundaries and social borderlands. For them, the meaning and the material effect of Japanese women's language flows not from any obligatory or one-to-one correspondence with attributes of a female role, but from border tensions concerning various social divides that are culturally complex and impossible to reduce simply to gender difference, which the discourse of women's language would precisely compel them to do.

The chapter described Ikegami-san and Tanabe-san, who resisted women's language to distance themselves from their mothers' generation. Sugimoto-san and Fujiwara-san, working women, performed a women's language whose excess, to brilliant effect, asserted the difference between them and women reproducing the traditional ideology of gender and kinship. Sawada-san actively acquired feminine speech forms as part of a strategy of class mobility and cultural citizenship. For white women studying Japanese, performing Japanese women's language is about performing a gendered identity of the racial/national other and thus an unsettling act of racial mimicry, whose inevitable failure assures both their whiteness and their claimed autonomy from patriarchy. The last example was drawn from a U.S. classroom, where some American female students studying Japanese refused to learn women's language because, for them, it was a reflection of non-Western (Oriental) sexism, while the Japanese instructor attempted to present it as "culture."

These are performative histories of women's language situated in its multiple displacements with multiple vectors. The women I have described engage with the discourse of women's language and (re)write its history in their everyday performance of it in intensely local settings. They are the subjects of the discourse of women's language. But, at the same time, the simple fact that the body of a subject exists and does things in a densely historical and material world of ongoing contingency inevitably means that the discourse of women's language and its regulatory effects are regularly exceeded. Such subjects produce the *agent*-like effects of *defamiliarizing* and *decentering* women's language. And their performative acts expose the trace of its incessant ideological working to contain unassimilable and unnameable others and their historical realities and temporalities. This is how the abject returns. It returns in unintended places without any trumpet announcement—even without acts of "everyday resistance"—simply and quietly pointing to the void and absence in the discourse that claims its own plentitude and ontology. Such a "gap" was once and originally occupied by the abject but was evacuated (abjected) as inessential, extra, and unintelligible, so that the discourse could attain its essential unity. And this gap was laid bare through the "performative" moments and spaces—as Bhabha (1990a:297) puts it—that belong to the temporality of those women's experience of women's language.

AFTERWORD

This Vicarious "Japanese Women's Language"

No one can seriously doubt that Japan has exhibited both particularities and universalities in its encounter with and experience of modernity and modernization since 1868. This is because modernization is always both local and global—in non-Western places such as Japan, but also of course, in modernity's supposed core, the industrial and postindustrial West. This book has examined one of those specificities of the Japanese modern— the linkage between three elements: capitalism and state formation; the social organization and cultural constitution of gender; and language. While it is not at all unusual to find the first two elements—political economy and gender—linked in processes of modernization across the globe, their additional linkage to language in Japan is noteworthy. Women's language is unique, but not because of its claimed antiquity in premodern Japan, but rather because of its birth and functioning in modernity.

As with any claim of totality or essence, when women's language is claimed as "identity," it is important to remember that its possibility rests on the historical, cultural, and political abjection of certain people, ideas, events, and temporalities. My goal in this book has been to identify those who were abjected, to undo the process of such abjection both historically and ethnographically, and to reinstall these people in their original place in the discourse of women's language. Because they are excess to, but also, paradoxically, original in the *real* of women's language, tracing the abjected allows us to see not only how the ontology or essence of women's language is possible *only* by the compulsive repetition, both temporally and spatially, of exclusionary practices, but also how such practices are unstably predicated upon other equally unstable notions and exclusionary practices of the nation: modernity, tradition, culture, language, and women.

Women's language became a cultural "thing" and a target of governmental projects, not because women and men are naturally different or even culturally different ("in Japan"), but because complex historical and material forces involving class, region, nation, and race colluded in the discourse that gave cultural and political life to "women's language." This means that a critical analysis of women's language through a single system of oppression such as sexism—a framework that sees only gender at work in "women's language"—cannot account for the power of this discourse. This is not to say that women's language has nothing to do with sexism and male domination. But what constitutes sexism is a broader historical and political network of power, so that women's language cannot simply be posited against "men's language." As I have shown, what is critical to recognize is that women's language creates *hierarchy among women* and unevenly scatters their positionalities vis-à-vis gender politics. Women's language hails those who are socially named into "women," regardless of their class, region, race, or sexual orientation and, upon interpellating them, ranks and hierarchicalizes them. This book is meant to foreground the epistemic violence beyond *gender* that is inherent in the idea of women's language.

Yet the discourse itself is unstable and not best understood as a grid imposed on agents. The assertion of the naturalness and timelessness of women's language is, in fact, threatened by, if never completely reversed by, contingent enactments of women's language by actual women in the real, material world. These enactments dislocate the terms in which women's language is to be cited and disrupt its linear and singular temporality (a temporality which upholds that of the nation) and thus historicize women's language in local, ongoing contexts. Such situated performative histories and temporalities can be understood as the strategic failure of discourse, by which we witness the fundamental impossibility of any complete and perfect identification with the subject position designated by the discourse. These are the moments when the abject returns to haunt the supposedly stable subject of the Japanese woman, laying bare the fundamental contradiction of women's language. But since, as I pointed out above, language and gender are inextricably tied to the political economy of capitalist growth and nationalism, much more is at stake in the failure of the discourse than simply the idea that women's language exists.

The idea of discursive strategic failure also complicates our familiar notion of agency, accorded to bourgeois citizens, neoliberal actors, and even "subjects" in much critical theory. This book shows that if we seek to understand power, it is important to avoid romanticizing the sovereign subject through notions of oppositional consciousness, choice, transgression, or difference. None of the women I describe in my ethnography at May Japan Limited *speak against* women's language. Instead, the women I worked with show us moments of contingency that amount to blind spots in the discourse that regulates the mode and location of women's language. These women come from positions that the discourse of women's language fails to name, and it is this unnameability itself that constitutes the disruption of the discourse.

As I said above, the discourse of women's language goes beyond both gender and language understood as autonomous systems, and my analysis has examined how the temporality semiotically encoded in the indexical order of women's language is informed by and informs the temporality of Japan's national modernity. My aim has been to identify the cultural logic in the relationship between the temporality produced in microlinguistic processes and the temporality inherent in the logic of larger capitalist political-economic processes. Whether one is talking about the historical takeoff of Japanese modernity and nationalism or about "late" Japanese capitalist modernity, the linkage among gender, language, and national identity invokes a linear temporality of progress, with tradition and modernity at opposite ends. This temporal imaginary is ideologically encoded in the indexical order of women's language through the semiotic process of inversion and reification. Thus, critical analysis of gender and language in Japan inevitably entails a genealogy of national modernity and its historical narrative. In doing this, I have aimed to renew the importance of the analytical concepts of temporality and historicity in linguistic analysis as well as in social analysis.

Important sociolinguistic work on language and gender in Japan has emerged that seeks to illuminate the diverse social locations where gender and sexuality are linguistically constructed. Critically responding to the conflation of ideology and practice, for example, the contributors in Okamoto and Smith (2004) collectively demonstrate the disjuncture and tension between them and thus highlight the figures of speakers who are not simply duped by ideology.[1] I join such critics in arguing that we need

---

1. The range of new critical approaches presented in this collection includes studies of aging (Matsumoto 2004), female dialect speakers (Sunaoshi 2004), sexual minorities (Lunsing and Maree 2004), female adolescents' use of male first-person pronouns (Miyazaki 2004), language policy regarding women during the Second World War (Washi 2004), and

to seek within the broader social and historical context the conditions enabling the diverse locations and modes of the linguistic construction of gender and the gendered construction of linguistic practice in modern Japanese society. In order to achieve this goal, language, or the idea of language, needs to be historicized. It needs to be genealogically undone to show that all historical narratives are the product of projects and struggles over what is to be memorialized and what is to be forgotten.

Most importantly, however, my aim here has been to retell the story of Japanese women's language in a way that makes intelligible the epistemological shift in its vicarious and estranged experience, in which the indissoluble disjuncture between the subject position designated by the discourse and the situated citations of it performed by actors enters deeply into their historical consciousness. From this ground of knowledge and experience, I argue, we see the extent to which what we identify as "women's language" has neither an organic body to inhabit nor a concrete origin to claim, but is a powerful effect of a system of citations and a network of media that belong to forces and institutions of modernity that link gender, the nation, and capitalism.

Like the women I described in this book, I, too, speak within the discourse of Japanese women's language—even when speaking or writing English—by using the very term and category "women's language" and other associated idioms. At the risk of reproducing it, however, I hope my re-citing of the story of women's language will be "a repetition in difference," whose insertion into the discourse contributes to denaturalizing it and to creating a new condition of its existence, so that, as Butler (1993a, 1993b) would put it, we can turn the experience and the domain of the abject into a site of critical epistemology and a political platform. And we can turn such epistemological dissonance into a theory to understand this vicarious Japanese women's language, which is not yours, but which speaks for you and to you, as the voice of a citizen, a consumer, and "the Japanese woman."

---

others. These studies represent productive responses to new theoretical developments in the field of gender and language in the United States and Europe since the 1990s (Bucholtz and Hall 1995; Eckert and McConnell-Ginet 1992; Gal 1991), which call for more practice-oriented and ethnographically based research that highlights the diverse modalities of the linguistic construction of gender identity, its micro and macro processes of forging resistance and agency, and the operation of social power. See also Washi's (2000) study of the relationship between women's language and the emperor system *(tennōsei)*, and Nakamura's (1995, 2001) sustained theorization and critique of "Japanese women's language."

Bibliography

Adorno, Theodor
    1990 The Curves of the Needle. Thomas Levin, trans. *October* 55:48–55.

Agha, Asif
    2003 The Social Life of Cultural Value. *Language and Communication* 23 (3/4):231–73.

Ahearn, Laura M.
    2001 Language and Agency. *Annual Review of Anthropology* 30:109–37.

Allison, Anne
    1994 *Nightwork: Sexuality, Pleasure, and Corporate Masculinity in a Tokyo Hostess Club*. Chicago: University of Chicago Press.

Althusser, Louis
    1971 Ideology and Ideological State Apparatuses. In *Lenin and Philosophy and Other Essays*. Pp. 127–88. New York: Monthly Review Press.

Anderson, Benedict
    1983 *Imagined Communities: Reflections on the Origin and Spread of Nationalism*. London: Verso.

Appadurai, Arjun
    1996 *Modernity at Large: Cultural Dimensions of Globalization*. Minneapolis: University of Minnesota Press.

Austin, John Langshaw
    1962 *How to Do Things with Words*. Cambridge, MA: Harvard University Press.

Bachnik, Jane, and Charles J. Quinn
    1994 *Situated Meaning: Inside and Outside in Japanese Self, Society, and Language*. Princeton: Princeton University Press.

Bakhtin, Mikhail
    1981 *The Dialogic Imagination*. Michael Holquist, ed. Cary Emerson and Michael Holquist, trans. Austin: University of Texas Press.

Barthes, Roland
 1977 The Photographic Message. In *Image, Music, Text*. S. Heath, trans. Pp. 15–31. New York: Hill and Wang.
 1982 Myth Today. In *A Barthes Reader*. Susan Sontag, ed. Pp. 93–149. New York: Hill and Wang.

Baudrillard, Jean
 1981 *For a Critique of the Political Economy of the Sign*. C. Levin, trans. St. Louis, MO: Telos Press.
 1983 *Simulations*. P. Foss, P. Patton, and P. Beitchman, trans. New York: Semiotext(e) Inc.
 1988 Simulacra and Simulation. In *Jean Baudrillard: Selected Writings*. M. Poster, ed. Pp. 166–84. Stanford: Stanford University Press.

Bauman, Richard, and Charles L. Briggs
 1990 Poetics and Performance as Critical Perspectives on Language and Social Life. *Annual Review of Anthropology* 19:59–88.

Befu, Harumi
 2001 *Hegemony of Homogeneity: An Anthropological Analysis of Nihonjinron*. Melbourne: Trans Pacific Press.

Benjamin, Walter
 1968 The Work of Art in the Age of Mechanical Reproduction. In *Illuminations*. Pp. 217–52. New York: Schocken Books.
 1973 *Charles Baudelaire: A Lyric Poet in the Era of High Capitalism*. London: NLB.
 1978 *Reflections: Essays, Aphorisms, Autobiographical Writings*. E. Jephcott, trans. P. Demetz, ed. New York: Harcourt Brace Jovanovich.
 1999 *The Arcades Project*. H. Eiland and K. McLaughlin, trans. Cambridge, MA: Belknap Press.

Bennett, Tony
 1994 The Exhibitionary Complex. In *Culture/Power/History: A Reader in Contemporary Social Theory*. Nicholas B. Dirks, Sherry B. Ortner, and Geoff Eley, eds. Pp. 123–54. Princeton: Princeton University Press.

Bestor, Theodore C.
 1988 *Neighborhood Tokyo*. Stanford: Stanford University Press.

Bhabha, Homi
 1990a DissemiNation: Time, Narrative, and the Margins of the Modern Nation. In *Nation and Narration*. H. K. Bhabha, ed. Pp. 291–322. New York: Routledge.
 1990b *Nation and Narration*. New York: Routledge.
 1994 *The Location of Culture*. New York: Routledge.

Bourdieu, Pierre
 1977 The Economics of Linguistic Exchanges. Richard Nice, trans. *Social Science Information* 16 (6):645–68.

1984 *Distinction: A Social Critique of the Judgment of Taste.* R. Nice, trans. Cambridge, MA: Harvard University Press.

1990 *In Other Words: Essays towards a Reflexive Sociology.* M. Adamson, trans. Stanford: Stanford University Press.

1991 *Language and Symbolic Power.* Gino Raymond and Matthew Adamson, trans. J. B. Thompson, ed. Cambridge, MA: Harvard University Press.

Briggs, Charles L., and Richard Bauman
1992 Genre, Intertextuality, and Social Power. *Journal of Linguistic Anthropology* 2 (2):131–72.

Brinton, Mary
1991 Sex Differences in On-the-Job Training and Job Rotation in Japanese Firms. *Research in Social Stratification and Mobility* 10:3–25.

1993 *Women and the Economic Miracle: Gender and Work in Postwar Japan.* Berkeley: University of California Press.

Bucholtz, Mary, and Kira Hall
1995 Introduction: Twenty Years after Language and Woman's Place. In *Gender Articulated: Language and the Socially Constructed Self.* K. Hall and M. Bucholtz, eds. Pp. 1–24. New York: Routledge.

Buck-Morss, Susan
1989 *The Dialectics of Seeing: Walter Benjamin and the Arcades Project.* Cambridge, MA: MIT Press.

Butler, Judith
1990 *Gender Trouble: Feminism and the Subversion of Identity.* New York: Routledge.

1993a *Bodies That Matter: On the Discursive Limits of "Sex."* New York: Routledge.

1993b Imitation and Gender Insubordination. In *The Lesbian and Gay Studies Reader.* H. Abelove, M. A. Barale, and D. M. Halperin, eds. Pp. 307–20. New York: Routledge.

1997 *Excitable Speech: A Politics of the Performative.* New York: Routledge.

Calhoun, Craig, ed.
1992 *Habermas and the Public Sphere.* Cambridge, MA: MIT Press.

Carter, Erica
1984 Alice in the Consumer Wonderland. In *Gender and Generation.* A. McRobbie and M. Nava, eds. Pp. 185–214. London: Macmillan.

Chakrabarty, Dipesh
2000 *Provincializing Europe: Postcolonial Thought and Historical Difference.* Princeton: Princeton University Press.

Chatterjee, Partha
1990 The Nationalist Resolution of the Women's Question. In *Recasting Women: Essays in Indian Colonial History.* Kumkum Sangari, ed. Pp. 233–53. New Brunswick, NJ: Rutgers University Press.

1993 *The Nation and Its Fragments: Colonial and Postcolonial Histories.* Princeton: Princeton University Press.

Chion, Michel

1994 *Audio-Vision: Sound on Screen.* C. Gorbman, trans. New York: Columbia University Press.

1999 *The Voice in Cinema.* C. Gorbman, trans. New York: Columbia University Press.

Chuō Kōron Henshūbu

2001 *Ronsō chūryū hōkai* [Debate: The collapse of the middle class]. Tokyo: Chuō Kōron Shinsha.

Clifford, James

1992 Traveling Cultures. In *Cultural Studies.* L. Grossberg, C. Nelson, and P. A. Treichler, eds. Pp. 96–116. New York: Routledge.

Cowie, Elizabeth

1978 Woman as Sign. *M/F* 1:49–63.

Crary, Jonathan

1990 *Techniques of the Observer: On Vision and Modernity in the Nineteenth Century.* Cambridge, MA: MIT Press.

Dean, Mitchell

1999 *Governmentality: Power and Rule in Modern Society.* Thousand Oaks, CA: Sage.

Debord, Guy

1977 *Society of the Spectacle.* Detroit: Black and Red.

de Certeau, Michel

1984 *The Practice of Everyday Life.* Steven Rendall, trans. Berkeley: University of California Press.

1986 *Heterologies: Discourses on the Other.* Minneapolis: University of Minnesota Press.

1988 *The Writing of History.* New York: Columbia University Press.

De Grazia, Victoria

1996 Nationalizing Women: The Competition between Fascist and Commercial Cultural Models in Mussolini's Italy. In *The Sex of Things: Gender and Consumption in Historical Perspective.* V. de Grazia, ed. Pp. 337–58. Berkeley: University of California Press.

de Lauretis, Teresa

1984 *Alice Doesn't: Feminism, Semiotics, Cinema.* Bloomington: Indiana University Press.

Derrida, Jacques

1976 *Of Grammatology.* Baltimore: Johns Hopkins University Press.

1977 *Limited Inc.: abc.* Baltimore: Johns Hopkins University Press.

1982 *Margins of Philosophy.* Alan Bass, trans. Chicago: University of Chicago Press.

Doane, Mary Ann
  1992 Film and the Masquerade. In *Femme Fatales: Feminism, Film Theory, Psychoanalysis*. Pp. 17–32. New York: Routledge.

Dolar, Mladen
  1996 The Object Voice. In *Gaze and Voice as Love Objects*. Renata Salecl and Slavoj Žižek, eds. Pp. 7–31. Durham, NC: Duke University Press.

Duara, Prasenjit
  1998 The Regime of Authenticity: Timelessness, Gender, and National History of Modern China. *History and Theory* 37 (3):287–308.

Eckert, Penelope, and Sally McConnell-Ginet
  1992 Think Practically and Look Locally: Language and Gender as Community-Based Practice. *Annual Review of Anthropology* 21:461–90.

Errington, James Joseph
  1988 *Structure and Style in Javanese: A Semiotic View of Linguistic Etiquette*. Philadelphia: University of Pennsylvania Press.

Fabian, Johannes
  1983 *Time and the Other: How Anthropology Makes Its Object*. New York: Columbia University Press.

Foucault, Michel
  1965 *Madness and Civilization: A History of Insanity in the Age of Reason*. New York: Vintage.
  1972 *The Archaeology of Knowledge*. A. M. Sheridan Smith, trans. New York: Pantheon Books.
  1977a Nietzsche, Genealogy, History. In *Language, Counter-Memory, Practice: Selected Essays and Interviews by Michel Foucault*. D. F. Bouchard, ed. D. F. Bouchard and S. Simon, trans. Pp. 139–64. Ithaca: Cornell University Press.
  1977b What Is an Author? In *Language, Counter-Memory, Practice*. Pp. 113–38.
  1978 *The History of Sexuality*. R. Hurley, trans. New York: Pantheon Books.
  1979 *Discipline and Punish: The Birth of the Prison*. A. Sheridan, trans. New York: Vintage Books.
  1980 *Power/Knowledge: Selected Interviews and Other Writings by Michel Foucault, 1972–1977*. Colin Gordon, trans. New York: Pantheon Books.
  1982 The Subject and Power. In *Michel Foucault: Beyond Structuralism and Hermeneutics*. Hubert L. Dreyfus and Paul Rabinow, eds. Pp. 208–26. Chicago: University of Chicago Press.
  1991 Governmentality. In *The Foucault Effect: Studies in Governmentality*. G. Burchell, C. Gordon, and P. Miller, eds. Pp. 87–104. Chicago: University of Chicago Press.

Fraser, Nancy
  1990 Rethinking the Public Sphere: A Contribution to the Critique of Actually Existing Democracy. *Social Text* 8–9 (3–1):56–80.

Freud, Sigmund
    1990 The Uncanny. In *Art and Literature*. Vol. 14, *The Penguin Freud Library*. Albert Dickson, ed. Alix Strachey, trans. Pp. 335–76. Harmondsworth, UK: Penguin.
Friedrich, Paul
    1989 Language, Ideology and Political Economy. *American Anthropologist* 91:295–312.
Fujii, James
    1993 *Complicit Fictions: The Subject in the Modern Japanese Narrative Prose*. Berkeley: University of California Press.
Fujita, Kuniko
    1991 Women Workers and Flexible Specialization: The Case of Tokyo. *Economy and Society* 20 (3):260–82.
Fujitani, Takashi
    1996 *Splendid Monarchy: Power and Pageantry in Modern Japan*. Berkeley: University of California Press.
Fukama, Naiki
    1878 *Danjo dōkenron* [The theory of gender equity]. Shibaku, Tokyofu: Yamanaka Ichibei.
Fukaya, Masashi
    1981 *Ryōsai kenbo shugi no kyōiku* [The education of the "good wife and wise mother"]. Tokyo: Reimei Shobō.
Fukei no shokugyō chōsa [A survey on the father's occupation]
    1901 *Fujo shimbun*, August 26, 2.
Futabatei, Shimei
    1906 Yoga gembun'itchi no yurai [The origin of my gembun'itchi]. *Bunshōsekai* 1 (3):11–13.
Gal, Susan
    1989 Language and Political Economy. *Annual Review of Anthropology* 18:345–67.
    1991 Between Speech and Silence: The Problematics of Research on Language and Gender. In *Gender at the Crossroads of Knowledge: Feminist Anthropology in the Postmodern Era*. M. di Leonard, ed. Pp. 175–203. Berkeley: University of California Press.
Garon, Sheldon M.
    1987 *The State and Labor in Modern Japan*. Berkeley: University of California Press.
    1993 Women's Groups and the Japanese State: Contending Approaches to Political Integration, 1890–1945. *Journal of Japanese Studies* 19 (1):5–41.
Gengo no daraku [The corruption of language]
    1906 *Jokan* 16 (8):1–2.
Gluck, Carol
    1985 *Japan's Modern Myths: Ideology in the Late Meiji Period*. Princeton: Princeton University Press.

Goffman, Erving
  1981 *Forms of Talk*. Oxford: Blackwell.

Gordon, Andrew
  2002 The Short Happy Life of the Japanese Middle Class. In *Social Contracts under Stress: The Middle Classes of America, Europe, and Japan at the Turn of the Century*. Olivier Zunz, Leonard Schoppa, and Nobuhiro Hiwatari, eds. Pp. 108–29. New York: Russell Sage Foundation.

Gramsci, Antonio
  1971 *Selections from the Prison Notebooks*. Q. Hoare and G. Nowell-Smith, trans. and eds. London: Lawrence and Wishart.

Gumperz, John
  1982 *Discourse Strategies*. Cambridge: Cambridge University Press.

  1992 Contextualization and Understanding. In *Rethinking Context: Language as an Interactive Phenomenon*. Alessandro Duranti and Charles Goodwin, eds. Pp. 229–52. Cambridge: Cambridge University Press.

Gupta, Akhil, and James Ferguson
  1997 *Anthropological Locations: Boundaries and Grounds of a Field Science*. Berkeley: University of California Press.

Habermas, Jürgen
  1989 *The Structural Transformation of the Public Sphere: An Inquiry into a Category of Bourgeois Society*. Thomas Burger, ed., with Frederick Lawrence. Cambridge, MA: MIT Press.

Haig, John H.
  1990 A Phonological Difference in Male-Female Speech among Teenagers in Nagoya. In *Aspects of Japanese Women's Language*. S. Ide and N. H. McGloin, eds. Pp. 123–68. Tokyo: Kurosio Publishers.

Hall, Stuart
  1993 Encoding, Decoding. In *The Cultural Studies Reader*. S. During, ed. Pp. 90–103. New York: Routledge.

Hanks, William F.
  1989 Text and Textuality. *Annual Review of Anthropology* 18:95–127.

  1996 *Language and Communicative Practices*. Boulder, CO: Westview Press.

Hansen, Miriam
  1991 *Babel and Babylon: Spectatorship in American Silent Film*. Cambridge, MA: Harvard University Press.

  1993 Early Cinema, Late Cinema: Permutations of the Public Sphere. *Screen* 34 (3): 197–210.

Harootunian, Harry
  1988 Visible Discourses / Invisible Ideologies. *The South Atlantic Quarterly* 87 (3):445–74.

  2000a *History's Disquiet: Modernity, Cultural Practice, and the Question of Everyday Life*. New York: Columbia University Press.

2000b *Overcome by Modernity: History, Culture, and Community in Interwar Japan*. Princeton: Princeton University Press.

Harvey, David
1989 *The Condition of Postmodernity: An Enquiry into the Origins of Cultural Change*. Cambridge: Blackwell.

Hasegawa, Yoko
1996 The (Non-Vacuous) Semantics of TE-Linkage in Japanese. *Journal of Pragmatics* 25:763–90.

Haug, Wolfgang Fritz
1986 *Critique of Commodity Aesthetics: Appearance, Sexuality, and Advertising in Capitalist Society*. Minneapolis: University of Minnesota Press.

Hida, Yoshifumi
1988 Yamanote no kotoba no keisei [The formation of the language of Yamanote]. *Bungaku* 53 (11):16–34.

Hill, Jane H.
1998 "Today There Is No Respect": Nostalgia, "Respect," and Oppositional Discourse in Mexicano (Nahuatl) Language Ideology. In *Language Ideologies: Practice and Theory*. Bambi B. Schieffelin, Kathryn Ann Woolard, and Paul V. Kroskrity, eds. Pp. 68–86. New York: Oxford University Press.

Hill, Jane H., and Judith T. Irvine, eds.
1993 *Responsibility and Evidence in Oral Discourse*. New York: Cambridge University Press.

Hirao, Taro
1929 *Hirao sanpei shōten gojūnenshi* [Hirao Sanpei Company Limited, the history of the first fifty years]. Tokyo: Hirao Sanpei Shōten.

Hirata, Oriza
1998 *Engeki nyūmon* [Introduction to drama]. Tokyo: Kōdansha

Honda, Masuko
1990 *Jogakusei no keifu* [The genealogy of the schoolgirl]. Tokyo: Seidosha.

Horii, Reiichi
1993 Joseigo no seiritsu [The establishment of women's language]. *Kokugogaku* 12 (5): 100–108.

Huyssen, Andreas
1986 Mass Culture as Woman: Modernism's Other. In *Studies in Entertainment: Critical Approaches to Mass Culture*. Tania Modleski, ed. Pp. 188–207. Bloomington: Indiana University Press.

I, Yonsuku
1996 *"Kokugo" to iu shisō: Kindai nihon no gengo ninshiki* [National language as a social thought: The understanding of language in modern Japan]. Tokyo: Iwanami Shoten.

Ide, Risako, and Tomomi Terada
1998 The Historical Origins of Japanese Women's Speech: From the Secluded

Worlds of "Court Ladies" and "Play Ladies." *International Journal of the Sociology of Language* 129:139–56.

Ide, Sachiko
1979 *Onna no kotoba, otoko no kotoba* [Women's speech, men's speech]. Tokyo: Nihon Keizai Tsūshinsha.
1982 Japanese Sociolinguistics: Politeness and Women's Language. *Lingua* 57:357–85.
1993 Sekai no joseigo, nihon no joseigo: joseigo kenkyū no shintenkai o motomete [Women's language in the world, women's language in Japan: Towards new developments in the study of women's language]. *Nihongogaku* 12:4–12.
1994 Women's Language in Women's World. Paper presented at the Third Berkeley Women and Language Conference, University of California, April 10.

Ide, Sachiko, Motoko Hori, Akiko Kawasaki, Shoko Ikuta, and Hitomi Haga
1986 Sex Differences and Politeness in Japanese. *International Journal of the Sociology of Language* 58:25–36.

Ide, Sachiko, and Naomi Hanaoka McGloin, eds.
1990 *Aspects of Japanese Women's Language*. Tokyo: Kuroshio Publishers.

Iida, Yuko
1998 *Karera no monogatari: Nihon kindai bungaku to jendā* [His stories: Japanese modern literature and gender]. Nagoya-shi: Nagoya Daigaku Shuppankai.

Inoue, Mariko
1996 Kiyokata's Asasuzu: The Emergence of the Jogakusei Image. *Monumenta Nipponica* 51 (4):431–60.

Irvine, Judith T.
1989 When Talk Isn't Cheap: Language and Political Economy. *American Ethnologist* 16:248–67.

Irvine, Judith T., and Susan Gal
2000 Language Ideology and Linguistic Differentiation. In *Regimes of Language: Ideologies, Politics, and Identities*. P. V. Kroskrity, ed. Pp. 35–84. Santa Fe: School of American Research Press.

Ishiguro, Tadanori
1911 Chikagoro no onna no kotobazukai [Recent language use by women]. *Fujin sekai* 6 (13):28–30.

Ishikawa, Sadayuki
1972 Kindaigo no "teyo, dawa, noyo" (*Teyo, dawa,* and *noyo* in modern Japanese]. *Kaishaku*:18 (10):22–27.

Ishino, Hiroshi, and Minako Yasuhira
1991 Linguistic Awareness of the Japanese and the Future of the Japanese Language. *The NHK Annual Bulletin of Broadcasting Culture Research* 36:83–114, 149.

Isoda, Koichi
   1979 *Shisō to shite no Tokyo: Kindai bungaku shiron nōto* [Tokyo as a social thought: Working notes on modern literature]. Tokyo: Kokubunsha.

Itoh, Makoto
   1994 Is the Japanese Economy in Crisis? *Review of International Political Economy* 1 (1):29–51.

Ivy, Marilyn
   1995 *Discourses of the Vanishing: Modernity, Phantasm, Japan*. Chicago: University of Chicago Press.

Iwaya, Sazanami
   1904 Hatsu no butōkai [The first ball]. *Jogaku sekai* 4 (4):155–73.

Jakobson, Roman
   1971 [1957] Shifters and Verbal Categories. In *Roman Jakobson, Selected Writings*. Vol. 2, *Word and Language*. S. Rudy, ed. Pp. 130–47. The Hague: Mouton.

   1981 [1960] Concluding Statement: Linguistics and Poetics. In *Roman Jakobson, Selected Writings*. Vol. 3, *Poetry of Grammar and Grammar of Poetry*. S. Rudy, ed. Pp. 18–51.The Hague: Mouton.

Jameson, Fredric
   1981 *The Political Unconscious: Narrative as a Socially Symbolic Act*. Ithaca: Cornell University Press.

Jay, Martin
   1988 Scopic Regimes of Modernity. In *Vision and Visuality*. H. Foster, ed. Pp. 3–28. New York: New Press.

Jogakusei kotoba [Schoolgirl speech]
   1905 *Yomiuri Shimbun*, March 16.

Jogakusei no gengo [The schoolgirl's language]
   1905 *Jokan* 15 (4):197.

Joseph, John Earl, and Talbot J. Taylor
   1990 *Ideologies of Language*. New York: Routledge.

Kamei, Hideo
   1993 Buntai no naka no kigō: Kindaiteki buntaishi saikoo no tameni [Symbols in styles: Toward the rethinking of the history of modern stylistics]. *Bungaku* (Winter): 2–14.

Kanai, Yoshiko
   1987 *Aisareru ofisuredī no hanashikata manā* [Desirable manners of speaking for office ladies]. Tokyo: Daiwa Shuppan.

Kaplan, Caren
   1987 Deterritorializations: The Writing of Home and Exile in Western Feminist Discourse. *Cultural Critique* 6:187–98.

Karatani, Kojin
   1993 *Origins of Modern Japanese Literature*. Brett de Bary, trans. Durham, NC: Duke University Press.

Karlin, Jason G.
   2002 The Gender of Nationalism: Competing Masculinities in Meiji Japan. *Journal of Japanese Studies* 28 (1):41–77.

Katayama, Seiichi
   1984 *Kindai nihon no joshi kyōiku* [Women's education in modern Japan]. Tokyo: Kenpakusha.

Kato, Emiko
   2000 *Ojō-sama kotoba sokushū kōza* [Ojō-sama language quick study course]. Tokyo: Discover 21.

Kato, Hiroyuki
   1902 Kokugo chōsa ni tsukite [On the survey of national language]. *Kyōiku jiron* 622:4–6.

Kawaguchi, Yoko
   1987 Majiriau danjo no kotoba: jittai chōsa ni yoru genjō [The blending of men's and women's languages: The reality based on empirical research]. *Gengoseikatsu* no. 429:34–39.

Kawamura, Kunimitsu
   1993 *Otome no inori: Kindai josei imēji no tanjō* [The maiden's prayer: The birth of the image of modern women]. Tokyo: Kinokuniya Shoten.

Keen, Donald
   1984 *Dawn to the West: Japanese Literature of the Modern Era*. New York: Holt, Rinehart, and Winston.

Kelly, William W.
   1986 Rationalization and Nostalgia: Cultural Dynamics of New Middle-Class Japan. *American Ethnologist* 13 (4):603–18.
   2002 At the Limits of New Middle Class Japan: Beyond "Mainstream Consciousness." In *Social Contracts under Stress: The Middle Classes of America, Europe, and Japan at the Turn of the Century*. Olivier Zunz, Leonard Schoppa, and Nobuhiro Hiwatari, eds. Pp. 232–54. New York: Russell Sage Foundation.

Kerr, Derek
   2002 The "Place" of Land in Japan's Postwar Development, and the Dynamic of the 1980s Real-Estate "Bubble" and 1990s Banking Crisis. *Environment and Planning D* 20:345–374.

Kikuchi, Yuho
   1971 [1903] Chikyōdai [Sisters]. In *Meiji katei shōsetsu shū*. Vol. 93, *Meiji bungaku zenshū*. Pp. 89–240. Tokyo: Chikuma Shobo.

Kikuzawa, Sueo
   1929 Fujin no kotoba no tokuchō ni tsuite [On the characteristics of women's language]. *Kokugo kyōiku* 14 (3):66–75.

Kimura, Ryoko
   1992 Fujin zasshi no jōhō kūkan to josei taishū dokushasō no seiritsu: Kindai

nihon ni okeru shufu yakuwari no keisei tono kanren de [The development of the information space in women's magazines, and the female mass readership: In conjunction with the formation of the role of housewives in modern Japan]. *Shisō* no. 821:231–52.

Kindaichi, Haruhiko
    1988 *Nihongo* [Japanese language], vol 1. Tokyo: Iwanami Shinsho.

Kindaichi, Kyosuke
    1942 *Zōho kokugo kenkyū* [Studies of national language, additional supplement]. Tokyo: Yakumoshorin.

Kokugo Chōsa Iinkai
    1908 *Kōgohō torishirabe ni kansuru jikō* [Notes on the survey of the grammar of colloquial Japanese]. Tokyo: Monbushō.

    1916 *Kōgohō* [The grammar of colloquial Japanese]. Tokyo: Kokutei Kyōkasho Kyōdō Hanbaisho.

    1949 [1902] Kokugo Chōsa Iinkai Ketsugi Jikō [Resolutions of the National Language Research Council]. In *Kokugo chōsa enkaku shiryō* [Documents for the history of the national language survey]. Monbushō Kyōkashokyoku Kokugoka, ed. P. 59. Tokyo: Monbushō Kyōkashokyoku Kokugoka.

    1986 [1906] *Kōgohō chōsa hōkokusho* [The report of the national language survey]. Tokyo: Kokusho Kankōkai.

Kokugo Shingikai [National Language Council]
    1998 Kokugo Shingikai dai ichi iinkai, dai 13 kai giji yōshi [Minutes of the 13th meeting of the National Language Council (the First Committee)]. April 14. http://www.mext.go.jp/b_menu/shingi/12/kokugo/gijiroku/005/980401.htm (accessed April 1, 2005).

    2000 Gendai shakai ni okeru keii hyōgen [Deferential expressions in modern (Japanese) society]. Publication of Bunkachō [Agency for Cultural Affairs]. December 8. http://www.mext.go.jp/b_menu/shingi/12/kokugo/toushin/001216.htm (accessed April 1, 2005).

Komatsu, Sumio
    1988 Tokyōgo ni okeru danjosa no keisei: Shūjosi o chūsin to shite [The formation of gender differences in the Tokyo dialect: Centering on the sentence-final particles]. *Kokugo to kokubungaku* 65:94–106.

Komori, Yoichi
    1988 *Kozō to shite no katari* [Narrative as a structure]. Tokyo: Shinyosha.

    1992 Buntai to Aidentitii [Style and identity]. *Gekkan gengo*. October, 48–55.

    2000 *Nihongo no kindai* [The modernity of Japanese language]. Tokyo: Iwanami.

Kondo, Dorinne
    1990 *Crafting Selves: Power, Gender, and Discourses of Identity in a Japanese Workplace*. Chicago: University of Chicago Press.

Kotobazukai [Language use]
    1892 *Jokan* no. 8:74.

Kōtō jogakkō kenkyūkai [The study of women's high schools]
   1994 Tokyo: Ōzorasha.

Koyama, Shizuko
   1991 *Ryōsai kenbo to iu kihan* [The norm of a good wife and wise mother]. Tokyo: Keiso Shobō.
   1999 *Katei no seisei to josei no kokuminka* [The construction of the home and the nationalization of women]. Tokyo: Keisō Shobō.

Kristeva, Julia, and Leon S. Roudiez
   1980 *Desire in Language: A Semiotic Approach to Literature and Art*. Oxford: Blackwell.

Kristof, Nicholas D.
   1995 Japan's Feminine Falsetto Falls Right Out of Favor. *New York Times* 145 (December 13):A1.

Kroskrity, Paul V.
   2000 *Regimes of Language: Ideologies, Polities, and Identities*. Santa Fe: School of American Research Press.

Kuno, Susumu
   1973 *The Structure of the Japanese Language*. Cambridge, MA: MIT Press.

Kyōiku jiron
   1899 Kabayama bunsō chihō shigakukan kaigi (Meiji 32 nen 7 gatsu 11 nichi) deno enzetsu [Speech by Kabayama, Minister of Education, at the Regional Conference for Academic Affairs Observers, July 11, 1899]. *Kyōiku jiron*, July 11, 22–23.

Labov, William
   1972 *Sociolinguistic Patterns*. Philadelphia: University of Pennsylvania Press.

Lacan, Jacques
   1977 *The Four Fundamental Concepts of Psycho-Analysis*. London: Hogarth Press.

Lam, Alice
   1992 *Women and Japanese Management: Discrimination and Reform*. London: Routledge.

Lebra, Takie Sugiyama
   1976 *Japanese Patterns of Behavior*. Honolulu: University Press of Hawaii.
   1992 Gender and Culture in Japanese Political Economy: Self Portrayals of Prominent Business Women. In *The Political Economy of Japan*. Vol. 3, *Cultural and Social Dynamics*. S. Kumon and H. Rosovsky, eds. Pp. 364–419. Stanford: Stanford University Press.

Lee, Benjamin
   1997 *Talking Heads: Language, Metalanguage, and the Semiotics of Subjectivity*. Durham, NC: Duke University Press.

Levin, David Michael
   1993 *Modernity and the Hegemony of Vision*. Berkeley: University of California Press.

Lucy, John A.
　1993 Reflexive Language and the Human Disciplines. In *Reflexive Language: Reported Speech and Metapragmatics*. J. A. Lucy, ed. Pp. 1–32. New York: Cambridge University Press.

Lukács, György
　1968 *History and Class Consciousness*. Cambridge, MA: MIT Press.
　1971 *The Theory of the Novel: A Historico-Philosophical Essay on the Forms of Great Epic Literature*. London: Merlin Press.

Lunsing, Wim, and Claire Maree
　2004 Shifting Speakers: Negotiating Reference in Relation to Sexuality and Gender. In *Japanese Language, Gender, and Ideology: Cultural Models and Real People*. S. Okamoto and J. Shibamoto Smith, eds. Pp. 92–109. New York: Oxford University Press.

Lynch, Deidre, and William B. Warner
　1996 *Cultural Institutions of the Novel*. Durham, NC: Duke University Press.

Makazekoikaze
　1904 [Publication advertisement for the novel *Makazekoikaze*]. *Fujinkai* 3 (1):3.

Mani, Lata
　1987 Contentious Traditions: The Debate on *Sati* in Colonial India. *Cultural Critique* (Fall):119–58.

Marchand, Roland
　1985 *Advertising the American Dream : Making Way for Modernity, 1920–1940*. Berkeley: University of California Press.

Maree, Claire
　1997 Jendā no shihyō to jendā no imisei no henka: Eiga *Shinjuku Boys* ni okeru onabe no baai [Gender indexicality and the shifting meanings of gender: The case of an *onabe* in the documentary film *Shinjuku Boys*]. *Gendai shisō* 25 (13):263–78.

Martin, Samuel E.
　1975 *A Reference Grammar of Japanese*. New Haven: Yale University Press.

Marx, Karl
　1976 *Capital: A Critique of Political Economy*, vol. 1. Ben Fowkes, trans. New York: Penguin.
　1981 *Capital: A Critique of Political Economy*, vol. 3. David Fernbach, trans. New York: Penguin.

Mashimo, Saburo
　1969 *Fujingo no kenkyū* [The study of women's language]. Tokyo: Tokyōdō Shuppan.

Matsumoto, Yoshiko
　2004 Alternative Femininity: Personae of Middle-aged Mothers. In *Japanese Language, Gender, and Ideology: Cultural Models and Real People*. S. Okamoto and J. Shibamoto Smith, eds. Pp. 240–55. New York: Oxford University Press.

Maynard, Senko K.
    1999 Grammar, with Attitude: On the Expressivity of Certain *da* Sentences in Japanese. *Linguistics* 37 (2): 215–50.

McClintock, Anne
    1995 *Imperial Leather: Race, Gender, and Sexuality in the Colonial Conquest*. New York: Routledge.

Miki, Hiroko
    1986 Kindai fujin zasshi kankei nenpyō [The chronology of publications related to modern women's magazines]. In *Nihon no fujin zasshi, kaisetsu* [Japanese women's magazines, comments]. K. Nakajima, ed. Pp. 167–219. Tokyo: Ōzorasha.

Miller, Scott J.
    1984 Japanese Shorthand and *Sokkibon*. *Monumenta Nipponica* 49 (4):471–87.

Miyajima, Tatsuo
    1988 Shōsetu no kōgoka [The colloquialization of novels]. In *Gengo no henka*. *"Kotoba,"* series 28. Pp. 68–80. Tokyo: Bunkachō.

Miyazaki, Ayumi
    2004 Japanese Junior High School Girls' and Boys' First-Person Pronoun Use and Their Social World. In *Japanese Language, Gender, and Ideology: Cultural Models and Real People*. S. Okamoto and J. Shibamoto Smith, eds. Pp. 256–74. New York: Oxford University Press.

Mogami, Katsuya
    1986 Hataraku josei no kotoba no ishiki [The language awareness of working women]. *The NHK Monthly Report on Broadcast Research*. November, 14–28.

Mohanty, S. P.
    1989 Us and Them: On the Philosophical Bases of Political Criticism. *Yale Journal of Criticism* 2 (2):1–31.

Molony, Barbara
    1995 Japan's 1986 Equal Employment Opportunity Law and the Changing Discourse on Gender. *Signs* 2 (1995):268–302.

Monbushō
    1904 *Jinjō shōgaku tokuhon* [Elementary primers]. Tokyo: Nihon Shoseki.
    1964 *Gakusei kyūjū nen shi* [School system, the history of the first ninety years]. Tokyo: Monbushō.

Morino, Muneaki
    1991 Joseigo no rekishi [The history of women's language]. In *Kōza nihongo to nihongo kyōiku*. 10: *Nihongo no rekishi* [Japanese and Japanese language education series. Vol. 10, The history of the Japanese language]. Pp. 225–49. Tokyo: Meiji Shoin.

Mouffe, Chantal
    1988 Hegemony and New Political Subjects: Toward a New Concept of Democracy. In *Marxism and the Interpretation of Culture*. Cary Nelson and Lawrence Grossberg, eds. Pp. 89–104. Urbana: University of Illinois Press.

Mulvey, Laura
    1989 Visual Pleasure and Narrative Cinema and Afterthoughts. In *Visual Pleasure and Narrative Cinema*. Pp. 14–38. Bloomington: Indiana University Press.

Muta, Kazue
    1996 *Senryaku to shite no kazoku: Kindai nihon no kokumin kokka keisei to josei* [Family as a strategy: The modern Japanese nation state and women]. Tokyo: Shinyōsha.

Nagamine, Shigetoshi
    1997 *Zasshi to dokusha no kindai* [The modernity of magazines and their readers]. Tokyo: Nihon Editor School Shuppan.

Nagasaki, Kazunori
    1986 *Miryokuteki josei wa hanashi jōzu* [Attractive women are raconteurs]. Tokyo: Mikasa Shobō.

Nakajima, Kuni
    1986 Kaisetsu [Comments]. In *Nihon no fujin zasshi* [Japanese women's magazines]. K. Nakajima, ed. Pp. 1–166. Tokyo: Ōzorasha.
    1989 Kindai nihon ni okeru fujin zasshi, sono shūhen: "Fujin zasshi no yoake" ni yosete [The surroundings of women's magazines in modern Japan: On the occasion of publication of "The Dawn of Women's Magazines"]. In *Fujin zasshi no yoake*. Kindai josei bunkashi kenkyūkai, ed. Pp. 1–17. Tokyo: Ōzorasha.

Nakamura, Momoko
    1995 *Kotoba to feminizumu* [Language and feminism]. Tokyo: Keisō Shobō
    2001 *Kotoba to jendā* [Language and gender]. Tokyo: Keisō Shobō.

Natsume, Soseki
    1985 [1909] *Sanshiro*. Tokyo: Horupushuppan.

Negt, Oskar, and Alexander Kluge
    1993 *Public Sphere and Experience: Toward an Analysis of the Bourgeois and Proletarian Public Sphere*. P. Labanyi, J. O. Daniel, and A. Oksiloff, trans. Minneapolis: University of Minnesota Press.

Noguchi, Takehiko
    1994 *Sanninshō no hakken made* [Up until the discovery of the third-person pronoun]. Tokyo: Chikuma Shobō.

Noguchi, Yukio
    1994 The "Bubble" and Economic Policies in the 1980s. *Journal of Japanese Studies* 20 (2):291–329.

Nolte, Sharon H., and Sally Ann Hastings
    1991 The Meiji State's Policy toward Women, 1890–1910. In *Recreating Japanese Women, 1600–1945*. G. L. Bernstein, ed. pp. 151–74. Berkeley: University of California Press.

Ochs, Elinor
    1990 Indexicality and Socialization. In *Cultural Psychology*. James W. Stigler,

Richard A. Shweder, and Gilbert Herdt, eds. Pp. 287–308. Cambridge: Cambridge University Press.

1992 Indexing Gender. In *Rethinking Context: Language as an Interactive Phenomenon*. Alessandro Duranti and Charles Goodwin, eds. Pp. 335–58. Cambridge: Cambridge University Press.

Ogasawara, Yuko
 1998 *Office Ladies and Salaried Men: Power, Gender, and Work in Japanese Companies*. Berkeley: University of California Press.

Ogawa, Kikumatsu
 1962 *Nihon shuppankai no ayumi* [The course of the Japanese publishing industry]. Tokyo: Seibundō Shinkōsha.

Ogawa, Naoko, and Janet Shibamoto Smith
 1997 The Gendering of the Gay Male Sex Class: A Preliminary Case Study Based on Rasen no Sobyō. In *Queerly Phrased: Language, Gender, and Sexuality*. A. Livia and K. Hall, eds. Pp. 402–15. New York: Oxford University Press.

Ogino, Hajime
 1896 Joshi no gengo no tsukaikata [Women's language use]. *Jokan* no. 175:3–5.

Okamoto, Shigeko
 1995 "Tasteless" Japanese: Less "Feminine" Speech among Young Japanese Women. In *Gender Articulated: Language and the Socially Constructed Self*. K. Hall and M. Bucholtz, eds. Pp. 297–325. New York: Routledge.

Okamoto, Shigeko, and Shie Sato
 1992 Less Feminine Speech among Young Japanese Females. In *Locating Power: Proceedings of the Second Berkeley Women and Language Conference*. K. Hall, M. Bucholtz, and B. Moonwomon, eds. Pp. 478–88. Berkeley: Berkeley Women and Language Group, University of California.

Okamoto, Shigeko, and Janet Shibamoto Smith, eds.
 2004 *Japanese Language, Gender, and Ideology: Cultural Models and Real People*. New York: Oxford University Press.

Okano, Kyuin
 1902 Hyōjungo ni tsuite [On standard language]. *Gengogaku zasshi* 3 (2):32–40.

Omori, Maki
 1993 Gender and the Labor Market. *Journal of Japanese Studies* 19 (1):79–102.

Ong, Aihwa
 1987 *Spirits of Resistance and Capitalist Discipline: Factory Women in Malaysia*. Albany: State University of New York Press.

Onna tachi no kotoba bumi kotoba [Women's written language]
 1892 *Jokan* no. 8:75–76.

Ortner, Sherry
 1991 Reading America: Preliminary Notes on Class and Culture. In *Recapturing Anthropology*. R. G. Fox, ed. Pp. 163–90. Santa Fe: School of American Research Press.

Otsuki, Fumihiko
　1917 *Kōgohō bekki* [Supplement to the grammar of colloquial Japanese]. Tokyo: Dai Nihon Tosho Kabushiki Kaisha.
Ozaki, Koyo
　1994 [1888] Hayari kotoba [Vogue speech]. In *Koyo zenshū*, vol. 10. Ooka Makoto et al., eds. Pp. 4–5. Tokyo: Iwanami Shoten.
Peirce, Charles S.
　1931 *Collected Papers of Charles Sanders Peirce*. 8 vols. Charles Hartshorne, Paul Weiss, and Arthur W. Burks, eds. Cambridge, MA: Harvard University Press.
Philips, Susan U.
　1986 Reported Speech as Evidence in an American Trial. In *Georgetown University Round Table on Languages and Linguistics*. Deborah Tannen and James Alatis, eds. Pp. 154–70. Washington, DC: Georgetown University Press.
Pollock, Friedrich
　1976 [1955] Empirical Research into Public Opinion. In *Critical Sociology: Selected Readings*. P. Connerton, ed. Pp. 225–36. New York: Penguin Books.
Pollock, Griselda
　1988 *Vision and Difference: Femininity, Feminism, and Histories of Art*. New York: Routledge.
Povinelli, Elizabeth
　1999 Grammaires intimes: Langage, subjectivité, et genre: Compte rendu anthropologique et psychoanalytique. Special issue, Christine Jourdan and Claire Lefebvre, eds. *Anthropologie et Societés* 23 (3):121–47.
　2001 Sexuality at Risk: Psychoanalysis (Meta)pragmatically. In *Homosexuality and Psychoanalysis*. Tim Dean and Christopher Lane, eds. Pp. 387–411. Chicago: University of Chicago Press.
Pratt, Mary Louise
　1987 Linguistic Utopias. In *The Linguistics of Writing: Arguments between Language and Literature*. Nigel Fabb, Derek Attridge, Alan Durant, and Colin MacCabe, eds. Pp. 48–66. New York: Methuen.
　2002 Modernity and Periphery: Toward a Global and Relational Analysis. In *Beyond Dichotomies: Histories, Identities, Cultures, and the Challenge of Globalization*. Elizabeth M. Mudimbe-Boyi, ed. Pp. 21–48. Albany: State University of New York Press.
Ragsdale, Kathryn
　1998 Marriage, the Newspaper Business, and the Nation-State: Ideology in the Late Meiji Serialized *Katei Shosetsu*. *Journal of Japanese Studies* 24 (2):229–55.
Reijōsaikun no kotoba [Daughters' and wives' language]
　1896 *Waseda bungaku*, February, 148.
Robertson, Jennifer
　1998a It Takes a Village: Internationalization and Nostalgia in Postwar Japan.

In *Mirror of Modernity: Invented Traditions in Modern Japan.* S. Vlastos, ed. Pp. 209–39. Berkeley: University of California Press

1998b *Takarazuka: Sexual Politics and Popular Culture in Modern Japan.* Berkeley: University of California Press.

1999 Dying to Tell: Sexuality and Suicide in Imperial Japan. *Signs* 25 (1):1–36.

Rofel, Lisa
1999 *Other Modernities: Gendered Yearnings in China after Socialism.* Berkeley: University of California Press.

Rohlen, Thomas
1974 *For Harmony and Strength: Japanese White-Collar Organization in Anthropological Perspective.* Berkeley: University of California Press.

Rose, Nikolas
1999 *Powers of Freedom: Reframing Political Thought.* New York: Cambridge University Press.

Rosenberger, Nancy Ross
1992 *Japanese Sense of Self.* New York: Cambridge University Press.

Rumsey, Alan
1990 Wording, Meaning, and Linguistic Ideology. *American Anthropologist* 92 (2): 346–61.

Sakai, Naoki
1988 Modernity and Its Critique: The Problem of Universalism and Particularism. *The South Atlantic Quarterly* 87 (3):475–504.

1992 *Voices of the Past: The Status of Language in Eighteenth-Century Japanese Discourse.* Ithaca: Cornell University Press.

1996 *Shizansareru nihongo, nihonjin* [The stillbirth of the Japanese language and the Japanese]. Tokyo: Shinyōsha.

Sakakura, Atsuyoshi
1964 Hanasuyōni kaku to iukoto: Gembun'itchi to Shoyo, Shimei [Write as you speak: Gembun'itchi and Shoyo, Shimei]. *Kokugo kokubun* 33 (7):25–31.

Sakamoto, Hideko
1951 *Kōkoku gojūnenshi* [The history of the first fifty years of advertisement]. Tokyo: Nihondenpōtsūshinsha.

Sakuma, Kanae
1936 *Gendai nihongo no hyōgen to gohō* [The expression and usage of modern Japanese language]. Tokyo: Kōseikaku.

Sato, Barbara Hamill
2003 *The New Japanese Woman: Modernity, Media, and Women in Interwar Japan.* Durham, NC: Duke University Press.

Sato, Haruo
1998 [1941] Shōsetsu [The novel]. In *Kokugo bunka kōza.* Vol. 4, *Kokugo geijutsu hen.* Toshiaki Sakuragi, ed. Pp. 71–98. Tokyo: Asahi Shimbunsha.

Sato, Rika Sakuma

   1995 Shashin to josei: Atarashii shikaku media no tōjō to "miru/mirareru" jibun no shutsugen [Photography and women: The advent of the new visual media and the emergence of the seeing/seen self]. In *Onna to otoko no jikū: Nihon joseishi saikō* [Time space of gender: Redefining Japanese women's history]. N. Kono, ed. Pp. 187–237. Tokyo: Fujiwara Shoten.

   1996 Kiyoki shijōde gokōsai o: Meiji makki shōjo zasshi tōshoran ni miru kyōdōtai no kenkyū [Correspondence columns of Japanese girls' magazines, 1902–13]. *Joseigaku* 4:114–41.

Sato, Toshiki

   2000 *Fubyōdō shakai nihon: sayonara sōchūryū* [The unequal society, Japan: Farewell to all-middle-class society]. Tokyo: Chūō Kōron Shinsha.

Saussure, Ferdinand de

   1959 *Course in General Linguistics*. New York: Philosophical Library.

Schieffelin, Bambi B., Kathryn Ann Woolard, and Paul V. Kroskrity

   1998 *Language Ideologies: Practice and Theory*. New York: Oxford University Press.

Scott, Joan Wallach

   1996 After History? *Common Knowledge* 5 (3):9–26.

Shibamoto, Janet S.

   1985 *Japanese Women's Language*. New York: Academic Press.

   1987 Japanese Sociolinguistics. *Annual Review of Anthropology* 16:261–78.

Shibamoto Smith, Janet S.

   1992 The Giving of Evidence: A Study of Sentence Extensions and Gender in Japanese. *Journal of Japanese Linguistics* 14:67–90.

Shibatani, Masayoshi

   1990 *The Languages of Japan*. New York: Cambridge University Press.

Shikitei, Sanba

   1952 [1813] *Ukiyoburo* [The bathhouse of the floating world]. Tokyo: Iwanami Shoten.

Shindo, Masahiro

   2000 *Besutoserā no yukue: Meiji Taisho no ryūkō shōsetsu* [The trajectory of best sellers: Popular novels in Meiji and Taisho]. Tokyo: Kanrin Shobō.

Shiraki, Susumu

   1970 Nihongo ni okeru joseigo no seiritsu to sono haikei no kōsatsu [The study of the establishment of women's language in Japanese language and its background]. *Kokubungaku kenkyū* 6:155–66.

Siegal, Meryl

   1994 Second Language Learning, Identity, and Resistance: White Women Studying Japanese in Japan. In *Cultural Performances: Proceedings of the Third Berkeley Women and Language Conference*. M. Bucholtz, A. C. Liang, L. A. Sutton, and C. Hines, eds. Pp. 642–50. Berkeley: Berkeley Women and Language Group, University of California.

Sievers, Sharon L.
  1983 *Flowers in Salt: The Beginnings of Feminist Consciousness in Modern Japan.* Stanford: Stanford University Press.
Silverberg, Miriam
  1991a Constructing a New Cultural History of Prewar Japan. *Boundary 2* 18 (3):61–89.
  1991b Modern Girl as Militant. In *Recreating Japanese Women, 1600–1945.* G. L. Bernstein, ed. Pp. 239–66. Berkeley: University of California Press.
  1995 Advertising Every Body: Images from the Japanese Modern Years. In *Choreographing History.* S. Foster, ed. Pp. 129–247. Bloomington: Indiana University Press.
Silverman, Kaja
  1988 *The Acoustic Mirror: The Female Voice in Psychoanalysis and Cinema.* Bloomington: Indiana University Press.
Silverstein, Michael
  1976 Shifters, Linguistic Categories, and Cultural Description. In *Meaning in Anthropology.* K. H. Basso and H. A. Selby, eds. Pp. 11–55. Albuquerque: University of New Mexico Press.
  1979 Language Structure and Linguistic Ideology. In *The Elements.* P. R. Clyne, W. Hanks, C. Hofbauer, eds. Pp. 193–247. Chicago: Chicago Linguistic Society.
  1981 The Limits of Awareness. Sociolinguistic Working Paper No. 84. Austin, TX, Southwestern Educational Development Laboratory.
  1993 Metapragmatic Discourse and Meta-Pragmatic Function. In *Reflexive Language: Reported Speech and Metapragmatics.* J. A. Lucy, ed. Pp. 33–58. Cambridge: Cambridge University Press.
  1996 Indexical Order and the Dialectics of Sociolinguistic Life. In *Salsa III: Proceedings of the Third Annual Symposium about Language and Society, Austin, TX.* Rebecca Parker, Risako Ide, and Yukako Sunaoshi, eds. Pp. 266–95. Austin: Department of Linguistics, University of Texas.
  2000 Whorfianism and the Linguistic Imagination of Nationality. In *Regimes of Language: Ideologies, Politics, and Identities.* Paul V. Kroskrity, ed. Pp. 85–138. Santa Fe: School of American Research Press.
Silverstein, Michael, and Greg Urban
  1996 *Natural Histories of Discourse.* Chicago: University of Chicago Press.
Smith, Henry D., II
  1986 The Edo-Tokyo Transition: In Search of Common Ground. In *Japan in Transition: From Tokugawa to Meiji.* M. B. Jansen and G. Rozman, eds. pp. 347–74. Princeton: Princeton University Press.
Smith, Robert J.
  1983 Making Village Women into "Good Wives and Wise Mothers" in Prewar Japan. *Journal of Family History* (Spring):70–84.

Smith, Robert J., and Ella Lury Wiswell
  1982 *The Women of Suye Mura*. Chicago: University of Chicago Press.
Spivak, Gayatri Chakravorty
  1988 Can the Subaltern Speak? In *Marxism and the Interpretation of Culture*. C. Nelson and L. Grossberg, eds. Pp. 271–316. Urbana: University of Illinois Press.
  1990 *The Post-Colonial Critic: Interviews, Strategies, Dialogues*. Sarah Harasym, ed. New York: Routledge.
Statistics Bureau, Management and Coordination Agency
  various years *Annual Report on the Labor Force Survey*. Tokyo: Management and Coordination Agency, Statistics Bureau.
Stoler, Ann Laura
  1991 Carnal Knowledge and Imperial Power: Gender, Race, and Morality in Colonial Asia. In *Gender at the Crossroads of Knowledge: Feminist Anthropology in the Postmodern Era*. Micaela Di Leonardo, ed. Pp. 51–101. Berkeley: University of California Press.
Sturtz Sreetharan, Cindi
  2004a Japanese Men's Linguistic Stereotypes and Realities: Conversations from the Kansai and Kanto Regions. In *Japanese Language, Gender, and Ideology: Cultural Models and Real People*. Shigeko Okamoto and Janet Shibamoto Smith, eds. Pp. 275–90. New York: Oxford University Press.
  2004b Students, Sarariiman (pl.), and Seniors: Japanese Men's Use of "Manly" Speech Register. *Language in Society* 33:81–107.
Sunaoshi, Yukako
  2004 Farm Women's Professional Discourse in Ibaraki. In *Japanese Language, Gender, and Ideology: Cultural Models and Real People*. Shigeko Okamoto and Janet Shibamoto Smith, eds. Pp. 187–204. New York: Oxford University Press.
Suzuki, Kenji
  1989 *Sutekina anata o tsukuru josei no utsukushii hanashikata* [The beautiful manner of speaking for women that makes you attractive]. Tokyo: Gotō Shoin.
Suzuki, Tomi
  1996 *Narrating the Self: Fictions of Japanese Modernity*. Stanford: Stanford University Press.
Takasaki, Midori
  1988 Mosakuki no joseigo [Women's language at the searching stage of its future direction]. *Kotoba* 9:23–40.
Takeuchi, Kyuichi
  1907 Tokyo fujin no tsūyōgo [The common language among women in Tokyo]. *Shumi* 2 (11):24–26.
Tamanoi, Mariko
  1998 *Under the Shadow of Nationalism: Politics and Poetics of Rural Japanese Women*. Honolulu: University of Hawai'i Press.

Tanahashi, Junko
  1911 Chikagoro no onna wa tadashii kotoba o tsukawanu [Women nowadays do not use the correct language]. *Fujin sekai* 6 (13):54–56.

Tannen, Deborah
  1989 *Talking Voices: Repetition, Dialogue, and Imagery in Conversational Discourse*. New York: Cambridge University Press.

Taussig, Michael T.
  1993 *Mimesis and Alterity: A Particular History of the Senses*. New York: Routledge.

Terada, Tomomi
  1993 Nihon ni okeru joseigo kenkyūshi [The history of the studies of Japanese women's language in Japan]. *Nihongogaku* 12:262–309.

Tokyo Tōkei Kyōkai
  1912 *Tōkei shūshi* [Journal of statistics] 376:27.

Trudgill, Peter
  1972 Sex, Covert Prestige and Linguistic Change in the Urban British English of Norwich. *Language in Society* 1:179–95.
  1974 *The Social Differentiation of English in Norwich*. Cambridge: Cambridge University Press.

Tsubouchi, Shoyo
  1886 *Shōsetsu shinzui* [The essence of the novel]. Tokyo: Shōgetsudō.
  1930 *Kaki no heta* [The navel of persimmons]. Tokyo: Azusa Shobō.

Tsurumi, E. Patricia
  1990 *Factory Girls: Women in the Thread Mills of Meiji Japan*. Princeton: Princeton University Press.

Twine, Nanette
  1991 *Language and the Modern State: The Reform of Written Japanese*. New York: Routledge.

Uchida, Roan
  1984 [1894] Bungakusha to naru hōhō [How to become a literary scholar]. In *Uchida Roan zenshū*. Vol. 2, *Bungei hyōron kenkyū, 2*. T. Nomura, ed. Pp. 175–299. Tokyo: Yumani Shobō.

Ueda, Kazutoshi
  1895 Hyōjungo in tsukite [On standard language]. *Teikoku bungaku* 1 (1):14–23.
  1968 [1894] Kokugo to kokka to [National language and the nation-state]. In *Meiji bungaku zenshū*. Vol. 44, *Ochiai Naobumi, Ueda Kazutoshi, Haga Yaichi, Fujioka Sakutaro shū*. Senichi Hisamatsu, ed. Pp. 108–13. Tokyo: Chikuma Shobō.

Ueno, Chizuko
  1987a Genesis of the Urban Housewife. *Japan Quarterly* 34 (2):130–42.
  1987b The Position of Japanese Women Reconsidered. *Current Anthropology* 28 (4):75–84.

1988 *Joen ga yononaka wo kaeru* [Women's network changes society]. Tokyo: Nihon Keizai Shimbunsha.

1989 Women's Labor under Patriarchal Capitalism in the Eighties. *Review of Japanese Culture and Society* 3 (1):1–6.

1998 *Nashonarisumu to jendā*: Engendering nationalism. Tokyo: Seidosha.

Urla, Jacqueline
 1993 Cultural Politics in an Age of Statistics: Numbers, Nations, and the Making of Basque Identity. *American Ethnologist* 20 (4):818–43.

Voloshinov, V. N.
 1973 *Marxism and the Philosophy of Language*. Ladislav Matejka and I. R. Titunik, trans. New York: Seminar Press.

Wacquant, Löic
 1991 Making Class: The Middle Class(es) in Social Theory and Social Structure. In *Bringing Class Back In: Contemporary and Historical Perspectives*. S. G. McNall, R. F. Levine, and R. Fantasia, eds. Pp. 39–64. Boulder, CO: Westview Press.

Walkowitz, Judith R.
 1992 *City of Dreadful Delight: Narratives of Sexual Danger in Late-Victorian London*. London: Virago Press.

Warner, Michael
 1990 *The Letters of the Republic: Publication and the Public Sphere in Eighteenth-Century America*. Cambridge, MA: Harvard University Press.

Washi, Rumi
 2000 Nyōbōkotoba no imisayō: tennōsei, kaisōsei, sekushuariti [The signification of the language of court ladies: The emperor system, stratification, and sexuality]. *Joseigaku nenpō* 21:18–35.

 2004 "Japanese Female Speech" and Language Policy in the World War II Era. In *Japanese Language, Gender, and Ideology: Cultural Models and Real People*. Shigeko Okamoto and Janet Shibamoto Smith, eds. Pp. 76–91. New York: Oxford University Press.

Watt, Ian P.
 1957 *The Rise of the Novel: Studies in Defoe, Richardson, and Fielding*. London: Chatto and Windus.

Wetzel, Patricia J.
 2004 *Keigo in Modern Japan: Polite Language from Meiji to the Present*. Honolulu: University of Hawaii Press.

Wetzel, Patricia J., and Miyako Inoue
 1999 Vernacular Theories of Japanese Honorifics. *The Journal of the Association of Teachers of Japanese* 33 (1):68–101.

Williams, Raymond
 1973 *The Country and the City*. New York: Oxford University Press.

Wilson, Elizabeth
  1991 *The Sphinx in the City: Urban Life, the Control of Disorder, and Women*. London: Virago.
Woolard, Kathryn A.
  1998 Introduction: Language Ideology as a Field of Inquiry. In *Language Ideologies: Practice and Theory*. Bambi B. Schieffelin, Kathryn A. Woolard, and Paul V. Kroskrity, eds. Pp. 3–48. New York: Oxford University Press.
Woolard, Kathryn A., and Bambi B. Schieffelin
  1994 Language Ideology. *Annual Review of Anthropology* 23:55–82.
Yamamoto, Masahide
  1965 *Kindai buntai hassei no shiteki kenkyū* [The historical study of the emergence of modern styles]. Tokyo: Iwanami Shoten.
  1971a *Gembun'itchi no rekishi ronkō* [The historical consideration of gembun'itchi]. Tokyo: Ōfusha.
  1971b Kindaishōsetsu no joseigo [Women's language in modern novels]. *Kaishaku*, December, 1.
  1978 *Kindai buntai keisei shiryō shūsei: hassei hen* [The collection of the material on modern styles: The emergence]. Tokyo: Ōfusha.
  1979 *Kindai buntai keisei shiryō shūsei: seiritsu hen* [The collection of the material on modern styles: The establishment]. Tokyo: Ōfusha.
  1981 *Gembun'itchi no rekishi ronkō: zoku hen* [A sequel to the study of the history of gembun'itchi]. Tokyo: Ōfusha.
Yamamura, Kozo
  1997 The Japanese Political Economy after the "Bubble": Plus Ça Change? *Journal of Japanese Studies* 23 (2):291–331.
Yanagihara, Yoshimitsu
  1908 Teyodawa kotoba no kairyō: mazu hyōjungo o tsukure [The reform of teyo-dawa speech: First, establish the standard Japanese language]. *Jokan* 18 (1):13–15.
Yoda, Tomiko
  2000 Literary History against the National Frame, or Gender and the Emergence of Heian Kana Writing. *Positions: East Asia Cultures Critique* 8 (2):465–97.
Yoneyama, Lisa
  1999 *Hiroshima Traces: Time, Space, and the Dialectics of Memory*. Berkeley: University of California Press.
Yoshida, Sumio, and Yuichi Inokuchi
  1972 *Meiji ikō kokugo mondai shoan shūsei, jōkan* [The collection of documents on national language issues since the Meiji period, first volume]. Tokyo: Kazama Shobō.
  1973 *Meiji ikō kokugo mondai shoan shūsei, gekan* [The collection of documents

on national language issues since the Meiji period, second volume]. Tokyo: Kazama Shobō.

Young, Robert

2001 *Postcolonialism: An Historical Introduction*. Malden, MA: Blackwell Publishers.

Žižek, Slavoj

1996 "I Hear You with My Eyes," or, the Invisible Master. In *Gaze and Voice as Love Objects*. Renata Salecl and Slavoj Žižek, eds. Pp. 90–128. Durham, NC: Duke University Press.

2000 *Enjoy Your Symptom!: Jacques Lacan in Hollywood and Out*. New York: Routledge.

Index

Abjection: and agency, 23, 24, 277; Butler on, 10–11, 281; and discourse analysis, 17; epistemology of, 12, 17, 21, 24, 281; and national modernity, 26, 31, 197; and nation-state formation, 12, 17, 114; and normativity, 11, 12, 15, 164, 196; and performativity, 277; and return of the abject, 31, 33, 277, 279; and standard Japanese language, 196–97; and women's language, 11, 12, 14, 15, 17, 21–23, 26, 31, 33, 114, 277–79
Acoustic mirror, 68, 73
Acoustic presence, 26, 39, 47, 52, 55
Address, forms of, 254
Adorno, Theodor, 51
Advertising: film actresses represented in, 142, 145, 147; geishas represented in, 142, 145; intertextual disguise in, 140; schoolgirl speech in, 27–28, 69–70, 112, 119, 120, 139–40, 142, 145, 147, 150, 157; schoolgirls represented in, 43, 69, 136, 142; social tableaux in, 140, 145; women's language in, 7–8, 19, 104, 105, 147; in women's magazines, 19, 27–28, 69–70, 104, 105, 110, 113, 117, 119, 120, 135–50, 152–54
Affectivity, 76–77
Agency: and abjection, 23, 24, 277; and resistance, 21, 23, 71, 73, 281n1; and schoolgirl speech, 71–72, 73–74, 120; and subject formation, 71–72, 73; and women's language, 21, 22, 23–24, 250–51, 277
Agha, Asif, 155n28
Ahearn, Laura M., 72n49
Allison, Anne, 208n2
Alterity: and de Certeau's theory of writing, 48, 51–52; and linguistic modernity, 48, 50, 52, 53; and literary modernization, 92; and print media, 48–49, 53; and reported speech, 49–50; and subject formation, 48, 49, 53; of women, 48, 52–53; and women's language, 33, 215, 252, 277. *See also* Other
Althusser, Louis, 66
American Indian languages, 168n8
Anderson, Benedict, 24, 48, 65, 78, 92n25, 129, 151
Appadurai, Arjun, 273n9
Auditory practices: and female hysteria, 52, 56; and linguistic ideology, 39; and modernity, 40–41; schoolgirl speech as object of, 26, 38–41, 54, 56, 70–71, 72
Austin, John Langshaw, 20n17, 185n20
Authorship: Foucault on, 50; and literary commodification, 120; and readers' correspondence columns, 128–29, 174; Voloshinov on, 120
Auxiliary verbs, 7n6, 86n14; and literary modernization, 89, 93–96; and school-

309

Auxiliary verbs *(continued)*
    girl speech, 54, 61–63, 108; and women's language, 233, 244, 245, 259, 267, 270n4

Bachnik, Jane, 218n1
Bakhtin, Mikhail, 49n24, 50, 97, 140
Barthes, Roland, 54n31, 77, 95, 130
Baudrillard, Jean, 43n11, 135, 183n18, 201
Bauman, Richard, 20n16, 49n23, 85n11, 105, 149n25
Befu, Harumi, 167n5
Benjamin, Walter, 41, 113, 120–21, 136, 154
Bennett, Tony, 104
Bentham, Jeremy, 55, 90
Bestor, Theodore C., 273
Bhabha, Homi K., 31, 33, 40n5, 73, 91, 215, 277
Binaries: and center/periphery relation, 247; and discourse analysis, 23; and gender difference, 4, 6, 9, 12, 14, 114; and intratextual hierarchy, 52; and linguistic research, 214; and women's identity, 81
Body: and de Certeau's theory of writing, 51; responsibilized, 164, 182, 200; speaking, 19, 22, 23, 31, 73, 112, 125, 130, 131
Bourdieu, Pierre, 106, 133, 183, 201
Bourgeoisie: and family relations, 46, 100, 125, 151, 154; and interiority, 122, 124; and literary modernization, 84; and male subject, 49, 53, 90n21; and public sphere, 53, 127, 129; and schoolgirl speech, 58, 122, 157. *See also* Middle class
Briggs, Charles L., 20n16, 49n23, 85n11, 105, 149n25
Brinton, Mary, 171n12, 208n2
Bubble economy, 29, 164, 170, 171n11, 173n14, 175, 195, 201
Bucholtz, Mary, 28n1
Buck-Morss, Susan, 120, 121
Buddhism, 115, 167
Butler, Judith, 10–11, 21, 22, 98n28, 108, 203, 251, 266, 281

Calhoun, Craig, 90
Capitalism: and Debord's theory of the spectacle, 43; and family relations, 46, 47; and gendered division of labor, 46, 47, 80–81, 100, 117, 167, 173; and literary style, 120–21; and Marx's theory of commodity fetishism, 43, 49, 109; and modernization, 109, 166, 278; and nation-state formation, 79; and the novel, 78, 83; and print media, 26, 78, 79, 83, 99, 102, 105, 115, 116, 120–21, 151, 181; and social inequality, 166; and women's language, 4, 5, 12, 25, 77, 147, 169, 278, 281, 282; and women's magazines, 102, 115, 116, 120–21. *See also* Market relations
Captions, photographic, 130–31, 133, 139, 151
Carter, Erica, 150
Chakrabarty, Dipesh, 196
Chatterjee, Partha, 81, 166
Chinese language, 63–65, 139
Chion, Michel, 55
Christianity, 115
Christian missionaries, 43, 64
Cinema, 44n14, 68
Citation: and contextualization, 20–21, 55; de Certeau on, 50n25; Derrida on, 20; and schoolgirl image, 43; and schoolgirl speech, 38, 39, 54, 70, 72–73, 108, 109; and women's language, 21–23, 24, 31, 33, 163, 203, 216, 217, 241, 244, 252, 260, 264–66, 273, 276, 281
Citizenship, 42, 46, 65, 79, 83, 150, 247, 272, 277
Class, social: and consumerism, 200–201; and linguistic differentiation, 103; and marriage, 58; and schoolgirl speech, 37, 57–60, 66, 133; and upward mobility, 200–203; and women's language, 100, 103, 200–203, 246–48. *See also* Middle class; Working class
Clerical workers, 208–11, 213, 223, 255
Clifford, James, 273n9
Code-switching, 233, 255, 260
College graduates, 208–13, 253, 259, 269
Colloquial Japanese language, 26, 78, 83–85, 88–89, 91, 139, 269
Colonialism, 48, 69, 77, 83
Commodification, 101, 104, 109, 120–21, 154, 200, 203; of desire, 28, 70, 108, 109, 133, 140, 147
Commodity fetishism, 43–44, 49, 109, 151, 154, 155, 159
Commodity spectacle, 151, 154
Communication: narrative, 129; non-reciprocal, 54–55, 72. *See also* Metacommunication

Confession, 122–24, 142, 150, 157
Confucianism, 42n7, 45, 46, 80
Consumerism: and class mobility, 200–201; and gender equality, 173; and nationalism, 150, 151, 153–55; and schoolgirl speech, 27–28, 69, 110, 123, 124, 145, 150, 154–55, 157; and subject formation, 157; and women's language, 7–8, 25, 28, 103–4, 105, 147, 155, 157; and women's magazines, 27–28, 110, 117, 123, 124, 133, 136, 145, 149, 150, 151, 153–55, 157, 202
Consumers: interpellation of, 145, 147; schoolgirls as, 27–28, 109, 123, 124, 136; women as, 8, 25, 29, 42, 69, 99, 104, 105, 112, 154–55, 173, 202
Contextualization, 20, 49, 55, 56, 264, 265
Copies: as originals, 8, 11, 21, 43, 98n28, 103; preceding originals, 9, 10, 266
Copulas, 7n6, 86n14, 131
Corruption, linguistic: and schoolgirl speech, 19, 37, 40n5, 60, 61, 62, 66, 69, 70, 115, 150, 169; and women's language, 2, 19, 20, 29–30, 37, 165, 168–70, 174, 175, 177, 178, 180, 181, 182, 198, 260, 272
Counterpublic sphere, 102, 110, 112, 127–30
Cowie, Elizabeth, 44
Crary, Jonathan, 41
Cross-cultural relations, 3, 274–75, 277

Dean, Mitchell, 164
Debord, Guy, 43, 44n13
de Certeau, Michel, 48, 49n24, 50, 51, 66–67, 105
Defamiliarization, 33, 215, 252, 264, 273
Defoe, Daniel, 84
de Grazia, Victoria, 150
de Lauretis, Teresa, 44n14
Democracy, 42, 79, 90, 115, 127, 166, 182, 188–89, 246–47
Derrida, Jacques, 9, 10, 20, 23, 52n29, 68n47, 85n10, 98n28, 108
Desire, commodification of, 28, 70, 108, 109, 133, 140, 147
Dialects, Japanese, 6, 82, 89, 91, 102, 103, 147, 181, 193, 197; working women as speakers of, 247, 267, 269–72
Dialogue: intersubjective, 72; in novels, 19, 26, 65, 92, 93, 98, 99, 101, 111, 119, 122, 125, 142, 149; and schoolgirl speech, 64, 65, 70, 108, 111, 119–22, 125, 142, 149; in self-help books, 200; in television dramas, 183
Diaries, 111, 119, 122–25
Disciplinary practices: and female consumption, 108; Foucault on, 95n26, 99, 164n2; and language use, 184; and scholarly discourse, 193, 197; and women's education, 46; and women's language, 12, 30, 98–99, 197
Discourse analysis, Foucauldian, 15–17, 22–23
Disembodied speech, 55, 91, 105, 112, 129–30
Doane, Mary Ann, 44n14
Doi, Takeo, 218n1
Dolar, Mladen, 40, 68, 69n48
Domestic novels, 65, 99–102, 119, 120, 142
Domestic sphere, 19, 100, 104, 118, 125, 250
Duara, Prasenjit, 170
Dutch language, 86nn12, 14

Eckert, Penelope, 28n1
Economic growth, 25, 29, 45, 167, 170–71, 175, 201, 209
Edo period, 42n7, 84, 91, 93
Education, women's: and citizenship, 42, 46; and Confucianism, 42n7, 45, 46; curriculum of, 45, 46; and economic growth, 47; and English language, 63–64; and Enlightenment, 38, 42; and family relations, 41–42, 46, 47; and female subject formation, 38, 42; and gender construction, 38, 42; and kango (Chinese-derived words), 63–64; and missionary schools, 45, 64; and modernization, 25, 38, 42, 43, 69, 80; and occupational opportunity, 208–13; and public opinion surveys, 187; and social elite, 25, 38, 42n6, 43; state's role in, 38, 39, 42, 46, 102; and Westernization, 45; and women's magazines, 115, 116, 117
Egalitarian division of labor, 223–24
Elite, social: and economic disparity, 201; and male response to schoolgirl speech, 58, 60, 63, 66, 70, 72; schoolgirls as members of, 25, 38, 42n6, 43
Empty signifiers, 33, 44, 105, 215
English language, 63–64, 86nn, 128, 155n28, 281
English speakers, as students of women's language, 274–75, 277
Enlightenment, 25, 38, 42, 115

Entextualization, 49, 85, 105
Epistles, 83, 108, 119, 122, 124, 125
Equal Opportunity Employment Law, 29, 32, 163, 171–72, 175, 184, 188, 209, 210
Errington, James Joseph, 47n20
Essentialism, 25, 75–76, 77, 106, 165, 170, 228
Ethnography, 4, 11, 31, 51, 52n29, 66–67, 81n4, 207, 280. *See also* Field research
Etiquette books, 18, 108, 155n28
Eurocentrism, 71

Fabian, Johannes, 5n5
Failure, discursive, 11, 21, 24, 279
Family relations: bourgeois, 46, 100, 125, 151, 154; and capitalism, 46, 47; and commodification, 151, 154; and domestic novels, 99–100; linguistic parody as critique of, 262, 264, 265; and middle class, 166, 259; and modernization, 81n4, 167; and nuclear family, 47, 100, 167, 259; and women's education, 41–42, 46; and women's magazines, 118, 125, 154
Female intellectuals, 40n5, 93
Female office workers. *See* Working women
Female subject formation: and agency, 71–72, 73; and literary practice, 95; and modernization, 38, 40, 79, 80–81; and nation-state, 80, 109; and schoolgirl speech, 27, 71–72, 73, 98–99, 102, 110, 115, 119, 122, 125, 127, 157; and women's education, 38, 42; and women's magazines, 110, 115, 119, 122, 125, 127
Feminine speech, 37, 62, 63, 70, 77, 168, 169n9, 185, 198–99, 202; parody of, 262, 264; and working women, 260, 262, 264, 267, 269–71, 277
Femininity, 14, 175n15, 250, 260
Feminism, 44n14, 47n18, 110, 195, 196, 275
Feminization, 67n45, 98, 99n29
Ferguson, James, 273n9
Fetishization, 57, 168. *See also* Commodity fetishism
Fielding, Henry, 84
Field research, 4, 207–8, 213–16
Final particles: and gender identity, 2, 76–77, 93–96, 98, 99; and literary modernization, 93–96, 98, 99, 100, 102; and schoolgirl speech, 53–54, 76–77, 86n14, 98, 99; and women's language, 7n6, 14, 76–77, 98, 100, 237, 243, 244, 257, 263, 267, 268
First person, 14, 90, 269, 280n1
Foreign-affiliated firms, 208–9
Foucault, Michel: on authorship, 50; on bourgeois interiority, 122; on confession, 124; on disciplinary practices, 95n26, 99, 164n2; on discourse, 15–17, 22, 189; on genealogy, 25, 77; on history, 77, 105; on madness, 72; on normativity, 164, 169; on panopticon, 55, 90; on power, 72, 79, 95n26, 99
Fraser, Nancy, 90
Freud, Sigmund, 41
Friedrich, Paul, 107
Fujii, James, 83n6
Fujitani, Takashi, 41
Futabatei, Shimei, 84, 87n15, 97

Gal, Susan, 48n21, 57n32, 107, 281n1
Garon, Sheldon M., 117n8
Gaze, metalinguistic, 78. *See also* Male gaze
Geishas, 43n10, 58, 59, 60, 75, 86n13, 142, 145
Gembun'itchi (language-modernization) movement: and alterity, 92; and colloquial speech, 26, 50, 78, 83–85, 88–89, 91, 139; and commodification, 101; and dialogues, 92, 93, 98, 99, 101, 119; and final particles, 93–96, 98, 99, 100, 102; and Futabatei's *Ukigumo*, 84, 87n15, 97; and indexicality, 51, 98; and institutional policy, 88–89; as linguistic technology, 89, 90; and linguistic transparency, 78, 90, 91–92, 106; and male gaze, 92–93; and male subject formation, 90, 92, 129; narrating voice in, 90, 91–92; and nationalism, 83, 87; and national subject formation, 26, 90, 92, 93, 95, 120; and the novel, 78, 83, 84, 92, 93, 95, 97–102; and omniscient voice, 92; and panopticon, 90; and phonocentrism, 85; and phonograph, 101; and popular culture, 101; and realism, 26, 50, 83, 89n19, 90, 92, 101; and schoolgirl speech, 39, 97–98; and standard Japanese language, 26, 50, 87–89, 91, 95, 129; and third-person voice, 90; and Tsubouchi's literary criticism, 84; and Ueda's concept of

national language, 87–88; and utterance endings, 85–86, 89, 93–96, 119, 246; and women's language, 26, 93, 105, 275; and women's reported speech, 93–98, 119
Gender blending in language use, 194–95
Gender construction: historicized study of, 281; and modernization, 38, 79, 80–81; and nation-state formation, 79, 109; and women's education, 38; and women's magazines, 110, 122. *See also* Subject formation
Gender difference: and domestic novels, 65, 100; and forms of address, 254; and ideology, 13, 100; and nationalism, 168, 170; and national language policy, 198–99; and occupational hierarchy, 209–13, 220, 240; and public opinion surveys, 185–92, 198, 199; and scholarly research, 2, 13–14, 103, 193–96; and temporality, 168, 198; Western theoretical model of, 195–96; and women's language, 1–2, 4, 9, 13–15, 28, 169–70, 175, 185–99
Gender equality: and consumerism, 173; and Enlightenment, 42; and female employment, 29, 163, 171–72, 175, 184, 188, 209, 210, 253, 258, 259; feminists' demand for, 47n18; and national language policy, 198, 199; and public opinion surveys, 185; and women's language, 3, 37, 163, 198, 199
Gender identity: and affectivity, 76–77; and commodification, 104; and final particles, 2, 76–77, 93–96, 98, 99; and indexicality, 2, 76–77, 95, 98, 105, 106, 113–14, 244, 272; and public sphere, 102; and women's language, 9, 198, 274, 277
Gender markers, 2, 24, 114, 147, 198, 241, 244, 251, 272
Gender relations: and capitalist division of labor, 46, 47, 80–81, 100, 117, 167, 173; and working women, 29, 173, 253–54
Genealogy: Foucauldian, 25, 77; and historicization, 106, 281; of women's language, 25, 26, 77, 104, 106, 147
Generational difference, 259–60, 276
Gesaku (Edo-period popular literature), 84
Goffman, Erving, 262
"Good wives and wise mothers," 28, 38, 46, 47n18, 80, 81n4, 100, 110, 117–18, 150–51, 153–55
Gordon, Andrew, 167n6
Government. *See* State
Gramsci, Antonio, 87n16
Gumperz, John, 264
Gupta, Akhil, 273n9

Habermas, Jürgen, 90, 92n25, 127
Haig, John H., 27n6
Hall, Mary, 28n11
Hall, Stuart, 113nn2–3
Hanks, William F., 20n16, 49n23, 78, 85n11
Hansen, Miriam, 102n33, 127
Harootunian, Harry, 5, 6, 41, 71, 166
Harvey, David, 29
Hasegawa, Yoko, 61n36, 62n39
Hastings, Sally Ann, 81n4, 153
Haug, Wolfgang Fritz, 105n34, 154
Hida, Yoshifumi, 91
Hierarchy: and classification of speech styles, 249; corporate, 209–13, 224, 226n10, 229, 233, 240, 241, 247, 254n1; among female and male workers, 209–13, 220, 240; between narrative subject and object, 27, 92; between researcher and subject, 214; social, 233, 246, 247; between speech and writing, 52n29, 85; among women via women's language, 12, 28, 279
Hill, Jane H., 18n14, 49n23, 97n27, 165n3
Historicization, 25, 31, 106, 215, 216, 276, 279, 281
History effect, 76–77
Honda, Masuko, 64, 102n32
Honorifics: and national language policy, 246; and schoolgirl speech, 60–61, 86, 87n15, 89, 97, 100, 103, 108; and women's language, 131, 139, 175, 190, 192, 200, 202; and women's language used by working women, 233, 237, 239, 240, 244–46, 248–50, 255, 257, 260, 262–63, 265, 267
Horii, Reiichi, 75n2
Housewives: and advertising, 69, 142; and employment, 229; and gendered division of labor, 167; leisure-class, 262, 266; middle-class, 125, 142, 164, 195, 202, 250, 260; and women's education, 42; and women's language, 164, 181, 194, 195, 259, 260, 262; and women's magazines, 116, 117, 125

Huyssen, Andreas, 65n43
Hysteria, 52–53

Iconicity, 48, 140, 246
Ide, Risako, 75n2
Ide, Sachiko, 2n2, 47n19, 75n2, 193, 195
Ideology: and gender difference, 13, 100; linguistic, 17–18, 39, 51, 57n33, 78, 184; linguistic parody as critique of, 264, 265; and national subject formation, 109; productionist, 21–22; and realism, 92; and women's magazines, 115
Iida, Yuko, 65, 99n29
Imperialism, 28, 153, 154
Indexicality: and affectivity, 76–77; and code switching, 260; and contextualization, 55, 56; and gembun'itchi (language-modernization) movement, 51, 98, 101; and gender identity, 2, 76–77, 95, 98, 105, 106, 113–14, 244, 272; and history effect, 76–77; and indexical inversion, 51, 169n9; and indexical labor, 27, 113, 150; and intertextuality, 149–50; and metapragmatics, 55, 56, 57n33; Ochs's model of, 76; and photographic captions, 130, 131; and schoolgirl speech, 56–57, 60, 65, 66–67, 70, 98, 101, 108–10, 113–14, 129, 131, 135, 140, 149–50, 157; and women's language, 27, 75–78, 98, 105, 106–7, 169, 200, 244, 246, 273, 280; and women's magazines, 27, 113, 129, 131, 135, 140, 149–50
Individualism, 71, 83, 218
Industrialization, 26, 47, 77, 79, 166
Inokuchi, Yuichi, 89n18, 91n22
Inoue, Mariko, 43
Intellectuals: female, 40n5, 93; male, 25, 26, 37–40, 54, 56–71, 93, 109–10; organic, 87n16; state, 87
Interpellation, 5, 28, 40, 42, 53, 66, 145, 147
Intersubjectivity, 72
Intertextuality, 113, 140, 142, 149–50, 151, 154, 157
Intratextual hierarchy, 51–52
Irvine, Judith T., 18n14, 48n21, 49nn22–23, 57n32, 97n27, 107
Ishiguro, Tadanori, 55, 58
Ishikawa, Sadayuki, 98
Ishino, Hiroshi, 192
Isoda, Koichi, 91
Iterability, 20, 21, 26, 98n28, 108

Itoh, Makoto, 171n11
Ivy, Marilyn, 3n4, 11n8, 85n10, 167n6
Iwamoto, Yoshiharu, 115n5
Iwaya, Sazanami, 121

Jakobson, Roman, 48n21, 51n27
Jameson, Fredric, 57
Jay, Martin, 71
Joseph, John Earl, 17n12

Kamei, Hideo, 95
Kanai, Yoshiko, 200
Kango (Chinese-derived words in Japanese), 63–65
Kaplan, Caren, 273n9
Karatani, Kojin, 51n26, 83n6, 124n16
Karlin, Jason G., 67n45, 100
Kato, Emiko, 202–3
Kawaguchi, Yoko, 194
Kawamura, Kunimitsu, 102nn31–32, 114n4, 125, 129, 150
Keen, Donald, 91n24
Kelly, William W., 167n6
Kikuchi, Yuho, 99–100
Kikuzawa, Sueo, 2, 192
Kimura, Ryoko, 114n4
Kindaichi, Haruhiko, 168n8
Kindaichi, Kyosuke, 2
Kluge, Alexander, 127
Komatsu, Sumio, 94, 96
Komori, Yoichi, 83n6, 92, 100
Kondo, Dorinne, 273
Konoe, Atsumaro, 153
Kosugi, Tengai, 101
Kotobazukai (language use), 184, 232, 234, 235, 240–41, 248
Koyama, Shizuko, 42, 81n4
Kristeva, Julia, 149n25
Kristof, Nicholas D., 3
Kroskrity, Paul V., 17n12
Kuno, Susumu, 61n36

Labor market, 29, 171n12, 172–73, 195, 212, 259
Labov, William, 27n6
Lacan, Jacques, 68, 72n51, 189n21
Lam, Alice, 172n12
Language reform, 50, 81–83, 87–88. *See also* Gembun'itchi (language-modernization) movement
Lebra, Takie, Sugiyama, 218n1, 227n12, 231n15

Lee, Benjamin, 49, 92
Leisure activity, 104
Leisure class, 262, 264, 265, 266
Léry, Jean de, 51
Levin, David Michael, 71
Lévi-Strauss, Claude, 52n29
Liberalism, 25, 42, 45, 79, 90, 100, 115, 127
Literary criticism, 84
Love, romantic, 27, 100, 101
Lucy, John A., 18nn13–15, 47n20, 97n27, 264n2
Lukács, György, 78
Lunsing, Wim, 273n8, 280n1
Lynch, Deidre, 91

Maejima, Hisoka, 83n7
Magazines, women's: advertising in, 19, 27, 69–70, 104, 105, 110, 113, 117, 119, 120, 135–36, *137–38, 139*, 139–40, *141*, 142, *143–44*, 145, *146*, 147, *148*, 149–50, *152*, 153–54; and capitalism, 102, 115, 116, 120–21; confessional style in, 122–24, 142, 150, 157; and consumerism, 27–28, 110, 117, 123, 124, 133, 136, 145, 149, 150, 151, 153–55, 157, 202; dialogue-based prose in, 119–22, 125, 142, 149, 157; diary style in, 111, 119, 122–25; and domestic sphere, 118, 125; editorial policies of, 117–19; epistolary style in, 108, 119, 122, 124, 125; and family relations, 118, 125, 154; and female subject formation, 27, 110, 115, 119, 122, 125, 127; and housewives, 116, 117, 125; and indexicality, 27, 113, 129, 131, 135, 140, 149–50; and intertextuality, 113, 140, 142, 149–50, 151, 154, 157; mass circulation of, 110, 114, 117, 119, 120, 128n19; and middle-class women, 27, 69, 110, 117, 125, 142, 154; and modernity, 112–13; and modernization, 115, 116; moga identity in, 133, 135, 142, 147; and motherhood, 118; and nationalism, 115, 118, 150, 151, 153–55; and national subject formation, 104, 150–51, 154; nonlinear reading demanded by, 113, 149; otome identity in, 125, 126, 129, 130; paratexts in, 111, 115, 121, 130; photography in, 104, 111, 113, 118, 130–31, *132*, 133, *134*, 135, *135, 153, 155, 156, 158*; and public sphere, 102, 108, 110, 112, 127–30; readers' correspondence in, 70, 102, 103, 104, 105, 106, 119, 125–30, 150, 157; serialized novels in, 103, 111, 113, 119, 120, 121, 125, 142, 149, 150, 157; and sexuality, 133, 135; as virtual community, 70, 102n33, 129, 159; and Westernization, 136; and women's education, 115, 116, 117; women's language in, 19, 27, 28, 102–4, 105, 200, 202; and working women, 116, 117, 142. *See also* Schoolgirl speech, in magazines
Makaseru management style, 226–28
Male anxiety, 44, 59–60, 66, 109
Male gaze, 27, 43, 54–55, 92
Male intellectuals, 19, 25, 26, 37–40, 54, 56–71, 93, 109–10
Male office workers: and gender-based occupational hierarchy, 209–13, 220, 240; and language use, 248–49, 271; and relations with female coworkers, 239–41, 253–54
Male subject formation: and cinema, 68; and literary modernization, 90, 92, 129; and public sphere, 129; and race, 53; and schoolgirl speech, 26, 39, 40, 66, 68; and standard Japanese language, 129–30
Managerial class, emergence of, 47
Managerial positions, women in: case study of work performed by, 220–29; and Equal Employment Opportunity Law, 32, 172; and makaseru management style, 226–28; and on-the-job-training, 240; and personal appearance, 217–18; and personal narrative, 219, 229–32; and promotion, 231–32, 234, 235, 239–40; represented in popular media, 32; and women's language, 31–33, 217, 220, 232–51, 272
Managerial practices, 209, 220–29, 235
Mani, Lata, 81
Marchand, Roland, 140
Maree, Claire, 273n8, 280n1
Market relations, 5, 42, 49, 78, 102, 182, 200; and women's magazines, 109, 114, 125, 128, 135, 150, 154
Marriage: and social class, 58; and working women, 173, 213, 220, 229, 230, 231, 258, 265
Marx, Karl, 43–44, 105n34, 159
Masculine speech, 64, 174, 175, 185–89
Masculinization, 67n45
Mashimo, Saburo, 75n2

Mass culture, 14, 65n43, 69, 91, 114
Mass media, 29, 78, 79, 202, 208, 247; and women's magazines, 110, 114, 117, 119, 120, 128n19
Matsumoto, Yoshiko, 280n1
May Japan Limited, Inc. (MJL), 31–32, 207–13, 217–26, 229, 231, 235, 252–53
Maynard, Senko K., 86n14
McClintock, Anne, 151, 168, 170
McConnell-Ginet, Sally, 281n1
McGloin, Naomi, 195
Meiji period: and language reform, 81–83, 87; and modernization, 25, 38, 44, 79, 81; reactionary movement in, 44–45; and schoolgirl speech, 38, 39, 42, 44, 47, 57–58, 60, 61, 69, 70, 72–73, 163, 174; and social class, 58–60; state in, 38, 44–45, 79; and Westernization, 44–45, 67n45, 136; and women's education, 25, 38, 42, 45; and women's language, 103; women's magazines in, 114, 115, 116, 122, 123, 126; and women's visibility, 60
Meiji Restoration, 58, 79
Metacommunication, 102n33, 111n1, 128, 140, 149
Metalanguage, 18, 27, 53, 82, 92, 111, 112, 119, 140, 157, 214, 215
Metalepsis, 22, 50
Metanarrative, 83
Metapragmatics: and citationality, 21; and contextualization, 55, 56, 264n2; and disembodied voice, 55, 91; and indexicality, 55, 56, 57n33; and linguistic ideology, 18; and schoolgirl speech, 39, 40, 53, 56–57, 63, 65, 66, 69, 70, 147; and standard Japanese language, 91; and women's language, 19, 30–33, 48, 82, 103, 104, 106, 163, 174, 215, 233–34, 266, 273
Mid-career employment, 211–12, 229, 238n20, 266
Middle class: and center/periphery relation, 247; and commodification, 154; and family relations, 167, 259; and industrialization, 47; men as members of, 90; and the novel, 78; and standard Japanese language, 14, 90–91, 165n4, 193, 196, 197, 247; and urbanization, 47
Middle-class women: and consumerism, 8, 154; as housewives, 125, 142, 195, 202, 250, 260; interpellation of, 42; novelistic representation of, 101; as office workers, 246–47, 259, 272; and public opinion surveys, 185; and resignification of schoolgirl speech, 108–9; and women's education, 46, 47; and women's language, 19, 22, 27, 28, 37, 70, 100, 147, 164, 165n4, 181, 246–48, 272; and women's magazines, 27, 69, 110, 117, 125, 142, 154
Miki, Hiroko, 116n5
Mill, John Stuart, 42
Miller, Scott J., 84n9
Mimicry, 63–64, 67n45, 78, 109, 215, 277
Miyajima, Tatsuo, 89
Miyazaki, Ayumi, 280n1
Mockery, 261–66
Modernity: and alterity, 48, 50, 52, 53; and auditory practices, 40–41, 71; co-eval, 5–6; Harootunian on, 5, 41; and the novel, 78, 83; and reported speech, 50; and schoolgirl image, 43, 136; and schoolgirl speech, 26, 39–41, 66, 67–68, 69, 71, 73–74, 97–98, 109; and temporality, 24, 30, 39–40, 66, 67, 165, 166, 168, 195, 196, 215, 216, 271–72, 280; and visual practices, 41, 71; and women's language, 3–6, 24, 26, 112, 147, 165, 166, 196–97, 215, 216, 250, 272, 278–81; and women's magazines, 112–13
Modernization: and capitalism, 109, 166, 278; and Enlightenment, 38; and family relations, 81n4, 167; and female subject formation, 38, 40, 79, 80–81; and gender construction, 38, 40, 79, 80–81; and language reform, 50, 81–83, 87–88; and middle class, 167; and nationalism, 166; and national subject formation, 48, 79, 80; state's role in, 38; and women's alterity, 48; and women's education, 25, 38, 42, 43, 69, 80; and women's language, 24, 25, 26, 27, 77–78, 103, 104–5, 166, 167, 169, 278; and women's magazines, 115, 116. See also Gembun'itchi (language-modernization) movement
Moga identity, 133, 135, 142, 147
Mohanty, S. P., 276
Molony, Barbara, 172n12
Morality in domestic novels, 99–100
Mori, Arinori, 83n7

Mothers and motherhood: and capitalist social relations, 80–81; and citizenship, 42, 46; novelistic representation of, 100; and "wise mothers" ideologeme, 28, 38, 46, 47n18, 80, 81n4, 100, 110, 117–18, 150–51, 153–55; and women's education, 38, 41, 46, 47, 80; and women's magazines, 118
Mouffe, Chantal, 105n34
Mourning rituals, 25, 29–31, 163–65, 174–75, 202
Multinational corporations, 208
Mulvey, Laura, 44n14
Muta, Kazue, 81n4

Nagamine, Shigetoshi, 102, 117
Nagasaki, Kazunori, 200
Nakajima, Kuni, 115, 116, 118n9
Nakamura, Momoko, 28n11
Narrative: and alterity, 49; and field research, 215, 219; and literary modernization, 27, 90, 91–92; personal, 6–9, 219, 229–32, 269–73; and public opinion surveys, 188; and schoolgirls' correspondence columns, 129; schoolgirl speech as object of, 57, 58–59
Nationalism: and Anderson's theory of writing, 48; and consumerism, 150, 151, 153–55; and fetishization, 168; and gembun'itchi (language-modernization) movement, 83, 87; and gender difference, 168, 170; and modernization, 166; and the novel, 83; and Sino-Japanese War, 45; and temporality, 168; and women's language, 4, 168, 280; and women's magazines, 115, 118, 150, 151, 153–55
National Language Council, 164, 184, 197–99, 246, 250
National Language Research Institute, 103, 184
National Language Studies (Kokugogaku), 75, 86n13
National subject formation: and literary practice, 26, 90, 92, 93, 95, 120; and modernization, 48, 79, 80; and women's language, 155; and women's magazines, 104, 150–51, 154
Nation-state: and Anderson's theory of writing, 48; and female subject formation, 80, 109; formation of, 26, 79, 83, 166; and language reform, 87, 89; and women's education, 42; and women's language, 4, 12, 15, 20
Natsume, Soseki, 93
Naturalism, 89n19, 97
Negt, Oskar, 127
Neogrammarian theory of language, 88
Neoliberalism, 164, 189, 200, 201–3
Newspapers: and capitalist relations, 79; and domestic novels, 99; readers' correspondence columns in, 175–82; and schoolgirl speech, 30, 48–49, 62, 65; and women's language, 175–82
Nihonjinron, 166
Noguchi, Takehiko, 90n20
Noguchi, Yukio, 171n11
Nolte, Sharon H., 81n4, 153
Nonreferential forms, 53–55
Normativity, 164–65, 169–70, 180–81, 193, 196–99, 233
Novels: and Anderson's theory of writing, 48–49; capitalist context of, 78, 83; dialogue in, 19, 26, 65, 92, 93, 98, 99, 101, 111, 119, 122, 125, 142, 149; domestic, 65, 99–102, 119, 120, 142; and gembun'itchi (language-modernization) movement, 50, 78, 83, 84, 92, 93, 95, 97–102, 129; and modernity, 78, 83; and national subject formation, 26, 90, 92, 93, 95; and nation-state formation, 83; and realism, 50, 78, 83, 105; schoolgirls' consumption of, 65; schoolgirl speech in, 65, 98, 119, 120, 157; schoolgirls represented in, 43, 99; women represented in, 93, 97, 98, 99–101; women's consumption of, 99–102; women's language in, 92, 93, 95, 97–102, 103, 105; in women's magazines, 103, 111, 113, 119, 120, 122, 125, 142, 149, 150

Objet petit a, 68–69
Ochs, Elinor, 57n32, 76
Ogasawara, Yuko, 208n2
Ogawa, Naoko, 273n8
Ogino, Hajime, 64
Ojō-sama language, 202–3
Okamoto, Shigeko, 14n10, 270, 280
Okano, Kyuin, 90
Okumura, Ioko, 153
Omori, Maki, 172n12
Ong, Aihwa, 228n13
Opinion polls. *See* Public opinion surveys

Orientalism, 275
Ortner, Sherry, 220
Other: and schoolgirl speech, 39, 56, 57, 69, 70, 71, 73, 109, 110; and women's language, 33, 215, 252, 277. *See also* Alterity
Otome identity, 125, 126, 129, 130
Otsuki, Fumihiko, 86n13
Ozaki, Koyo, 57–58, 98

Panopticon, 55, 90
Paratextual genres, 111, 115, 121, 130
Parody, 18, 202, 203, 262, 264, 266
Patriarchy, 12, 28, 29, 68, 71, 125, 154, 208n2, 277
Performativity: and abjection, 277; Bhabha on, 24, 31, 33, 277; Butler on, 22, 23, 24, 215; and literary modernization, 92; and pedagogical/performative split, 24, 33, 216, 273; and public opinion surveys, 175n15; and reported speech, 18, 73; and schoolgirl speech, 73, 108; and temporality, 24; and women's language, 19, 22, 23, 24, 31, 33, 215, 216, 264, 265, 273, 277, 279
Peripheral relations: and linguistic differentiation, 103, 147, 197; with metropole, 123, 197, 247, 271–72; and schoolgirl speech, 66, 67–68, 71, 73, 169; and standard Japanese language, 270–73; and women's language, 3, 6, 103, 147, 169, 197, 271–73
Petite bourgeoisie, 27, 46, 90
Philips, Susan U., 97n27
Phonemes, 51, 53
Phonocentrism, 85
Phonograph, 101, 105
Photography, 43, 105; and photographic captions, 130–31, 133, 139, 151; in women's magazines, 104, 111, 113, 118, 130–31, *132*, 133, *134*, 135, *135*, *153*, 155, *156*, *158*
Pitch, 2, 3, 255, 262
Plain style in language use, 236–37, 242–46, 249, 256–58, 263
Polite forms: and literary modernization, 86, 87n15, 89; and professionalism, 248–49; and schoolgirl speech, 60, 61, 108, 119, 130; and women's language, 1, 2, 13, 14, 106, 184n19, 185n20, 195, 202; and women's language used by working women, 232–36, 239–46, 248–49, 255–57, 259, 263, 267–68, 270n4
Political-economic relations: and de Certeau's theory of writing, 48; and schoolgirl speech, 70, 71, 73, 74; and Spivak's theory of subaltern speech, 73; and women's language, 107, 163, 165, 203, 278–80
Pollock, Griselda, 44
Pragmatic salience, 47–48
Pratt, Mary Louise, 71, 247
Print media: and alterity, 48–49, 53; and Anderson's theory of writing, 48–49; and capitalism, 26, 78, 79, 83, 99, 102, 115, 116, 120–21, 151, 181; and public sphere, 53, 90n21, 126; and schoolgirl speech, 37, 40, 44, 57, 65, 69–70, 72–73, 102, 106, 108, 112; Warner's study of, 53, 126; and women's language, 102–4, 105, 106. *See also* Magazines; Newspapers
Private sphere, 59–60, 127n19, 195
Prostitutes, 44, 56, 58, 75, 115n5
Psychoanalysis, 44n14, 66–67n44, 68; Freudian, 41; Lacanian, 68, 72n51, 189n21
Public opinion surveys, 2, 19, 30, 163, 174, 182–92, 197–98, 199
Public sphere: bourgeois, 53, 127, 129; and counterpublic sphere, 102, 110, 112, 127–30; and disembodied speech, 112, 129–30; Habermas on, 127; Hansen on, 127; men's participation in, 90, 129; and middle class, 90; Negt and Kluge on, 127; and print media, 53, 90n21, 126; private sphere conflated with, 59–60; private sphere excluded from, 127n19; and public opinion surveys, 189; and readers' correspondence columns, 174, 181; schoolgirl speech in, 102, 108, 112, 127–30; schoolgirls' visibility in, 43, 44, 59–60; and standard Japanese language, 112; Warner on, 53, 90n21; and women's language, 14, 29, 163; and women's magazines, 102, 108, 110, 112, 127–30; women's participation in, 29, 60, 90n21, 102, 195

Quinn, Charles L., 218n1
Quotation: de Certeau on, 50–51; and parodies of women's language, 264,

266; and transition from quoted to quoting voice, 27–28, 110–11, 114, 120, 122, 127, 157

Race, 15, 22, 42, 52, 78, 106, 147, 215, 229n13, 274–77, 279
Ragsdale, Kathryn, 99
Rakugo (storytelling performance), 84
Readers' correspondence columns: and authorship, 128–29, 174; decline of women's language cited in, 30, 163, 174–82; in newspapers, 175–82; and public sphere, 174, 181; in women's magazines, 70, 102, 103, 104, 105, 106, 119, 125–30, 150, 157
Realism, 26, 50–51, 78, 83, 89n19, 90, 92, 101, 105, 119
Reification, 4, 14, 18, 26, 49, 72, 73, 92, 101, 108, 273n8, 280
Reported speech, 18–20, 26, 49–51; and gembun'itchi (language-modernization) movement, 93–98, 119; and photographic captions, 130, 131; and pictorial reporting, 120, 121, 131; and schoolgirl speech, 37, 50, 70, 73–74, 110, 119, 120, 130, 131
Resignification, 21, 24, 25, 27, 28, 70, 98, 101, 108–9, 110, 113, 117
Resistance, 11n8, 12, 32, 78, 106, 196–97, 260, 266, 276–77; and agency, 21, 23, 71, 73, 281n1
Responsibilized subjects, 164, 181, 182, 189
Robertson, Jennifer, 67n45, 124n17
Rofel, Lisa, 71
Rohlen, Thomas, 207n1
Rose, Nikolas, 164n2, 182
Rosenberger, Nancy Ross, 218n1, 238n19
Rousseau, Jean-Jacques, 42
Rumsey, Alan, 17n12
Russo-Japanese War, 47, 87, 116, 153

Sakai, Naoki, 50, 81, 166
Sakakura, Atsuyoshi, 84
Sakuma, Kanae, 61n36, 62
Samurai, 42n7, 55, 57, 59, 66, 79, 80, 86nn12–14, 91, 95, 98, 103
Sato, Barbara Hamil, 114n4
Sato, Haruo, 97
Sato, Rika Sakuma, 43n10, 102n33, 114n4, 116n7
Sato, Shie, 270
Sato, Toshiki, 201

Saussure, Ferdinand de, 9–10, 51
Schieffelin, Bambi B., 17n12, 78
Scholarly literature, 1–2, 13–14, 164, 167, 174, 192–97
Schoolgirls: acoustic presence of, 26, 39, 47, 52, 55; aesthetic representation of, 43, 99; as consumers, 27–28, 109, 123, 124, 136; as copies without originals, 43; and Debord's theory of the spectacle, 43–44; as empty signifiers, 44; and male gaze, 43; and Marx's theory of commodity fetishism, 43–44; print media read by, 65, 69–70, 102–3; and public sphere, 43, 44, 59–60, 102; as social category, 38, 41–42, 70, 97
Schoolgirl speech: as acoustic mirror, 68, 73; in advertising, 69–70, 112, 119, 120, 139–40, 142, 145, 147, 150, 157; and agency, 71–72, 73–74; and auditory practices, 26, 38–41, 54, 56, 70–71, 72; auxiliary verbs in, 54, 61–63, 108; citation of, 38, 39, 54, 70, 72–73, 108, 109; and commodity fetishism, 159; commonness attributed to, 40, 56; and consumerism, 69, 110, 123, 124, 145, 154–55, 157; containment of, 39, 40, 53, 56, 57, 63, 70; and contextualization, 56; converted from sound to sign, 40, 56, 69; English words in, 63–64, 128; female educators' response to, 40n5, 61n38, 110; and female subject formation, 27, 71–72, 73, 98–99, 102, 110, 115, 119, 122, 157; and fetishization, 57, 168; film actresses as speakers of, 142, 145, 147; and final particles, 53–54, 98, 99; and honorifics, 60–61, 86, 87n15, 89, 97, 100, 103, 108; and indexicality, 56–57, 60, 65, 66–67, 70, 98, 101, 108–10, 113–14, 129, 131, 135, 140, 149–50, 157; kango (Chinese-derived) words in, 63–65; and linguistic corruption, 19, 37, 40n5, 60, 61, 62, 66, 69, 70, 115, 118, 150, 169; linguistic features of, 37, 47–48, 53–54, 60–63; and literary modernization, 39, 97–98; low-class connotation of, 25, 26, 27, 37, 56, 57, 58–60, 66, 70, 98, 169; male intellectuals' relation to, 19, 25, 26, 37–40, 47, 54, 56–71, 72, 109–10; and male subject formation, 26, 39, 40, 66, 68; masculine speech doubled in, 64, 69;

Schoolgirl speech *(continued)*
  metapragmatics of, 19, 39, 40, 53, 56–57, 63, 65, 66, 69, 70, 147; and modernity, 26, 39–41, 66, 67–68, 69, 71, 73–74, 97–98, 109; nonreferential properties of, 53–54, 56; origin narrative for, 57, 58–59, 98; and otherness, 39, 56, 57, 69, 70, 71, 73, 109, 110; and peripheral relations, 66, 67–68, 71, 73, 169; phonological contraction in, 61–62, 63; and polite forms, 60, 61, 108, 119, 130; and pragmatic salience, 47–48; and print media, 37, 40, 44, 57, 65, 69–70, 72–73, 102–3, 106, 108–9, 112 (*see also under* magazines); as psychic object, 66, 68; and reported speech, 37, 50, 70, 73–74, 110, 119–21, 130, 131; and resignification, 27, 28, 108–9, 110, 113, 117; strangeness attributed to, 25, 37, 38, 57, 59, 63, 98; syntactic ambiguity in, 62–63; and uncanniness, 41, 64, 66, 69; unpleasantness attributed to, 37, 40, 63, 64, 67, 69, 71; and utterance endings, 47–48, 53–54, 55, 62, 63, 98, 119, 128, 131, 157; vulgarity attributed to, 25, 26, 27, 37, 40, 56–63, 65, 70, 98, 105, 147, 157, 163, 164, 174; women's language based on, 25, 27, 28, 37, 98, 105, 113–15, 147, 155, 157, 159, 164; working women as speakers of, 147
Schoolgirl speech, in magazines: and advertising, 27, 69–70, 112, 119, 120, 139–40, 142, 145, 147, 150, 157; and agency, 120; and confessional style, 122–24, 142, 150, 157; and consumerism, 27–28, 110, 123, 124, 133, 150, 157; and counterpublic sphere, 102, 110, 112, 127–30; and dialogue, 108, 111, 119–22, 125, 142, 149; and diary style, 111, 119, 122–25; and epistolary style, 108, 119, 122, 124, 125; and female subject formation, 27, 110, 115, 119, 120, 122, 125, 127; and indexicality, 113, 129, 131, 135, 140, 149–50; and linguistic corruption, 115, 118, 150; as metalanguage, 111, 112, 119, 140, 142, 157; and moga identity, 133, 135, 142, 147; and narrative communication, 129; and otome identity, 125, 126, 129, 130; and photographic captions, 130–31, 133; and play scripts, 111, 121; as quoting voice, 27–28, 102, 110–11, 114, 120, 122, 125, 157; and readers' correspondence, 70, 102, 106, 119, 125–30, 150, 157; and reported speech, 119, 120, 121, 130, 131; and resignification, 27, 110, 113, 117; and serialized novels, 119, 121, 125, 150, 157; and short stories, 119, 121
Scott, Joan Wallach, 106
Self-help books, 29, 200–203, 254, 301n64
Self-regulating subjects, 164, 189, 199
Sexism, 12, 178, 179, 180, 182, 195, 196, 250, 275, 279
Sexuality, 11, 44, 46, 81, 273n8, 280
Shakespeare, William, 97
Shaseibun school, 89n19
Shibamoto, Janet S., 2n2, 14n10, 47n19, 267n3, 273n8, 280, 302
Shibatani, Masayoshi, 245n23
Shifters, linguistic, 48
Shikitei, Sanba, 93, 95
Shimoda, Utako, 40n5, 61n38
Shindo, Masahiro, 100
Shiraki, Susumu, 75n2
Siegal, Meryl, 274
Silverberg, Miriam, 145n23, 150
Silverman, Kaja, 68
Silverstein, Michael, 18nn13–15, 39, 47n20, 48n21, 49n23, 53n30, 57nn32–33, 63, 78, 85n11, 92, 140, 219n2, 264n2
Simulacra, 43n11
Sino-Japanese War, 45, 47, 87
Smith, Henry D., 91n24
Smith, Robert J., 81n4
Social change: and decline of women's language, 30; and emergence of women's language, 25, 104–5; and gender blending in language use, 194–95; schoolgirl speech as indicator of, 59–60, 65–66
Sovereignty, 10, 32, 72, 73, 182, 189, 250, 251, 259, 280
Spectacle, 43–44, 101, 151, 154
Speech acts, 185n20, 213
Spencer, Herbert, 42
Spivak, Gayatri Chakravorty, 22n18, 73
Standard Japanese language: and genbun'itchi movement, 26, 50, 87–89, 91, 95, 129; and language reform policy, 50, 82–83, 87–89; and male office workers, 271; and male subject formation, 129; and metapragmatics, 91; and middle class, 14, 90–91,

165n4, 193, 196, 197, 247; and other, 70; and peripheral relations, 270–73; and public opinion surveys, 185; and public sphere, 112; and scholarly research, 193; and subject formation, 91, 95; Tokyo as locus of, 90–91, 185, 193, 247, 272–73; and working women, 217, 270
State: and language reform, 87–89, 91; and modernization, 38, 79, 80; and national language policy, 164; and women's education, 38, 39, 42, 46, 80, 102. *See also* Nation-state
Stoler, Ann Laura, 81
Sturtz Sreetharan, Cindi, 271n5
Subaltern speech, 10n7, 71, 106
Subject formation: and agency, 71–72, 73; alterity as condition of, 48, 49, 53; Bhabha on, 40n5; and consumerism, 157; and modernization, 38, 48; and nonreciprocal communication, 72; and productionist ideology, 21–22; and standard Japanese language, 91, 95; and women's alterity, 48; and women's education, 38. *See also* Female subject formation; Male subject formation; National subject formation
Sunaoshi, Yukako, 280n1
Supplementarity, 9–10, 85
Suzuki, Kenji, 200
Suzuki, Tomi, 124n16

Taisho period, 114, 122
Takasaki, Midori, 194
Takehisa, Yumeji, 118
Takeuchi, Kyuichi, 58
Tanahashi, Junko, 40n5
Tannen, Deborah, 97n27
Tape recorder in field research, 213–14
Taussig, Michael T., 109
Taylor, Talbot J., 17n12
Tele-technology, 48–49, 50, 70, 73
Television, 6–8, 32, 183, 272, 273
Temporality: and dialectal speech, 271–72; and gender difference, 168, 198; and modernity, 24, 30, 39–40, 66, 67, 165, 166, 168, 195, 196, 215, 216, 271–72, 280; and nationalism, 168; and performativity, 24; and women's language, 24, 165, 169, 183, 195, 198, 215, 216, 251, 252, 260, 277, 279, 280

Terada, Tomomi, 75n2, 167n7
Teyo-dawa speech. *See* Schoolgirl speech
Third person, 82, 90, 130
Tocqueville, Alexis de, 42
Tokugawa period, 79, 86nn12–13
Tokyo: and center/periphery relation, 123, 247, 271; commodity display in, 124; disreputable neighborhoods in, 58; economic transformation in, 47; as locus of standard Japanese language, 90–91, 185, 193; as locus of women's language, 8; middle class in, 8, 90–91
Trade dispute as moral crisis, 45
Translation, 42, 82, 92, 97
Transparency, linguistic, 51, 78, 90, 91–92, 106
Trudgill, Peter, 271n6
Tsubouchi, Shoyo, 84, 97
Tsurumi, E. Patricia, 102
Turgenev, Ivan, 97
Twine, Nanette, 83n8, 86nn12–13

Uchida, Roan, 65
Ueda, Kazutoshi, 87–88
Ueno, Chizuko, 42, 80n3, 167
Uncanny, 41, 64, 66, 68, 69
Unnamability, 15, 275, 280
Urban, Greg, 18nn13–14, 49n23, 85n11
Urbanization, 47, 90, 272
Urla, Jacqueline, 182
Utopian language, 247
Utterance endings: and classification of speech styles, 244–46; and gembun'itchi (language-modernization) movement, 85–86, 89, 91, 93–96, 246; and gender identity, 76, 93–96; and gender neutrality, 244, 249, 256–57; male office worker's use of, 248–59; and photographic captions, 130, 131; and schoolgirl speech, 47–48, 53–54, 55, 62, 63, 98, 119, 128, 131, 157; and women's language, 6, 7n6, 76, 186–87, 200, 202; and women's language used by office managers, 217, 232–36, 242, 244–47, 249–50; and women's language used by office workers, 255–57, 260, 262–63, 270

Virtual community, 70, 102n33, 129, 159
Visual practices: and gender, 44n14; and modernity, 41, 71

322 INDEX

Voice: disembodied, 55, 91, 105, 129–30; narrating, 90, 91–92; nonreferential aspects of, 54
Voloshinov, V. N., 18, 37, 49n24, 97, 120, 131, 252

Wage labor, 43, 47, 99, 167
Walkowitz, Judith R., 44n15
Warner, Michael, 53, 54, 90, 126
Warner, William B., 91
Washi, Rumi, 280–81n1
Watt, Ian P., 78
Westernization, 4, 19, 44–45, 67n45, 87, 136, 166
Wetzel, Patricia J., 245n23
Whitney, William D., 83n7
Williams, Raymond, 123
Wilson, Elizabeth, 44n15
Wiswell, Ella Lury, 81n4
Women: alterity of, 48, 52–53; as citizens, 42, 46, 65; as college graduates, 208–9, 253, 259, 269; and Confucianism, 42n7, 46, 80; as consumers, 8, 25, 29, 42, 69, 99, 104, 105, 112, 154–55, 173, 202; education of (see under Education); as educators, 40n5, 61n38, 110; as geishas, 43n10, 58, 59, 60, 75, 86n13, 142, 145; as "good wives and wise mothers," 28, 38, 46, 47n18, 80, 81n4, 100, 110, 117–18, 150–51, 153–55; and hysteria, 52–53; as intellectuals, 40n5, 93; magazines for (see under Magazines); as members of leisure class, 262, 264, 265, 266; and modernization, 38, 79, 80–81; and nation-state formation, 79; novelistic representation of, 93, 97, 98, 99–101; as objects of male anxiety, 44, 59–60; as prostitutes, 44, 56, 58, 75, 115n5; and public sphere, 29, 60, 90n21, 102, 195; sexuality of, 44, 46, 81, 273n8; as signs, 44; writing practiced by, 63. See also Housewives; Middle-class women; Mothers; Working women
Women's language: and abjection, 11, 12, 14, 15, 17, 21–23, 26, 31, 33, 114, 277–79; and advertising, 7–8, 19, 104, 105, 147; and agency, 21, 22, 23–24, 250–51, 277; and alterity, 33, 215, 252, 277; authenticity of, 170, 203; and capitalism, 4, 5, 12, 25, 77, 147, 169, 278, 280, 281; and citation, 21–23, 24, 31, 33, 163, 203, 216, 217, 241, 244, 252, 260, 264–66, 273, 276, 281; as civilized speech, 167–68n8; and class difference, 100, 103; and class mobility, 200–203; and consumerism, 7–8, 25, 28, 103–4, 105, 147, 155, 157; and cross-cultural relations, 3, 274–75, 277; decline of, 2, 3, 19, 29–31, 37, 163, 169, 182, 196, 198, 203; defamiliarization of, 33, 215, 252, 264, 273; and discursive failure, 11, 21, 24, 279; as disembodied speech, 105; emergence of, 70, 77–78, 104–5, 275; essentialist account of, 25, 31, 75–76, 77, 106, 165, 170; as fakery, 203; and fetishization, 168; final particles in, 7n6, 76–77, 98, 100, 237, 243, 244, 257, 263, 267, 268; foreigners as speakers of, 274–75, 277; and gembun'itchi (language-modernization) movement, 26, 93, 105, 275; gender as insufficient category for, 9, 215, 244, 251, 279, 280; and gender difference, 1–2, 4, 9, 13–15, 28, 169–70, 175, 185–99; and gender equality, 3, 37, 163; and gender identity, 9, 198, 274, 277; as gender marker, 114, 198, 241, 244, 251, 272; genealogy of, 25, 26, 77, 104, 106, 147; and generational difference, 259–60, 276; historical continuity attributed to, 25, 75–76, 77, 106, 164–65, 167–70; housewives as speakers of, 164, 181, 194, 195, 259, 260, 262; and indexicality, 27, 75–78, 98, 105, 106–7, 169, 200, 244, 246, 273, 280; and linguistic corruption, 2, 19, 20, 29–30, 37, 165, 168–70, 174, 175, 177, 178, 180, 181, 182, 198, 260, 272; as masculine speech, 174, 175, 185–89; and metapragmatics, 19, 30–33, 48, 82, 103, 104, 106, 163, 174, 215, 233–34, 266, 273; middle-class women as speakers of, 19, 22, 27, 28, 37, 70, 100, 147, 164, 165n4, 181, 246–48, 272; mockery of, 261–66; and modernity, 3–6, 24, 26, 112, 147, 165, 166, 196–97, 215, 216, 250, 272, 278–81; and modernization, 24, 25, 26, 27, 77–78, 103, 104–5, 166, 167, 169, 197, 278; mourning rituals for, 25, 29–31, 163–65, 174–75, 202; and nationalism, 4, 168, 280; and national language policy, 164, 197–99; and national subject formation,

155; and normativity, 164–65, 169–70, 180–81, 193, 196–99, 233; and the novel, 93, 95, 97–102, 103, 105; office managers as speakers of, 31–32, 217, 220, 232–51, 272; office workers as speakers of, 19, 33, 252–73, 276–77; parody of, 18, 202, 203, 262, 264, 266; and performativity, 19, 22, 23, 24, 31, 33, 215, 216, 264, 265, 273, 277, 279; and peripheral relations, 3, 6, 103, 147, 169, 197, 271–73; and political-economic relations, 107, 163, 165, 203, 278–80; and print media, 102–4, 105, 106; and public opinion surveys, 2, 19, 30, 163, 174, 182–92, 197–98; purity attributed to, 3n4, 9, 19, 30, 169–70, 174–75, 202, 203, 260; and readers' correspondence columns, 30, 163, 174–82; as representation of Western women's speech, 97, 275; and resignification, 25, 27, 28, 70, 98, 101, 109, 110, 113, 117; and responsibilized subjects, 164, 181, 182, 189; roughness attributed to, 174–76, 178–82, 190, 191; and scholarly literature, 1–2, 13–14, 164, 167, 174, 192–97; schoolgirl speech as basis for, 25, 27, 28, 37, 98, 105, 113–14, 147, 155, 157, 159, 164; and self-help literature, 29, 30, 164, 200–203, 254; teleological account of, 75–76, 77, 169n9; and temporality, 24, 165, 169, 183, 195, 198, 215, 216, 251, 252, 260, 271–72, 277, 279, 280; unnamability of subject position in, 15, 275, 280; vulgarity attributed to, 174–80; and women's magazines, 19, 27, 28, 102–4, 105, 200, 202. *See also* Feminine speech; Honorifics; Polite forms; Utterance endings

Woolard, Kathryn Ann, 78

Working class, 6, 9, 12, 48, 127, 181, 197; women as members of, 21, 105n34, 110, 147, 181

Working women: case study of work performed by, 220–29, 253; and childrearing, 213, 220, 258; as college graduates, 208–13, 253, 259, 269; and dialectal speech, 247, 267, 269–72; and economic growth, 29, 170–71; and Equal Opportunity Employment Law, 29, 163, 171–72; and foreign-affiliated firms, 208–9; and gender relations, 29, 173, 253–54; hiring of, 29, 171n12, 209–12, 229; and management style, 226–29; and marriage, 173, 213, 220, 229, 230, 231, 258, 265; and mid-career employment, 211–12, 229, 238n20, 266; and occupational hierarchy, 209–13; and personal appearance, 217–18, 253, 262; and personal narrative, 219, 229–32, 269–73; promotion of, 29, 171n12, 209, 212, 227n11, 231–32, 234, 235, 239–40; and public opinion surveys, 185; recruitment of, 171n12, 172, 210–13, 228n13; as reserve workforce, 170–72; salaries received by, 212–13; and schoolgirl speech, 147; and self-help books, 200; and standard Japanese language, 217, 270; and women's language used by office managers, 31–33, 217, 220, 232–51, 272; and women's language used by office workers, 19, 33, 252–73, 276–77; and women's magazines, 116, 117, 142

World War I, 47, 69

Writing: Anderson's theory of, 48; de Certeau's theory of, 48, 50, 51–52; hierarchy between speech and, 52n29, 85; and hieroglyphic script system, 85; women's practice of, 63

Yamada, Bimyo, 87n15
Yamamoto, Masahide, 83n8, 86nn, 87n15, 89
Yamamura, Kozo, 171n11
Yanagihara, Yoshimitsu, 62–63
Yasuhira, Minako, 192
Yoda, Tomiko, 63n41
Yoneyama, Lisa, 11n8
Yoshida, Sumio, 89n18, 91n22
Young, Robert, 16

Zizek, Slavoj, 68, 72n51

Compositor:	Integrated Composition Systems
Indexer:	Andrew Joron
Text:	10/13 Galliard
Display:	Galliard
Printer and binder:	Maple-Vail Manufacturing Group